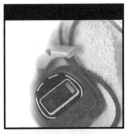

On Time Within Budget

Software Project Management Practices and Techniques

Third Edition

E. M. Bennatan

Wiley Computer Publishing

John Wiley & Sons, Inc.

NEW YORK · CHICHESTER · WEINHEIM · BRISBANE · SINGAPORE · TORONTO

Publisher: Robert Ipsen
Editor: Robert M. Elliott
Managing Editor: John Atkins
Text Design & Composition: Publishers' Design and Production Services, Inc.

This book is printed on acid-free paper. ∞

Published by John Wiley & Sons, Inc.

Published simultaneously in Canada.

This publication is designed to provide accurate and authoritative information in regard to the subject matter covered. It is sold with the understanding that the publisher is not engaged in professional services. If professional advice or other expert assistance is required, the services of a competent professional person should be sought.

Library of Congress Cataloging-in-Publication Data:

Bennatan, E. M. (Edwin M.)
    On time within budget : software project management practices and techniques / E. M. Bennatan.—3rd ed.
      p.   cm.
    Includes bibliographical references and index.
    ISBN 0-471-37644-2 (pbk : alk. paper)
    1. Computer software—Development—Management.   I. Title.
  QA76.76.D47 B454 2000
  005.1'068'4—dc21   00-027330

Printed in the United States of America.

10 9 8 7 6 5 4 3 2 1

Contents

Acknowledgments

The US Department of Defense (DOD) standards DOD-STD-267A and DOD-STD-268 and the related Data Item Descriptions have been referenced and quoted with the permission of the US Department of Defense, Space and Naval Warfare Systems Command.

Figures 10.1 and 10.2 and the text in Table 10.1 are copyright © The Software Engineering Institute (SEI), and are reprinted with the permission of The Software Engineering Institute.

The IEEE software engineering standards have been referenced and the following texts have been quoted with the permission of the Institute of Electrical and Electronics Engineers, Inc. (IEEE): All are copyright © Institute of Electrical and Electronics Engineers, Inc. 1999.

I should like to acknowledge the extensive help provided by Amir in the review and compilation of the text. I am grateful for his many useful suggestions.

I should also like to acknowledge Sharon and Talya for not disturbing the writing of this text.

Lastly, and most importantly, I fondly acknowledge the encouragement of Irit, without which this text would never have been written.

E. M. Bennatan

Preface to the First Edition

This is a book about software project management; it is not another book on software engineering. There are already many excellent reference books on software engineering (see the reference list at the end of this book). The objective of this book is to present software development from the *manager's perspective*, rather than from the *developer's perspective*.

The book concentrates, in a single volume, many modern software management practices and techniques that have been developed and refined over the past decade. Project management is presented as an acquired skill and not a gift from birth. Certainly, project management requires management talent, but this in itself is not enough. The effective application of modern software development procedures requires *professional* managers.

As this is a practical text (and not a theoretical work), many methods and techniques are described without their theoretical basis. However, extensive references are provided throughout the book for those interested in the theoretical background. A comprehensive list of references and recommended reading appears at the end of the book.

Occasionally, the reader may find some text repeated in the book. This occurs in order to resolve what is often called the *five finger* predicament. This condition occurs when each of the reader's five fingers needs to be inserted into a book as place markers while the reader struggles back and forth between chapters in order to cover a specific topic. This book attempts to reduce the need for place markers by repeating a short explanation of any major topic that is referenced, even though the topic is discussed in detail elsewhere.

Throughout the book the items *work month* and *work year* have been used in place of the older items *man month* and *man year*. These terms are discussed in detail in Section 10.5.3.

Intended Audience

On Time Within Budget: Software Project Management Practices and Techniques is intended for a varied audience. First and foremost, the text is intended as a reference source for practicing software project managers, and as such it is organized so that a major subject is covered in each chapter (excluding Chapter 1). This is further discussed in the following explanation of the organization of the book.

The book is also intended as a class textbook. Each chapter (except for Chapter 1) is followed by several exercises which cover the technical material discussed in the chapter and which encourage students to put into practice what they have learned. There are also numerous class projects, which are geared toward team solutions that can later be presented, discussed, and compared by the teams in class.

Finally, the book may serve as a reference for software engineers who would like to expand their knowledge into areas of technical project management.

Preface to the Second Edition

The second edition of *On Time Within Budget: Software Project Management Practices and Techniques* has undergone several changes. Many subjects have been updated and expanded and several new subjects have been added.

Firstly, a new chapter has been added on software project management in a client/server environment. This reflects the trend toward the development of software both for and on client/server platforms. As client/server systems become more prevalent the special problems they pose (such as the independence of the client or the management of a geographically distributed development team) also become more prevalent.

Methods for measuring the level of a software development organization are also covered, with Carnegie Mellon's SEI five-level scale presented and explained.

The landmark IEEE 1074 standard for software life cycle processes is covered and an overview of the individual processes is presented.

The discussion of the IEEE standards has been updated to reflect the complete suite of IEEE software standards published in 1993.

European software development standards are now also addressed, with emphasis on the ISO 9000 software standards.

Lastly, those readers familiar with the first edition will notice that the numbering of some of the chapters has changed. The client/server chapter has been inserted as Chapter 7, and all subsequent chapters have moved up by one.

Preface to the Third Edition

The third edition of *On Time Within Budget: Software Project Management Practices and Techniques* is significantly revised and updated. New subjects and references have been added and the content of the chapters has been changed.

A new chapter (Chapter 10) on Organizational Excellence covers Software Engineering Institute's (SEI) assessments and the Project Management Institute (PMI). This chapter reflects the new thinking in project management, emphasizing the importance of the development maturity of organizations. A closing chapter (Epilogue) also proposes some new ideas on how the book's methods can be put into practice.

The chapter on standards (Chapter 9) has been rewritten so that the ISO standards now play a central role alongside the new four-volume IEEE standards. Major new sections cover such topics as legal perspectives in software development, software availability and reliability, international perspectives, reuse, and component-based development.

Finally, the all-important customer perspective has been given prominence throughout the book.

Organization of the Book

Generally, the thirteen chapters appear in logical order and provide a step-by-step entry into the realm of software project management. An extended summary appears at the end of each chapter and can be used either as a memory refresher or as an initial source of information. The reader is urged to try some of the exercises at the end of each chapter. These exercises will assist the reader in understanding many of the ideas and techniques presented in the chapter.

Chapter 1 introduces the concept of software project management. The chapter discusses many difficulties experienced by project managers in gaining support from higher management for the introduction of new development procedures.

Chapter 2 briefly summarizes many common software development problems that are elaborated on throughout the book. The chapter is divided into two sections. The first section is intended for readers who are unfamiliar with the fundamental problems of software management. The second section is intended for new and experienced project managers alike. This section discusses a method of combating the problems discussed earlier, called risk analysis. Experienced project managers may choose to skip over Chapter 1 and the first section of Chapter 2.

Chapter 3 discusses software development under contract. The chapter describes how software project contracts are awarded, how proposals are prepared, how a proposal document should be constructed, and how relationships should be established between customer and developer. This chapter also describes the request for proposal (RFP) document and the selection process after the proposals have been submitted. The chapter concludes with a discussion of common software legal issues.

Chapter 4 describes the basic software development cycle and the phased approach to software development. Newer methodologies, such as rapid prototyping and the Spiral model, are also discussed. The basic phases are described from the project manager's perspective, emphasizing the atmosphere and problems of each phase. This chapter also covers the IEEE 1074 standard for software life cycle processes. The chapter concludes with a discussion of the customer perspective, cultural issues, reliability, availability, and ease of use.

Chapter 5 presents some of the basic principles of managing people. Specific aspects related to managing software engineers—such as the considerable difference in productivity among software engineers and the temperament of programmers in general—are covered.

Chapter 6 addresses one of the most difficult problems of software development: how to manage large software projects. The chapter explains how large projects can be divided into small manageable pieces using the "divide and conquer" approach. The chapter also discusses software reuse and component-based development.

Chapter 7 introduces the software project manager to project management in a client/server environment. This chapter addresses management issues related to client/server development and target environments, and discusses the many advantages and disadvantages of each. The chapter also covers design considerations specific to the development of a client/server project.

Chapter 8 describes three of the basic management support functions: configuration control, quality assurance, and software testing. The chapter also discusses the relationships between these functions.

Chapter 9 presents a general overview of software development standards. Two standards in particular are discussed in detail: the ISO standards and the IEEE standards. The US Department of Defense (DOD) standard 2167, though now defunct, is discussed due to the central role it played in software development.

Chapter 10 discusses organizational excellence in software development and covers the Software Engineering Institute's Capability Maturity Model and the Project Management Institute's (PMI) body of knowledge. The chapter centers around the role that process excellence in an organization plays in producing good software.

Chapter 11 discusses scheduling and the project development plan. Several scheduling and planning techniques are described, including the classic Gantt and PERT charts and the work breakdown structure (WBS). The chapter concludes with a discussion of the importance of customer involvement in preparing the project plan.

Chapter 12 contains detailed descriptions of several methods and techniques for the preparation of estimates. The chapter includes methods for estimating the size of a project and the project development schedule including COCOMO and COCOMO II, and Function Point Analysis, as well as technical estimates, such as memory and disk requirements. The chapter also explains how experience can be used to improve estimates, and how estimates can be refined as project development progresses.

The Epilogue provides a number of hints and ideas on how best to implement the methods described in the book.

Trademarks

Ada is a registered trademark of the US Government, Ada AJPO.

LAN Manager is a trademark of Microsoft Corporation.

Macintosh is a trademark of Apple Computer, Inc.

Motif is a trademark of Open Software Foundation, Inc.

MS-DOS is a trademark of Microsoft Corporation.

NetWare is a registered trademark of Novell, Inc.

PC-DOS is a trademark of International Business Machines Corporation.

PDP is a trademark of Digital Equipment Corporation.

Pentium is a trademark of Intel Corporation.

Power PC is a trademark of Motorola, Inc.

SNA is a trademark of International Business Machines Corporation.

Sparc is a trademark of Sun Microsystems, Inc.

UNIX is a trademark of American Telephone and Telegraph Corporation.

VAX is a trademark of Digital Equipment Corporation.

VMS is a trademark of Digital Equipment Corporation.

MS-Windows, MS-Project, and MS-Outlook are trademarks of Microsoft Corporation.

Windows NT is a trademark of Microsoft Corporation.

X-Windows is a trademark of the Massachusetts Institute of Technology.

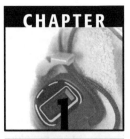

Introduction to Software Project Management

One of the most amazing things about the Y2K scare is how readily people accepted the fact that a software bug could bring the world to an unprecedented level of disruption (at least in peace time). The media was full of stories about people hoarding supplies and preparing for chaos. Even reasonable people printed out their bank statements during the final bank days of the millennium just in case the bank's data base failed. Now, in retrospect, this all seems absurd. But the question remains, how did so many people come to believe that software could be so unreliable and could cause such damage?

Modern society cannot function today without software, and there is no alternative. But as society's dependence on software has grown so has its distrust, and not without good reason. Examining the record of software projects reveals a mixed bag of successes and failures.

Examples of major software schedule overruns and even project abandonment are numerous. Watts Humphrey (1999a) describes the initial estimates he used at IBM for a major new feature of the OS/360 operating system: it ended up costing almost three times as much as originally estimated. Humphrey relates that later analysis of the overrun uncovered planning and estimation practices that ignored the complete project and only addressed individual tasks. There were no plans for system testing, integration, documentation, and other major phases of software development that together formed most of the effort. There was no overall project plan.

This IBM story occurred in the early days of software development. Twenty-five years later another often-quoted example attracted attention: the opening of the city of Denver's new airport in the early nineties was delayed time and time again (at a cost of more than one million dollars a day) awaiting the delivery of the 193 million dollar software for the baggage handling system (see Gibbs 1994). The repeated delays reached a point where the airport planners reluctantly admitted that they could no longer predict when the airport would open. Clearly something in this project plan was very wrong, too.

Debacles such as these have led to a bleak perception of the state of software development. In their notable tutorial on software engineering, Dorfman and Thayer (1997) state: "Even in today's society, software is viewed with suspicion by many individuals, such as senior managers and customers, as being somewhat akin to 'black magic.'"

Software development is certainly not black magic. Not all software projects end in disaster. There are enough real-life success stories throughout the business world to unquestionably demonstrate that software projects *can* be completed on time. The tools for success are there. The methods, practices, and processes are there.

This book addresses methods and techniques for the planning and management of a successful software development project. It presents a practical "how to" approach rather than a theoretical approach, though extensive references are provided for those interested in the theory behind the methods. The main objective is to concentrate, in a single volume, a description of many of the tools and procedures that have evolved for such software management activities as:

- Estimation of project cost
- Preparation of development schedules
- Application of effective development standards
- Preparation and evaluation of proposals

The software project manager is thus provided with the means to make software development more successful, with the three famous objectives in mind—to develop software:

1. On schedule
2. Within budget
3. According to requirements

These objectives cannot be met with the crude development methods of the early days of computers. New methods have had to be devised to improve significantly the way software is developed. This chapter discusses the state of the art, the role of project management in achieving these objectives, and proposes a means of gaining support for the introduction of modern software development methodologies.

1.1 Advances in Software Engineering

Impressive strides have been made in the past decade toward improving the way software is developed. Witness the enormous growth in the amount of software being delivered and that in fact much of the world could not function today without the software that drives its economy and administration. In fact, software has now changed position with hardware as the main component of computer-based systems (see Figure 1.1).

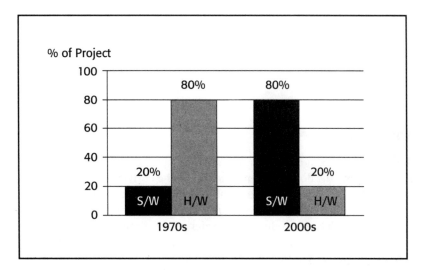

Figure 1.1   The changing role of software in hi-tech projects.

Many organizations such as the IEEE, the ACM, Carnegie Mellon's Software Engineering Institute (SEI), the Project Management Institute (PMI), and the European-based ISO, have conducted landmark research in the areas of software engineering and management and many of the major commercial software corporations have applauded their work. The tools are undoubtedly there, but the question is, are they being applied?

"Since the early days of software development, our industry has been the outstanding example of poor performance. Even today, few expect software to be delivered on time and, when the products finally arrive, they often have lots of defects." This quote from Watts Humphrey (1999b) provides a dim view of the state of the art of software engineering. He continues: ". . . as tough as this work is today, it will not get any easier."

If indeed software development won't get any easier, then software developers and managers must get better. They must take advantage of the new methods being developed and they must learn not only from mistakes, but from successes too. Success need not be an act of chance. Cost, completion date, and quality of software development can become more controlled.

Many advances have occurred in recent years in the way software is developed. The development environment has undergone significant change over the past decade. Distributed development using client/server and Internet-based systems has changed the way projects are developed and managed. However, client/server environments, with their increased level of developer independence, have solved some problems and produced new ones. This is particularly true in the Internet, for which much of the new software is being developed.

Until such time as reusable software and automatic software development begin to replace software engineers, software will continue to be developed by people. In the meantime, the required increase in productivity and reliability, and the general success of software development, must remain the responsibility of the software project manager.

This section discusses the progress being made in several areas of software engineering: in process, metrics, testing, tools, project cycle time, and in people management. The advances are discussed from a manager's perspective: how can they improve the overall performance of the project? The topics are then further discussed in more detail in later chapters.

1.1.1 Advances in Process

More than anything else, it is the advances in process that have moved software development from an art form into the domain of engineering. In the early days, asking a programmer when he would complete his assignment was rather like asking Rembrandt when he would complete his painting. You were apt to get an answer like: "I'll let you know when I'm finished!" With the introduction of orderly process into software development, this is no longer the case. The primary objective of process is to make software development more deterministic and thus more controllable.

The IEEE led the way in formalizing software process with its landmark Software Engineering Standards first published in 1984. This modest, though important milestone included just five software topics: testing, requirements, configuration management, quality assurance, and—to make sure we all spoke the same language—a glossary of software engineering terminology.

What distinguished the IEEE standards from other related works (such as the early US Department of Defense standard 2167 [1988a]) was that they were easy to use and they included many examples and guidelines. By the end of the nineties the IEEE had published several new editions of the standards, which evolved into a comprehensive and detailed set of four volumes (IEEE 1999). This provided an excellent reference for anyone wishing to implement an orderly software development process.

In the area of life cycle models, alternatives to the classic Waterfall Model gained popularity. Winston Royce defined the Waterfall Model in 1970 (Royce 1970) and it has remained the backbone of software life cycle models ever since. Most, if not all newer models seem to incorporate variations of the Waterfall Model within. Some of the newer models range from *rapid prototyping* and the *spiral model* to the utopian *automatic software synthesis*, which is based upon a highly automated development environment capable of transforming formal requirements into operational code (see Comer 1997). These newer life cycle models, radical as some may be, still need to maintain the cloak of formality necessary to be able to incorporate them into an orderly development process (and this is particularly important with prototyping models that tend to encourage corner cutting).

Many research and engineering institutes have made significant contributions to the modern software development process. Carnegie Mellon University's Software Engineering Institute (SEI) has pioneered the field of *organization assessment* discussed in Chapter 10. SEI's assessment process responds to the question: How does one measure the degree to which an organization is in fact using an orderly software development process? The SEI's Capability Maturity Model (CMM) has gained significant popularity in recent years almost as a de facto standard for assessing and improving software processes (see Herbsleb 1996). CMM grades an organization on a level of 1 to 5, which corresponds to its level of maturity as a software development organization.

1.1.2 Advances in Metrics

Metrics, the measurement of software development activities, brought about a significant step forward in project management. Measurement produces data, that in turn is the raw material which information is made of. This type of development information sired the school of *management by data.*

The idea behind management by data is simple; so simple, in fact, that one wonders how it took so long to gain ground in project management. Basically stated, management by data means that any decision, assessment, estimate, or conclusion about a project must always be based upon supporting data. This approach therefore requires that project-related data be collected systematically and consistently, so that critical aspects of the project can be measured.

Gone are the subjective estimates, the hopeful forecasts, the controversial decisions, and the ambiguous status reports. In their place, every major project activity is based upon data and thus can be substantiated and justified. Regrettably, this is not only idealistic but even somewhat impractical. You never have all the data you need, data is rarely one hundred percent reliable, and no two managers will consistently draw the same conclusions from the same data. Nonetheless, management by data is generally far superior to management by gut feeling.

Despite the limitations of management by data, the collection of project metrics as an aid to project management has gained support in recent years. Realistically, metrics, coupled with experience, combined with common sense, all in reasonable measure, is a good basis for good decision making.

Significant work has been done in defining standards for metrics collection and usage, and these are discussed in more detail in Chapter 10.

1.1.3 Advances in Testing

Testing is a less exciting facet of software development. This is possibly one of the reasons why it has never been one of the more successful activities in the development cycle. Many of the advances in testing are not really new; they have been around for many years. What is new is that their importance has now gained increased recognition.

New emphasis has been placed on several areas of testing: independent testing, traceability, and phase containment:

- *Independent testing* is an age-old theory that has proven itself time and time again. Simply stated, developers cannot test their own software well. They become blinded by their intimate involvement in what they are doing and cannot see what an outsider would see immediately. That is why outside, independent testers find problems that the developers cannot find.

- *Traceability* is the ability to determine that each feature has a source in requirements and each requirements has a corresponding implemented feature.

- *Finding and correcting faults* as close to the point of their introduction as possible is also a concept that has gained prominence. This principle has led to the concept of *phase containment*: the detection and correction of errors within the development phase in which they were introduced.

These and other modern principles of software testing are discussed in detail in Chapter 8.

1.1.4 Advances in Software Tools

Good software development tools can ease some of the tribulations of software development. The wide variety of tools available today can be categorized as:

- Process automation tools (such as automatic testers, code generators)
- Utilities (such as word processors, requirements/design aids, compilers)
- Project data management tools (such as configuration managers, project data repositories)
- Product applications (such as data base managers, communications packages)

Tools in software development serve a purpose that is similar to that of tools in any other field. They make the work more productive, easier to perform, and less error prone. They are essential for effective project management.

The increasing sophistication and availability of the PC has also made development tools more accessible. Though Microsoft has been a major source for advanced development tools (e.g., MS-Project or MS-Outlook), many other companies have developed a wide variety of development tools for the PC too. This has made development tools more accessible and more available to software developers.

In addition to software development tools becoming more available,[1] they have also become more integrated and more supportive of teamwork. A good set of requirements, design, and test tools, for example, should (and can) interact with the same data base, so that data can be entered only once. They should also have a similar look and feel: commands should be similar, help screens should be common, and they should merge seamlessly together into a unified suite. They should also support networking so that a team of developers can communicate easily while using the tools.

The availability of *integrated* tool sets has been one of the most significant recent advances in this field (see Bawtree1999). Integration not only provides ease of use, it also saves time and reduces the risk of error due to incorrect data entry. At last, software tool sets are beginning to look more like a well-fitted carpentry shop and less like a supermarket.

1.1.5 Advances in Cycle Time Reduction

Determining the scope of a software project is not the responsibility of only the project manager. The scoping of a project may require business and marketing considerations (such as when the product must reach the market), senior management decisions (such as the prioritization of resources), and possibly contractual considerations (in cases where software is being developed under contract).

Though the business and marketing factor has always been a major driver in determining project scope, the importance of this perspective has grown in recent years. In

---

[1]See Software Methods and Tools at: http://www.methods-tools.com/html/tools.html

many areas of business, time to market has become an overriding consideration. This has led to the evolution of such development methods as rapid prototyping and rapid application development, all to aid the ageless goal of cycle time reduction.

Cycle time reduction (or simply developing software faster) has been a major topic since the early days of programming. As software development became more process oriented the proponents of cycle time reduction became more concerned. Even though process did indeed combat project overruns (though not always as successfully as had been hoped), the consensus was that software development was taking too long and in many cases had become *process-heavy*.

Initiatives such as 10X cycle time reduction never did achieve their goal and did little more than skim the surface of the problem. Rapid prototyping provided one solution by breaking one of the age-old rules of prototyping: thou shalt not market the prototype. In fact, rapid prototyping coupled with an iterative approach to product development was able to provide a way to quickly get early versions of the product to market. Many companies, such as Microsoft, had been using this approach for several years (a good example is the DOS operating system). The basic idea was that a product can reach the market early if its functionality can be minimized to the bare essentials. Subsequent releases of the product would then provide increasing feature sophistication. The price to be paid by the development organization would be more overhead due to the many releases, but the benefit would be the ability to release the product early. In addition to the obvious competitive business advantage, early to market would also provide early user feedback and thus ultimately a better product.

Rapid prototyping and other methods of cycle time reduction are described in Chapter 8.

1.1.6 Advances in People Management

Chapter 5, which discusses management of software engineers, provides data on the wide variation of software developers' productivity, which is characterized by a factor of 25 to 1. A simplified view of this data would imply that major productivity improvements are possible if only we could move everyone closer to the 25 factor number.

To what extent a 25-fold improvement in team productivity can be achieved is debatable, but it is widely believed that significant improvements *can* be achieved through modern people-management practices.

Modern approaches to people management attach increasing importance to the composition of the development team and the interaction between the team members. Sawyer and Guinan report in the *IBM Systems Journal* (Sawyer and Guinan 1998) that "social processes such as the level of informal coordination and communication, the ability to resolve intergroup conflicts, and the degree of supportiveness among the team members, can account for 25 percent of the variations in software product quality." In other words, improvements in these areas can increase the effectiveness of the team by 25 percent.

But how can team members be motivated to even greater heights? Ben Rich wrote *Skunk Works* in 1994 after his team at Lockheed developed the Stealth fighter plane—a masterpiece of modern technology. Rich explained the management technique he had used to build the plane with a small team of highly dedicated engineers. His remarkably successful technique led to the popularity (in North America) of the term *Skunk Works*

Team. As Rich describes (Rich and Janos 1994), "We encouraged our people to work imaginatively, to improvise and try unconventional approaches to problem solving, and then got out of their way."

Creating a sense of ownership among the development team is achieved by "getting out of people's way" and letting developers make their own decisions—even their own mistakes. One of the highest forms of motivations is the feeling that the project is *yours*.

For software development teams, the same rules hold as for fighter plane engineers: productivity can be increased through creating small, dedicated project teams and providing ownership through delegation.

1.2 Project Success and Failure

The previous section discussed the evolution of software development into an engineering discipline. As we have seen, this evolved together with the appearance of new systematic development methodologies (see also Shaw 1990). The goal of these new methodologies has been to make software development more successful. If success is to be measured in terms of the three previously mentioned objectives (on schedule, within budget, according to requirements), then failure should mean the failure to achieve even one of these objectives. However, success and failure are not that easily defined.

Many studies have shown that project success and failure is a question of perception (see Pinto and Mantel 1990). A project may be perceived as having failed in one environment while in another it may be perceived as having succeeded. Simply stated, one customer may be pleased with the outcome of a project, while another customer may not. Hence, project success or failure is not only related to the three basic development objectives, it is also related to the expectations of the customer.

This ambiguity can best be avoided if a single goal is set and if it is set by the customer, not the development team. This means that ultimately the success or failure of a project is determined by the satisfaction of the party that requested its development (i.e., the customer).

The unfortunate stories mentioned in the introduction to this chapter prompt the question: just what is the proportion between well-managed software projects and failures? Do failures get more prominence because they render more piquant stories?

The figures for the nineties look like this: Keil reports that in 1995, annual US spending on software projects reached approximately 250 billion dollars, with an estimated 175,000 projects (Keil et al. 1998).[2] During the same period, US companies spent an estimated 59 billion dollars in cost overruns and another 81 billion dollars on cancelled software projects.

These are not pretty figures. However, modern software project management practices also have countless real-life successes to recount. The total dependency of the Western World on software is witness enough to the fact that there must be quite a few success stories, too. So what type of learning experiences should the software project manager seek?

---

[2]Quoted by Keil from Johnson 1995.

Andrew Nolan, reporting on his *learning from success* method at Rolls Royce's software engineering and assessment department (Nolan 1999) emphasizes this point: "Many organizations habitually focus on their failures, believing that to improve they must 'learn from their mistakes.' . . . Moving your business process away from an undesired outcome is not the same as moving toward a desired one."

It is the project manager's responsibility to take advantage of industry-wide experience and not just to learn from mistakes but also to learn from successes.

1.3 The Role of the Software Project Manager

Industry-wide experience is an excellent source of knowledge. However, to be able to manage a software project successfully, the manageer requires many other talents and skills. The Project Management Institute (PMI 1996) provides the following definition of project management:

> *Project management is the application of knowledge, skills, tools, and techniques to project activities in order to meet or exceed stakeholder[3] needs and expectations from a project.*

It includes planning, organizing, staffing, monitoring, controlling, and leading a project. Clearly, it is no longer sufficient to be a good software developer in order to be a good software project manager. Specific management skills are required from the initial stages of the project in such areas as:

- **Leadership and Guidance**: This includes providing direction to the team, fulfilling the role of facilitator so that the team members can successfully perform their tasks, continuously being informed on the real status of the project, and ensuring that correct decisions are made to achieve efficiency throughout the course of the project.

- **Planning**: This includes the preparation of good estimates, the maintenance of the development schedule and the efficient assignment of personnel. Planning is one of the most important management activities, for a project without a good plan is like a foreign voyage without a good map.

- **Customer Relations**: In all projects, contact with the customer is an essential management activity. All projects have a customer: either a formal business customer or an internal organization customer. This aspect of management includes ensuring continuous interaction with the customer, accurately documenting the customer's requirements, controlling changes required by the customer, and reporting status and organizing reviews and product demonstrations.

- **Technical Leadership**: Good technical leadership is usually a desirable quality in effective software management. This often requires the ability to provide guidance in the solution of technical problems that arise during project development.

---

[3]A stakeholder is an individual or organization that is involved in or may be affected by project activities.

It does not necessarily mean the provision of the actual solution itself. However, one must beware of becoming the meddlesome manager who cannot break free of having been a technical expert in the past.

- **Senior Management Liaison**: The project manager is the development team's chief representative when interacting with senior management. This includes carrying out policy decisions, reporting project status, and negotiating project and team related issues.

Though decision making has classically been a central responsibility of project managers, modern approaches to management strongly support delegation of decision making and chart more of a guidance role for managers. This is especially true for teams of software developers, as discussed in Chapter 5.

The software project manager also has the responsibility to ensure that the project is developed in an orderly manner. As we have seen, an attempt has been made in recent years to standardize the software development process and to create a strict development environment in which software projects are easier to estimate and control. However, this has led to a new problem: developers have complained that they were spending too much time on documentation and too little on the actual development of software. When taken to extremes, standards can stifle creativity and can be excessively confining.

Clearly, a middle ground should be sought between the two extremes: the free-style project, which is impossible to schedule and estimate, and the over-standardized over-documented project, in which exaggerated effort is spent on overhead and paperwork. Project management is a delicate balance between an orderly development process and common sense (this dilemma is further discussed in the Epilogue to this book).

It is the project manager's responsibility to prevent over-process—to ensure that the process is adapted (or tailored) to the size and type of the project being developed. Several software standards specifically support tailoring, from the early US Department of Defense (DOD) software development standards (DOD 1988a) to the modern IEEE standards (IEEE 1999)—within, of course, certain limitations (see Chapter 9).

When taken to extremes, not only standards can become ridiculous, so can other areas of process. At a recent project management course, one of the participants asked: how often should project meetings be held for small projects (he meant a *team of two people!*)?

Adapting standards to fit the project and determining the correct level of process needed for a project is the project manager's responsibility. This and other software project principles are highlighted in the following examples.

1.4 Two Examples

The following two cases demonstrate some of the pitfalls of software projects. The first demonstrates the failures of a project and the second illustrates the failures of project management itself.

The first example highlights what kind of problem can occur with weak, sloppy, or ineffective development practices due to poor design, implementation and testing. Figure 1.2

```
■■■■■■■■■■■■■■■■■■■■■■■■■■■■■■■■■■■■■■■■■■■■■■■■■■
  NCI Account: 1S777531                    Statement Date
  Telepone:                                May 11, 1998

  ☎ NCI Customer Service: 1 800 999-1909   Page 3 of 3          NCI
  ─────────────────────────────────────────────────────────

  Taxes and Surcharges.................................   $.01
  Current Charges                                         $.01

  Taxes and Surcharges
  Long Distance service
  Federal, State & Local Surcharges...................    $.01
  Total Taxes and Surcharges                              $.01

                                             End of Invoice.
                                             Thank You for Choosing NCI.
```

Figure 1.2   Copy of a bill received from the NCI phone company.

is a copy of a bill received from the NCI phone company. It was followed in later months by bills for two and then three cents. Clearly it cost the company much more to generate and send out the bills, not to mention the cost of monitoring them within the billing system, to ensure that they were paid.

The generation of such output from NCI's billing system could indicate a host of interesting problems. The actual design flaw that generated these bills could be little more than harmless in itself, except that it immediately raises a question: What other, possibly more severe problems, may be hiding behind this one?

In his paper on software defects, Watts Humphrey (1999c) rhetorically asks: "Why not just worry about the serious defects?" and goes on to explain why this is not possible: ". . . some of the most trivial-seeming defects can have the most dramatic consequences."[4]

What should a good project manager have done to prevent problems of this sort? One would suspect that the software project that produced this output could have benefited from better inspections in all phases of development.

The second example illustrates several common project management errors that can ultimately lead to the failure of a software project. The project starts off with several basic wrong decisions related to the launching of the project, which in turn lead to more wrong decisions as the project progresses.

---

[4]Humphrey provides an example from an executive of a major manufacturer who recounted that the three most expensive defects his organization had encountered were an omitted line of code, two characters interchanged in a name, and an incorrect initialization. Each of these caused literally millions of dollars of damage.

Technology Associates Inc. (TAI) is a company that specializes in the development and manufacturing of communications equipment. TAI has a large software department that is responsible for the development of software for communications equipment. The manager of the software department learned that corporate management was looking for an outside software company to develop a time and attendance system for TAI.

TAI's software department took the initiative, prepared a proposal to develop the system, and submitted it to corporate management. According to the proposal, two months would be devoted to consulting the personnel department, the financial department, and the department managers to define the requirements for the system. The development team would then develop the system during the following six months (the total development time would be eight months).

The software department estimated that a team of four people would be required to produce the requirements and to develop the system. The idea to use an outside software company was put aside, and the software department's proposal was accepted by corporate management. A development budget was approved to cover two and a half work years, or four people for eight months. The software department proceeded to establish a project team, and selected a project manager from one of the communications projects to lead the team.

As the end of the initial two-month period drew near, it became evident to the project manager that much more time was needed to determine and document the requirements. The project manager's options were:

1. Request an extension for the schedule and an addition to the development budget.
2. Use the existing partial requirements.

The department manager wanted to demonstrate that his department was capable of developing both embedded communications software and information systems. Therefore the project manager and his team were urged to choose option 2. This was based on the premise that if the project was late and over budget, it would be considered a failure, and future information systems would then be contracted to an outside software company.

The time and attendance system was developed based on the incomplete information that was accumulated during the initial two-month period. When the system was installed, the personnel department found it inadequate because it could not handle two employee entries and exits on the same day. The financial department found that the system only reported hours worked, and not the time of day at which the hours were worked. This meant that overtime could not be calculated correctly.

All the other departments found several major problems with the system. In short, the system fell far short of what the company needed.

The software department proposed correcting the problems and requested a budget for the development of a new, improved version. However, dissatisfaction was such that corporate management decided to offer the development of an entirely new system to an outside software company. The software company that was selected successfully developed the system. Surprisingly, this time the cost was less than the budget requested by TAI's software department for correcting the problems in the original system.

This (true) example demonstrates several major project management errors:

- Experience in one area of software (embedded communications systems) is not sufficient for the successful development of software in an entirely different area (information systems).

- A project manager should avoid committing to either development schedule or budget before the project has been adequately defined. In most cases, a firm commitment can be given only after the requirements are concluded.

- If the requirements of a project are not met, then adhering to the budget and schedule becomes meaningless.

- A customer or user will not always provide the correct requirements (e.g., hours worked also requires time of day). It is often the developer's responsibility to ask the right questions in order to collect the necessary information.

- It is sometimes better to develop a new system from scratch than to try to salvage a poorly developed system.

1.5 Gaining Acceptance for New Development Procedures

As we have seen in the previous TAI project example, pressure to meet budget and schedule can sometimes create disasters if other project aspects remain fixed (e.g., quality, functionality, and development resources). Such pressure is not uncommon, and, admittedly, is often justified. As discussed in Section 1.1.5, there are solutions to cutting development time that do not compromise crucial aspects of the project (such as quality, basic functionality, etc.). Critical project problems of this nature require a basic understanding by senior management of software development methods, otherwise creative solutions cannot gain their support.

One of the obstacles that project managers often have to overcome is the lack of support from senior management for modern development methods. Applying effective methodologies is not easy when senior management disputes their need. This leads project managers to a classic dilemma: how to stand up for what they believe is best and still retain their positions as project managers.

Clearly the many methods and techniques described in this book are effective only when they are *used*. The following section discusses methods to assist the project manager in gaining acceptance from senior management for the application of new methods.

1.5.1 Luck as a Factor in Software Development

As a software project manager you may, from time to time, be confronted by people who will tell you (and your boss) how they developed a software project without using any orderly development methods. And, of course, they will always tell you how they succeeded in producing the software in a fraction of the time it would have taken them had they used an orderly process, the kind that you support.

This can be a difficult situation to combat, particularly in front of a doubting audience. This is because occasionally such unlikely stories are true!

Actually, the explanation is surprisingly simple. Consider, for example the following scenario.

> *You are crossing Fifth Avenue in New York City during lunch time. Being a reasonably careful person, you first search out a pedestrian crossing. You then wait until the green "WALK" light comes on, and then, remembering that traffic lights are considered by New York drivers to be no more than a recommendation, you look left then right then left again.*[5]
>
> *Satisfied that all is clear you safely cross Fifth Avenue to the other side. While you are involved in this exploit, a friend of yours, without hesitating, races across Fifth Avenue and surprisingly makes it safely to the other side. He then proceeds to taunt you for wasting time with all the precautions that you took.*
>
> *You may be tempted for a brief moment to wonder if he is right.*

The parallel in software is that occasionally you may rush through a software project without using any orderly development methods, and you may be lucky enough to succeed. However, in most cases, like the person rushing across Fifth Avenue, you will be hit by a bus!

We all know that occasionally people are lucky. But, as a professional engineering manager, you cannot base your project development plan on sheer luck. The business case for developing a software project is based on the fact that there is a reasonable chance for success. If, in throwing care to the wind, you can promise no more that a poor gamble, then it makes little business sense to develop your project. An orderly development process is like an insurance policy; it greatly reduces risk, but for a price. The recent history of software development has demonstrated time and time again that this price is well worth paying.

1.5.2 Overcoming Resistance

Senior management (and sometimes other software engineers) occasionally use the following arguments against the use of modern software development methodologies:

1. These methods are all *theoretical*; in the "real world" things are done differently.

2. Project managers are too formalistic; they request everything in writing and make an issue out of every small change.

3. We don't have time for all this paperwork.

4. We can't afford the luxury of these lengthy procedures. We have always developed software without all this overhead.

5. This is a business, not a university. We will lose money and customers if we start wasting time on all these methods.

6. The methods are good, but unfortunately, now is not the right time to implement them. We hope to be able to use them some day, but not just yet.

---

[5]Readers have written pointing out that Fifth Avenue is a one-way street and therefore there is no need to look left and right. Clearly these are people who know little about New York drivers.

7. None of our engineers is familiar with these new methods. It will take too long and will cost too much to start retraining them.

The following are some of the recommended responses to the above arguments:

1. The record of software development in the real world has not been too good. In fact, the old methods have only too often led to disaster. There have been successes, but the hit rate of successes versus failures is much too low.

   Any effective method contains some theory, just as these software development methods do. These methods have been successfully applied by other similar companies, and have produced a drastic reduction in the cost of software development and a significant rise in the quality of software.

2. Orderly written record keeping is beneficial for everyone: the development team, the customer, and senior management. It assures that verbal communications have been understood correctly. If changes and other instructions are not documented and approved, then the development may proceed in the wrong direction. No one can be sure that all changes, large and small, will be remembered later when the project is completed. A documented list of approved changes provides traceability and accountability.

3. This may be a valid claim; paperwork should be kept to a minimum (it occasionally is exaggerated). However, surprisingly enough, paperwork in moderation actually saves time and does not waste it. For example, undocumented decisions often need to be repeated and verbal specifications lead to conflicting interpretations. The lack of documentation is usually most time-consuming during the integration and test phases, when the system design is recorded only in the mind of the developers.

   Also, an undocumented project is a nightmare to maintain. After project completion, when the developers disperse, all that is left is the product and its documentation. Without documentation, the product is no more than a mystery.

4. A question to reflect on is: ". . . and just how successful has our software development really been?" This argument is best challenged with a prepared file of information that documents the problems the company has experienced with previous projects. The objective is to prove that a new approach to software development is not a luxury but a necessity.

5. Arguments are most difficult to challenge when there is an element of truth in them, specifically when a company intends to develop its own new methodology. Though many companies do carry out research in software engineering, this is hardly necessary in all companies. There exist adequately documented methodologies, standards, and guidelines (see IEEE 1987b) to enable them to be easily applied in any company, without the need to redevelop them.

   Customers are lost not only due to an extended development schedule, but also due to poor quality and unsatisfied technical needs. The trade-off is heavily inclined toward a longer development schedule in exchange for a better software product.

   Also, short development schedules are often misleading, due to the additional time required to correct a poor software product after its first release (see the "Slick Terminal" example in Chapter 9).

6. Why not just yet? Is there any real basis for the claim that a more suitable time will appear later? On the contrary, the more time and effort invested in poor development methods, the more difficult they are to change.

   The best way to respond to this argument is to provide business reasons that explain why new development methods should be adopted as quickly as possible. The prepared file, mentioned in the response to argument 4, will be helpful, together with information collected from other companies. The objective is to demonstrate that orderly development procedures will increase the quality of the company's software product while reducing the cost of development.

7. The importance of investing in training rarely needs to be established; this is a widely accepted notion. This argument may be difficult to challenge when new development methods are presented as a *major* change of direction.

The best response depends on the specific situation. If the new methods do indeed represent a major change of direction, then most probably the company has been experiencing many software development problems. The responses to arguments 4 and 5 are then appropriate.

If the new methods do not really represent a major change of direction, then this should be demonstrated using data from previous projects. The basic idea is to show that, although several current development procedures are fine, significant improvement can be achieved through the introduction of some new methods.

All arguments against new development methodologies should only be challenged after adequate preparation. This usually means:

- Collecting data on previous software development projects within the company.

- Collecting data on similar companies that have adopted new development methods.

- Collecting documented reports, texts, and other written evidence (beware of being too theoretical).

- Obtaining the support of other software development experts, either from within the company, or from without.

All the data should be studied, and notes should be prepared that substantiate the need for new development methods. The bottom line should be that *the application of new, effective software development procedures is in the interest of the company.*

Having gained the necessary approval from senior management, the software project manager can move on to the application of the methods described in the following chapters. The first step, understanding the basic software development problems, is discussed in Chapter 2.

1.6 Summary

Even though software has no alternative to which it can be compared, there is a basic assumption that software costs more than expected.

Examining the record of software projects reveals a mixed bag of successes and failures. There are enough real-life success stories throughout the business world to unquestionably demonstrate that software projects *can* be completed on time. There exist methods, techniques, standards, and tools that, when applied correctly, promote the successful development of a software project, with the three famous objectives in mind—to develop software:

1. On schedule

2. Within budget

3. According to requirements

There have been impressive strides made in the past decade toward improving the way software is developed. In fact, software has now changed position with hardware as the main component of computer-based systems. Significant progress has been made in several areas of software engineering, including process, metrics, testing, tools, project cycle time, and people management.

The primary objective of process is to make software development more deterministic. In order to be able to measure the extent to which a development organization has implemented orderly process, the SEI's Capability Maturity Model (CMM) grades an organization on a level of 1 to 5, which corresponds to its level of maturity as a software development organization.

One of the basic principles of modern testing theory states that testing should occur at the end of each phase of software development (called *phase containment*), not just at the end of the project. Phase containment's main objective is to prevent errors from propagating into other development phases, and thus to make the correction at the point where the cost is least.

In several areas of business, time to market has become an overriding consideration emphasizing the importance of cycle time reduction. Rapid prototyping coupled with an iterative approach to product development has been able to provide a way to quickly get early versions of the product to market.

There is a wide variation of software developers' productivity, which is characterized by a factor of 25 to 1. Productivity can be increased through creating small dedicated project teams and providing ownership through delegation.

It is the project manager's responsibility to take advantage of industry-wide experience, and not just learn from mistakes but also learn from successes. To be able to manage a project effectively, specific management skills are required in such areas as leadership and guidance, planning, customer relations, technical leadership, and senior management liaison.

Project management is a delicate balance between orderly development process and common sense. The middle ground should be sought between the free-style project, which is impossible to schedule and estimate, and the over-standardized, over-documented project, where an exaggerated effort is spent on overhead and paperwork.

Ultimately, the business case for developing a software project is based on the fact that there is a reasonable chance for success. It is modern software project management practices that provide the potential for success.

Exercises

1. Section 1.1 discusses how software has changed position with hardware as the main component of computer systems. Spend time in a local library or on the Internet to locate at least two major computer products in which software has overtaken hardware as the primary component. Summarize the impact this has had on the organization developing the product, on the development facilities, and on the customer and end-user.

2. Review the first example (the NCI bill) in section 1.4.

   (a) Based on your set of assumptions about how this occurred, prepare a formal analysis of the problem (sometimes called a *post mortem*). List your findings and recommendations. Estimate the possible total cost of the problem to NCI. What other problems might this bill be indicative of?

   (b) Dates in Europe are written *dd/mm/yy* in contrast to *mm/dd/yy* in the United States. Discuss the possible results of two significantly different cases in which a software product implements the date in the wrong format. Would this always be a trivial problem?

3. Review Boehm's four rapid application development (RAD) categories. As project manager for the TAI project discussed in section 1.4, you need to decide which form of RAD is best suited to minimize development time. Add assumptions as needed and recommend the RAD approach that your development team will use. Explain your decisions, the pros and cons that you have considered, and how you plan to organize the project to support the form of RAD you have chosen.

   Explain your reasons for rejecting other forms of rapid development.

4. The Sales Department of your company has just announced the signing of a large contract for the delivery in twelve months of a new corporate software communications. The new software system is a modification of an existing communications system, with new features to be added for fast Internet connection, fax electronic routing and storage, and improved data security capabilities. This will be your company's flagship product release and everyone (developers, marketing, management, customers, and the competition) is anxiously waiting to see how this project turns out.

   Six months into the project, the status indicates that the project is going to be five months late. This is due to errors in estimating the complexity of the new features. All phases of testing are now taking longer than originally anticipated. Some members of senior management claim that part of the lateness is due to the heavy process overhead. If process was eliminated or reduced, they claim, the project could be completed earlier.

   As project manager, prepare your response to these claims. Write a memo laying out your position and include the justification for your recommendations. Suggest steps that may be taken to alleviate the situation with the customer.

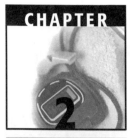

CHAPTER

2

Software Development Problems: An Ounce of Prevention

At a recent course on software project management, one of the participants asked:

We have several major problems in a project that I am managing. We don't have any orderly documentation, or a development plan, and the project is way over budget and behind schedule. How do I apply all the methods and techniques that I have learned here, in order to get the project back on schedule?

This is not an uncommon situation, where a magical remedy is sought for a near-disastrous situation. Poorly managed projects can run into delays and budget overruns of two or even three hundred percent, and in some cases may even be abandoned. Most modern project management methods are primarily concerned with preventing (and not correcting) these types of problems.

Preventing problems is easier and less costly than solving them. Effective preventive measures should:

- Locate problems and potential problems early
- Resolve problems before they get out of hand
- Plan ahead for potential problems

Problems become more costly to resolve as the project progresses into advanced development stages. Neglected problems may also propagate into other areas of the project, making them much more difficult to correct. It is therefore important to establish procedures for the early location and correction of problems.

This chapter explains the causes of some of the more common types of software development problems and discusses their effect on the development process. The chapter also discusses the anticipation of problems in order to minimize their impact on the project. Later chapters address methods of preventing the problems described here from occurring.

2.1 Basic Problems

There are several basic problems that a project manager is likely to find in any software project. These basic problems are caused by the following situations that can always be expected to occur:

- Incomplete, unclear, or inadequate requirements
- Dependence on external sources (vendors, subcontractors, etc.)
- Difficulties in concluding the project
- Frequent replacement of the development personnel (staff turnover)

Other basic problems are often produced by common errors of management, such as:

- Poor estimates
- Inadequate tracking and supervision
- Uncontrolled changes
- Poor testing procedures
- Poor development documentation

The best way to locate a problem early is to go looking for it. Clearly, the first place to look is where problems most frequently occur. For example, frequent and unchecked changes to the requirements specification are notorious as a major source of design problems. Unsupervised subcontractors and vendors are one of the most common sources of surprises, particularly when they report technical problems and delays at the very last moment. For the project manager, knowing where to look is therefore as important as knowing what to do.

2.1.1 Problems Related to Project Requirements

The project requirements specification describes the product to be produced by the development group (see Chapter 4). If the requirements are not adequately specified, then nothing short of pure luck will assure that the product meets the needs of the customer.[1] The following examples describe some of problems related to poor requirements specification.

---

[1] The term *customer* here is used in its broadest sense to include a formal customer, the marketing department, the users group, management, etc.

Features are missing. The customer was sure that certain missing features would be included in the product, based on informal discussions (often with the wrong people), memos, comments, and remarks at meetings, but not based on a formal requirements specification.

Unnecessary features have been included. The development team was sure that the customer would be overjoyed with the extra features that were added to the product (usually without consulting the customer). An example might be the addition of password security access to the system when the customer wanted the system to be readily accessible to anyone.

Features that work differently than expected. The customer inadequately explained the need for a feature, and so the development team interpreted the requirement according to their own understanding. An example might be a requirement to "update the data base regularly." The developers produced a system that updates the data base once a day, while the customer meant once an hour.

Necessary features that nobody thought about. The customer is not necessarily a computer expert, and therefore may not be aware that a specific feature is needed. An example would be the need for adequate backups; the customer may assume that backups are unnecessary because, if computer service is interrupted (say by a power failure), then the loss of one or two memory resident transactions will not be a problem. However, the customer may not have considered the fact that disk drives can also crash and lose all their data.

Clearly, poorly specified requirements are as much a problem to the developer as they are to the customer. The developer, however, is often in a better position than the customer to compile the requirements. Usually, the best requirements specification is the result of a joint effort by both the developer and the customer, with the actual document being written by the developer and being approved by the customer (this is discussed further in Chapter 4).

2.1.2 Frequent Changes

It is extremely rare to find a well-planned software project come to a successful conclusion with a requirements specification labeled version 1.0. Changes are inevitable throughout the software development cycle. However, in most cases, the later a change is introduced, the more costly it is to implement.

A reasonable number of changes should be manageable. It is when the flow of changes turns into a torrent that they become a problem. Even a single change can be a problem if it is requested well into the development of the project and if it results in a major change of direction. Excessive changes produce what is commonly referred to as the "moving target syndrome." The project manager is continually changing direction, and the development team becomes both confused and demotivated.

Changes can disrupt the project if they are not adequately documented and monitored. Changes, in reasonable numbers, must be managed using a systematic change control mechanism. This method, within the configuration control organization, is discussed in Chapter 7.

When projects are difficult to specify at the beginning (such as in research and development projects), the problem of changes can also be dealt with by selecting an appropriate evolutionary development model such as rapid prototyping or a spiral model (see Chapter 4). This enables the development team together with the customer to "learn as they go."

2.1.3 Estimates and Related Problems

Good estimates are important, because they form the foundations of a good project development plan. This plan, prepared by the project manager, is produced during the initial stages of the project, and includes estimates related to:

- The project development budget
- The project development schedule
- The required development resources (development staff, development equipment, etc.)

Technical estimates are also produced during the design phase, and include

- The characteristics of the software (estimates of memory size, data base size, etc.)
- The characteristics of the required target hardware (estimates of CPU speed, input/output capacity, disk drive capacity, communications characteristics, etc.)

Estimates are the basis for many technical and management decisions. Poor estimates lead to poor decisions. A poor estimate can be either too high or too low, and the subsequent decisions produce either a waste or a shortage of a development resource. This produces planning errors, such as:

- Schedules that are much too short or highly exaggerated
- Budgets that are much too low or greatly inflated
- Under- or over-staffing

and technical design errors, such as:

- Targeting computers that are much larger (and more expensive) than necessary, or that are incapable of supporting the application being developed

Problems that result from low estimates are usually more critical than problems that result from high estimates. Realizing this, estimators commonly add uncertainty factors (of say 30 percent) to their estimates, assuming that it is better to be too high than too low. However, even though a high estimate may not cause a project to fail, it may prevent the project from ever getting launched at all.

Many methods have been developed to produce various types of estimate at different stages of the project (see Chapters 11 and 12). However, even well-prepared estimates can lead to problems if they are not updated on a regular basis. Clearly, better and more complete information produces better estimates. Therefore, as the project moves forward and more information becomes available, estimates should be reviewed and refined. This leads to the reassessment of development decisions, enabling potential problems to be addressed early, before they become critical (see Section 2.2 on risk analysis).

2.1.4 External Sources

Project development problems are usually easiest to manage when all the development factors are controlled by project management. This, however, is not always the case. Many projects are dependent on various external sources, such as:

- Subcontractors
- Equipment vendors
- Parallel development projects
- Service providers (maintenance, training, installation, etc.)
- Support functions (telephone communications, networks, data providers, etc.)

The dependence on external sources must be reflected in the project development plan. This means incorporating within the plan commitments and estimates received from other sources. Consequently, the estimates in the plan can be no better than the estimates received from the other sources.

Reliance on external sources can cause the following problems:

- Schedule delays, owing to late delivery of project components.
- Poor quality and design of development equipment and external project components.
- Incompatible external components, owing to departure by the external developer or vendor from the agreed or published specification.
- Poor product support for external components.

By being aware of these potential problems, the project manager can assure that they are adequately addressed in the contract or agreement with the external source. These problems can often be averted by including in the contract penalties for delays in delivery or flaws in the product (see Chapters 3 and 11). Early warnings can be detected by regularly reviewing the work being developed by the subcontractor and requesting regular progress reports.

2.1.5 Concluding a Software Project

As all project managers know, projects are difficult to start. Experience shows that they are often no less difficult to end. Toward the end of a project, there is always a tendency for various interested parties to emerge with new requirements, comments, changes, and other last-minute activities. This is especially true for *fixed price* projects being developed for a customer under contract (see Chapter 3).

The main problems related to the conclusion of a project are:

- Disputes between customer and developer regarding the interpretation and the provision of all required features.
- Attempts to include last-minute changes.
- System failures and design defects located during system installation and test.
- Difficulty in keeping the development team together and motivated. As tension lessens toward the end of the project, there is a corresponding reduction of enthusiasm among the remaining development team members.

It is the responsibility of the project manager to assure the orderly and successful conclusion of the project. This is achieved through detailed planning at the start of the project, and effective project management throughout the project. Specifically, this requires that:

- Acceptance test plans must be prepared, documented, and approved by the customer well before the end of the project.

- Staffing levels and assignments must be scheduled, taking into account the gradual reduction in the development team size toward the end of the project.

- The release of the product must be well planned, including packaging, production of documentation, training, installation, and an orderly transition to the maintenance and support phase.

The successful conclusion of a project starts at the other end of the development cycle: at the beginning. Poor requirements specifications, test plans, or development plans all lead to major problems at the conclusion of the project.

2.1.6 Staff Recruitment and Turnover

The difficulty in recruiting development team members is one of the first problems encountered by the software project manager. Before any project can be launched, the initial development team must be established. And the problems do not end once the team is in place. Keeping the team together is often as difficult as establishing it.

The demand for software engineers exceeds the supply. This is not a new problem. In 1985 Frenkel reported that the demand for software engineers was growing exponentially, while productivity was rising at a rate of about 5 percent a year (Frenkel 1985). This situation is no better at the beginning of the twenty-first century. US and European universities are not producing software engineers at a rate sufficient to close the gap between supply and demand. In fact, not only is the gap not being closed, it is widening at a concerning rate.

The average amount of time a software engineer remains at a job decreases as the demand for engineers grows. This is not only caused by migration of software engineers *between* companies, but also by migration within companies, as these companies attempt to make more efficient use of their engineers. Migration *within* companies is not only due to the shortage of software engineers but also to their relatively high cost. This means that even in cases where additional engineers are available in the job market, their cost may inhibit additional hiring.[2]

Staff turnover is in itself a major problem. The stability of the development team contributes significantly to the morale and motivation of the team, and thus to the success of the project. The problems related to staff recruitment and frequent turnover include:

---

[2]Basic economics dictates that when engineers are available, their cost should decrease (based on the supply and demand within the job market). However, in recent years the supply of software engineers has never been sufficiently high to cause this effect, except for brief periods of time in isolated locations.

- A significant investment is required in the learning curve and training for new development team members.

- Frequent staff turnover reduces team spirit and negatively affects team motivation.

- Recruitment is often costly and time-consuming, requiring several interviews and possibly recruitment fees.

- Frequent staff turnover produces a lack of consistency in the development of the project.

Of all software development problems, those related to the development team are often perceived as the most critical. The team members are the most important development resource, for it is they who contribute most to the success or failure of the project.

2.1.7 Tracking and Supervision

Tracking and supervision are management tasks. When problems arise in these and related areas, they are often the consequence of inappropriate and ineffective project management procedures. One of the most common results is that the project manager is unaware of the existence of major problems at the stage when they can best be contained and corrected.

Effective tracking and supervision require direct contact between project management and the development team (see Chapter 8). One of the major causes of tracking and supervision problems is the *ivory tower syndrome*, where a permanent rift exists between project management and the rest of the development team. This leads to:

- An inaccurate or non-existent flow of information, contributing significantly to poor management decisions.

- Uncoordinated development, a situation that is often depicted as one development team developing two different projects. It occurs when uncoordinated and unsupervised development team members proceed in different directions.

- Schedule delays and budget overruns, both of which are caused by poor estimates based on incorrect information.

Information is the basic ingredient of any type of management. Therefore, poor supervision coupled with an inadequate flow of information are at the core of poor project management. The above three problems describe the general outcome of poor management. The list of resulting problems could just as easily cover almost every type of project development problem. Methods for establishing effective channels of information and well-organized reporting procedures are described in Chapter 5.

2.2 Risk Analysis

Foresight is an excellent management quality that can often be cultivated with experience. Indeed, in many cases, problems can be anticipated. In such cases, the manager can plan for the possibility that a problem will occur by estimating its probability, evaluating its impact, and preparing solutions in advance. This is referred to as *risk analysis*, and is an effective means of combating potential development problems.

Performing risk analysis means being prepared. It is a form of insurance, the basic idea being that if a problem occurs, a solution is readily available. Like all insurance, risk analysis usually comes with a price. The cost of preparing for the occurrence of a problem is primarily the cost of having the alternative solution at hand, even though the problem may or may not occur. In some cases, the cost may be minimal: the time needed to analyze and document the solution, and the time to track the problem. In other cases, the cost may be substantial: for example, the price of an alternative piece of development equipment. In any case, a problem that has been analyzed and resolved ahead of time is far simpler to resolve than a problem that occurs unexpectedly.

This section provides some basic techniques for management of risks. The formal theory of risk management, though more extensive, essentially produces the same results. An overview of risk management is presented in the following section, along with several references for more extensive theory. Readers seeking a practical technique can go directly to Section 2.2.2.

2.2.1 The Theory of Risk Analysis

Risk Analysis and its variant theory Risk Management have been a favored area of research for many years. In software, there have been many notable contributions to the theory, including works by Capers Jones (1994), and Barry Boehm and Tom DeMarco (1997).

Interest in the field was stimulated by an early understanding that software development would never be deterministic. The impact of external events on development would always be unpredictable, and therefore most suited for a statistical or probability model.

Carnegie Mellon's Software Engineering Institute (SEI) has made significant contributions to the field, particularly in the area of practical methodologies[3] (see Higuera and Haimes 1996).

Higuera identifies three groups of practices within the framework of software risk management:

1. **Software Risk Evaluation (SRE):** assessing the existence of risks, analyzing them, and providing mitigation plans.

2. **Continuous Risk Management (CRM):** preparing plans to manage risk, and implementing them as a continuous risk management process.

3. **Team Risk Management (TRM):** bringing about joint management of risks in a collaborative fashion (including all partners in a program).

Higuera finds that the need to manage risk increases as systems become more complex (see Figure 2.1).

As systems become more complex, risks increase both in number and in complexity. A simple example is that the risk of new hardware being late is much more severe in a $20 million project than in a $20 thousand project.

---

[3]For more information on SEI's work on risk management, see also: http://www.sei.org/programs/sepm/risk/risk.mgmt.overview.html

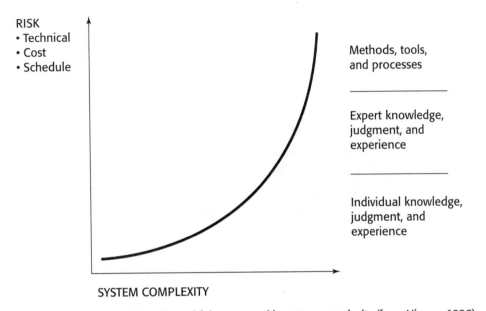

Figure 2.1   The need to manage risk increases with system complexity (from Higuera 1996).

For large projects, risk identification becomes a major issue. Keil conducted a survey of forty software project managers from around the globe, to identify a universal set of risk factors that could be used much like a checklist (see Keil et al. 1998). The survey found that in terms of identifying and rating risk factors, there were nearly a dozen factors that three panels (from three different countries) viewed as important (see Figure 2.2), suggesting the existence of a universal set of risks with global relevance. Interestingly, risks that were viewed to be most serious were often seen as being outside the direct control of the project manager.

Additional research into risk analysis addresses behavioral risks such as: shoot the messenger, make emotional risk decisions, be reactive not proactive (see Gemmer 1997). These types of risk are frequently more dangerous than the technical ones. It is therefore essential for an organization to foster an environment where risk management is considered good practice, and not a matter of needless concern or of "raining on the parade."

In an excellent FAQ,[4] the SEI summarizes the meaning of successful risk management:

> *A successful risk management practice is one in which risks are continuously identified and analyzed for relative importance. Risks are mitigated, tracked, and controlled to effectively use program resources. Problems are prevented before they occur and personnel consciously focus on what could affect product quality and schedules.*

[4]SEI's Frequently Asked Questions (FAQs) about risk management can be found at: http://www.sei.cmu.edu/programs/sepm/risk/risk.faq.html

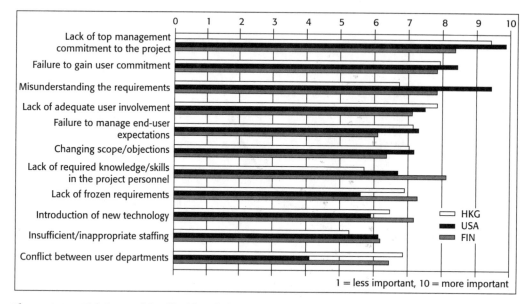

Figure 2.2 Risk factors identified by all three panels ordered by relative importance.

Techniques for achieving this are described in the following sections.

2.2.2 Anticipating Problems

The first stage of risk analysis requires a review of all project technical and administrative plans in order to identify potential problems. It includes:

- The project development plan
- The requirements specification
- The design specification

All major dependencies in the project development plan are examined and evaluated. Examples may be the dependence on external sources such as subcontractors, vendors and suppliers, and service providers. Problems will arise if external components or services are not provided on time, or if they do not function as expected.

The project design specification is a detailed plan of how the requirements are to be implemented. The implementation decisions involved may contain potential problems. For example, problems will arise if the selected hardware turns out to be inadequate—perhaps the CPU is too slow, the LAN is not sufficiently reliable, or the server cannot support all the clients in the network.

A list of all anticipated problems is then compiled, identifying each problem and describing its potential effect on the project. Table 2.1 presents an example of an anticipated problem list.

The anticipated problem list should be compiled with the participation of the principal members of the project development team. Other people may also be invited to contribute to the list, based on their experience and technical or administrative knowledge.

Table 2.1   Example of an Anticipated Problem List

PROBLEM	DESCRIPTION
1 Late delivery of the development computer	If the development computer is not delivered by June 1, as planned, the integration phase will be delayed.
2 Internet communications too slow	Information to be posted and downloaded from the Internet site is too slow and cannot support the amount of data to be transmitted.
3 No operating system expert	The system requires changes to the standard operating system. John Adams is the only OS expert in the company, and he may not be available for this project.
4 System response time too slow	The required system response time to the input may exceed the 5 seconds specified in the requirements.
5 High staff turnover	The schedule is tight with only minimal slack time. If there is more than average staff replacement during development, we will slip the schedule.
6 Communications too slow	The standard communications package is too slow. The design is based on the new binary communications package. This package has never been used with this system, and may not be suitable.
7 Late delivery of the data base subsystem	The data base subsystem is subcontracted to Software Developer Inc. (SDI), which has committed to delivery by April 15. SDI may not deliver on time, thus delaying the final integration and test phase.

This might include people from other project teams, support groups, the company's legal department, or the purchasing department.

While the objective is not to list every conceivable problem that a particular project might experience, it is necessary to identify those problems that should reasonably be considered in relation to the project. In any event, the following analysis stage is designed to isolate only those problems that could have significant impact on the project, and that can reasonably be expected to appear.

2.2.3 The Analysis Stage

The analysis of the anticipated problems list requires the evaluation of each problem in order to:

1. Estimate the probability that the problem will occur

2. Estimate the impact of the problem on the project

3. Attribute a measure of severity to the problem

The probability and the impact should be estimated by more than one person. All items on the list are best estimated during a single problem evaluation meeting to assure that the relative severity between problems is not distorted. The objective is to avoid situations in which late delivery by supplier A is estimated at 0.8 by one estimator, and late delivery by supplier B is estimated at 0.6 by another, while both estimators would agree that the probability is equal. Having both persons in the same room at the same time reduces this relative distortion.

A simple and effective way of producing the measure of severity for each anticipated problem is to:

1. Assign an expectation number between 1 and 10 based on the probability that the problem will occur, with 10 representing high probability, and 1 representing low probability (e.g., multiply the probability by 10).

2. Assign a number between 1 and 10 based on the impact of the problem on the project, with 10 representing high impact and 1 representing low impact.

3. Multiply the value produced in step 1 by the value produced in step 2 to produce the measure of severity for the problem.

Table 2.2 presents an example of the calculation of the measure of severity, using the anticipated problems described in Table 2.1.

After the measure of severity has been calculated for each anticipated problem, the list is sorted according to the severity of the problems, with the most severe problem at the top of the list. A decision can then be made that any problem with a severity level less than some value (say 10), will not be considered. The remaining problems are then evaluated and a detailed course of action, called a *contingency plan*, is selected for each problem. The information is then entered into a *contingency table*. For each entry in the table, a member of the development team is assigned to be the *tracker*, to track the problem and to alert project management when the contingency plan needs to be put into effect. This stage is demonstrated in Table 2.3.

Table 2.2 Example of the Calculation of Measure of Severity

PROBLEM	EXPECTATION	IMPACT	SEVERITY
1 Late delivery of the development computer	6	5	30
2 Internet communications too slow	4	2	8
3 No operating system expert	5	5	25
4 System response time too slow	5	3	15
5 High staff turnover	5	8	40
6 Communications too slow	2	8	16
7 Late delivery of the data base subsystem	3	9	27

Table 2.3 Example of a Contingency Table

PROBLEM	SEVERITY	CONTINGENCY PLAN	TRACKER
5 High staff turnover	40	Allocate bonuses for successful project completion.	J. Smith
1 Late delivery of the development computer	30	Request night shift on development system of another project.	H. Brown
7 Late delivery of the data base subsystem	27	Design a data base subsystem simulator to be used for integration.	W. Alda
3 No operating system expert	25	Locate an OS expert outside the company, and hire as a consultant.	H. Brown
6 Communications too slow	16	Contract the company that developed the binary communications package to adapt the package to this project.	H. Troy
4 System response time too slow	15	Enter a CPU upgrade agreement clause in the computer purchase contract.	Y. Knot
2 Internet communi- cations too slow	8	(not considered)	

Risk analysis is first performed as early in the project as possible, but no later than the end of the requirements phase (see Chapter 4). However, risk analysis is not a one-time activity. As the project progresses, additional problems may be anticipated and other problems may need to be removed from the problem list. As new information becomes available, the evaluation of the severity or the probability may be improved. Therefore, the risk analysis tables should be reviewed and updated periodically and whenever a significant event occurs (e.g., a subcontractor announces a schedule delay, or a major design decision is found to be incorrect).

2.2.4 Implementing Contingency Plans

Contingency plans are implemented in one of the following instances:

1. The anticipated problem occurs, or becomes imminent.

2. The contingency plan requires advance preparation.

Generally, contingency plans can be perceived as plans of action that are shelved for possible use later . However, in some cases, the plan is implemented *before* the anticipated problem occurs, such as when a simulator is developed in case the delivery of a critical component is delayed. Then, if the component is delivered on time, the simulator can be discarded.

As an example of the complete process, let us consider a communications project involving a central computer connected by a wide area network to several small computer sites. Two potential problems have been identified:

- The two computers have different architectures that may interpret the designated communications protocol differently (e.g., the order of two byte words may be reversed—LSB MSB instead of MSB LSB).

- The selected phone company may not be able to install test lines in time for the integration phase.

Tables 2.4, 2.5, and 2.6 are the risk analysis tables for the communications project. If the availability of communications lines is delayed this will be slightly more damaging to the project than the incompatible protocol problem. The tracking of this problem has been assigned to William Doo. It is his responsibility to assure that lines are ordered from two other phone companies (for the integration phase only). If the preferred phone company is ready on time, then the orders from the other two companies will be canceled and possibly a cancellation fee paid.

Another engineer, Indira Hope, is responsible for tracking the incompatible communications protocol problem. She must assure that a simple ASCII communications package is ordered for both computers. The cost of the ASCII packages will be wasted if the selected binary protocol works. The alternative ASCII solution will most certainly be much slower, but it will provide a temporary solution until the incompatibility problem is resolved.

Table 2.4   Anticipated Problem List

PROBLEM	DESCRIPTION
1 Incompatible communications protocol	The two computers have different architectures that may interpret the designated communications protocol differently.
2 Test line late for integration	The selected phone company may not be able to install test lines in time for integration.

Table 2.5   Measure of Severity

PROBLEM	EXPECTATION	IMPACT	SEVERITY
1 Incompatible communications protocol	5	8	40
2 Test line late for integration	8	6	48

Table 2.6 Contingency Table

PROBLEM	SEVERITY	CONTINGENCY PLAN	TRACKER
2 Test line late for integration	48	Order line from two additional phone companies.	Will Doo
1 Incompatible communications protocol	40	Use an ASCII communications package.	I. Hope

2.3 Summary

Modern project management methods are primarily concerned with *preventing* (and not *correcting*) project development problems. Preventing problems is easier and less costly than solving them. Effective preventive measures should:

- Locate problems and potential problems early
- Resolve problems before they get out of hand
- Plan ahead for potential problems

There are several basic problems common to almost all software projects. Most of these problems are derived from:

- Incomplete, unclear, or inadequate requirements
- Dependence on external sources (vendors, subcontractors, etc.)
- Difficulties in concluding the project
- Frequent replacement of the development personnel (staff turnover)
- Poor estimates
- Inadequate tracking and supervision
- Uncontrolled changes
- Poor testing procedures
- Poor development documentation

The best way to locate a problem early is to go looking for it. Clearly, the first place to look is where problems most frequently occur. For example, frequent and unchecked changes to the requirements specification are notorious as a major source of design problems. Unsupervised subcontractors and vendors are one of the most common sources of surprises, because they often report technical problems and delays at the very last moment. For the project manager, knowing where to look is therefore as important as knowing what to do.

Knowing what to do includes being prepared for the appearance of a problem. In many cases, problems can be anticipated. The project manager can plan for the possibility that a problem will occur by estimating its probability, evaluating its impact, and preparing alternative solutions. This is referred to as risk analysis, and is an effective means of combating potential development problems.

Performing risk analysis means being prepared. It is a form of insurance, the basic idea being that if a problem occurs, a solution is readily available. Like all insurance, risk analysis usually comes with a price. The cost of preparing for the occurrence of a problem is primarily the cost of having the alternative solution at hand. In some cases, the cost may be minimal: the time needed to analyze and document the solution, and the time to track the problem. In other cases, the cost may be substantial: the price of an alternative piece of development equipment. In any case, a problem that has been analyzed and resolved ahead of time is simpler to resolve than a problem that occurs unexpectedly.

Exercises

1. A new cable television service company is preparing to establish service in eight months' time. The company provides service to subscribers for a fixed monthly fee that depends on the extent of the service that they have ordered. The company also screens new movies, each of which can be viewed by a subscriber by telephone request to the company.

   The company is now in the process of ordering equipment, purchasing facilities, and signing up customers. A software company has been contracted to develop a billing system for the subscribers. The system will interface with the equipment to receive information on new movie screenings, and it will interface with the customer data base for regular monthly billing information.

   Prepare a list of the 10 most critical problems that you anticipate in the development of the billing project. Discuss the reasoning behind your selection of problems.

2. Calculate a measure of severity for each of the potential problems you identified in Exercise 1. Explain your assignment of project impact and probability values.

   Suggest an alternative method for assigning a measure of severity to anticipated problems that also takes into consideration the cost of preparing the contingency plans.

3. Suggest contingency plans for the anticipated problems you identified in Exercise 1. Consider two different alternative plans for each problem. Consider the cost of each alternative plan, and then select the best one based on the alternative method for assigning measures of severity that you suggested in Exercise 2.

   Prepare a contingency table containing the contingency plans that you have selected.

4. As a class exercise: divide the class into groups of three or four students. Assign Exercises 1, 2, and 3 to each group. Ask each group to present their risk analysis to the rest of the class. Discuss (a) the different anticipated problem lists, (b) the different contingency plans, and (c) the different methods for assigning a measure of severity (did any two groups suggest similar methods?).

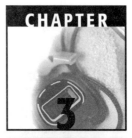

CHAPTER 3

Software Development Contracts and Other Legal Issues

Owing to the rapid advances in technology during the last several decades, it has become increasingly necessary for high-technology organizations to specialize in specific, well-defined areas. Specialization has not only defined many new branches of engineering, it has also defined areas of expertise within the engineering disciplines. This is especially true of software engineering.

Frequently, organizations that do not specialize in software development hire other organizations that do so to develop software for them. Even organizations that do develop their own software may decide to hire outside specialists in specific areas. IBM hired Microsoft to develop the PC–DOS operating system, because Microsoft had experience in developing microcomputer systems and IBM did not.

This chapter deals with the relationship between customer and software developer, and provides some guidelines on how to avoid the classic pitfalls resulting from conflicting interests. Though many of these problems are common to all customer-developer relationships, some issues are specific to software development. The development of software is much less deterministic and more risky than other areas of technology. This often leads to misunderstandings and disagreements that could have been avoided if they had been anticipated and contained early enough.

To standardize our terminology, the organization to whom a proposal is being submitted will be referred to as the *customer*, and the organization submitting the proposal will be referred to as the *proposer*. Other terms commonly used elsewhere for the proposer include *bidder*, *vendor*, or *contractor* and for the customer *requestor* or *issuer*.

The organization submitting the winning proposal, after being selected, will be referred to as the *developer*.

3.1 The Cost-Plus versus Fixed Price Dilemma

There is often a real or imagined conflict of interest between the developer and the customer. The customer wants to spend less and the developer wants to earn more. As we shall see, a good relationship between developer and customer need not necessarily lead to this conflict of interest.

There are basically two types of contractual relationship between the customer and the developer:

1. Cost-plus (also called time and material), and

2. Fixed price

Most other relationships are some kind of combination of these two.

3.1.1 The Cost-Plus Contract

Cost-plus is a contractual relationship in which the developer is paid for the cost of the services provided and in addition is allowed an agreed profit margin. This is rather like renting a car; the customer pays for the time that the car is used (by the hour, day, week, etc.), and for any other expenses such as insurance and gasoline. Thus, in a cost-plus contract the total cost of the project is only known after the project has been completed.

As an example, company Alpha may contract software company Beta to develop a system. Company Beta will be paid $120 by company Alpha for each hour invested by their engineers in the project. An additional 20 percent may then be added to cover managerial, secretarial, and other office services. Additional expenses incurred by company Beta for the benefit of the project would then be reimbursed by company Alpha. These expenses might cover such areas as:

- Special-purpose development equipment (computers, compilers, networks, etc.)
- Travel expenses incurred by employees of company Beta for the benefit of the project
- Target equipment procured by company Beta for the use of company Alpha
- Services from other outside sources requested by company Beta for the project

The customer, company Alpha, may require the developer, company Beta, to receive prior authorization before incurring any single expense exceeding $400, and any expense in excess of a $10,000 monthly total. Such authorization should always be in writing. This defines a basic cost-plus contractual relationship between the two companies.

In many cases, cost-plus can be the most appropriate way to contract development work. However, there are numerous potential problems. A conflict of interest may arise due to the developer's lack of motivation to complete the project as quickly as possible, or due to the customer's reluctance to authorize additional expenses.

Cost-plus is often appropriate for small, undefined projects, for which it is difficult to identify the project's requirements in advance. In fact, in many cases the requirements phase of a project is offered as a cost-plus contract, and the remaining phases are contracted at a fixed price. The requirements phase is then used to bring the rest of the project to a sufficiently well-defined state, from which it can then be contracted at a fixed price. Occasionally, one company is awarded a cost-plus contract for the requirements phase, and another company is awarded the remaining phases as a fixed price contract.

Cost-plus may be preferred by the customer who wants to retain control of the development process. In some cases, the developer is perceived as an extension of the customer's organization, and the development activities are managed by the customer.

A cost-plus contract should cover the following issues:

- List of persons to be assigned to the project
- Work definition
- The percent of time each person is assigned to the project
- Hourly or daily work rate for each person
- Administrative overhead
- Authorized expenses to be reimbursed
- Billing procedure
- Payment procedure
- Termination procedure

The percentage of time each person is assigned to the project may be 100 percent for some engineers, and 50–60 percent for experts in specific areas. This assignment percentage may also be quoted in terms of maximum or minimum, meaning that, for example, a quality assurance engineer will devote no more than 20 hours a week to the project, and no fewer than 10 hours a week to the project.

The billing rate may be a fixed rate for all persons assigned to the project, or individual rates may be set for each person or class of people. For example, for each hour worked on the project, the developer will bill $120, irrespective of who worked that hour. Or the contract may stipulate that design engineers bill at $140 per hour, less experienced developers at $70 per hour, documentation writers at $50 per hour, and so forth. The most difficult cost-plus contract billing rate method is the individual billing method, in which Frank Jones is billed at $100 per hour, John Smith at $75, and so forth. This means that each time a person is replaced or added to the project, the hourly rate must be renegotiated.

For a software development organization, there can be real advantages in cost-plus contracts. These include:

- No financial or business risk
- Acquisition of knowledge and experience at the expense of another organization

However, as in most cases, these advantages come with some disadvantages, which include:

- Low business profit
- Possible staff discontent
- Reduced control of staff and development work
- Potential friction with the customer due to a lack of well-defined goals
- Contract continuity is not assured

Most employees prefer a clear definition of the hierarchy to which they belong. In a cost-plus contract, the employee may work within the customer's hierarchy, while belonging to the developer's hierarchy, and this can cause discontent.

In general, from the developer's perspective, a cost-plus contract is a solid, low-profit, no-risk business relationship.

From the customer's perspective, the advantages of a cost-plus contract are:

- Retention of control over development
- No commitment needed for a full project contract
- A possible reduced business risk (due to the ability to terminate the contract at any time with no penalty)

The customer's possible disadvantages are:

- Increased development costs
- Customer's assumption of development risks
- Increased involvement in development
- Potential friction with the developer due to a lack of well-defined goals

For the customer, the desirability of a cost-plus contract is difficult to establish. Clearly, this is dependent on the type of project and the conditions under which it will be developed, as well as on other non-technical business considerations.

3.1.2 The Fixed Price Contract

A fixed price contract is a commitment by the developer to provide an agreed product or service for an agreed fee, within an agreed schedule. This is similar to purchasing a bus ticket, for which the bus company agrees to take the customer to a specific destination within a published timetable, and for an agreed fee. Of course, travelers can elect to rent a car instead of purchasing a bus ticket, and then drive to their destinations themselves. However, this may turn out to be more expensive, and requires of the traveler some prior skills and knowledge, such as driving skills and knowledge of the route to the destination. So travelers (or customers) must decide between providing the service themselves and contracting someone else to provide the service.

A fixed price contract can only be applied to a well-defined project. Both customer and developer must be able to define the final deliverable product or service. Once this has been achieved, one of the main weaknesses of the fixed price contract will have been removed.

The advantages of a fixed price contract for the developer include:

- Full control of the development process
- Potentially higher business profit
- Commitment for a complete project

The commitment for a complete project is a significant advantage over cost-plus contracts that may end at any time, at the customer's discretion. Of course, fixed price contracts also have some disadvantages for the developer, which include:

- Assumption of business and development risks
- Potential friction with the customer due to:
  —continuing requirement changes
  —project completion criteria
  —interpretation of requirements
- Potential business loss

A successful software organization will often prefer a fixed price contract. These are usually the projects that build a company's professional reputation, and generate profit to enable growth. Unfortunately, these are also the projects that generate loss, and that often severely harm a company. Stiff competition for an important contract occasionally tempts a company to underbid, which ultimately generates losses for the developer.

It is almost inevitable in any project that the developer will be requested to change the requirements during development. Such changes are usually associated with additional cost to the customer, and are invariably a cause of disagreement between developer and customer. This is often due to unclear or ambiguous requirements, which in turn lead to disagreements regarding the criteria for project completion. This, essentially, returns the contract to an insufficiently defined state.

From the customer's perspective, the advantages in a fixed price contract include:

- A fixed budget for the project
- Most of the development risks are transferred to the developer
- Minimal involvement in the development process

The disadvantages to the customer are:

- Reduced control of the development process
- Risk of late delivery by the developer
- Potential friction with the developer due to:
  —high cost of requirement changes
  —unclear project completion criteria
  —interpretation of requirements

Even though the interests of the developer and the customer may be different, fixed price contracts are still often preferred by both parties. If the project is sufficiently detailed and clear, and if the relationship between the two parties is well defined, then fixed price contracts can be beneficial to both the developer and the customer.

3.2 Other Customer-Developer Relationships

Cost-plus and fixed price are two of the traditional contractual relationships between developer and customer. There are many variations of these two basic relationships, including various combinations that are tailored to suit specific projects. Some of these relationships are associated with the roles of customer and developer, and attempt to provide more incentives for the developer to support the customer's objectives beyond contractual obligations.

Additional types of customer-developer relationship include:

- Combinations of fixed price and cost-plus
- Joint ventures
- Royalty agreements
- Long-term commitments

As mentioned in Section 3.1, a contract can combine cost-plus and fixed price, where the requirements are developed at cost-plus and the remainder of the project is developed at fixed price.

Joint ventures are instances where the customer-developer dividing line can become hazy, and many of the previously discussed advantages and disadvantages may not apply. There are many cases where some form of joint venture may be desirable for both parties, such as when the developer wants to retain rights to the product, or when the developer joins the customer in funding part of the development effort.

One way the customer can offer the developer moderate participation in the business aspect of the project is by substituting royalties as partial payment. This generates an added dimension to the developer's interest in the success of the project. The royalties are usually such that the failure of the project would produce less revenue for the developer than a straightforward fixed price contract, and the success of the project will increase the developer's revenue.

Long-term relationships are often important for the developer. In many cases, long-term commitments are also in the customer's interest. This occurs when the developer, by being awarded the initial contract, gains, through acquired knowledge, a major advantage over others for subsequent development work. Clearly, when the developer successfully completes a large and complex project, a significant advantage is then acquired over other companies with respect to future extensions of the project. A long-term commitment may then be of mutual interest to both parties, wherein the customer is assured future services from the developer and the developer is guaranteed a long-term revenue commitment.

3.3 The Request for Proposal

Software development under contract starts with the selection of the software developer by the customer. A *request for proposal*, or *RFP* (also called in Europe an *invitation to tender*) is the beginning of the selection process. To understand how an RFP should be prepared, we will first review the steps leading up to the decision to request proposals.

In the phased approach to software development, the pre-project phase is often referred to as the *concept phase*. This is the stage where the idea behind the project crystallizes and takes form, and decisions are made by the organization as to whether or not to proceed with the project. This is also the stage where the organization decides whether the project can be developed in-house, or whether it will be contracted out to another company.

RFPs are not only issued for complete projects; they may also be issued for software maintenance of an existing system, or for a single phase of a project. All well-prepared RFPs must contain the same basic information; incomplete RFPs result in incomplete proposals.

3.3.1 Some Basic Issues

Before hiring the development services of another organization, some basic issues need to be considered:

What are the objectives of the project?

Which organizations are to be considered for the job?

What type of contract will be offered (fixed price, cost-plus, etc.)?

What responses must be received from potential developers so that they can be considered?

When must the developer selection process be completed?

When must the project be completed and when must intermediate components be ready?

Who, within the organization, will be assigned the responsibility of selecting the developer?

What budget range will be allocated for the contract?

All of the above issues must be adequately addressed before taking the next step: the preparation of the RFP.

3.3.2 Preparation of the RFP

A good request for proposal is one that will draw the best responses (proposals). The preparation of a good RFP often requires the cooperation of many people, each of whom is assigned responsibility for specific sections of the RFP.

An RFP should include the following sections:

1. *Statement of the problem and project objectives.* This section provides general background information, including a description of the problem that is to be solved. The section should provide all relevant details necessary to understand the problem, including diagrams, reports, and examples.

2. *Technical requirements.* This section describes specific technical requirements of the system, such as:
   - Interfaces to existing systems
   - Data base requirements (such as required capacity, data relationships, etc.)
   - Communications and network architecture
   - Military, government, or other required standards
   - Required development methodologies
   - Reliability of the system
   - Timing constraints
   - Programming language
   - Host computer

3. *Administrative information.* This section provides information regarding the physical submission of the proposal, such as:
   - Who may respond to the RFP
   - How to request clarifications or additional information
   - Date and location of a scheduled meeting with all potential proposers
   - The proposal selection criteria

   This section may also contain a provision to the effect that the organization issuing the RFP will not be obliged to select the lowest cost proposal, or any other proposal.

4. *Cost requirements.* All financial issues are addressed in this section. This includes the pricing structure required in the proposal, as well as any specific information that is to be addressed in the proposal (such as justification of costs, or separate pricing for each phase). This section may also specify what type of development contract will be offered (cost-plus, fixed price, royalties, etc.).

5. *Referenced documents.* This section contains a list of all relevant documents addressed in the RFP, such as standards, existing system documentation, various product literature, etc.

6. *Required deliverables.* This section contains an initial version of the statement of work (SOW). This is mainly a list of the main project deliverables, such as documentation, software, training, and any relevant hardware or equipment. This section may also discuss the required warranty for the delivered system.

7. *Required proposal format.* The required standard format for the proposal is described in this section. This includes the required content of:
   - The technical proposal
   - The management proposal
   - The pricing proposal
   - The statement of work

   An example of a proposal outline appears in Section 3.4.

   This section also contains a list of all information that should be appended to the proposal. Apart from the basic proposal (according to the format described above) this may include the latest financial report of the proposer's organization, or the proposer's technical credentials.

8. *Submission schedule and decision schedule.* The critical dates relating to the RFP are described in this section. This includes the latest date for submission of the proposal, and the expected date by which a selection will be made. This may also include a tentative schedule for the completion of the development work.

One of the objectives of the RFP is to ease the task of comparing different proposals. This task can become extremely difficult if all proposals are constructed differently, or if they are based on very different assumptions. Section 3 of the outline refers to a meeting with all potential proposers. This meeting provides an opportunity to assure that all proposers have a common basis of understanding, and results in their proposals being easier to compare. This is also achieved by requiring the standardized proposal format, referred to in Section 7 of the RFP. Table 3.1 contains a general outline of an RFP.

Table 3.1   General Outline for an RFP

1. Statement of the problem and project objectives
   - description of current state
   - description of the problem
   - support documentation
     - reports
     - diagrams
     - examples
   - objectives

2. Technical requirements
   - interfaces to existing systems
   - data base requirements
   - communications and network architecture
   - military or government standards
   - reliability of the system
   - timing constraints
   - programming language
   - host computer

3. Administrative information
   - who may respond to the RFP
   - how to request clarifications or additional information
   - date and location of a scheduled meeting with all potential proposers
   - the proposal selection criteria
   - other administrative information

4. Cost requirements
   - pricing structure
     - services
     - products
     - procurement
   - justification of costs
   - separate pricing for each phase

   - type of development contract offered
   - cost comparisons of alternative solutions

5. Referenced documents
   - standards
   - existing system documentation
   - product literature

6. Required deliverables
   - documentation
   - software
   - training
   - relevant hardware or equipment
   - warranty for the delivered system
   - development and test tools

7. Proposal format
   - technical proposal
   - management proposal
   - pricing proposal
   - statement of work
   - supplements and appendices
     - financial report of proposer's organization
     - the proposer's technical credentials
     - résumés of key personnel

8. Submission schedule and decision schedule
   - latest date for submission of the proposal
   - expected date by which a selection will be made
   - preferred schedule for the completion of the development work

3.3.3 Issuing the RFP

There are three basic methods for distributing an RFP:

- According to a limited distribution list
- According to a broad distribution list
- To all who request it

A limited distribution list contains only those organizations that have been selected according to a specific set of criteria. Various government agencies maintain a list of authorized companies for each class of RFPs. This method precludes organizations that have little chance of being selected.

A broad distribution list includes any organization that has any chance of being selected. For an organization to be added to the list, it need only request it. Broad distribution lists may be appropriate for small projects, projects requiring no special expertise, or projects for which few appropriate organizations have been located.

It is not uncommon for initial RFP information to be advertised in the press or in professional journals. These announcements contain a short description of the RFP and invite companies to request a copy of the full RFP. This approach is often appropriate when new potential proposers are being sought.

Whichever distribution method is selected, the organization issuing the RFP must remember that the issuing procedure does not end with the distribution of the RFP. The issuing organization should be ready to provide any additional information and clarifications that may be requested. One way to achieve this, which has already been mentioned, is to schedule a meeting with all potential proposers in order to provide clarifications and to answer any questions. This meeting is also an opportunity for the proposers to tour the target plant and to see at first-hand the problems that will be resolved by the project.

3.4 The Proposal

The various types of proposal can be divided into two basic categories:

- Solicited proposals
- Unsolicited proposals

The solicited proposal responds either to a formal RFP or to a specific invitation to submit a proposal, while the unsolicited proposal is usually initiated by the proposer. There are, of course, various combinations of the two, such as the strange but common situation in which a company is urged to submit an unsolicited proposal, or when an unsolicited proposal triggers the issuance of a formal RFP.

3.4.1 The Unsolicited Proposal

Unsolicited proposals are much less formal than the solicited proposal, and they are often no more than a first step leading to more formal negotiations. An unsolicited proposal should contain the following basic sections:

1. Justification for the submission of the proposal

2. A description of the problem that is to be solved

3. A description of the proposed solution

4. A description of the proposer's organization

5. A general overview of the cost of the proposed solution

The justification section is vital, as it explains why the customer should read on. This section may proclaim, for example, that the proposer has developed a new and successful technology that would benefit the customer and could be adapted to the needs of the customer's organization. The main objective is to provide an answer to the customer's question: "Why has this company approached me, and why is it to my benefit to read the proposal?"

Sections 2 and 3 describe the way the proposer's specialized knowledge will be applied to the problems of the customer's organization. This requires the proposer to study the customer's organization in order to assure the proposal provides a real solution to a real problem.

The precise cost of the solution need not be provided at this stage. An unsolicited proposal is rarely accepted the first time around. Its main objective is to generate interest. If the proposal generates sufficient interest, the proposer will be invited to discuss the proposal, and will then resubmit to the customer a more detailed version of the proposal.

3.4.2 Solicited Proposals

A solicited proposal is initiated by the customer as a response to a formal RFP or to some other form of invitation to submit a proposal. Contrary to the informal nature of the unsolicited proposal, the solicited proposal is complete and detailed, and its content is often binding on the proposer.[1]

Together with the request to submit a proposal, the customer may also specify exactly how the proposal is to be prepared and submitted. An example of a formal proposal format appears in Table 3.2.

One basic area in which solicited and unsolicited proposals differ is in the need to be competitive. Solicited proposals must be capable of competing successfully with other proposals. This means that the preparation of a solicited proposal must be regarded as a mini-project in itself, and as such requires the formation of a proposal preparation team.

3.4.3 The Proposal Preparation Team

The formation of a proposal board is fundamental to any organization that expects to respond successfully to an RFP. This board designates a person whose job it is to locate suitable RFPs and submit them for discussion, based on a set of guidelines established by the board. These guidelines should address RFPs that:

---

[1]The proposal as a binding document is further discussed and illustrated in the introduction to Chapter 12.

- Are within the company's line of business

- Are within specific limits of size (projects that are not too small and not too large)

- Do not obviously preclude the company (e.g., requiring special expertise or security clearance)

Based on its evaluation of the RFPs submitted, the proposal board decides which RFPs will be responded to by the company.

The proposal board then selects a team for the preparation of each proposal. This team may contain a single person, or many team members, depending on the size of the proposed project. The team draws from the experience and expertise of all company employees, and, if necessary, may engage the services of outside experts to assist in the preparation of the proposal.

The basic knowledge required within a proposal preparation team includes:

- Technical knowledge relating to each separate area addressed by the proposal

- Project management, including estimation and planning

- Financial knowledge, including budgeting and finance planning for the whole project

- Familiarity with the customer's organization

- Experience in writing proposals

One member of the team will be designated team leader, or coordinator, by the proposal board. After the team has been assembled, its first two assignments should be:

1. An initial review of the RFP

2. The preparation of a schedule for the completion of the proposal, and the assignment of responsibilities

The preparation of a good proposal costs money, and should be regarded as an investment. If it is done well, it can produce a profit. An inadequate proposal budget will reduce the chances of producing a winning proposal. The members of the proposal preparation team should be dedicated to the task, and they must be provided with adequate resources.

The process of submitting proposals has been significantly influenced by the US Department of Defense—probably the largest customer for contracts in the world. DOD proposals commonly required a major investment by the proposer. This practice became customary after the Second World War when the DOD began issuing giant RFPs. According to Silver (1986), proposals in high technology and aerospace industries were budgeted at around 2 percent of the amount of the contract. Today, the range of proposal cost is commonly 1 percent to 10 percent. The higher the cost of the contract, the lower the percentage that is devoted to the preparation of the proposal.[2]

---

[2]Silver presents a project contract range of $10K to $2B, with a proposal cost range from 1 percent to 20 percent in the United States, and a contract range of $10K to $1B with a proposal cost range of 1 percent to 10 percent in Europe. With regard to most projects, which fall between $250K and $100M, he presents a proposal cost range of 0.5 percent to 8 percent in the United States, and 1 percent to 2.5 percent in Europe.

3.4.4 The Proposal Format

A good proposal should provide answers to six basic questions: *who, what, why, how, when,* and *how much.* Responses to these questions simply refer to:

1. *Who* is the organization submitting the proposal?
2. *What* is being proposed?
3. *Why* is the proposal being submitted?
4. *How* will the proposed work be implemented?
5. *When* will it be developed and delivered?
6. *How much* will it cost?

The *why* question is important for an unsolicited proposal, and provides the basis for its submission. A response to an RFP would simply state that "This proposal is being submitted in response to Acme Inc.'s request for proposal No. 456 of 5 June . . ."

The other five questions are addressed in the five main components of the proposal:

1. The technical proposal (*what, how*)
2. The management proposal (*how, when*)
3. The pricing proposal (*how much*)
4. The statement of work (*what, when*)
5. Executive summary

and in the supplements, which include:

- Company background and experience (who)
- Qualifications of key personnel
- Exhibits and relevant documents

The executive summary is especially important for large and complex proposals, because not all selection board members will read the proposal. The summary should be between one and six pages in length, and should include references to specific areas in the full proposal that provide more detail.

Tables 3.2, 3.3, and 3.4 present examples of outlines for the technical, management, and pricing proposals for a software project.

Table 3.2 Sample Outline for a Technical Proposal

1. Overview of the problem to be solved
2. Overview of the proposed solution
3. Components to be purchased
4. Components to be developed

(continues)

Table 3.2   (*continued*)

5. Equipment
   - infrastructure
   - computer hardware
   - communications and networks
   - test and verification equipment
   - other special equipment
   - interfaces to other systems

6. Software components
   - general description of the software system
   - detailed description of each major software component
   - interfaces to other systems
   - data bases
   - use of existing software components
   - reusability of software components to be developed

7. Human engineering and user interfaces

8. Special considerations
   - reliability
   - timing
   - data integrity
   - backup and recovery

Table 3.3   Sample Outline for a Management Proposal

1. Development tools and utilities

2. Development environment

3. Personnel requirements and development team structure

4. Development methodology

5. Development phases

6. Reviews

7. Reporting
   - types of reports
   - report formats
   - reporting frequency
   - distribution list

8. Subcontractors

9. Standards

10. Testing
    - testing stages
    - formal testing procedures
    - error detection and correction

11. Quality control

12. Configuration management

13. Maintenance

14. Schedule
    - major activities list
    - milestones
    - dependencies
    - staffing

15. Risk management

Table 3.4 Sample Outline for a Pricing Proposal

1. Type of contract (fixed price, cost-plus, etc.)	6. Warranty
2. Development cost by project component	7. Profit
3. Subcontractor costs	8. Total project cost
4. Procurement costs	9. Type of financing (negative, positive)
5. Overhead	10. Payment schedule
	11. Billing and administration

3.4.5 The Statement of Work

The statement of work (SOW) is the basis of the contract between the proposer and the customer, and is often incorporated into the contract. The SOW contains a detailed list of all work to be performed by the proposer for the benefit of the customer.

The SOW starts as a general list of required deliverables in the RFP. A more detailed version of the SOW is submitted as part of the proposal, and is still considered only an initial description of the work to be performed. The binding version of the SOW is finalized during contract negotiations, or after the detailed project requirements have been completed.

Table 3.5 presents an example of an SOW outline for a software project. The list of items varies considerably, depending on the type of project being developed; for exam-

Table 3.5 A Sample SOW Outline for a Software Project

1. Referenced documents • requirements specification • existing system description • customer's RFP • developer's proposal • vendor's and developer's technical literature	6. Procurement
	7. Supervision of subcontractors
	8. Documentation • development documentation • user documentation • maintenance documentation • other technical documentation
2. Software deliverables • functionality (as documented in the requirements specification) • list of major software components	9. Testing • alpha testing • beta testing • acceptance tests (ATP)
3. Equipment and hardware deliverables • functionality (as documented in the requirements specification) • list of major hardware components	10. Installation
	11. Maintenance services
	12. Other services and deliverable items
4. Training • user courses • operator training • installation training	13. Method of delivery • software • documentation • hardware
5. Market research	

ple, not all projects include the delivery of hardware components, and not all projects require training or installation.

The basic guideline for the preparation of the SOW is that any activity, service, or product required by the customer, and agreed to by the developer, must be included. This means that there can be no binding work items that were informally understood, or agreed to verbally, which do not appear in the SOW. The formal SOW must include all and only the work to be performed. This condition prevents misunderstandings and disagreements later, after the project begins.

3.5 The Proposal Review and Selection Process

After the proposals have been submitted, the review and selection process begins. This section discusses the review process from a technical perspective. Undeniably, the review process is far from being purely technical. Few proposal selection processes are totally objective. Selection boards are composed of people, all of whom come with their own preferences and inclinations.

In fact, there are many cases where the proposal selection process is totally subjective. This includes cases of personal influence, familiarity, and friendship between customer and contractor, unfounded bias in favor of one company, or unfounded prejudice against another.

Such situations are difficult to overcome, and often more difficult to discover. These situations can be combated with some degree of effectiveness through psychological sales and marketing techniques that are beyond the scope of this book.

3.5.1 The Proposal Selection Board

A proposal selection board is a group of people appointed to review and evaluate proposals, and to recommend one of the proposals according to a predetermined set of criteria. This may be a set of general guidelines, or an extremely formal set of evaluation factors and procedures.

Many large organizations have formalized the proposal evaluation procedure.[3] This usually includes three separate channels for technical, management, and cost evaluation. Each component of the proposal is graded according to a specific evaluation procedure, and a combination of the individual grades produces the final grade for the proposal.

Proposals for small and large projects alike should be evaluated according to a systematic and relatively objective procedure. Based on its evaluation, the proposal selection board then submits its recommendation, together with a summary of the data, calculations, and evaluations that led to the selection. Frequently, two or three recommendations are submitted, and a second iteration is started with the selected companies to choose the winning proposal.

---

[3]For example, the US DOD has issued Directives 5000.1 *Major Systems Acquisition*, and 4105-62 *Proposal Evaluation and Source Selection*, and DOD FAR Supplement 15.6 *Source Selection*. NASA has issued Directive 5103.6a *Source Evaluation Board Manual*, and FAR Supplement 18-16.608-70 *Proposal Evaluation*.

This list of companies for the second iteration is often referred to as the *short list*, and the second round of proposal discussions is referred to as the *best and final*.

3.5.2 Proposal Evaluation Method

Most proposal evaluation methods are based on some variation of the weighted technique, whereby a number of factors score points that are then weighted and combined to provide an overall grade for the proposal.

Silver (1986) suggested a rating technique for each factor that is similar to Table 3.6. Note that the description of the lower ratings takes into account that an opportunity may be provided to the proposer to correct the item being scored.

The rating technique described in Table 3.6 is then applied to each major component of the proposal, and a weighted average is then calculated. As an example, the four major components of the proposal may be weighted as follows:

Technical	35%
Management	25%
Cost	30%
Company background	10%

This means that more importance is attached to the technical component of the proposal than to any other component.

The weighted average can be further refined. An additional acceptance criterion may state that any proposal that rates less than 5 out of 10 in any one major component will be rejected, irrespective of its final weighted score. This means, for example, that no matter how good the technical, management, and cost proposals are, if the company background is weak, the overall proposal will be rejected.

Table 3.6 A Sample Rating Scale for Proposal Evaluation

GRADE	RATING	DESCRIPTION
9–10	Superior	High degree of expertise, knowledge, or competence; highly acceptable; comprehensive; leaves very little else to be desired
7–8	Good	Satisfactory level of expertise or knowledge; acceptable; comprehensive; generally does not require additional information or clarification
5–6	Fair	Minimally acceptable level of expertise or knowledge; requires additional information or clarification
3–4	Poor	Below minimally acceptable level; requires considerable improvement; indicates a low level of expertise or knowledge
0–2	Rejected	Lack of capability to perform the work; data cannot be evaluated or is not provided

Table 3.7   Management Proposal Items—Evaluation Weights

1. Schedule		23%
final completion date	12%	
likelihood	5%	
milestones	4%	
level of detail	2%	
2. Staffing		16%
key personnel	11%	
development team structure	5%	
3. Development control		17%
quality control	7%	
testing	7%	
configuration management	3%	
4. Subcontractors		12%
5. Maintenance		10%
6. Risk management		8%
7. Development methodology		5%
8. Development environment		5%
9. Development tools and utilities		4%
		100%

Table 3.7 presents an example of the weighted items within the management component of the proposal. Similar tables should be prepared for the items comprising each of the major components of the proposal. Both the list of items to be scored and the individual weights may be tailored for each RFP, but this tailoring should be done in advance of the evaluation and selection process. A general master version of the evaluation tables should be maintained as a basis for each new project.

3.6 Some Additional Proposal Considerations

Software development is much less deterministic than other areas of high technology. It is usually much easier to estimate the factors of a hardware or electronics development project than the factors of a software project. Experience has shown that substantial software project overruns have been much more frequent, and much more extensive, than in other areas of technology. This means that software proposals require special attention in specific areas, such as scheduling, risk analysis, personnel management, and costing. These areas are important in *any* area of technology development, but much more so in the development of software.

Both the customer and the proposer must be aware of these and other special peculiarities of software development. The customer should devote special attention to these areas when evaluating proposals, just as the proposer should devote special attention to them when preparing a proposal.

3.6.1 Issues Relating to the Customer

When preparing an RFP, one of the customer's most common dilemmas is just how much detail to provide. Too much detail may discourage proposers from offering their own solutions, while too little detail may generate unsuitable solutions due to lack of information. The customer usually has some idea of how the problem should be solved. If the customer's ideas are firm, then these ideas need to be detailed in the RFP. However, if the proposers are given the freedom to propose their own solution, then one of these solutions may be considerably better than the one visualized by the customer.

The customer has many other concerns, such as what happens if the requirements change. To what degree will the RFP lock the customer into an airtight solution that will be difficult to change? Or what happens to an urgent project that simply does not provide enough time to complete a good proposal evaluation procedure? The following is a summary of these and other issues that should be addressed *before* the RFP is released.

1. **The degree of detail.** Specific problems usually require specific solutions. If the problem is narrow and well defined, or if the customer has a specific solution in mind, then considerable detail should be developed in the RFP.

2. **Evaluating the proposals.** Objective evaluation of the proposals is not easy to achieve. At least two people should evaluate and score each item in the proposals, and an average should be calculated. If the scores differ greatly, then a third (and even fourth) person should score the item, and the two (or three) closest scores should then be averaged.

3. **Changes to the requirements.** The formal project agreement between the developer and the customer should allow for a reasonable number of changes (early in the project). This requirement can be included as part of the RFP. The application of the term *reasonable* should take into consideration the customer's valid need to correct errors in the project requirements on the one hand, and the developer's need to avoid disruption of the cost and schedule calculations on the other.

4. **Gaining time.** The process of issuing an RFP, evaluating proposals, and completing negotiations can be time-consuming. In some cases the project may be urgent, with the development work subject to a critical time frame.

   One of the ways to save time is for the customer to permit development work to start immediately upon the selection of the winning proposal. This is usually done by issuing a letter of intent (LOI) to the selected developer. The customer's risk in an LOI can be reduced by limiting the developer to a specific budget until the final contract is signed.

5. **Joint proposals.** One of the main problems with a joint proposal is the lack of a clear definition of responsibility. Joint proposals must always assign overall responsibility to one party. Other participants in the proposal, such as subcontractors, should be defined.

3.6.2 Issues Relating to the Proposer

There is no sure method for writing a winning proposal. Questions regarding technical and architectural issues, the inclusion of options, or the submission of multiple solutions depend on the type of proposal and the circumstances within which it is being submitted. The following are some general guidelines for the preparation of a proposal.

1. **The appearance of the proposal.** The outside appearance of the proposal is almost as important as its content. Few slovenly, haphazard proposals are selected as winning proposals. Significant attention should be devoted by the proposer to the cosmetics of the text, graphics, binding, slides, and any accompanying verbal presentations.

2. **Optional requirements.** An RFP may also include *optional* requirements. These are additional features or capabilities that are not absolutely necessary for the completion of the project, but are what is often referred to as *nice to have*. A proposal that includes the optional features may gain points with the proposal review board.

   Optional features are best addressed within a supplementary section of the proposal, and should be priced and scheduled separately.

3. **All requirements.** A proposal need not respond to *all* the RFP requirements. It must, however, reference all requirements to demonstrate that they have not been overlooked. Deviations from the RFP must be justified and explained.

4. **Alternative solutions.** A proposal may include more than one proposed solution. However, alternative solutions must be submitted separately, so that they can be addressed and evaluated separately.

   Alternatives need not repeat complete sections in the first solution proposed; they can reference them (e.g., "The development team organization for the Distributed Processing solution will be the same as for the Centralized System solution.").

5. **Professional tools.** Automated utilities and tools should be used to assist in the preparation of a proposal. Apart from the obvious word processors and spelling checkers, such tools as scheduling packages, design and requirement generators, graphics packages, and so forth can save a significant amount of effort and time in preparing a professional proposal.[4]

3.7 Legal Perspectives

The previous section discussed software development under contract. Contracts are legal documents and are often best dealt with through legal counseling. Contracts are not the only area where proposers and software developers come into contact with the legal profession. Most of the legal issues are related in some manner to questions of ownership.

[4]For a review of the most recent tools, see the Project Management Institute's (PMI) Internet site, at: http://www.pmi.org/publict/pmnetworkonloine/productnews.htm and see Software Methods and Tools at: http://www.methods-tools.com/html/tools.html

When a proposer or development organization supplies a software product, there immediately arise issues of ownership. Who owns the rights to software being supplied? Who owns the rights to software packages, components, and support software that has been incorporated into the software product? These rights of ownership are not very different than the ownership of any kind of property.

Software is one of the few products that can be stolen and left intact, at the same time. At least superficially that is the way it would appear. The illegal copying of software has been romanticized: software is not *stolen*, it is *pirated*. This word play somehow makes the offense appear less severe. It is, though, extremely frustrating for software developers to have worked hard to produce a software product only to have it blatantly plagiarized.

The law does offer protection through various forms of intellectual property safeguards. In fact, in the last two decades software development has evolved from being virtually a legally defenseless enterprise to one in which almost every innovation is a candidate for patent protection (see Nichols 1999).

This section provides a general overview of some of the most common legal problems facing software contract proposers and, in fact, any type of software developer. For a more detailed and authoritative source, see Fishman (1998).

3.7.1 Software Contracts and Agreements

There are many areas in software development where formal binding agreements are required. In all such cases, formal legal counsel should be sought. This is especially true of large contracts and RFPs. The impact of an agreement or contract often goes way beyond the original intent of the parties. A famous example of how software development agreements can produce surprising outcomes is the story of IBM's first PC operating system.

In the early eighties IBM produced the first version of today's PC (though they were preceded by Apple Computer, which developed the first home computer). IBM, a giant corporation, turned to Microsoft, then a very small software company, to develop the PC's operating system, DOS. The agreement between IBM and Microsoft was an amazing achievement for Microsoft. While being commissioned to develop DOS for IBM's PC, Microsoft was allowed to retain the rights to develop their own parallel version, MS-DOS. If not for this agreement, it is debatable whether Microsoft would have reached its extraordinary level of success, eventually surpassing IBM in its stock value.

Remarkably, a similar agreement was concluded between the two companies several years later for IBM's OS2 operating system.

Unfortunately, it is not uncommon for legal issues to complicate relationships between parties involved in the development of software. Major technology corporations regularly assign legal counsel to work alongside development managers in formalizing relationships, in order to prevent loss of valuable intellectual property. The following are some examples of areas where formal agreements are often required:

- Agreements with software contractors, vendors, and suppliers: such as software development contracts, approved supplier agreements, and maintenance and support agreements.

- Exchanges of information with co-developers: this includes nondisclosure agreements (NDAs) and various types of partnership agreements.

- Provision of early marketing information to distributors and customers: this covers sales agreements, exclusivity agreements and, in this case too, nondisclosure agreements.

- Employment agreements: including ownership of original ideas and software inventions, information disclosure restrictions, and noncompetition agreements.

There is one challenge that will be familiar to many software managers who have developed long-term (more than one year) projects. Close to the beginning of the project, decisions must be made about the version of commercial components that will be used in the project. This includes the operating system, data base manager, communications package, user interface application, and also hardware interfaces and platforms. A year or more later, these software and hardware product suppliers may have produced new versions, yet they must be willing to continue to support the previous versions that were selected at the beginning of the project. Alternatively, they must declare that their products are backward compatible. These are formal commitments that are best ensured in a legal agreement, for without such an agreement the project could be doomed to failure.

3.7.2 Ensuring Software Rights

Many aspects of software development are considered *intellectual property*, a term that describes products containing unique content resulting mainly from thought process. Intellectual property is an asset than can be copied or imitated, in contrast to more tangible assets such as real estate property.

Protection for software can be sought through such remedies as:

- patents
- copyrights
- trade secrets
- copy prevention methods (modules and logic to be included in the software product)

The following summary is based on Nichols (1999):

A *patent* is a legal monopoly granted for the use, manufacture, and sale of an invention. The term *invention* includes applicable original software. To qualify for a patent, the technology in question must be original and not currently available to the public. An idea is considered available to the public if it has been disclosed anywhere in the world and is part of the body of available knowledge. One of the central features of patent law is that the holder can prevent the use of the patented software even by others who discover the same idea independently.

A *copyright* is a legal device that enables the copyright owner to control how the work is used. It provides exclusive rights to the owner. In contrast to patents, copyrights are easy to obtain. In fact there are cases in which copyright protection is automatic. Under US law, a copyright requires minimal originality and protection lasts for 75 years.

A derivative of a copyrighted work can escape copyright infringement with just a small number of changes. Consequently, copyrights are not suitable for invisible or abstract work such as data structures or software algorithms. Copyrights have been applied successfully to such general concepts as the look and feel of a user interface (this, for example, prevents competitors from copying the appearance of Microsoft's Windows operating system even if they use different code).

The owner of a software copyright owns (and hence can sell) various exclusive rights, such as the right to copy the software; the privilege to further develop, expand, or make derivatives of the software; and the right to sell the software.

The law also provides protection of *trade secrets* provided the secret remains confidential. This can be accomplished with nondisclosures and employment agreements. Trade secret protection is not difficult to acquire but the protection it offers is limited. It is a reasonably good alternative to a patent especially when a patent cannot be obtained.

Software, similar to books, music, and other intellectual property, is difficult to control on a worldwide basis (see Philips 1998). This is especially true since the advent of the Internet, where software can be downloaded, exchanged, and copied, with virtually no visibility to controlling agencies. Many countries have mutual copyright and patent agreements that provide protection for work that was developed in one country from being used illegally in another. There are, though, many countries that do not respect or enforce intellectual property rights (or IPR) and some of them have become major international centers of illicit software products.

There are other international patent considerations. Most countries will not grant patents for software that was publicly disclosed any time prior to filing. However, US patent law provides a one-year grace period allowing software developers to disclose their inventions or offer them for sale for up to one year before applying for a patent.

Even considering the limitations of a patent, it is still a good legal resort for protecting software. Graham (1999) reports that toward the end of the nineties software patents accounted for 15 percent of the 120,000 US patents being granted annually.

The encouragement of patent proposals by engineers is a management responsibility. However, the actual identification, preparation, and submission of a proposal can only be performed by the engineers who produce the innovative research and development work. Graham strongly recommends that *patents be filed early, even before software is coded*. He believes that patents will only be submitted if developers are encouraged to do so. Many organizations have incentive programs, with substantial monetary awards, to encourage engineers to submit patent proposals.

3.7.3 Legal Requirements in Software Development

The previous sections discussed how to protect your rights in developing software. The other side of the coin is how you need to take the rights of others into consideration while developing software. This section discusses some of the pitfalls of these, often thorny, legal issues. Failure to address them early in the project can be costly later on. This is particularly true in cases of:

- **Commercial software products:** These are products that are often sold together with other software components developed by others (operating systems, data base managers, user interfaces, etc.)

- **Projects with considerable involvement of external parties:** When teams from different companies and organizations join together to develop a product, there is always a risk of one party infringing on the ownership rights of another.

- **Projects that produce new technology:** New technology is continually being developed throughout the world and there is always a risk that innovative ideas are not really innovative; they may have already been developed and patented elsewhere.

- **Large software projects with significant budgets:** The larger the budget, the more software is being developed, and consequently the greater the risk of legal infringement.

There are not many software projects that do not fall into at least one of these categories. Therefore, *virtually all software projects must consider legal requirements early in the development phase.* The best place to do this is in the software requirements specification (see Chapters 4 and 9).

In addition to the legal software rights and contracts discussed earlier, software requirements must consider such areas as:

- Third-party software such as data bases, user interfaces, operating systems, etc., and the restrictions they may apply to the software product being developed.

- The implications of the inclusion of public domain and open-source software, such as operating systems, graphic characters and pictures, utility packages, and other software applications.

- Warranties and the consequences of the software failing to perform: Examples are critical financial software or life-support equipment software.

- Expiration and validity issues: When do the developer's responsibilities (if any) expire? When do warranties and maintenance responsibilities of third parties expire? What legal commitments must third parties provide for maintenance of their software?

- Unintentional violation of rights: methods of prevention.

These issues translate into legal requirements, and just like any other requirement, must be reflected in the requirements, design, and implementation phases of the software project. It is the responsibility of the project manager to ensure that this happens: that third-party contracts and agreements adhere to legal requirements, that intellectual property is protected, that copyright notices are inserted throughout the documentation and code, and that significant legal issues are brought to the attention of the development organization's legal counsel.

These requirements, as well as other legal issues, must be reviewed during project audits and reviews just like any other requirement or major issue. For large or sensitive projects, it is desirable to have legal counsel present during the review.

3.8 Summary

This chapter deals with the relationship between customer and software developer, and the preparation, submission, and evaluation of proposals. It also provides some guidelines on how to avoid the classic pitfalls resulting from the conflicting interests of the customer and the developer. Though many of these problems are common to all customer-developer relationships, some issues are specific to software development.

There are basically two types of contractual relationship between the customer and the developer:

1. Cost-plus (also called time and material), and

2. Fixed price

Most other relationships are some kind of combination of these two.

Cost-plus is a contractual relationship where the developer is paid for the cost of the services provided and in addition is allowed an agreed profit margin. Cost-plus is often appropriate for small, undefined projects, when it is difficult to identify the project's requirements in advance.

Cost-plus may be preferred by the customer who wants to retain control of the development process.

A fixed price contract is a commitment by the developer to provide an agreed product or service for an agreed fee, within an agreed schedule. If the project is sufficiently detailed and clear, and if the relationship between the two parties is well defined, then fixed price can be beneficial to both parties.

There are many variations of these two basic relationships, including various combinations that are tailored to suit specific projects.

Software development under contract starts with the selection of the software developer by the customer. This is usually accomplished by issuing a request for proposal (RFP).

There are two basic categories of proposal: solicited proposals and unsolicited proposals. The solicited proposal responds either to a formal RFP or to a specific invitation to submit a proposal, whereas the unsolicited proposal is usually initiated by the proposer.

After their submission to the customer, all proposals are reviewed by a selection board.

Proposals for small and large projects alike should be evaluated according to a systematic and relatively objective procedure. Frequently, two or three recommendations are submitted, and a second iteration is then started with the selected companies to choose the winning proposal and to produce an agreed development contract.

Software development under contract is also a legal issue that often requires legal counsel. However, contracts are not the only area where software developers come into contact with the legal profession. Most of the legal issues are related in some manner to questions of ownership.

Many aspects of software development are considered *intellectual property*, a term that describes products containing unique content resulting mainly from thought process. Protection for software intellectual property can be sought through such remedies as:

- patents
- copyrights
- trade secrets
- copy prevention methods (modules and logic to be included in the software product)

The other side of the coin is how you need to take the rights of others into consideration when developing software. Virtually all software projects must consider legal requirements early in the development phase. The best place to do this is in the software requirements specification. These requirements, as well as other legal issues, must be reviewed during project audits and reviews just like any other requirement or major issue. For large or sensitive projects it is desirable to have legal counsel present during the review.

Exercises

1. The Acme Trucking Company has a fleet of 500 trucks, with 30 truck depots around the country. Acme dispatches trucks on delivery routes. Each trip begins at the closest depot to the start of the route that has an available truck, and ends at the closest depot to the end of the route. Acme wants to develop a computerized dispatching system to optimize the use of their trucks.

   Discuss the advantages and disadvantages to Acme, and to a project developer, assuming different types of development contracts.

2. Prepare an RFP for Acme's truck scheduling project. Include the Technical Requirements section, the Required Deliverables section, and the Administrative Information section, and an outline for all other major RFP sections.

3. Prepare a proposal to be submitted to Acme for the truck scheduling project. Include the technical proposal, the statement of work, and the executive summary, and an outline for all other major sections (including supplements).

4. Prepare the review and selection method and criteria for Acme's proposal selection board. Assign the weights for the four major components of the proposal and for the weighted items within each major component.

   Discuss any special review and selection criteria, such as minimum grades for certain items, or major components.

   Explain the reasoning behind the review method that you have described.

5. As a class exercise, select one of the RFPs prepared in Exercise 2 as the RFP for the Acme truck scheduling project. Designate three to five proposal preparation teams to prepare proposals in response to the RFP.

Designate a proposal review board to review the proposals and to select the winning proposal.

Discuss the review and selection procedure.

6. Prepare a list of legal requirements for the Acme truck project. Consider areas where intellectual property may be generated. Propose two different types of contracts that would address issues of the IPR in very different ways.

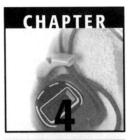

4

The Software Development Cycle: Variations on a Waterfall Theme

Software development, just like most other activities, has a beginning, middle, and end. The end of one development phase is sometimes perceived as being linked to the beginning of a new development phase, thus producing a cycle of beginning—middle—end, link, beginning—middle—end, link, and so forth. This view of software development is referred to as *the software development life cycle*.

There are many variations of the software development life cycle. Figure 4.1 presents a simple life cycle that was common during the first few decades of software development. In those early days of software development, the programmer would create programs by iterating from code to fix then back to code, and then to fix again, until something acceptable was (hopefully) produced. At the start of the cycle, there was usually no clear concept of what was required, and the basic development procedure was a form of "let's see what we can do" approach.

The software development method represented by the development cycle in Figure 4.1 is often referred to as the *code and fix method* (for obvious reasons). Software development methodologies have come a long way since the days of code and fix, though it is surprising how much software is still being developed this way.

Successful management of any project, especially software projects, requires planning, and planning is impossible with code and fix, which is totally unpredictable. Management of software development within an engineering discipline is based on a much more orderly set of development phases. These phases of the development cycle do not represent the classic activity called *programming*. In fact, programming (or coding) is

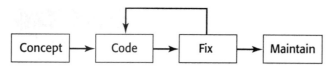

Figure 4.1   The code and fix method.

just one of the many development phases of the life cycle, and it has become a relatively small one, too, as is evident from Table 4.1.

The numbers in Table 4.1 are derived from the general shift in emphasis to software planning (requirements and design) and testing. Commercial data processing systems, with some exceptions, still spend a significant amount of development time in the programming and unit testing phase. Real-time systems are often more complex, and may include extensive hardware/software integration. This usually requires more planning and more integration and testing.

The data in Table 4.1, of course, represents a generalization; commercial data processing systems can be just as complex as a real-time system (see Section 4.4 for further discussion of this topic). Defense systems require high reliability and are usually closely supervised by the customer, leading to a significant increase in the time spent in planning. Most interestingly, Internet-based systems are often heavy users of Java, Pearl, and other very high-level languages. This reduces the amount of time spent on programming and increases the relative amount of time spent on planning and design.

Figure 4.2 presents an early basic phased model of a software development cycle. This model, called the Waterfall model, got its name from the way in which each phase cascades into the next (due to overlapping), as demonstrated in Figure 4.3. Some interpretations of the Waterfall model, like the one that follows, combine the top level design and the detailed design phases into a single design phase, and the integration and test phases into a single phase. In fact, there are many variations of the classic Waterfall model, but they are all based upon a systematic transition from one development phase to the next, until the project is complete.

Many modern development methodologies do not move from one phase to the next like the Waterfall model. Rapid prototyping, for instance, iterates in a mini-development phase until a system prototype is developed (see Fig. 4.4). After the prototype is complete, the Waterfall approach can then be implemented to complete the full system. Rapid prototyping is particularly helpful in projects where the requirements are difficult

Table 4.1   Estimated Percentage of Time Spent in Each Major Software Development Phase

	PLANNING	CODE AND UNIT TEST	INTEGRATION AND TEST
Commercial data processing	25%	40%	35%
Internet-based systems	55%	15%	30%
Real-time systems	35%	25%	40%
Defense systems	40%	20%	40%

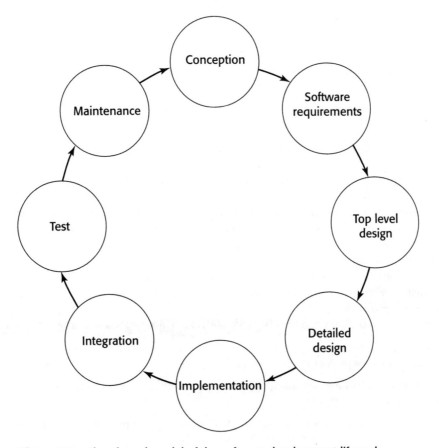

Figure 4.2   The phased model of the software development life cycle.

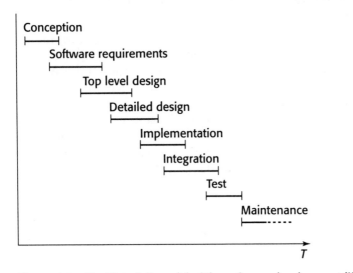

Figure 4.3   The Waterfall model of the software development life cycle.

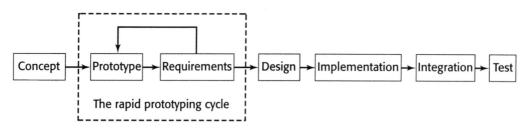

Figure 4.4   Rapid prototyping followed by the phased method.

to specify. The prototype can be used as a tool for analyzing and determining what the requirements should be.

Rapid prototyping is an instance of rapid development techniques in general. Another is the Spiral model described below. These techniques are extremely useful in reducing development cycle time.

The methods that rapidly produce software products are varied and are collectively referred to as rapid application development (RAD). They are often the models of choice for fast development cycles (when an early version of the software is required as quickly as possible).

In his review of RAD, Barry Boehm (Boehm 1999) describes its various forms as:

1. **Dumb RAD:** when a decision maker sets an arbitrarily short deadline for completing a software project (to be avoided).

2. **Generator RAD:** involves using application generators such as spreadsheets, fourth-generation languages, etc.

3. **Composition RAD:** uses small "tiger teams" to rapidly compose a small to moderately large application in three to five months.

4. **Full-scale RAD:** based on several cycle time reducing strategies, such as task elimination, reducing rework using techniques for defect and risk avoidance, and staff motivation techniques.

Boehm is also the father of the Spiral model, another way of producing early results. The Spiral model iterates between the requirements, design, and implementation phases, and it has gained increasing popularity in recent years. The model, described by Boehm as early as 1988 (Boehm 1988), is an excellent model for an evolutionary product. It produces intermediate versions of the software and continues iterating until the final system is complete. Within each iteration, the Spiral model follows a phased approach similar to the Waterfall model. The Spiral model is illustrated in Figure 4.5.

Different models may be suitable for different software projects or for different software development organizations. However, a good model must include certain fundamental features.

Some of these basic features are discussed in IEEE Standards 12207 and 1074 (IEEE 1999) which discuss Software Life Cycle Processes, their development and implementation. These standards describe the processes that are required for the development of software and they specify the activities that must be included in the life cycle model. These standards are discussed further in Section 4.7 and in Chapter 9.

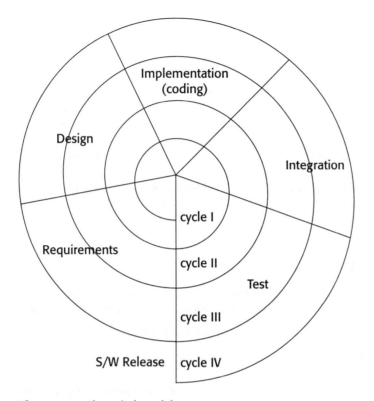

Figure 4.5   The spiral model.

Most modern software development models, and certainly those following IEEE Standard 1074, include some form of the basic phased model. It is therefore important to understand the different phases and how they relate to one another. This chapter describes some of the management issues associated with the phased models, including the atmosphere and the problems that characterize each phase.

4.1 The Concept Phase

The Waterfall model begins with an initial *concept phase*, during which the need for the software system is determined and the basic concept of the software system evolves. This phase provides the basis for:

- The preparation of a request for proposal (RFP); the RFP is useful when projects are contracted out to other developers (see Chapter 3).
- The definition of the software requirements (the next phase).
- Initial planning and preparation of estimates; this often serves as an early version of the project development plan.

The concept phase produces two types of project documents:

- The product description
- A concept document

The product description is primarily a marketing document, and is used as a future product announcement or as a general overview of the product. The concept document is a technical document and forms the basis for the main technical activities of this phase (RFP, initial planning). The concept document is also one of the main sources of reference for the production of the software requirements during the next phase of the project.

The concept phase is not a mandatory formal development phase. It is often conducted informally, before any commitment is made to further development of the project.

4.1.1 The Atmosphere during the Concept Phase

The atmosphere of the concept phase is variable, based on the ups and downs of indecision and hesitation. Thus, this initial phase of the project is usually characterized by:

- The desire of the technical staff to get the project moving.

- Lack of full commitment on the part of management; only initial budgets are usually allocated at this phase.

- Frustration of management; due to the inability of the technical staff to provide management with anything more than rough estimates.

- Frustration on the part of the development team, due to the inability of the customer (including management, marketing, and users) to provide accurate definitions of the required system.

All these are the product of a lack of commitment by the interested parties. The customer and management have not yet firmly made up their minds about whether they want to go ahead with the project. In addition, they are often not totally convinced of the importance of the concept phase, as there are very few visible results produced. The parties tend to be involved but not fully committed[1] to the project, and therefore expect results even though they haven't yet provided sufficient resources.

The allocation of a budget is always the firmest sign of commitment to a project, and the larger the initial budget, the firmer the commitment. The procurement of an initial project budget is often the project manager's first major task. This may be achieved as the result of:

- The preparation of a good concept document. A *good* concept document is the result of a comprehensive market analysis and user survey, and it includes a well-

---

[1]The concepts of *involvement* and *commitment* are often confused and used interchangeably. A famous anecdote emphasizes the difference between the two: in ham and eggs, the hen was involved, but the pig was committed!

written overview of the system's functional requirements. This document should also address the feasibility of the project.

- The establishment of a clear need for the system that is to be developed. One of the best ways to gain approval for a development project is to clearly identify and describe the problem for which the project will provide a solution.

- The provision of convincing initial estimates for the development of the project. No organization can commit to an unknown expenditure. If initial estimates cannot be prepared, then at the very least estimates for the requirements phase should be submitted (see Chapter 12 for a discussion of estimates).

4.1.2 Problems during the Concept Phase

Many problems during the concept phase are due to the difficulty in getting the project to move forward. This, clearly, is the result of the variable atmosphere described in the previous section.

This leads to the difficulty in obtaining a binding commitment from the customer and from top management.

The following problems are common during the concept phase:

- Many problems are related to establishing the initial project development team. Locating the right people for the project team is rarely an easy task. Indeed, locating a suitable project manager is not always an easy task.

- A common problem is either the lack or the excess of project leadership. In many cases the concept phase is led by many people; one may be responsible for market analysis, another for estimating, and yet another for producing the concept document. If there is a lack of coordination between those responsible for the various activities, it can produce many contradictions and bad initial decisions.

- When an initial team is in place and a rough development plan has been produced, it is not uncommon to find that there are many different ideas as to what the product should actually be. Producing an agreed concept document can often become a major problem. This problem can often be solved through the use of demo systems or prototypes.

Prototyping can be helpful when general agreement on the concept is difficult to reach. Concepts are often easier to consolidate when something concrete can be produced and reviewed by all interested parties.

4.2 The Software Requirements Phase

The software requirements phase, also called the definition phase, is the first formal mandatory phase of software development. This phase provides a detailed description of the software system to be developed. It is according to the requirements specification that the software product is tested at the end of the project to demonstrate that the required product has indeed been produced. The requirements specification answers the question *what* while attempting to avoid the question *how*.

The requirements phase forms the basis for:

- The first major system baseline (baselines are explained in Chapter 11)
- The design of the system (the next phase)
- The acceptance test procedures (ATP)

The requirements phase produces one main product document:

- The software requirements specification document

and two project planning documents:

- The project development plan
- The software test plan

The requirements phase formally concludes with the project's first major review: the software requirements review (SRR). It is this review that signs off the requirements specification and formally declares the requirements document as the first approved project baseline.

4.2.1 The Atmosphere during the Requirements Phase

The requirements phase is often perceived as the most important phase of the software development cycle (see the Epilogue). It is certainly one of the most difficult, due in part to the difficulty in documenting an agreed description of the software requirements. There is always a perceived (if not actual) conflict of interest between the customer[2] and the developer. The customer is reluctant to finalize the requirements because of the knowledge that once this is done any further changes may be costly. On the other hand, the developer needs to finalize the requirements as soon as possible because progress will be slow as long as the product is not fully defined; and this too is costly. Occasionally the atmosphere of the requirements phase becomes a form of tug of war between the customer and the developer. Preferably, this phase should be used to foster a cooperative relationship between developer and customer (see Section 4.9).

Cost-plus contracts, where the developer is paid by the hour or by the day (see Chapter 3), tend to have fewer conflicts of this type. However, cost-plus contracts leave the main responsibility for early closure of the requirements with the customer.

The requirements phase is thus characterized by:

- The risk of conflict between developer and customer in closing the requirements specification
- Disagreements over revised and binding estimates

and also by:

- Confusion due to shifting responsibilities and as yet unstaffed assignments

---

[2]The term *customer* is used here in its broadest sense and refers to the organization that requested the project, such as an external customer, marketing department, or users.

Closing and signing off the requirements is not always easy and requires experience, patience and firmness. It is the project manager's job, at some point, to be resolute and decisive in requiring all parties to sign off the requirements for the project. This is best achieved by explaining to the customer that lack of closure causes schedule delays, and schedule delays are costly.

4.2.2 Problems during the Requirements Phase

The occasional conflicts, disagreements, and confusion that characterize the atmosphere of the requirements phase are a major source of problems. The list could be long, but the most common problems are:

- Frequent requirements changes: during this stage there is often a seemingly endless flow of changes, making it difficult to compile the requirements specification.
- Requirements approval and sign-off: this phase cannot be completed without a formally approved requirements document.
- Requirements feasibility: sometimes this is difficult to determine before the implementation phase.
- Staffing: locating suitable development team members can be a difficult task. Assignment of team members should be completed during the requirements phase.
- Equipment procurement: budgeting and availability problems can disrupt equipment allocation plans.
- Binding estimates: if these have not already been provided, then they should be completed before the end of this phase.

As we have seen, obtaining formal approval for the requirements specification is the most difficult task of this phase. Usually, the requirements evolve gradually, with several draft versions of the specification converging to the final approved document. However, if major changes are introduced continuously, then not only will the document be difficult to compile, the project also will be difficult to plan. In such situations, prototyping can be most helpful in assisting the customer to determine the requirements.

The feasibility of requirements must be determined, when possible, before the requirements are closed. It is always costly to discover unfeasible requirements during later phases of the project.

The feasibility of requirements can be improved by:

- Using prototypes to test requirements.
- Temporarily involving experts in the feasibility analysis procedure.
- Requiring approval for alternate requirements if the original requirement is unfeasible.
- Making vague requirements contingent on certain outcomes (e.g., sufficient memory, or available CPU processing capacity). Whenever possible, vague or suspect requirements should be deleted.

An overview of the ingredients of a good requirements specification appears in Chapter 9.

Project planning progresses in parallel with the development of the requirements. Problems associated with the allocation of human and technical resources can delay the project. Finding good team members is always a problem for the project manager. However, once they are located and assigned, adequate development equipment must be available. Therefore, problems associated with the procurement of equipment become more severe as the development team grows.

Staffing problems can often be resolved by:

- Using temporary personnel
- Increasing the staff load later (not a desirable solution)
- Training existing available personnel

Equipment problems, too, can be resolved by:

- Using temporary equipment (loaned, or rented)
- Using software simulators in place of expensive equipment
- Obtaining an initial budget to fund basic development equipment

Equipment and staffing problems usually impact the estimates and the schedule in the project development plan. If equipment is late, or if staffing is slow, then estimates will need to be revised and schedules will have to be adjusted. These problems are discussed in detail in Chapter 11.

4.3 The Design Phase

During the design phase, the requirements are analyzed and the method of implementation is determined. Just as the previous requirements phase addressed the question *what?*, the design phase addresses the question *how?* The response to this question is documented in the software design specification document.

The design phase is often divided into two separate phases: top level design and detailed design. The dividing line between the two phases is set somewhat arbitrarily, based on the level of system decomposition (see Chapter 6). Figure 6.5 presents an example of the division of the design of a system into top level design and detailed design.

One of the advantages of using two design phases instead of one is that the first top level design provides an additional milestone at which the design approach can be evaluated and approved. This is especially important in medium and large projects (e.g., more than 18 work years) in which major design errors must be located as early as possible. When a major error is found at the end of the top level design phase, it is much easier to correct than if it is found after the whole design is complete. Consider the following example.

> *A company decides to link its eight facilities using a proprietary network. The company's communications team is entrusted with the project. The requirements are approved and signed off at the SRR, and the team proceeds to develop and assemble the inter-company network.*

At the next review, the Design Review, the architecture for the network is presented. The team has designed a network with eight local data bases interconnected. The equipment has been ordered, and development has started for the proprietary software. However, the design has been rejected.

The reason for the dissatisfaction with the design is that the distributed data bases will make it difficult for the teams to work in a distributed environment (with team members in different facilities). The solution would be costly, because it would require duplication of equipment at each facility. A single data base at one facility would be less costly and more reliable for backups.

The company must now decide either to incur the cost of changing the architecture, returning equipment (if possible), and rewriting the design specifications and some of the software, or to accept the current design.

If the distributed architecture decision had been discovered earlier, the preferred architecture could have been implemented at little or no cost. This could have been achieved with an early Preliminary Design Review.

The design phase provides the basis for:

- The second major system baseline

- The implementation of the system (the next phase)

- Updated development plan

The design phase produces the following documents:

- Design specification (for large projects: top level design specification and detailed design specification)

- Integration plan

- Test case specifications, describing in detail each individual low level test

The design specification document establishes the project's second major baseline. In the case of two design phases, the detailed design specification is regarded as the major design baseline, and the top level design specification is regarded as a secondary baseline.

At the end of this phase, many of the project's unknowns become known, thus providing a significant improvement in the development plan estimates. Various project development parameters, such as the integration schedule and resources, and the actual test cases for the test phase, can now be planned. The updated project development plan can therefore be regarded at this stage as being significantly more reliable.

Hence, in parallel with the design of the system, the following activities are also in progress:

- The development and integration platforms are installed. This includes all the equipment required for system development and integration.

- Estimates are significantly improved.

- Project risk analysis is reviewed and updated.

- The project development schedule is updated.

All of the above information is included in a new major revision of the project development plan.

The design phase concludes with the sign off of the design specification document. This usually occurs at a formal design review, referred to as the *Critical Design Review* (CDR). If an intermediate top level design specification is prepared, then this document is signed off at an initial *Preliminary Design Review* (PDR).

4.3.1 The Atmosphere during the Design Phase

The design phase is often a relatively confident and optimistic part of the development project. It is characterized by:

- Enthusiasm: the project gains momentum, budgets have been approved and are now being expended, and a new development team is in place.
- Delays: many changes in requirements and design are introduced, owing to:
  - late ideas
  - unfeasibility of requirements
  - additional new information
- Confusion: the team grows rapidly; project hierarchy and responsibilities are not yet clear

The design phase, for the project manager, is a period of organization during which the project team structure is finalized and the assignment of responsibilities is completed. These tasks must be completed by the project manager before the end of the design phase, because the confusion that may have accompanied the first two project phases cannot be carried over into the implementation phase.

4.3.2 Problems during the Design Phase

The main problems of the design phase are related to:

- Technical design issues
- Difficulties in staffing
- Procurement of development resources
- Customer relations

The technical design problems are concerned with both those derived from unfeasible requirements and those due to complex implementation and design decisions. It is during the design phase that all such problems should be resolved, because their resolution will become more costly as the project progresses.

Occasionally, staffing problems are carried over from the previous requirements phase. Some tasks will be hard to staff or slow to staff. It is therefore important for the project manager to attempt to assign people to all project positions as early as possible, even before the actual people are required. In fact, it is good practice to begin assigning people to positions well in advance of the date that people actually join the project.

Many of the problems related to procurement of development resources are also carried over from the previous phase. At this stage of the project, these problems are usually associated either with outside vendors and suppliers or with existing company equipment that is still tied up with other projects. As mentioned previously, many of these problems can often be resolved by equipment rentals or loans. However, the negative impact of such makeshift solutions increases as the project moves into more advanced development stages. In fact, these solutions, if not handled carefully, can lead to new problems:

- Rentals can be costly and can drain substantial amounts from the development budget.

- Loans can be retracted, leaving members of the development team without the necessary development facilities.

- Temporary makeshift solutions can lead to reduced quality and longer development time.

- This, in turn, will cause schedule slips.

Some customer—developer-related problems may still occur during the design phase. With the requirements now approved, much of the tension will have been eased, but when the design phase concludes with a formal review, the customer shares the responsibility for the design.

Continuous sharing of information with the customer is important. This is best achieved by designating one team member (possibly the project manager) to act as liaison with the customer. This reduces the points of contact between the team and the customer, while assuring that the customer has a single address for all requests and comments and for receiving information on the project's progress.

4.4 The Implementation Phase

During the implementation phase the software modules are coded and initial unit tests are performed. Unit testing is carried out by the programmer on each individual module immediately after it is coded. The modules are then approved by software quality control and submitted to configuration control (see Chapter 8 for a discussion of these control functions). Configuration control then releases modules for integration.

A detailed and well-structured design specification leads to relatively smooth and straightforward coding. Thus coding (or programming), which was originally perceived to be synonymous with software development, has become just a single phase in the software development cycle. In fact, the implementation phase is not even the longest phase. A common rule of thumb for estimating the software development cycle phases, uses a 40–20–40 division of effort and time (see Table 4.1). This means that about 40 percent of the time is devoted to specification (requirements and design), 20 percent to implementation (coding and unit testing), and 40 percent to integration and testing. Of course, the actual division of effort depends on the specific project and its type. As we have seen earlier, some projects (e.g., Internet-based projects) can require a significant

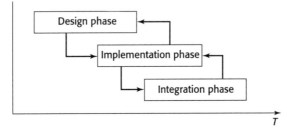

Figure 4.6   Overlapping of phases.

amount of time for planning and design and much less for coding, while others (commercial data processing) may behave quite the opposite.

The current trend is to attempt to reduce the 20 percent devoted to implementation, while increasing the 40 percent devoted to specification. One aspect of the reasoning behind this approach is that the earlier development phases are less costly than the later phases. The specification phases usually have lower staffing and less development equipment than the implementation phase. Also, as has often been demonstrated, when more effort is devoted to requirements and design, the integration phase is easier and more efficient.

The implementation phase links the design and integration phases of the system, and usually significantly overlaps each of these other two phases (see Figure 4.6). Overlapping will often occur when many parts of the system design are completed relatively quickly, leaving some design issues open for quite a while. In such cases, overlapping (rather than waiting for the design to be complete) can shorten the development schedule significantly.

Overlapping of the design and implementation phases requires great care to ensure that only design-complete modules are approved for early implementation. There is a risk that any later changes to the design of these modules may require re-coding, thus wasting resources.

There is also the risk of the design being changed without the code being changed. However, these risks are usually well worth taking. With good planning and automatic configuration control tools, these problems can be overcome.

On the other side of the implementation phase, overlapping of coding and integration is usually less risky and, if planned correctly, can be an excellent time saver. The order of implementation of the modules should be well planned to ensure that they are released in the order required for integration. This also means that implementation errors can be located during integration and fed back to the implementation phase.

The implementation phase includes the following main activities:

- The development of the software code
- Preparation for integration and test of the system (the next phase)
- The development of the maintenance plan

Apart from the actual code being written (and being well commented), some of the other documents that are developed during this phase include:

- The programmer's notebook, a file documenting coding decisions, unit tests, and resolution of implementation problems

- Maintenance plan and documentation, including all necessary documentation needed for system maintenance

- Initial versions of the user documentation, including reference manuals and operator guides[3]

During the implementation phase, the project enters a period of intense activity. The many other activities that are taking place include:

- The design phase is completed early during the implementation phase.

- The integration platform is put in place and integration begins.

- The test bed (test environment and equipment) is put in place in preparation for system testing.

- Risk situations may materialize and contingency plans are then put into action.

- The project plan is reviewed and updated.

4.4.1 The Atmosphere during the Implementation Phase

As we have seen, staffing reaches its peak during the implementation and integration phases. During implementation, the atmosphere is influenced by the many other activities going on in parallel. This atmosphere is characterized by:

- Pressure to get going and show something. This is often the result of a significant increase in the rate of expenditure, with little yet to show for the cost of development.

- Increased development team activity, with little free time left, as the delivery dates become close and more real.

In general, the implementation phase is a transitional period from specification to building. The atmosphere is heavily dependent on the success of the previous specification phases and the expected success of the following integration and test phases. Contributing factors include:

- Requirements may not yet be adequately defined.

- Insufficient resources have been assigned.

- Insufficient development time is available.

- Some technical problems may not yet be resolved.

- Management support may be lacking.

- Customer relations may be tense.

---

[3]The effect of the various schedule factors can be improved by dividing the project into components (e.g., data processing, communications, real-time) and applying the appropriate factors to each different type of component.

4.4.2 Problems during the Implementation Phase

If the design phase is implemented well, then most technical problems should be resolved by the end of design. If this is not so, then confusion may follow due to the necessity to program and solve technical problems simultaneously. Such situations often fall into the code and fix method (see Figure 4.1).

Other problems of the implementation phase include:

- Last-minute changes: this is a problem that can only be solved by assuring strict and orderly change control procedures.

- Interfacing and coordination between team members: this problem is particularly severe in large projects.

- Controlling and monitoring subcontractors and vendors.

The flow of changes is the scourge of engineering in general and of software development in particular. Clearly, changes must be permitted in moderation, but an unchecked flow of changes can bring a project to its knees. There is also the danger that, in large teams, some team member may be unaware of a particular change.

Communication between team members can be time-consuming. This communications overhead can be reduced in large teams by dividing the project into subsystems, with semi-independent teams assigned to each subsystem. Formal channels of communication are then defined between the smaller teams.

In some cases, subsystems can be assigned to subcontractors. However, controlling subcontractors and vendors may become a full-time job. Verbal and written reports are rarely sufficient; frequent visits to the development sites are often necessary to assure the availability of accurate information. In such cases, the developer becomes the customer in relation to the vendor or subcontractor.

4.5 The Integration and Test Phase

During the integration and test phase, the software modules are combined into a single system, and the functionality of the system is tested for compliance with the requirements. Integration starts with an initial version of the system that progressively increases in functionality until the full system is assembled. Each test stage then evaluates the performance of the system in order to identify problems that must be corrected before the system can be released.

The integration and test phase provides the basis for:

- The construction of the software system from the various software components

- The integration of the software and hardware equipment

- Determining whether the system has been developed according to the requirements specification

- Establishing the quality of the system

This phase is often divided into two separate and largely parallel phases: the integration phase and the testing phase. In large projects, this division is often necessary, especially when testing is carried out by a separate independent group (the *independent test team*) that works side by side with the developers—this is the preferred method. In smaller projects, the rationale behind the combination of the two activities into one phase is that integration cannot be successful without extensive testing being carried out in parallel. Therefore, if these two activities are performed by the same team, they are often best combined in a single phase (refer to Chapter 8 for a more detailed discussion of the software test team).

There are many techniques and methods of integration:

- top down
- bottom up

and an interesting approach referred to as

- inside out

The top down approach requires the core of the system (usually the central executive modules) to be implemented first.

They are then combined into a minimal system, using empty shell routines in place of the modules that have not yet been implemented. These empty shells of code that return fixed values and are devoid of any logic, are commonly called *stubs*. The stubs are then gradually replaced by the real modules, in a well-planned progressive build of the system, so that each new release of the system provides more functionality.

The bottom up approach starts from the individual modules at the lowest level (e.g., input/output drivers, formatters, data manipulators, and user/machine dialogues) and gradually binds them together in larger and larger groups until the full system is assembled.

The bottom up approach is rarely recommended as a comprehensive integration strategy; in most cases the top down approach is easier and more natural. However, in reality, most successful system integration strategies are a combination of the top down approach with a spattering of bottom up.

Inside out integration is common in the development of large data base systems, when the internal file structures are built first, after which the data processing logic is added, and finally the human interface is added. This approach is best when the system is logically comprised of succeeding layers of functionality, but its main drawback is that the human interface is usually the last to be integrated. This may require writing temporary test code to enable the output to be reviewed. Therefore, testing is often slow and difficult with the inside out approach.

Modern approaches to testing require each phase to be thoroughly tested before it is completed (not after). This prevents problems moving up from one phase to the next. This is called *phase containment* and is designed to locate and correct problems early (when they are less expensive to correct). Phase containment is discussed in more detail in Chapter 6.

Testing of the complete system starts with integration and continues until the final delivery of the system to the customer. The various types of testing include:

- *Integration testing*, performed by the system integrators.

- *Independent testing*, performed by an external test group to assure objective unbiased testing of the system.

- *Installation testing.* This includes general performance tests required whenever a version of the system is first installed in an operational environment. Many systems include a set of installation tests to ensure that the system has been installed successfully.

- *Alpha and beta testing.* These tests run in the system in a real (non-test lab) environment. Alpha testing tests the system without live data. Beta testing tests the system using live data, with constant supervision to correct any problems that may arise.

- *Acceptance testing.* This is the last milestone of the project, and its successful completion signifies the customer's acceptance of the developed product.

At the conclusion of the integration and test phase, all documentation must be complete and ready for delivery, including:

- Maintenance documentation

- Final user documentation

- All updated development documentation

- Test documentation and test reports

In parallel with integration and testing, the following managerial and nondevelopment activities take place:

- Final budgeting of the project: the cost of changes is determined, risk contingency activities are evaluated, and the budget is updated.

- Training is conducted for users, operators, customers, installers, maintenance engineers, and marketing engineers.

- Installation sites are prepared, and the infrastructure for hardware and special equipment is planned and installed.

- The development team size is reduced.

4.5.1 The Atmosphere during the Integration and Test Phase

Up to this point in the project life cycle, documents have been written, code has been developed and development equipment has been installed. Except for prototypes, nothing functional has yet been developed. The integration and test phase begins when staffing and budget expenditure are at their peak. Integration and testing is therefore often characterized by:

- Pressure to get something working. This began during the previous implementation phase, and now increases. Management has seen little of substance to justify their investment. Any schedule delays at this point can be critical. It is important for the project manager to produce an initial version of the system as soon as possible.

- Pressure to complete the project. This pressure appears towards the end of the project and becomes more intense if schedules begin to slip.

- Overtime. Calendar time is often more critical than development time (e.g., work months). The first solution for schedule slips is usually overtime.

- Conflicts with the customer. At last the customer can see an initial version of what the product will look like. At this point different interpretations of the requirements emerge, and often need to be resolved on a higher management level.

- Frustration. Solutions to integration problems and implementation bugs are often elusive, and may require a return to the design phase.

The integration and test phase is the most difficult to plan. It is also the most important to plan, because so much is actually going on. Many of the pressures of this phase can best be avoided by ensuring:

- Good design
- An efficient module coding plan
- A well-organized development team
- A good integration plan
- Suitable integration and test platforms

4.5.2 Problems during the Integration and Test Phase

It is during the integration and test phase that most of the development problems appear. It is payback time for poor phase containment. Events described earlier in the project as risks now materialize, and other unexpected problems inevitably occur. These problems include:

- Last-minute failures: design errors and implementation problems emerge. These are the types of problems that are difficult to uncover without an operational version of the system. They are therefore not discovered earlier in the project.

- Third-party problems, including late delivery from vendors and subcontractors and defects in their subsystems and components.

- Last-minute changes. This problem exists in all phases but becomes more severe as the project progresses. Changes now become much more costly.

- Budget overruns. This problem is derived from changes and design errors, as well as project planning errors.

- Staff motivation problems. These commonly occur toward the end of the project, during the final test stages.

- Project acceptance problems. This problem is particularly common in fixed price projects (see Chapter 3), when conflicts arise concerning the completion of the project.

Many of these problems can be avoided, or at least their severity can be reduced, by preparing for them early in the project. Just as risk management includes preparing

Table 4.2   Software Project Schedule Contingency Factors

TYPE OF SOFTWARE	ADDITION TO SCHEDULE
Small commercial data processing system	10%
Medium commercial data processing system	15%
Large commercial data processing system	20%
Communications system	33%
Internet-based software	15%
Scientific systems, compilers, etc.	25%
Operating systems	25%
Real-time systems	33%
User interfaces	15%
Hardware/software development	35%

contingency plans in case the risk event occurs, so the severity of any problem can often be reduced by planning for it ("what ifs").

As discussed previously, changes are inevitable, and are best handled through an orderly change control mechanism. This means that no change, without exception, can be accepted unless it is submitted through the change control channels.

Planning for last-minute failures and design errors is more difficult. A common solution to these types of problem is to accept the reality that failures and errors are inevitable. This means that they must be taken into account within the project schedule, even though they cannot be identified in advance. The traditional way of scheduling for unknown problems is to add a fixed percentage to the development schedule. A rule of thumb is to *add thirty percent for unexpected delays and unforeseen problems.*

Though a development organization will eventually accumulate the necessary information to define its own schedule contingencies, Table 4.2 is a good starting point. Chapter 12 discusses other more complex methods for improving estimates based on the type of project being developed.[4]

4.6 The Maintenance Phase

The maintenance phase completes the software development cycle and links the release of the completed software product with the development of a new product. The term *software maintenance* is controversial, because it implies a need to repair a product that has deteriorated. In mechanical or electronic systems, maintenance may

[4]In some sense software can be seen as changing if, due to a bug or a design error, it modifies itself (called "clobbering"). This can be prevented by storing software in read only memory (ROM).

require the repair or replacement of failed components, and preventive maintenance may require the servicing of components to prevent deterioration. However, software does not deteriorate. The vehicle that carries the software may deteriorate, but the software itself will not change[5] without human intervention.

The IEEE defines *software maintenance* (IEEE 1999) *as the process of modifying a software system or component after delivery to correct faults, improve performance or other attributes, or adapt to a changed environment.* This definition includes two basic components: (1) maintenance occurs after release of the product, and (2) it always involves changing the software that was released. Unlike hardware maintenance, none of these activities return the software to its previous state. Quite the opposite is true: the objective here is to modify the software.

Two other activities that are not mentioned in the IEEE definition are also part of maintenance:

- Maintaining updated documentation
- Updating user training courses

Modifying software includes all the characteristics of developing software. Modifications need to be formally described, designed, implemented, integrated, and tested. And of course, modifications need to be budgeted. It is therefore sound engineering practice to implement the maintenance phase as a series of small software projects.

Configuration control is particularly important during maintenance to manage the various changes to the software, and to control the many releases and versions of the system. This assures orderly periodic releases of the software, and avoids haphazard support and on-the-spot fixes that can turn into an engineering nightmare.

Project management is not always carried over from the development of the software product development to the maintenance phase. Maintenance requires a much smaller team, and a different type of management. In fact, a single maintenance group can be established to maintain several products, with common management, configuration control, installation and field engineers, and maintenance of documentation.

The documents that need to be updated during this phase include:

- Version release documentation
- Problem reports
- All development documentation
- All user documentation
- Maintenance logs and customer service reports

Maintenance continues for as long as the software product is installed and running. As the system ages, plans are prepared for a new development project to replace the aging system. At that time maintenance efforts are reduced to a minimum, due to the expectation that all required modifications and bug corrections will be included in the new system.

---

[5]Hewlett Packard, CISCO Systems, and Motorola, are examples of major corporations that have committed to 5NINES System Availability.

4.6.1 The Atmosphere during the Maintenance Phase

In many cases maintenance does not provide the challenge of new development. This can lead to an unstable maintenance team, with engineers frequently joining and leaving the team. Nevertheless, maintenance can provide many challenges, such as identifying critical problems, providing solutions, and suggesting improvements. In general, the maintenance phase is characterized by:

- A lack of enthusiasm, due, in some cases, to the lack of well-defined technical challenges.

- Pressure to provide quick fixes. In an orderly maintenance environment, problem corrections are rarely quick.

- Frustration due to a lack of adequate budgets. Maintenance activities are not always recognized as important, and are therefore often under-budgeted.

4.6.2 Problems during the Maintenance Phase

As we have seen, software maintenance includes all of the phases of a full development project. Therefore, many of the development problems prevalent during the basic development phases are common also in the maintenance phase. Other problems specific to this phase include:

- Insufficient knowledgeable maintenance engineers: this is due to the difficulty in recruiting engineers willing to accept maintenance tasks.

- Budgeting problems: associated with new releases of the system.

- Multiple patches on the existing system: after a while, even an orderly maintenance procedure can produce a patchwork software system. This often prompts the development of a new system.

- Lack of support equipment and test platforms; this problem, too, is often the result of insufficient budgets for maintenance activities.

For the maintenance manager, staffing the maintenance team is essentially a problem of creating an interesting and challenging assignment. This can often be achieved by assigning responsibility for a single project, or a well-defined part of a large project, to one software engineer. The assignment should include the identification of problems, provision of solutions, and suggestions for improvement within the engineer's area of responsibility. This approach promotes the engineer's dedication to the assignment and identification with the success of the maintenance effort.

Unlike staff motivation, budget and equipment problems are not primarily dependent on the maintenance manager. Budgets must be secured from higher management, and are often funded by the users of the system being maintained. Monthly or annual fees are a common way of budgeting maintenance.

The gradual evolution of a patchwork system has no real solution other than the eventual development of a new system. However, the many difficulties associated with a continuously evolving system can be significantly reduced by implementing an orderly configuration control program. As we have seen, maintenance without configuration control can become extremely difficult to manage.

4.7 IEEE Standard 1074: A Standard for Developing Software Life Cycle Processes

Strictly speaking, the maintenance phase is not the final phase in the life cycle of a software product. The final phase, often called *retirement,* heralds the end of the software's productive existence. Of the many life cycle models that deliver software from conception to retirement, the best are those that have well-defined processes associated with them.

A well-defined set of processes can be associated with many different software development life cycle models. In fact, one of these initial processes may be the selection of the best suited model from a set of candidate models. These required activities are described in the IEEE Standard 1074 (IEEE 1999) for software life cycle processes.

IEEE Standard 1074 was first published in 1990, with the stated purpose of defining the processes that are required for the development and maintenance of critical software. The standard has been updated several times. For non-critical software, the developer can tailor the standard to the level of the software project being developed.

Standard 1074 describes the mapping of activities into the chosen life cycle and the identification and documentation of standards and controls that govern the life cycle. This is achieved through six sets of processes:

- Life cycle model selection
- Project management
- Predevelopment processes
- Development processes
- Post-development processes
- Integral processes

Standard 1074 does not define how the activities related to each process are to be implemented; it describes what the activities are. The standard was reinforced in 1997 by standard 12207, which addresses implementation. Standard 12207 is an IEEE adoption of the ISO standard for software life cycles (see Chapter 9). The two standards overlap, to some extent, and in most cases either would suffice. Ultimately, it is the project manager who selects the appropriate model and implements of the processes.

Standard 1074 contains four basic steps:

1. Select the software life cycle model: decide which model will be used from a list of possible models.
2. Create a software life cycle: identify the list of activities that are required for the application of the model.
3. Place the activities in executable sequence: plan the execution of the activities.
4. Establish a software life cycle process: apply the activities to the project being developed.

The standard also includes two additional sections on the development of a list of activities not used ("not applicable" activities), and verification of mapping (making sure that no activities have been unintentionally omitted).

Standard 1074 also includes excellent guidelines and examples. A list of required tailorable activities is provided (this is actually the most extensive part of the standard), and examples are provided for each of the above basic steps.

The formal selection and implementation of life cycle models will not ensure the provision of a reliable software system. The life cycle model is the structure upon which the development process is applied. If the model is suitable for the type of project, then a good structure is in place upon which the software can be built. But it still must be built well. It must provide the software on time and according to requirements.

The following section discusses a different aspect of success based on a specific set of software requirements: reliability requirements. They are one of the project's next level building blocks after the appropriate life cycle model is in place.

4.8 Availability and Reliability Requirements

As modern society increases its dependency on computer systems, the availability of these systems increases in importance. Examples are telephony systems (as a customer, how long are you willing to do without telephone service?), financial data base systems (how long are you willing to wait for a withdrawal from your bank?), or credit approval systems (what would your level of satisfaction be if your credit card purchase was rejected due to the approval system failure?). There are also much more critical availability concerns in such fields as hospital equipment and aerospace flight systems. How are these systems perceived by customers?

Customers do not commonly perceive software as reliable, and this is a major cause of customer dissatisfaction. There are two fundamental conditions that must exist before software can be evaluated for customer satisfaction: (1) it must function when it is needed, and (2) when it functions it must do so correctly. This is the difference between availability and reliability.

These concepts are not new. For many years, high availability has been *demanded* by customers for life-support and mission critical systems. It is now also expected for communications systems (including Internet services), data base applications, and online services (such as banking and credit card validation). These computer-driven services have become indispensable in modern society. They have become basic requirements of all essential service software.

These requirements are simply that software (just like the hardware) must now provide continuous fail-free service. High availability and reliability of software is not just a case of preventing or overcoming software failures. It requires the correct attitude when architecting and designing the system.

Clearly, customer tolerance of software failures is declining. Humphrey (1999b) illustrates the situation well. Observing that, in the nuclear power industry, electromechanical instruments are being replaced by computerized controls, he asks: "If you lived next to a nuclear power plant, would you be happy with the traditional defect levels?"

4.8.1 System Reliability

The IEEE has produced a set of two documents on software reliability: a standard Std 982.1 and a guide Std 982.2 (IEEE 1999). For most purposes, these two documents provide an excellent overview of the theory and practice of software reliability which is formally defined as:

The probability that software will not cause the failure of a system for a specified time under specified conditions. The probability is a function of the inputs to, and use of, the system as well as a function of the existence of faults in the software. The inputs to the system determine whether existing faults, if any, are encountered.

A more straightforward definition provided in the guide simply states that *reliability* is an estimation of system failure-freeness.

The IEEE guide provides examples of why software fails:

1. Incompletely defining user needs and requirements

2. Omissions in the design and coding process

3. Improper usage of the system

4. Excessive change activity

The guide recommends the following three steps as a process strategy to improve software reliability:

1. **Do it right the first time.** Though somewhat patronizing, this slogan is well explained in the guide, which stresses the use of all means necessary to prevent faults by ensuring competent personnel, early user involvement, and modern development methods and tools.

2. **Detect it early, fix it as soon as practicable.** This step requires the use of reviews, prototyping, intermediate testing, and all the activities designed to promote phase containment.

3. **Monitor it.** This step refers to the continuous collection of data and its evaluation.

In addition, software reliability can be achieved through system reliability design methods such as fault tolerance—the protection of a system from faults through architectural design. This approach is based on the expectation that a system will fail. It therefore seeks to protect the system from faults by using such methods as multiple versions of software (or hardware) controlled by switching logic that moves from the failed version of the system to a different functioning version.

Architectural aspects of the reliability of a system can be predicted using modeling (called *probability modeling of software*). This is a mathematical technique based on various characteristics of the system, such as architecture and complexity.

4.8.2 System Availability

If you were told by your telephone company that it will provide you with 95 percent service availability, you might be impressed. But you shouldn't be. Providing 95 percent availability means that your phone will not work about 450 hours out of the year—that's well over half a month. During the nine-to five-office hours there could be over 100 hours when your phone would not work.

System availability has a simple mathematical definition: it is formally defined as *uptime/total-time*. It is the fraction or percentage of time that a system provides service out of the total amount of time within which it is being measured.

There are many methods for improving software system availability, most of which require that *software must be designed from the outset for high availability*. This is true of hardware, too, for it does little good if either the hardware or the software is designed for high availability, but not both (particularly in mission critical systems).

Courting the customer with promises of high availability has led to several major corporations subscribing to a new theory called "five nines system availability" (written "5NINES"). The theory is based on the concept that a high availability system can fail to provide service for no more than 5 minutes per year. A simple calculation shows that 5 minutes downtime out of the total number of minutes in a year is approximately 99.999% availability, hence, the name "five nines." Many telephone networks in developed countries approach 5NINES system availability.[6]

5NINES software availability is achieved through:

- Designing the system with no planned downtime (for software upgrades, for instance), and preventing unplanned downtime.

- Evaluating the expected availability of software before it is developed through mathematical modeling and prototyping. This approach can help select the best architecture for the application being developed.

- Demanding high availability from commercial off-the-shelf (COTS) software providers that become part of the software system being developed (operating systems, data base managers, etc.).

- The use of high availability hardware (without which high availability software would be meaningless).

- Simplicity and ease of use: elimination of human error. This is a major factor in high system availability, and is discussed in detail in the next section.

4.8.3 Ease of Use

The design of a software system can provide a development team with significant freedom of choice. Even though a requirements specification may contain design requirements, it is still project managers and their teams who make many, if not most, implementation decisions. One of the areas where this is most evident is the part of the system that is most visible: the user interface. In fact, the user interface *is* the system for the customer or end-user.[7]

---

[6]See Bruno von Niman's presentation (from Ericsson) on Usability at: http://www.nomos.se/newss/seminar/slides/tqm-bvn

[7]See J. Kirakowski (University of Cork, Ireland), background notes on the SUMI questionnaire, at: http://castor.ucc.ie/hfrg/questionnaires/sumi/sumipapp.html

Ease of use, or usability, intuitively describes the ease with which a customer can use a system correctly. The term is more formally defined as *the effectiveness, efficiency and satisfaction with which specified users can achieve specified goals in particular environments* (ISO 9241). For the software project manager, the intuitive definition is sufficient: *design your application for operational simplicity*. The question that then follows is: how do you objectively determine whether software is easy to use?

Several methods have been developed to measure usability. Kirakowski[8] has pioneered a method called Software Usability Measurement Inventory, or SUMI. The method measures usability based on a list of criteria:

- **Efficiency:** measures the degree to which users feel that the software assists them in their work.

- **Affect:** measures the user's general emotional reaction to the software (somewhat akin to *likeability*).

- **Helpfulness:** measures the degree to which the software is self-explanatory and also covers the *help* feature and the documentation.

- **Control:** measures the extent to which the user feels in control of the software (as opposed to being controlled by the software).

- **Learnability:** measures the speed and ease with which users feel that they have been able to master the software product, or to learn new features when necessary.

Other methods have been developed for specific classes of software. One such example is a method that measures users' satisfaction with Internet web site software.[9] In all cases, measurements are based on user feedback, usually through questionnaires.

Theories and methods for the measurement of usability are gaining recognition (see Madsen 1999). This is no coincidence, as the Internet, the personal computer, and data base applications are producing an explosive market growth for software and software-intensive products. As with system availability, *project managers will need to ensure that ease of use is designed into their software products*. This will be demanded by customers as their tolerance of cumbersome interfaces continues to decline.

A somewhat amusing but nonetheless true illustration of a challenging user interface is taken from a street bank-teller machine in Europe. After inserting a bank card and selecting English as the desired language, the machine actually displayed the following message:

> *Please enter your four-digit PIN and press enter. If this machine does not have an enter key then press continue except for newer machines for which no additional key needs to be pressed.*

---

[8]See Human Centered Measures of Success in Web Site Design, J. Kirakowski, et al., at: www.research.att.com/conf/hfweb/proceedings/kirakowski/

[9]See Human Centered Measures of Success in Web Site Design, J. Kirakowski, et al., at: www.research.att.com/conf/hfweb/proceedings/kirakowski/

4.9 Customer Perspectives

No software development cycle can be successful without making the customer a fundamental part of the process. The term *customer* is defined in Chapter 11, but the in broader context here it includes the end users.

Learning to know your customers is a winning strategy. This can provide a significant advantage in satisfying them. Commodity companies invest large amounts of money in collecting data about their customers. It helps them build the most suitable product for their market. Even when a project has a single customer, this is important.

In the nineties, when many large American and European telecommunications companies were cultivating new markets in Asia, their customers' cultural differences often produced unexpected situations. Western companies planned their telephone systems to work the same way in Asia as they did in Europe and America. But the protocol of conversation was different. A famous example was the call-waiting feature, popular in the West, but considered impolite in some parts of Asia.

This cultural blunder could have been identified during the requirements phase—if customers had been involved. And as we shall see, the customer should be involved in all phases of the development cycle. The significance of this approach is illustrated well in the following account related by a novice project manager at a recent seminar.

The software team was developing a new version of an aircraft maintenance system, and one of the developers went to speak to the users to collect impressions about the system. The project manager did not feel that he needed to go along. The developer returned with requests for new input fields, a request for a confirmation dialog before updating the data base, a complaint about the quality of some of the help screens, and a question about the need for password entry after each transaction. Most of these requests could have been addressed in the original requirements at no additional cost.

The project had not been difficult, it was well staffed and budgeted, it was completed on time, and yet it did not achieve customer satisfaction. The reason is clear.

4.9.1 International and Cultural Issues

In different countries people do things differently. There is nothing surprising in that statement. Why, then, are corporations always surprised when their software doesn't function well in other countries? One of the most notorious examples of this problem is also one of the most simple: date formats.

Does 4/5/2002 denote April fifth 2002 or May fourth 2002? Of course it depends where you come from; in North America it is April fifth while in Europe (and much of the rest of the world) it is May fourth.

The diversity of practices and cultures and its impact on products in general, and on software in particular, goes well beyond the date problem. Microsoft would have no more than a modest problem delivering its Windows operating system in English to a customer in, say, the Netherlands,[10] but it would have a major problem delivering it in English to France. And any general commodity software delivered in any language other

---

[10]There is, of course, a Dutch language version of Microsoft's Windows operating system.

Table 4.3   Colors in Various Cultures

COLOR	CHINA	JAPAN	EGYPT	FRANCE	UNITED STATES
Red	Happiness	Anger Danger	Death	Aristocracy	Danger Stop
Blue	Heavens Clouds	Villainy	Virtue Faith Truth	Freedom Peace	Sadness Melancholy
Green	Ming Dynasty Heavens	Future Youth Energy	Fertility Strength	Criminality	Novice Apprentice
Yellow	Birth Wealth Power	Grace Nobility	Happiness Prosperity	Temporary	Cowardice
White	Death Purity	Death	Joy	Neutrality	Purity

Adapted from Russo and Boor (1993) © 1993 Association for Computing Machinery, Inc., reprinted by permission.

than English (with the possible exception of Spanish) would have little chance of success in the United States.

Beyond language and dates, there are also presentation-style issues. Barber (1998) reports that on the Internet, there are patterns that reflect cultural practices and preferences. Middle Eastern sites in Arabic and Hebrew have a high frequency of orienting text, links, and graphics from right to left. While the left side of a web site may be the first focus of attention for an American, the right side would be the initial focus for a Middle Easterner, as Arabic and Hebrew are written from right to left.

Colors also have different meanings in different cultures (see Table 4.3). White, which is a sign of purity in America, and thus would be a favored background color in North America, signifies death in Japan.

The different interpretation of colors, features, and mannerisms should not come as a surprise. If software is to serve overseas markets, it must be designed to do so. *Software requirements specifications must contain sections on international requirements*, specifying the software product's target markets and the special considerations for those markets.

4.9.2 Customer Involvement

The annals of software are full of stories in which a development team confined itself to the lab and spent several months building a product that they believed was right for their customers, only to find that the customers did not want the product. This problem is not specific to software; it can happen with any type of product.

Customers should be involved in the development of a project from its earliest stages. As we have seen, during the initial concept phase, simple prototypes can be helpful in getting customer feedback on the product before it is built. User interface screens and sample outputs are excellent tools that allow the customer and end-user to evaluate the suitability of the product.

Customer involvement is essential especially during the requirements phase. A successful requirements specification, though usually written by the developer, is a joint effort by developer and customer. In cases of complex systems, about which the customer lacks the knowledge to fully understand the document, a separate layman's requirements document should be produced (see Chapter 9).

During design and implementation, customer input can be invaluable. *Customer involvement fosters an understanding of problems, decisions, and implementation issues, which in turn promotes higher customer satisfaction when the project is completed.*

Even good things have to be used in moderation; too much medicine can kill the patient. Admittedly, customer involvement, if not kept to a reasonable level, can begin to interfere with development. Use common sense. A good approach is *to define the level of customer involvement at the beginning of the project together with the customer.*

4.10 Summary

The software development life cycle includes all software development phases from the initial concept to the final delivery of the system. There are various different approaches to the software development cycle, including the primitive *code* and *fix* method, various iterative methods (such as rapid prototyping), and the phased approach. The phased approach to software development divides the development life cycle into:

- The concept phase
- The requirements phase
- The design phase
- The implementation phase
- The integration and test phase
- The maintenance phase

The phased approach (also called the Waterfall model) is included within most other software development methodologies. In fact, there are many variations of the classic Waterfall model, but they are all based upon a systematic transition from one development phase to the next, until the project is complete.

The Waterfall model begins with the initial *concept phase*, during which the need for the software system is determined and the basic concept of the software system evolves. This is followed by the requirements phase, which provides a detailed description of the software system to be developed. The requirements phase provides the project's first major baseline.

After the definition of the requirements, the design phase analyzes the requirements and determines the method of implementation. The design phase is often divided into two separate phases: top level design and detailed design. The dividing line between the two phases is set somewhat arbitrarily, based on the level of system decomposition. The system design provides the second major project baseline.

During the next phase, implementation, the software modules are coded and initial unit tests are performed. The modules are then approved by software quality control and submitted to configuration control. Configuration control then releases modules for integration.

During the integration and test phase, the software modules are assembled and the system gradually takes form. The system is then tested for compliance with the requirements specification.

Finally, the maintenance phase completes the software development cycle and links the release of the completed software product with the development of a new product. Software maintenance is involved with the correction of faults that existed in the software *before* its delivery, as well as changes to improve performance or to adapt the product to a changed environment.

A well-defined set of processes can be associated with many different software development life cycle models. These required activities are described in the IEEE standard 1074 for software life cycle processes. Standard 1074 does not define how the activities related to each process are to be implemented; it describes what the activities are. The implementation of the processes is defined by the project manager when selecting the specific life cycle model to be used.

Customers do not commonly perceive software as reliable, and this is a major cause of customer dissatisfaction. There are two fundamental conditions that must exist before software can be evaluated for customer satisfaction: (1) it must function when it is needed, and (2) when it functions it must do so correctly. This is the difference between availability and reliability.

Ease of use, or usability, intuitively describes the ease with which a customer can use a system correctly. The term is more formally defined as *the effectiveness, efficiency and satisfaction with which specified users can achieve specified goals in particular environments* (ISO 9241). For the software project manager, the intuitive definition is sufficient: *design your application for operational simplicity.*

Learning to know your customers is a winning strategy. This can provide a significant advantage in satisfying them. Customers should be involved in the development of a project from its earliest stages. A good approach is to define the level of customer involvement at the beginning of the project together with the customer.

Exercises

1. A large aircraft manufacturer has decided to permit engineers to work from their home. The engineers will be provided with a terminal and a modem, and they will dial into the company's computer from home.

   The aircraft manufacturer needs a communications and monitoring software package to manage the work being performed by the engineers. The package must include a sophisticated security feature that will prevent unauthorized people from dialing into the company's system, and will activate various alarms if unauthorized access is attempted. The system must also monitor the hours worked by the engineers from home, and it must provide resource sharing of common data files and software utilities. Finally, the package must contain both an online and a batch mode report feature to provide information on the use of the system by engineers from their home.

Analyze the software package and consider various methodologies for implementation. In particular, compare rapid prototyping with the Waterfall approach. Explain the advantages and disadvantages of each approach for this project.

2. Consider the overlapping of phases when applying the Waterfall method to the system described in Exercise 1. In particular, consider the overlapping of the implementation phase with the design phase.

Prepare a plan to code the modules so that the implementation phase can begin as early as possible. Explain which modules can safely be coded first, and discuss the possible risks.

3. As in Exercise 2, consider the risks of overlapping implementation with integration.

Prepare a plan to integrate the software modules so that integration can begin as early as possible. Explain which modules can safely be integrated first, and discuss the possible risks.

Compare the use of a top down integration plan to a bottom up plan and an inside out plan.

Describe which approach you would recommend for this project.

4. Discuss the main problems that you anticipate in the development of the system described in Exercise 1. In particular, consider the problems associated with the definition of requirements.

Who is the customer? Also, consider the integration and test problems in this project, and discuss the expected requirements changes. How will these problems best be handled?

5. Consider at least six additional features and improvements for the system described in Exercise 1. Prepare a long-range maintenance plan that includes new releases of the system with bug corrections and some new features in each new release.

The dial-in phone costs for the engineers have been overlooked, and cannot be reimbursed by the system. Propose a solution to this problem and schedule it in one of the new releases of the system.

6. Consider several different types of life cycle model that may be applied for the development of the project described in Exercise 1. Which of the IEEE 1074 standard processes are of particular importance for this project? Can any of the 1074 processes be tailored?

7. (1) Research your library or the Internet on the topic of 5NINES System Availability. Locate three organizations that have committed to the 5NINES program. Describe and compare (a) their reasons for joining the program, (b) their achievements and improvements to date, and (c) their customers' or users' response.

(2) Class debate: What is the role of software versus hardware in achieving 5NINES availability? What other factors impact availability?

(3) If three subsystems each achieve 99.999% availability, what is the availability of the overall system? Explain. What is the level of availability needed for each subsystem in order for the overall system to achieve 5NINES? Provide a general formula for n subsystems.

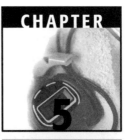

CHAPTER 5

Principles of Managing Software Engineers: Are They Really Any Different?

According to many studies, managing software engineers is more difficult than managing engineers in most other areas of technology. The typical software engineer (if such a person exists) is often characterized as being both artistic and logical, as well as possessive and temperamental. These traits can be found in any group of people, but they appear to be more prevalent among software engineers.

Software engineers are also widely diverse in their level of productivity. As far back as 1968, Sackman et al. documented the enormous difference in productivity between software programmers. Sackman reported productivity ratios of up to 25:1 for programming and 28:1 for debugging. All of the programmers taking part in the experiment were familiar with the application areas of the programs, leading Sackman to interpret the results as a range of their competence.

Sackman's results may be somewhat extreme, but several decades later his general conclusions are still often quoted. Even today, in an average project, it is not uncommon to find productivity ratios of 1:5. One of the targets of modern day software engineering has been to reduce this startling range of productivity among software developers. This has been done through more organized and systematic software development, much to the displeasure of the gurus at the high end of the productivity range. These software development methodologies have also reduced the impact of other human traits on the development process. This is achieved through the introduction of extensive documentation, reports, development standards and status meetings. These procedures, however, are but a few of the means for managing people.

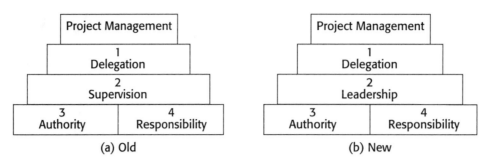

Figure 5.1   The four cornerstones of management.

People are managed within an organizational structure. This hierarchical structure has been regarded in the past as resting upon four cornerstones of management: delegation, authority, responsibility, and supervision (see Figure 5.1). Delegation bestows authority, and authority produces (and requires) responsibility. Both authority and responsibility, in classic management theory, require supervision.

Modern approaches to management shy away from the term supervision and regard it as condescending. A more progressive view replaces the term with leadership and the ability to facilitate. The basic assumption is that the need for supervision is a sign of poor management. Highly motivated people need leadership, not supervision.

Sawyer and Guinan (1998) in an analysis of the performance of software organizations found that organizational and social factors contribute significantly to the productivity and quality of projects. These factors can account for up to 25 percent of the variation in software product quality.

Most projects are organized as teams, with each team assigned specific functions within the project. Different types of project require different types of team structure. For example, a team of novice programmers requires a technical team leader, whereas a team of experts may require only an administrative team leader. It is the project manager's responsibility to select the structure best suited for the project.

This chapter deals with these people management issues. The main emphasis throughout the chapter is on software project-related issues. For a most enjoyable discussion on the behavior of software developers, the reader is referred to a classic in the field, *The Psychology of Computer Programming*, by Gerald Weinberg (Weinberg 1998).

5.1 The Software Project Organizational Structure

There are many ways to organize a software project. The larger the project the more critical the organizational structure becomes. Badly organized projects breed confusion, and confusion leads to project failure. Figure 5.2 describes the basic structure of a project in which below the project manager are just two general functions: development and support. This very basic software project structure was not uncommon in the early days of programming. It is still a valid project structure for very small projects (up to five developers), though occasionally it can still be found today in larger projects.

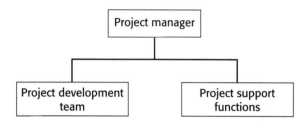

Figure 5.2   Basic structure of a development project.

Figure 5.3 describes a detailed organizational chart, including all major support functions. This organizational structure is suitable for medium to large projects (with a staff exceeding 20). Smaller projects may not require a deputy project manager or separate configuration control and quality assurance groups (see Chapter 8 for a detailed discussion of these topics).

Very large projects (with a staff exceeding 40 people) can often be managed more easily by dividing the project into sub-projects. Figure 5.4 presents the organizational chart for a large project. This chart includes both software and hardware development teams, and an integration group that is responsible for hardware/software integration as well as integration within each group.

As an example, consider the organization of a large satellite project. The project manager is in fact responsible for a number of projects: the ground control station, the rocket, and the satellite itself. This project could contain several hundred software developers. The software for all of these sub-projects is managed within a single project office. Each sub-project is then managed by a sub-project manager. An organizational

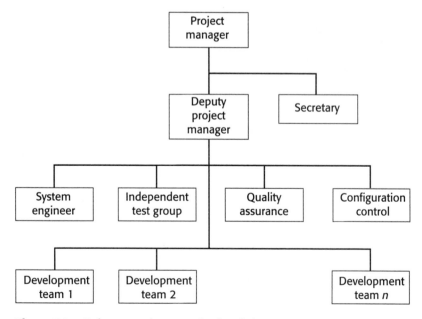

Figure 5.3   Software project organizational chart.

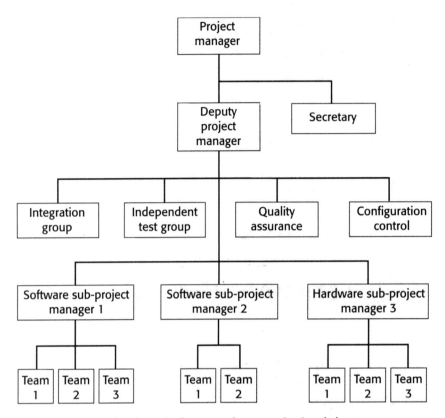

Figure 5.4 Large hardware/software project organizational chart.

chart similar to the one described in Figure 5.4 can be applied to the satellite project; the resulting chart is described in Figure 5.5.

Clearly the project's organizational structure is dependent on the type of project being developed. Some of the issues that must be considered are:

- **Project size.** The larger the project, the more important the organization. Large projects have significant human communications and coordination overhead, and therefore require more support functions.

- **Hardware/software development projects.** The simultaneous development of hardware and software is not easy. Planning, integration, and testing are much more complicated, and require dedicated support groups.

- **High reliability systems.** Any system that is sensitive to issues of reliability (such as defense or life-support systems) requires a major effort in quality assurance. These types of projects require a separate quality assurance organization.

- **Corporate structure.** The project's organization is largely dependent on the overall structure of the company within which the project is being developed. Many of the project support functions can be provided by centralized groups within the company. In fact, basic services, such as financial, secretarial, and legal services, are commonly provided by the parent or corporate organization.

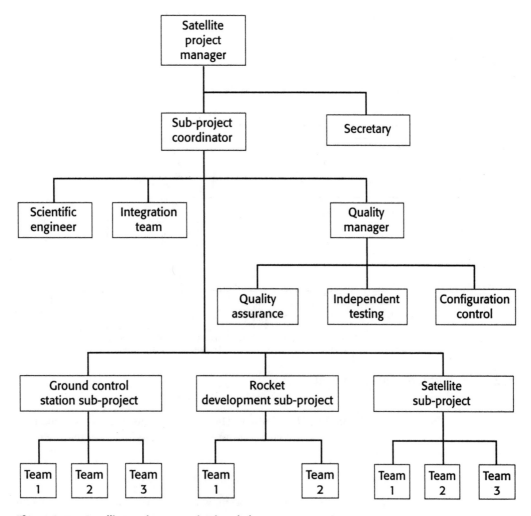

Figure 5.5   Satellite project organizational chart.

Corporate structure usually dictates one of two basic types of project organization: matrix or pyramid. Figure 5.6 describes the structure of a matrix organization (compare this to the pyramid structure in Figure 5.4). Within a corporate matrix organization, the project manager manages the technical activities of the project staff, while his or her involvement in nontechnical personnel issues (e.g., salary reviews, promotion, training) is minimal.

The advantages of a matrix organization are:

- **More expertise.** A matrix organization can maintain experts in specific fields (communications, data bases, graphics, etc.) who are then assigned to different projects. A single project cannot always afford the luxury of maintaining experts in all fields.

- **Flexibility.** It is easier to move people around from one project to another. This results in better utilization of the available expertise.

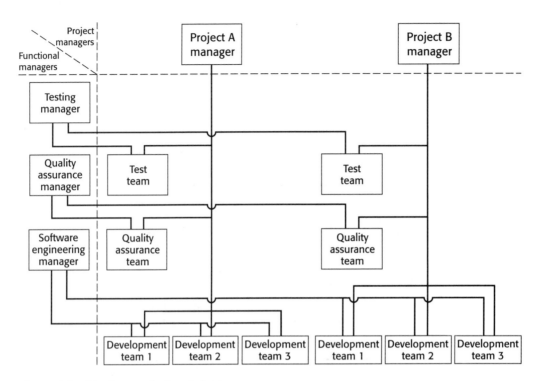

Figure 5.6 Matrix organizational chart.

- **Emphasis on managing the project.** The project manager is freed of many of the staff management tasks, leaving more time to concentrate on the technical aspects of the project.

However, matrix organizations also have significant disadvantages:

- **Less management authority.** Promotion, which is one of the primary tools for generating motivation, is taken out of the hands of the project manager. The manager has little influence on the developer's salary and professional role in the organization.

- **Lower staff loyalty.** All employees like to know exactly who their superior is. In a matrix organization, an employee has more than one superior. This causes a division of loyalty, and a weaker bond between employee and manager.

These disadvantages often outweigh the advantages of the corporate matrix organization. Motivation is a major factor in the success of a project, and anything that undermines motivation is certainly contrary to the best interests of the project. Unfortunately, the best interests of the project do not always completely coincide with the best interests of the company.

Pyramid organizations provide a clear, well-defined hierarchy in which all individuals know their own position and the positions of those above and below them. When promotion and status play a major role in generating motivation (and they often do), then the pyramid organization is most effective. Many other factors generate motivation: a sense of achievement, praise, and peer esteem are just a few (refer to Section 5.4 for further discussion of these topics). Though promotion and status are not always the most effective motivators, a project manager should rarely relinquish *any* effective management tool. Therefore, from the perspective of a single project, the pyramid organization is often the best.

5.2 The Team Structure

Except for very small projects (fewer than five developers), software projects are best organized into small development teams. The ideal size of a development team is between four and six developers. Larger teams restrict the ability of the team leader to function also as a developer, and thus increase management overhead and limit the team leader's technical involvement in the project.

Teams provide the project manager with many advantages, including:

- Easier and better management: the team structure easily supports delegation of authority.

- More effective exchange of information and ideas, due to broader familiarity within the team of each team member's tasks.

- Teams reduce the possibility of engineers becoming irreplaceable by sharing knowledge within the team. No single person becomes the only source of critical information.

- In small projects, there is stronger identification with the project. In large projects, developers tend to feel that they are just one of very many, and that their contribution to the project will go unnoticed. Smaller, more cohesive, teams can generate more dedication.

5.2.1 The Team Leader

The team leader serves as the main channel of information between the project manager and the team members. This does not mean that there is no direct communication between the project manager and the team members. However, if *all* communication was direct, then this would defeat the main purposes of the team structure: effective delegation of authority and responsibility (see Figure 5.1).

The team leader's role is:

- To represent the project manager, via delegation of authority
- To represent the team to the project manager
- To represent the team to other project teams and organizational functions

The team leader may also have other responsibilities, depending on the type of team structure. Figure 5.7 presents examples of two different team structures (these team structures are discussed later). All team leaders lead administratively; not all team leaders lead technically. Chief engineer teams require technical leadership, which, in turn, requires technical seniority. Both democratic and chief engineer teams require administrative team leadership.

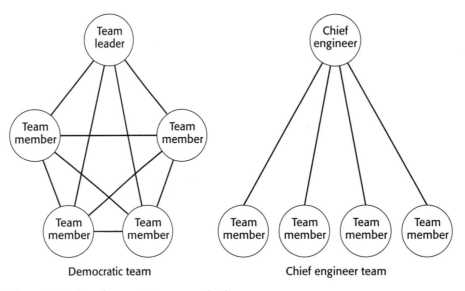

Figure 5.7 Development team organization.

It is the project manager's responsibility to select the teams and assign the team leader roles. This can (and usually should) be done in consultation with other experienced team leaders and senior project members. The team structure and assignment of key tasks is part of the project development plan, and should be completed as early as possible in the project development.

Team leaders should first be selected on the basis of their basic leadership abilities. If this ability is not inherent in the individual's character, then training will rarely be enough. A common error is to promote a good engineer only to have him then become a bad team leader.[1]

Team leadership is, first and foremost, a management function, and as such requires training. All team leaders should be formally trained in the basic management skills needed both for managing the team and for interfacing with project management. A capable, well-trained team leader becomes a successful extension of the project manager.

5.2.2 Democratic Teams

Strictly speaking, democratic teams do not have a *leader*; the function of the team leader role is more that of coordinator. In democratic teams, team leaders assign a small part of their time to:

- Representing the team in communications with the project manager and other teams
- Coordinating activities within the team
- Handling other administrative tasks, such as reports, scheduling, and monitoring activities

[1]See *The Peter Principle*, Peter and Hull (1970), for an interesting discussion of this phenomenon.

All technical decisions within a democratic team are made by the whole team. The team leader convenes meetings at which critical or urgent issues are discussed, but all team members take part in the decision-making process and assume responsibility for the outcome.

Democratic teams are often appropriate for groups of senior, experienced developers. The role of team leader then reduces the administrative overhead by assigning all the team's administrative tasks to a single team member.

The democratic team structure is particularly unsuitable for mixed groups, or groups comprised mainly of junior developers. In both these cases clear leadership is required.

5.2.3 Chief Engineer Teams

Chief engineer teams (also called chief programmer teams) provide clear leadership for the development team. The team leader's role is that of both coordinator (as in the case of democratic teams) and technical mentor. In complex projects, team leaders may be required to devote as much as 50 percent of their time to technical and administrative activities.

The main activities of the chief engineer team leader are:

- Assigning tasks and responsibilities to the team members

- Supervising the work of the team members

- Providing advice and guidance to the team members

- Administrative and coordination activities (similar to the democratic team leader)

Chief engineer teams are appropriate for mixed teams and teams that are mainly comprised of junior or inexperienced developers. The team leader functions as a first level manager, and therefore should have adequate training in basic management techniques.

Chief engineer teams can also be successful in teams of senior and experienced developers, but the role is often unnecessary. When this structure is applied to a team of experienced engineers, it becomes doubly important for the team leader to have basic management skills, without which friction can develop between the team members and the team leader. In this respect, leading a team of experienced professionals is more difficult than leading a team of beginners.

5.2.4 Expert Teams

Expert teams are small teams that are established to solve specific problems within a project. An expert team may be established during project development when a complex problem arises, and the team may then be disbanded when the problem is solved. In some cases, expert teams may support the project throughout the development cycle. The objective of an expert team is to concentrate expertise in a specific area of the project.

As an example, consider an automatic bank teller system with two major subsystems; the bank's central computer and the remote automatic teller. The development plan for these two subsystems has assigned the development of each subsystem to a separate team, but the size of the project cannot justify a separate integration team. The two teams have performed initial subsystem testing and integration using simulators. However, when the two subsystems are integrated together, the communication between them fails.

There is always a danger in such situations that each of the two teams will look for the problem in the other team's work. Even when the two teams cooperate well, differences in implementation (or in design) may make it difficult for the problem to be resolved. As the schedule begins to slip, this becomes a major concern to the project manager.

In such cases, the project manager may decide to establish an expert team to resolve the communications problem. The team would comprise two communications experts (possibly from outside the project staff) and two project engineers, one each from the two teams. This expert team would then concentrate its efforts on resolving the problem as quickly as possible, while the other two teams resume other development activities. After the communications problem between the two subsystems is resolved, the expert team can be disbanded.

In some respects, independent test teams and quality assurance teams can be viewed as expert teams (see Chapter 8 for a discussion of these topics). Independent test teams function primarily during the integration and test phases of the development cycle. The quality assurance team is an example of an expert team that functions throughout the project's development cycle.

An expert team frequently has highly experienced engineers. In such cases the team would most probably be constructed as a democratic team. In the preceding example, the team may be either a democratic team or it may be led by a senior communications expert.

5.3 Basic Reporting Techniques

For the project manager, it is essential to be constantly informed of the true status of the project. This is achieved by assuring the regular flow of accurate information from the development teams. Many of the methods of acquiring information are not objective and rely on the accuracy of the reports provided by the project developers themselves. They include:

- Periodic written status reports
- Verbal reports
- Status meetings
- Product demonstrations (demos)

Product demonstrations are particularly subjective, because they demonstrate only what the developer wishes to be seen. The project manager needs objective information. Such information can often be acquired from reports produced by support groups, such as:

- Quality assurance reports
- Independent test reports

Although reports and meetings are indeed useful sources of information, nothing can replace direct contact between the project manager and the development staff. Frequent informal talks with the developers are excellent sources of information, especially when held in an informal atmosphere (and not in the project manager's office).

The project manager must be on constant guard against an error commonly referred to as the "90/50 syndrome," which states that "it takes 50 percent of the time to complete 90 percent of the work, and an additional 50 percent of the time to complete the remaining 10 percent of the work." This means that project developers will begin to report quite early that they have "almost finished" their tasks. However, there is a great difference between "almost finished" and "finished."

Finishing a task—writing documentation and polishing off the last few problems—often takes longer than developers anticipate. This is because these activities produce very few visible results, and developers tend (wrongly) to associate work with results. Therefore, managers can obtain more information from developers by asking them how long they estimate it will take to finish, and not how much of their work has been completed.

5.3.1 Status Reports

Status reports should be required from *every* member of the development team, without exception. The reports should be submitted periodically, usually weekly or bi-weekly, and should contain at least the following four sections (see Figure 5.8):

1. **Red Flags.** Problems that require the immediate attention of the project manager.

2. **Activities during the report period.** Each subsection within this section describes a major activity during the report period. The description of each activity should be two or three lines long. Activities should be linked to the project task list or work breakdown structure (WBS) (see Chapter 11 for a description of the WBS).

3. **Planned activities for the next report period.** Each subsection within this section describes a major activity planned for the next report period. The description of each activity should be one to two lines long.

4. **Problems and general issues.** Each subsection within this section describes a major problem that either occurred during the report period, or that was reported previously and has not yet been resolved. This means that problems will be repeatedly reported until they are resolved. In particular, this section must explain why this report's Section 2 does not correspond to the previous report's Section 3. This section also includes general information such as vacation, staff recruitment, etc.

All reports should also contain:

- Date of report
- Report period (e.g., July 9 to July 13, 2003)
- Name of report (e.g., Communications Team Status Report)
- Name of person submitting the report

From: John Doe, Team Leader
To: Andrew Richardson, Project Manager
Date: June 16, 2003

User Interface Team: Weekly Status Report
For the period 9-13 June 2003

1.   Red Flags
1.1   Frank Smith has been transferred to another project. A replacement for Frank is needed urgently to ensure that we stay on schedule.
1.2   An agreement has not yet been signed with the company that will provide the screen interface generator. This tool is required by the team in three weeks.
:
:

2.   Activities during the report period
2.1   The design of the user help screens (activity 3.12.6) was completed on schedule. The design specs were submitted to configuration control.
2.2   Coding of the command-pass-through modules (activity 5.12) continues and is currently behind schedule by about 1 week. We have requested a software developer from the data base team for 3 days, to help get us back on schedule.
:
:

3.   Activities planned for the next report period
3.1   Coding of the command-pass-through modules (activity 5.12) will be completed, and unit tests will be started.
3.2   Two members of the team (Ed and Joan) will attend a two-day course on the programmer's interface to the new user interface package. This is an unscheduled activity that was approved at the last project meeting. This will not delay the schedule, due to the time-saving expected from the use of the new programmer's interface.
:
:

4.   Problems/Issues
4.1   An office has not yet been allocated for Joan, our new software developer. She is currently using a temporary office that needs to be vacated soon.
4.2   Transmission of large files via the company's intranet is too slow and consumes a lot of time. We would like to request the installation of a faster network link for at least one member of our team.
4.3   Ed will be taking a 3-day vacation next week
:
:

Figure 5.8   Example of a weekly status report.

The preparation of a periodic status report should take about 20 minutes, but not longer than 30 minutes. However, the very first time a report is prepared it will probably take longer.

Developers should submit their status reports to their team leader. The team leader then combines the reports of the team into a single status report, while maintaining the same report structure. This activity should take the team leader about 30 minutes, but not longer than 45 minutes (this is easily done when the reports are prepared and submitted by e-mail).

Each team leader submits the team status report to the project manager. The individual status reports need not be submitted; these should be filed and submitted to the project manager only on request.

The project manager also receives status reports from other project support personnel, such as the project systems engineer or the deputy project manager. The project manager then prepares the project status report by combining the individual reports that have been received into a single three-part report. The project status report is then submitted to top management.

Project status reports are not necessarily submitted with the same frequency as internal project status reports. Project reports may be submitted bi-weekly or monthly (see Chapter 11).

5.3.2 Project Status Meetings

Project status meetings should be held periodically, usually once a week. A good time for status meetings is either on the last day of the week, or at the beginning of the first day of the week. Status meetings also contribute to the atmosphere of order and control within the project, and should be held regularly, at a fixed time. Participants who cannot participate in the project status meeting may, with the project manager's approval, delegate participation to another member of their team.

The project manager prepares for the status meeting by reviewing the status reports submitted by the key project members (particularly scrutinizing the red flag section). Therefore the status reports should be submitted several hours (preferably one day) before the status meeting.

Project status meetings are attended by the key project members. The meeting begins with a report on project activities and general issues by the project manager, and a review of the previous meeting's action items. Then each participant should be given about five to ten minutes to report on the activity of his or her team or area of responsibility. The discussion of problems should not be restricted to the person reporting the problem and the project manager. All problems may be addressed by all participants, with possible assistance offered between team leaders, thus making their experience available throughout the project. It is preferable for the project manager to guide the team members toward solutions rather than present solutions to problems.

Solutions should be worked out whenever possible during the status meeting. Any problem not resolved within five minutes should be postponed for discussion by the relevant parties after the status meeting is over.

The proceedings of all project status meetings must be recorded. Verbatim minutes are not required, though the following items should appear in the record:

- Date of meeting
- Name of meeting
- Present (list of participants)
- Absent (list of absent invited participants)

- Action items (name, action, date for completion)

- Information items (major decisions and items discussed)

The record of the project status meeting should be distributed (e-mailed) as soon as possible, but no later than by the end of the day. This is particularly important when there are action items to be completed on the same day. When the project is sufficiently large to justify an administrative assistant (or secretary), then the minutes should be taken and distributed by the assistant. In smaller projects, the project manager can rotate this task each week between the participants.

5.4 General Guidelines for Managing Software Engineers

Many of the guidelines in this section are equally applicable to all types of engineer. However, owing to the diverse characteristics of software engineers, as discussed at the beginning of this chapter, good management techniques are more important in the management of software than in most other areas of technology. Therefore, a basic guideline for software managers is that education in the area of modern management methods, particularly in the management of people, is essential for success. This is true for team leaders and project managers alike.

Weinberg was one of the first to document the ego problem in software developers. Software is a very creative field and attracts very creative people. But creative people are also sensitive and their ego plays a major role in the way they regard their job.

One may assume that a good way to manage software developers would be to encourage them to redouble their efforts to find their errors. Perhaps the manager should walk among the developers each day and ask to see their errors. Weinberg observes that this method would fail by going precisely in the opposite direction to what our experience dictates, for the average person would view such an investigation as a personal trial. The solution is to foster an environment in which it is understood that producing software problems is not an offense but rather the inevitable product of software development. In this environment, everyone works together to try to reduce the number of software faults without ever assigning blame. This type of environment, promotes what Weinberg refers to as *egoless programming*.

Another mannerism to avoid is management by edict. Management by agreement is preferable. It is always best to have an engineer *accept* the assigned task. This provides what is commonly referred to as *ownership* of the task, and increases the motivation of the engineer significantly. In order to achieve this, engineers should be assigned tasks that they want whenever this is possible. When this is not possible, the project manager should candidly describe the options available and explain to the engineer why specific tasks are not available.

Responsibility must always go side by side with authority. All project staff members, no matter how junior, must be given authority to act within their area of responsibility. Quality assurance engineers must have the authority to approve or reject product components, and development engineers must have the authority to make design decisions related to the components that they are developing.

As a general rule, only outright errors should be corrected. This leads to one of the basic rules of project development: *a better way of doing something is not sufficient grounds for change*. In other words, if the manager feels that he or she could have made a better decision, but the current decision is acceptable, then the decision should not be changed.

Ownership is not related only to tasks, but also to the schedule and resources that go with the tasks. All schedules should be agreed to by the developers. In fact, schedule estimates should be prepared with the participation of the developers. This assures a commitment by the developer to adhere to the schedule.

Lastly, motivation is the single most important factor in the successful management of the development team. Motivation can be encouraged in many ways, such as:

- Salary and remuneration
- Advancement (promotion)
- Working conditions and environment
- Interest in the assigned work
- Peer esteem
- Appreciation
- Promoting a sense of achievement

Many managers make the mistake of assuming that the prime motivator is salary. This is not so. The most effective motivators are sense of achievement and appreciation (see Giegold 1982). This means that it is important to explain to the development team members just how important their work is to the project and the company (and possibly to the country or humanity, as in the case of the development of a life-support system). People are highly motivated when they believe that they are doing something important.

Appreciation is also a powerful motivator. For the project manager to drop by someone's office or workstation and say "thanks, you have been doing a great job" can do wonders. Other ways of showing appreciation are by issuing letters of appreciation with copies directed to higher management and to the personnel department, or by sending employees who have made an extraordinary effort on a weekend vacation. All these will increase motivation, not only for the individual employee being thanked, but for others throughout the project.

5.5 Summary

Managing software engineers is more difficult than managing engineers in most other areas of technology. Software engineers are widely diverse in their level of productivity. In an average project, it is not uncommon to find productivity ratios of 1:5. One of the targets of modern-day software engineering has been to reduce this range of productivity among software developers through more organized and systematic methods of software development.

There are many ways of organizing a software project. The most suitable project organizational structure depends on the type of project being developed. Large and complex projects require large organizational structures. Irrespective of project size, software projects should be organized into small development teams. Ideally, a software team will contain four to six developers, and will be led by a team leader.

There are three types of software team:

- Democratic teams, which are led administratively by the team leader. Technical decisions are made by all members of the team.

- Chief engineer teams (or chief programmer teams), with an experienced senior engineer who is responsibile for leading the team both administratively and technically.

- Expert teams are established to resolve special problems within the project. They may be disbanded when the special problem is resolved.

For the project manager, it is essential to be constantly informed regarding the true status of the project. There are many methods of acquiring information; most rely directly on the provision of information by the developers. However, frequent informal talks with the developers are also excellent sources of information, especially when held in an informal atmosphere (and not in the project manager's office).

Motivation is the single most important factor in the successful management of the development team. Many managers make the mistake of assuming that the prime motivator is salary. This is not so. The most effective motivators are sense of achievement and appreciation.

People are highly motivated when they believe that they are doing something important and when they feel that their effort is being recognized.

Exercises

1. You are project manager for a communications project linking all the stores in a large department store chain. Each store currently has its own computer, which is connected to the checkout registers. The management of the chain wants to install a central computer in the main office, and to connect all the store computers to the central computer via a wide area network. The central computer will receive real-time information on the transactions at the stores and will update a central inventory data base.

   Prepare a pyramid organizational chart for the store communications project. Explain the structure you have chosen, and why it is better suited than other possible organizational structures.

2. Plan the flow of information within the organization that you have proposed in Exercise 1.

   Which reports will be required, and how often will they be submitted? Which status meetings will be required, and how often will they be held? Who will attend? Suggest a varying frequency for the status reports and the status meetings, according to the different phases of development.

3. Prepare a matrix organizational chart for the project described in Exercise 1. Compare it to the pyramid structure you proposed in Exercise 1. Which is more suited to the project? What are the advantages and the disadvantages of each organizational structure for this project?

4. Propose the structure of the development and support teams for the project described in Exercise 1. Explain the structure you have chosen. Do you foresee a need for any expert teams during the development of the project?

5. Class project: divide the class into three or four groups of students. Assign Exercises 1, 2, and 4 to each group. Have each group present their solutions to the class.

   Compare the solutions proposed by each group. Discuss what makes each solution different from others.

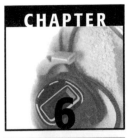

CHAPTER 6

How to Handle Large Projects: Divide and Conquer

Many complex objects can be viewed as a collection of numerous simpler objects. An appropriate example would be a complex chemical compound that is formed by various molecules, each of which is formed by combining various atoms. The atom, though itself divisible, can be regarded as the smallest particle of a chemical substance.

In a similar way, a complex project can be divided into simpler components. While the full project may be difficult to manage, each component will be easier to handle. Software projects can be decomposed into smaller components in order to provide better estimates of the amount of work involved, or in order to monitor the activities of the various development teams.

The decomposition of a software project is one of the software project manager's first tasks. However, the method of decomposition may differ from one project to another, depending on the project manager's actual objective. A functional decomposition of a project may not be the same as a design decomposition. A functional decomposition divides the project into its basic components from a user's perspective, while a design decomposition divides a project into its basic programming components or modules.

This chapter discusses methods for effectively managing complex software projects, and presents methods for decomposing projects into manageable components. The various types of project decomposition are also discussed, and the objectives of each type of decomposition are explained.

In addition, methods of simplifying the development of large projects by reusing software are also discussed. The ability to reuse components is one of the few ways work can be eliminated without reducing functionality or quality.

6.1 Stepwise Refinement

Intuitively, it would not appear reasonable to attempt to identify all project components in a single step. Clearly, an iterative procedure that would gradually provide more detail would be easier to use. Iterative methods of this kind are called *stepwise refinement,* as the decomposition is further refined in each succeeding step.

Figure 6.1 presents a general illustration of stepwise refinement. The system is initially divided into three top level components. In turn each top level component is further divided into lower level components, and so forth, until the lowest decomposition level is reached.

In a stepwise decomposition of a project, each component decomposes into the components directly below it, so that each step of the decomposition describes the full system, but at a different level of detail. In Figure 6.1, components 1, 2, and 3 comprise the complete system. For more detail we take the next decomposition step, and find that components 1.1, 1.2, 2.1, 2.2, 2.3, 3.1, and 3.2 now represent the whole system.

A stepwise refinement diagram looks similar to a hierarchical system chart. However, it is important to understand that stepwise refinement is basically different because the diagram's building blocks are different. A hierarchical system diagram describes the hierarchical relationship between components, so that each component in the diagram actually corresponds to a real component in the system. However, in a stepwise refinement diagram, a higher level component is only a name conveniently given to a group of real components that appear below it.

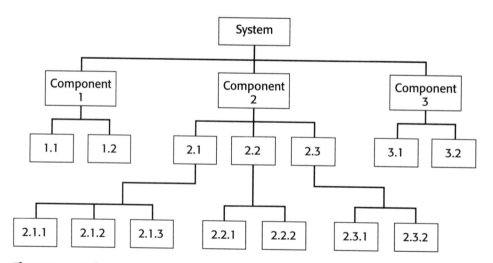

Figure 6.1   Software decomposition by stepwise refinement.

In Figure 6.2(*a*) the Controlled access system software has five low level software components: Visitor identification, Door lock control, Access file manager, Illegal access identification, and Alarm activation. Each of these five modules may correspond to an actual software module.[1] The two high level components, Access control and Alarm system, do not exist as actual software modules, and only appear as names given to the two groups of lower level components.

Figure 6.2(*b*) describes the same Controlled access system software, but this time it is represented as a hierarchical chart. Here, each component in the diagram represents a real software component. The System executive main Loop component calls three other components: Visitor identification, Door lock control, and Alarm activation. The Visitor identification component calls two components: Illegal access identification and Access file manager.

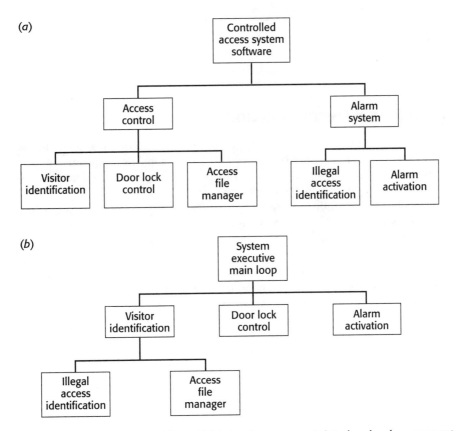

Figure 6.2 (*a*) Decomposition of high level components into low level components; (*b*) a hierarchical structure chart.

[1]This is, of course, a simplification of a real system. In reality, these five low-level components would be further decomposed into lower-level components.

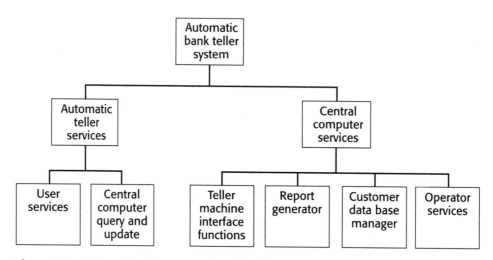

Figure 6.3   Automatic teller system—functional decomposition diagram.

6.1.1 Functional Decomposition

The functional decomposition of a software project is a division of the system into its operational components as they are seen by the user. Functional decomposition is part of the requirements phase of a project. The objective of this phase is to define all the characteristics of the system from the user's perspective.

Let us consider an automatic bank teller system. The ability to communicate online between the remote automatic tellers and the bank's central computer in order to provide updated account information is a functional characteristic of the system. This will usually be defined during the requirements phase of the development cycle. However, the method of transmission between the automatic teller and the central computer is not a functional characteristic of the system, because it is internal to the design and implementation of the system and is not apparent to the user. The method of transmission, including the communications protocol, will usually be defined during the design phase of the development of the system.[2]

Figure 6.3 presents an example of the functional decomposition of an automatic bank teller system into lower levels of functional components. In Figure 6.3 we have determined that there will be a customer data base, which could be viewed as a design decision. This is unavoidable. The functional decomposition is rarely completely devoid of all design considerations. As we will see, the functional decomposition is often a starting point for the initial design of the system.

---

[2]Implementation decisions may occasionally be dictated during the requirements phase, and are referred to as implementation requirements. This may include such features as the type of object computer, the programming language to be used, or the method of communications to be used. It is usually better to delay implementation decisions until the design phase whenever possible.

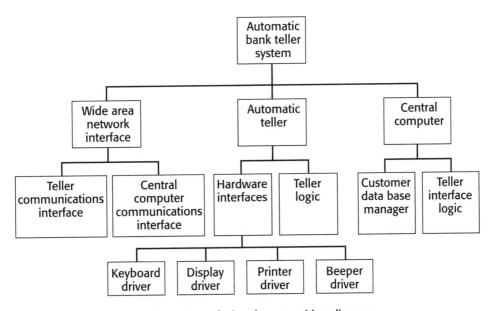

Figure 6.4   Automatic teller system—design decomposition diagram.

6.1.2 Design Decomposition

The design decomposition of a software system is a division of the system into lower level components that coincide with the actual software components of the system. In a full design decomposition of a software system, the lowest components correspond to programming modules (usually procedures, subroutines, or program functions).

Just as the requirements phase precedes the design phase, so the functional decomposition of a software system will usually precede the design decomposition. The functional decomposition will often provide much of the information necessary for the subsequent division of the system into the implementation components. In fact, the functional decomposition is often a good place to start when designing a software system, as the major functional components of a system will often correspond to the initial division of the system into subsystems or high level components.

Two of the main functions of an automatic bank teller system may be regarded as the central computer, where all the account information is stored and maintained, and the automatic teller machines that interface with the customers. The communications network that links the central computer with the teller locations may be defined as an additional high level component. This, then, would naturally be the first division of the system from a design perspective: (1) the automatic teller subsystem,[3] (2) the central computer subsystem, and (3) the communications network facility.

Figure 6.4 presents an example of the design decomposition of an automatic bank teller system into lower levels of design components. On the third level, the Automatic

---

[3]In large systems, subsystems often represent the first level decomposition of a system. This is further discussed in Section 6.3.

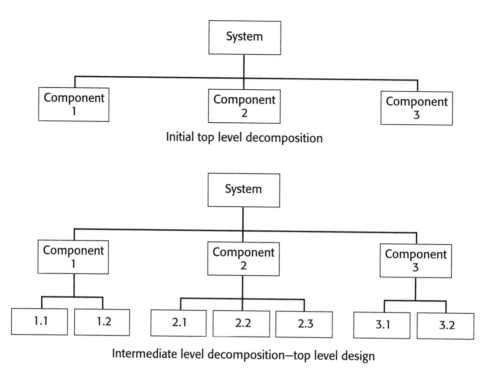

Initial top level decomposition

Intermediate level decomposition—top level design

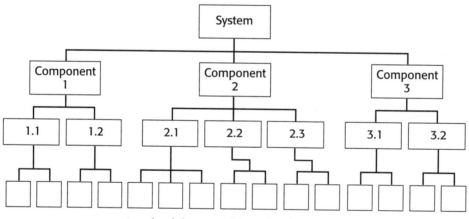

Low level decomposition—detailed design

Figure 6.5   Software decomposition by stepwise refinement with increasing detail.

teller component decomposes into the Hardware interfaces and the Teller logic. The next level may then decompose the Hardware interfaces into the Keyboard driver, the Display driver, the Printer driver, and the Beeper. At this level, these drivers may represent actual software modules.

An important point to remember is that in a design decomposition, only the lower level components are actually implemented. Higher level components represent a group of lower level components. This is illustrated in Figure 6.2(*a*), where the Access control and the Alarm system components represent two groups of lower level components (Visitor identification, Door lock control, etc.).

Design decomposition basically produces two types of system component: high level components and low level modules. Different software development standards use different terminology to identify the various levels of decomposition

A fully decomposed system, with all its low level components, is not always easy to grasp. This is especially true during the presentation of the system at a project review, when the system needs to be quickly understood by people who have not been involved in its design. On such occasions, the stepwise refinement technique is a convenient method for gradually presenting progressive detail by initially showing the first decomposition level, and then slowly revealing subsequent levels. This is demonstrated in Figure 6.5. At a convenient intermediate decomposition step, we can divide the design in two: the upper levels and the lower levels. This is used particularly when the design phase is implemented in two distinct stages: top level design and detailed design (see Figure 6.5).

6.2 The Work Breakdown Structure

So far we have discussed the division of a software *system* into either functional or design components. We will also consider the division of a software *project* into basic work components. The sum total of these work components covers all the tasks that need to be performed in order to complete the project successfully.

Large projects are difficult to manage. Without some basic order in the assignment of work tasks it is almost impossible to control the many people, materials, and functions that are involved in the development process.

6.2.1 Project Decomposition

Just like any other large, complex task, the development of a software project is more easily managed with the *divide and conquer* approach. Stepwise refinement, when applied to a software project, produces all the low level work tasks. This includes development tasks, managerial tasks, support tasks, and administrative tasks. The decomposition of a software project into tasks is referred to as the *work breakdown structure*, or the WBS.

Figure 6.6 presents an example of a work breakdown structure chart, and Table 6.1 presents the resulting work breakdown structure task list. The WBS task list contains all project work tasks, and can be used as a monitoring tool to monitor the status of assigned work tasks.

The initial WBS task list is often derived from the project schedule, which contains the project's activity list. The schedule activity list is similar to the WBS, though its purpose is different and it is usually less detailed. The schedule activity list is described in Chapter 11.

It is sometimes helpful to include the higher level task groups in the WBS task list (e.g., tasks 1, 2, 3, 2.1, 2.2, etc. in Table 6.1). This provides a useful traceback for each low level task in order to identify the task groups from which it was derived. However, inclusion of high level task groups in the WBS task list can also cause confusion, as

(a)

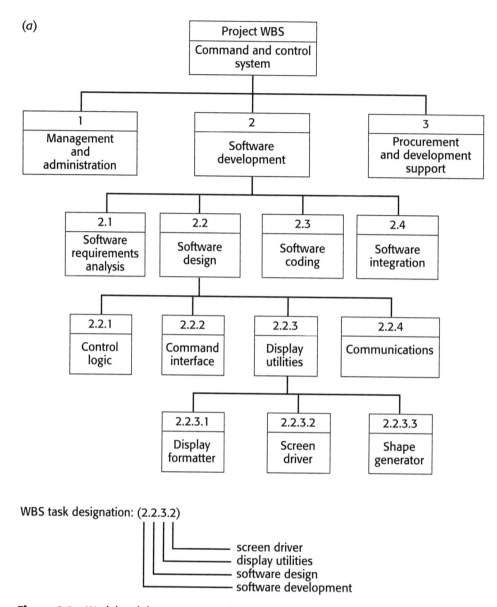

WBS task designation: (2.2.3.2)

- screen driver
- display utilities
- software design
- software development

Figure 6.6   Work breakdown structure: (a) task designation.

these items do not represent actual assigned tasks, and the *Status* and *Assigned to* attributes do not apply to them.

The WBS list of project tasks is derived from the *project's statement of work* (the SOW) that defines the scope of the project. The SOW is usually prepared before the official launching of the project (see Chapter 3), and is often part of the project contract between the customer and the developer. For internal projects, when an organization is funding its own development work, the SOW becomes synonymous with the Project

(b)

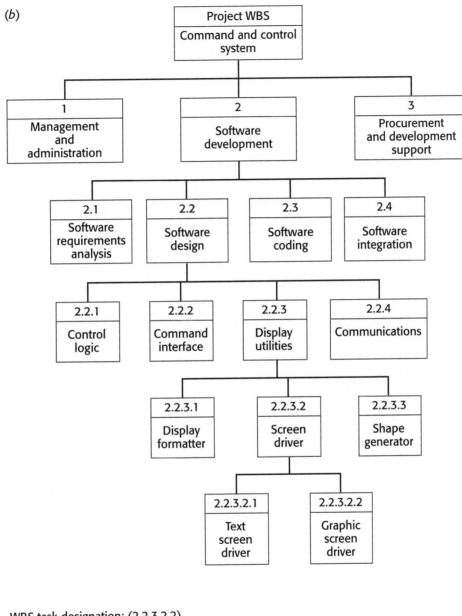

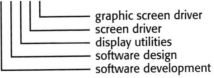

Figure 6.6 Work breakdown structure: (b) adding a task.

Table 6.1   Work Breakdown Structure Task List

TASK ID	DESCRIPTION	STATUS	ASSIGNED TO	COMMENTS
1.	Management and administration			
2.	Software development			
2.1	Software requirement analysis			
2.2	Software design			
2.2.1	Control logic			
2.2.2	Command interface			
2.2.3	Display utilities			
2.2.3.1	Display formatter	Complete	J. Smith	
2.2.3.2	Screen driver	Started	F. Brown	
2.2.3.3	Shape generator	Started	A. Black	
2.2.4	Communications			
2.3	Software coding			
2.4	Software integration			
3.	Procurement and development support			
.	.			
.	.			
.	.			

definition specification or a similar document that defines the scope of work for the software project manager.

6.2.2 The WBS as a Project Management Tool

The work breakdown structure defines all tasks to be performed during the development of the project. This will include tasks from such project categories as:

- Software development
- Installation

- Maintenance
- Management
- Training
- Procurement
- Documentation

These tasks are described in more detail in Table 6.2 (Section 6.3.4).

At all times, any work being performed by a member of the software project team must be part of a WBS task. No member of the team should ever perform any task that does not appear in the WBS list of tasks.

The WBS is a useful tool provided it is constantly updated. It should be updated periodically, together with the project development plan and the project schedule. It is reasonable to expect the WBS list to have tasks added, modified, or even removed as project development progresses.

The WBS is essentially a management tool that provides the ability to assign well-defined tasks to members of the development team. It is through the WBS that progress is monitored as tasks are completed and potential problems are discovered. New tasks that were overlooked are identified, and estimates are revised based on the actual resources used for completed tasks.

The WBS is also a budgetary tool that provides a means of charging each development activity to the appropriate section in the project budget. This is one of the basic methods for planning and monitoring project expenditure.

There are many computerized utilities available to support the maintenance of the WBS. These utilities run both on small PC type computers and large mainframes. WBS utilities are often available as part of a manager's general planning utility, and provide other scheduling and monitoring features, such as PERT analysis and report generation.

Other methods have been developed for managing the many low level work tasks that comprise a large project. There are several variations and enhancements of the work breakdown structure technique,[4] some using sophisticated tracking tools, others using special symbols and techniques to analyze and monitor the work task list.

6.3 Handling Large Projects

Clearly, small tasks are easier to handle than large tasks. As we have seen, this has been the reasoning behind the division of large projects into smaller components.

The way in which a system is decomposed contributes significantly to the software architecture. There is usually no such thing as a single correct architecture or a single correct decomposition. Figure 6.7 presents two possible high level decompositions of a controlled access system. Both appear to be reasonable divisions of the system, but the

---

[4]Alternate methods include the Wilson and Sifer (1990) model that replaces the WBS with a structured planning technique based on a hierarchy of work flow diagrams (WFDs), a form of network of tasks that includes each task's input and output. The Wilson and Sifer method is a highly formal method and is considerably more complex than the classic WBS.

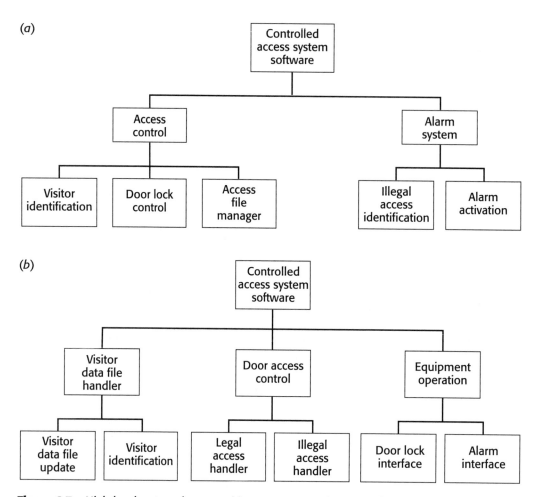

Figure 6.7 High-level system decomposition—two approaches. Two different system architectures—(*a*) and (*b*).

architecture in Figure 6.7(*b*) may require fewer interfaces between the main software components.

We will now consider some of the guidelines that should be followed when selecting a particular decomposition structure.

6.3.1 Subsystems

Large systems are often composed of major semi-independent components that may, themselves, be viewed as systems. An automatic bank teller system may be divided rather naturally into two subsystems: the main computer subsystem and the automatic teller computer subsystem. Thus, a subsystem contains most of the characteristics of a system, except that a subsystem is not intended to function on its own. When large software systems can be divided into subsystems, they discard some of the complexity that comes with largeness. The idea behind this approach is based upon the management of the development of each subsystem as a separate system, to the extent that this is possible. For each subsystem, a team leader or deputy project manager is assigned much of the responsibility for development, while responsibilities common to all subsystems are handled by central project management.

On a small-scale project, such as the automatic bank teller system discussed previously, two team leaders may be assigned responsibility for the two main components of the system. The project manager will then monitor the activities in each team, and will coordinate the technical and administrative interface activities between the teams. The assignment of software team leaders is further discussed in Chapter 5.

On a larger-scale project, such as the development of the software for the NASA space shuttle in the eighties, the project was so massive that it was, in fact, developed as several separate projects. A central office was responsible for the coordination and integration of all subsystems (both software and hardware). An insight into the magnitude of this complex project is provided in a paper by Madden and Rone (1984).

6.3.2 Guidelines for Functional Decomposition

As we have seen, the initial division of a software system is the functional decomposition, which corresponds to the structure of the software as it is perceived by the user. This division assists us in defining the requirements for the system and provides a method of identifying low-level functions and attributing them to major system functions.

Many texts propose that the functional decomposition of a system should follow the requirements analysis of the system. In many cases a general outline of the requirements will produce a high level functional diagram. From that point on, the refinement of the functional decomposition goes hand in hand with the analysis of the system. In fact, the generation of the functional diagram is often an iterative process, in which the diagram is repeatedly revised and refined, as more information becomes available.

The basic high level functional decomposition of a software system is often based on preconceived ideas that evolve during the conception phase. These ideas may then dictate a specific division of the system from which the functional decomposition evolves.

This initial division of the system is not always the most logical and appropriate from the developer's perspective. A large inventory system could initially be perceived as comprising:

- A human interface
- A data base
- A report generator
- Update logic

But the human interface may span a number of different computers, and part of it may be heavily integrated with the report generator. Major features, such as reliability and backup features, may have been overlooked. Therefore, a better division of the system might not define *human interface* as a high level function, preferring to include separate human interface low level functions within other major functions. Also, backup may be included in a high level *maintenance* function that would also cover data base compression and clean-up functions.

As a general guideline, no single functional decomposition should be selected just because it was conceived first.

As we have seen, a good functional decomposition is important, and may well determine the design and architecture of the system being developed. A sound strategy for defining a good software functional decomposition is to convene a meeting with the central participants in the project to discuss a number of different divisions of the system. A functional decomposition should then be selected based on:

- Reason (e.g., different computers usually support separate functions)
- Ease of implementation (e.g., a good functional decomposition will usually foster a good design)
- Comprehensiveness (have all functions been covered?)

Ease of implementation is dependent on design criteria, which are discussed next.

6.3.3 Guidelines for Design Decomposition

We have seen that the functional decomposition of a software system may be substantially different from the design decomposition of the system. However, a good functional decomposition will have taken into account design as the next development phase, and will often be a good starting point for the division of the system into high level design components.

The design decomposition of a system is only part of the full design of the software (there are many design methods—see Pressman [1992]). However, from the project manager's perspective, this is a crucial stage, because the design decomposition of a system determines the structure of the software as it will be built. The following is an overview of the basic design considerations that influence the method of system decomposition.

One of the early basic concepts of software engineering required a *structured* approach to the design and programming of software. The structured nature of the software is determined from the first stages of decomposition. In the early days of programming, this approach was championed by Dijkstra (1972). The main objective was to move software development (or simply *programming*, as it was then called) from immaturity to a fully developed engineering discipline. Many other structured design techniques have since been developed, but no single generally accepted standard has yet emerged.

As more experience was gained in the development of complex software projects, it became evident that the best design decomposition should strive to produce independent software components, or modules. Complex interfaces between modules were strongly discouraged, and such terms as low coupling, high cohesion, and information hiding became the basic building blocks for good software modular design.

Simply stated, a good design decomposition produces small, simple, independent modules. Of course, in any system no two modules are truly independent, so the term independent here should be interpreted as meaning *as independent as possible* within the constraints of the project being developed.

On the lowest decomposition level, the degree of independence of modules is referred to as the extent of *coupling* that exists in the design. Coupling measures such interdependent features as data, control, and module content (i.e. overlapping of module boundaries).

Probably one of the most fundamental principles in the design decomposition of software is centered around the concept of the *black box*. This principle, also referred to as *information hiding*, strives to produce modules that hide their design. Black boxes are only identified by their input and output, and not by the method that they use to generate the output from the input. Information hiding produces modules that hide their logic-flow, and their data structures, from each other. Though the term *black box* preceded the evolution of software engineering as a discipline, the concept of information hiding in software design was first formulated by Parnas (1972).

6.3.4 Guidelines for Decomposition of Work Tasks

We have seen that the work required to complete a project can be divided into a group of simpler well-defined tasks represented by the *work breakdown structure* or the WBS. The WBS is not a decomposition of the software produced by the project; it is a decomposition of the project itself, and includes such activities as management, procurement, installation and, of course, software development.

The design structure of the system produces low level *development* work tasks. Each low level module is assigned three basic work tasks: module design, coding, and unit testing. Additional development tasks such as prototyping, testing, and integration are derived from the other development phases.

Table 6.2 contains a typical list of high level WBS tasks to be included in the formal WBS task list (see Table 6.1). This is not an exhaustive list of all project development tasks, and not all projects will require all the tasks described. However, this table will be useful as a checklist to assist in locating tasks that may have been overlooked.

Nondevelopment activities, such as high level management WBS tasks, are standard, to a large extent, and any variance is determined by either the magnitude of the project or the introduction of a new management model. An example of a list of management WBS tasks appears in Table 6.3. This list contains many of the most important management tasks required for most software development projects. Those tasks that are mandatory for all projects are marked as such in the list.

Note that budget analysis and administration is not a mandatory management task, simply because not all projects administer their own budget. Some organizations have a financial officer responsible for the administration of project budgets.

Customer interface is a mandatory management task because all projects have a customer. In the case of company internal projects, high level management, together with the designated users of the system being developed, play the role of customer. It is usually they who specify the initial project requirements, and it is to them that the project manager must come for final approval and for final system acceptance.

Table 6.2   High Level Work Breakdown Structure Tasks

Software development
   Requirements analysis
   Prototype development
      Prototype specification
      Prototype design
      Prototype implementation
Design
   Top level design
   Detailed design
Implementation
   Coding
   Unit test
Integration
   Software integration
   Hardware/software integration
Testing
   Alpha testing
   Beta testing
   Acceptance
Installation
Maintenance
   Error correction
   Software enhancement
Management
   Planning
   Staffing
   Administration and services
   Budget administration
   Personnel management
   Quality assurance
   Configuration management
Training
Procurement
   Acquisition of development tools
   Acquisition of system components (off-the-shelf)
   Equipment selection
   Vendor selection
   Ordering procedure
   Inventory control
Documentation
   Technical writing
   Project publishing activities
   Development documentation
      Non-deliverable development documentation
      Deliverable development documentation
   Maintenance documentation
   User documentation

Table 6.3   Management and Administration Tasks

MANDATORY	MANAGEMENT TASK
✓	1. Planning
✓	2. Preparation of estimates
✓	3. Risk analysis and risk management
✓	4. Scheduling
	5. Staffing
	6. Budget analysis and administration
✓	7. Personnel management
✓	8. Task assignment
✓	9. Delegation of authority
✓	10. Assignment of development resources
	11. Supervision of development equipment maintenance
✓	12. Supervision and control of development
✓	13. Organization of reviews and formal presentations
	14. Establishment of standards and methods
✓	15. Quality assurance and control
✓	16. Configuration management and control
	17. Supervision of subcontractors and vendors
✓	18. Higher management interface and coordination
✓	19. Customer interface and coordination
✓	20. Reporting
	21. Administration and services

6.4 Component-Based Development

An excellent strategy in managing software projects, large or small, is the elimination of work. By identifying and removing unnecessary tasks, the work, cost, and risk can be reduced without losing functionality or quality. One way of achieving this is through the reuse of software components. This is well illustrated in the following case.

Control Systems Inc. (CSI) specialized in developing communications control centers, the kind used by railways, truck dispatch companies, and customer service centers. CSI's control centers displayed information regarding the locations of the company's vehicles, in real-time and on giant screens. CSI had developed its expertise over many years and had become one of the best providers of control center systems. But new rivals began appearing on the scene offering cheaper systems and using more aggressive sales techniques. CSI was loosing market share.

In 1994, CSI was greatly in need of a large new contract. In a bid for a major multimillion dollar contract, CSI was chosen for the best and final stage of negotiations, along with one other competitor. Though CSI had slashed its price from $34 million dollars to $25 million, it had learned that its competitor was offering a solution for $22 million.

The CSI proposal team was tempted to reduce its price to $22 million but was overruled by senior management, because at that price CSI would loose money. The proposal team convened a brainstorming session to come up with a winning strategy.

The team searched for areas where CSI had an advantage over its competitor. The team determined that CSI's best advantage was in the company's experience. It had developed many more similar systems than its competitor had. The team proposed that, contrary to previous practice, CSI would not build every component of the new system from the beginning but rather it would reuse components from previous systems, thus reducing development costs.

This strategy enabled CSI to reduce its price to $20 million, while still making a comfortable profit. CSI was awarded the contract.

CSI's solution seems so obvious, and yet most companies repeatedly try to reinvent the wheel time after time. In software, more than in hardware, there is a reluctance to reuse software components. This is a psychological problem more than anything else, for, as we have seen, the solution to the bystander is clear.

Reuse is possibly the single most important factor in reducing development time and in improving software quality. Though software reuse is definitely not a new concept, it has become practicable in recent years due to the growing acceptance of software component-based techniques.

The use of prebuilt and fully tested software components is called *component-based development* (CBD). The use of component-based development reduces the complexity of software development and is particularly effective in large software systems. This is because the larger the system, the more there is to save.

6.4.1 How Components Are Used

CBDs are software building blocks, and can almost be considered the software counterpart of hardware integrated circuits (ICs). They are produced by organizations that plan to reuse their own components, but they are also commercially available and can be purchased in much the same way as software applications and packages. Internal reused components are *inherited*, whereas external components are *acquired*. CBDs are often developed as *shelf* software components (to be used or sold later).

A CBD is about halfway between a software application and a library subroutine. Examples are algorithms, Java Beans, control elements (e.g. soft switches), communications stacks, and drivers. Though CBDs, like hardware ICs, may be stored for future use, unlike ICs, their use does not remove them from the store.

The example in the previous section (Control Systems Inc.) describes inherited reuse. The following true case describes the use of specially developed CBDs.

A company that produces 3-D graphic products (simulators, educational applications, and games) has several teams that develop products on a wide variety of hardware platforms. Because 3-D applications are complex and new graphic interfaces are being released every few months, the company decided to develop a set of 3-D graphic CBD modules. The modules provide various classes of interfaces to each type of graphic hardware. The teams develop their products with a standard API. When the products are ported to different platforms, the teams switch out the CBD modules and do not need to change the basic product software (see Figure 6.8).

Another familiar example of the implementation of the component-based development model is the Microsoft Windows plug-and-play concept. The idea behind this concept was to provide a modular-based applications interface that would plug into the operating system much the same as you would plug in an electric appliance at home. The application interface components that achieve this (the plugs) are available on the market.

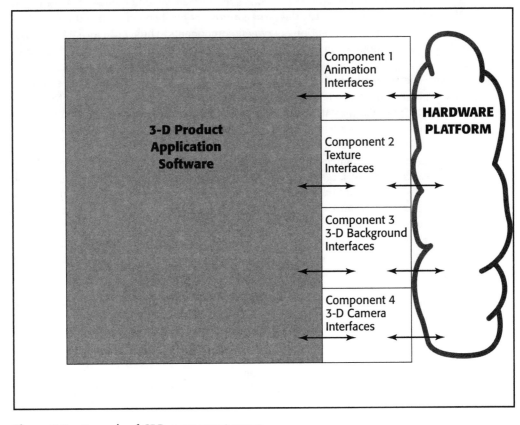

Figure 6.8   Example of CBD component usage.

The Internet is a most suitable environment for the use of CBD, due to the vast amount of interconnected software that exists on the Web. In fact, Java, the most common language on the Web, is one of the most suitable languages for CBDs.

6.4.2 CBD as a Formal Theory

Component-based development has a growing following. In addition to there being a web site[5] devoted to CBD, conferences have been held in the US and Europe devoted to the subject. Component-based theory has been formalized, and there are numerous texts that have been written on the subject (see Jell [1998] and Allen et al. [1998]). There are also several commercial companies that offer CBD components.

The IEEE has defined the way reuse modules should exchange information. The standard (Std 1420 [IEEE 1999]) defines the minimal set of information that reuse items need to be able to exchange to enable them to work together. A supplement to the standard defines a method for certifying that a reuse module conforms to the information exchange requirements. This facilitates the building of reuse libraries of modules that are guaranteed to work together. The modules (called *assets*) may be units of source code, documents, and any other unit of information that has the potential for being reused.

A number of research projects are in progress to promote and expand the theory of CBD. Krieger (Krieger and Adler 1998) has summarized the emergence of several new CBD-related expansions. Firstly, the term *containers* has been coined and it describes the shared context for interactions between components. Thus, in Figure 6.8, the four 3-D interface components may be considered to exist and operate within a single container.

A container is itself a higher level component (just as several building blocks when joined together can form a larger building block). In this context, each of the four components in Figure 6.8 may themselves also be containers, if they contain lower level components. As an example, the animation component (Component 1) may be a collection of low-level animation interfaces into the graphics hardware.

The concept of containers is important because it indicates where CBD could lead us. Successively making larger building blocks out of smaller ones could ultimately lead us to a software nirvana where applications are built by plugging (and playing) large software components into each other in much the same way as a modern modular stereo system is assembled.

Krieger's paper could indeed be an important milestone in that direction. Those skeptics who are recalling the promises of Ada[6] packages should give this idea one more try.

---

[5]The component-based development web site is located at: http://www.componentdevelopment.com

[6]The US Department of Defense (DOD) issued the Stoneman document in 1976, defining the "Requirements for Ada Programming Support Environments," and the "Steelman" document in 1978, defining the "Requirements for High Order Computer Programming Languages," which laid the foundations for the Ada language (named after Augusta Ada Byron, presumed to be the first computer programmer, and the daughter of the British poet Lord Byron). In spite of the massive support provided by the DOD, Ada's subsequent success (or lack thereof) is a most controversial issue.

It is catching on (possibly because, contrary to Ada, it is not supported by any government agency).

Finally, a note of caution. The concepts of reuse and component-based development include the use of software developed by others. This practice carries with it the potential for legal implications (see Chapter 3). Though this may not be an issue for reuse (from within the organization) it could well be an issue for software components acquired outside the organization. Such software should be acquired together with the same licenses and formal authorizations that accompany any other software product.

6.5 Summary

Complex software projects can be divided into simpler components, and though the full project may be difficult to manage, each component will be easier to handle. The decomposition of software projects into smaller components is helpful in monitoring the activities assigned to the various development teams. The method of decomposition may differ, depending on the project manager's objective.

Stepwise refinement is an iterative method for the decomposition of a project into manageable components. It is also a useful tool for the definition of the functional, design, and work decompositions of a software project. In a stepwise decomposition of a project, each component decomposes into the components directly below it. Each step of the decomposition describes the full system, but at a different level of detail.

The functional decomposition of a software project is a division of the system into its operational components; that is, those features that are seen by the user. The design decomposition of a software system is a division of the system into lower level components that coincide with the programming components of the system. The work breakdown structure (WBS) is the decomposition of a software project into low level work tasks.

Clearly, small tasks are easier to handle than large tasks, and this has been the reasoning behind the division of large projects into smaller components. Large systems are often composed of major semi-independent components, called subsystems, that may themselves be viewed as systems. When large software systems can be divided into subsystems, they discard some of the complexity that comes with largeness. The idea behind this approach is based upon the management of the development of each subsystem as a separate system to the extent possible.

The basic high level functional decomposition of a software system is often based on preconceived ideas that evolve during the conception phase. These ideas may then dictate a specific division of the system from which the functional decomposition then evolves. However, this initial division of the system is not always the most logical and appropriate from the developer's perspective. As a general guideline, no single functional decomposition should be selected just because it was conceived first.

The functional decomposition of a software system may be substantially different from the design decomposition of the system. However, a good functional decomposition will have taken into account design as the next development phase, and will often be a good starting point for the division of the system into high level design components. The high level design components are then further decomposed into successive lower levels that ultimately produce programming modules. A good modular design produces small, simple, independent modules.

The work breakdown structure is not a decomposition of the software produced by the project, but is a decomposition of the project itself, and includes such activities as management, procurement, installation and, of course, software development. Many of the WBS development tasks are derived from the development method that will be used, and from the design and architecture of the system.

An excellent strategy in managing software projects, large or small, is the elimination of work. By identifying and removing unnecessary tasks, the work, cost, and risk can be reduced without losing functionality or quality. One way of achieving this is through the reuse of software components.

The use of prebuilt and fully tested software components is called *component-based development* (CBD). CBDs are software building blocks, and can almost be considered the software counterpart of hardware integrated circuits (ICs).

Reuse is possibly the single most important factor in reducing development time and in improving software quality.

Exercises

1. Software Systems Inc. (SSI) is developing a special-purpose computer based on a common microprocessor. SSI has a cross compiler for the microprocessor that runs on its mainframe. The company has decided to develop a modest proprietary operating system for the new computer.

   Consider a simple single-user operating system. Prepare a proposal for the functional decomposition of the operating system using stepwise refinement. Describe the functional decomposition chart for the first three levels.

2. For the operating system described in Exercise 1, and based on the functional decomposition, prepare a design decomposition.

   a. Describe the design decomposition chart for the first three levels. Choose a single high level component and describe the full decomposition down to the software module level.

   b. Explain how you have taken into account the guidelines for independent modules. Explain how you have implemented the information hiding guidelines.

   c. Propose areas for reuse from similar projects. What components of the operating system would be candidates for external CBD module acquisition?

3. For the operating system described in Exercise 1, prepare a work breakdown structure chart for the first three levels and prepare a WBS tasks list.

   Explain why some of the tasks in Table 6.2 are not applicable to this project.

4. Consider the software for a satellite project, including the launching and tracking of the satellite, and the operation of the satellite during and after launch.

a. Identify the main subsystems in the project and explain the advantage that is to be gained by defining them as subsystems. Consider the pros and cons of using CBD modules in a project of this type.

b. Now consider a payroll system, including the staff file maintenance, issuance of payroll checks, etc. Would there be any advantage in defining subsystems for this project? Explain. How would the pros and cons for CBD modules be different for this project?

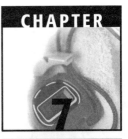

Software Project Management in a Client/Server Environment

Are client/server software projects easier or more difficult to manage than other types of projects? Well, firstly, it depends on whether you are developing *on* them or *for* them. In other words is your client/server system a development environment or is it a target environment?

Secondly, is your project well suited for this type of distributed environment or was it dictated by circumstance (i.e., you had no choice!)? Let us first understand how and why this distributed architecture evolved.

Some of the mainframes of just two decades ago would be easily shamed by the personal computers of today. The giant CDC 6000 series or the IBM 370 series would have a hard time competing today with many of the features of an Intel Pentium-based PC or Apple's iMac.

One of the first challenges to mainframes came from minicomputers such as Digital Equipment's PDP and VAX. The minicomputers competed well in price and software, but in performance they could not compete with the sheer power of their bigger brothers. The small computer's lack of power was mostly evident in two areas: number crunching and the number of users. As computers became even smaller, cheaper, and more versatile, the idea of connecting them together began to catch on. DEC had clusters, IBM had networks, and throughout the industry the battle raged between the proponents of distributed processing and the proponents of centralized processing. When the battle smoke subsided, the supporters of distributed networked computers had won and DEC was nowhere to be seen.

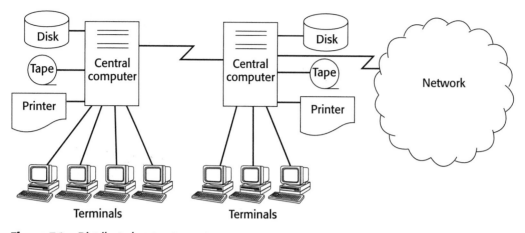

Figure 7.1   Distributed computer system.

The distribution of computing power started the evolution toward client/server systems. For the software project manager, this posed a new type of challenge. While the distributed system approach placed a computer in every department, the client/server approach placed a computer on every desk. Figure 7.1 presents a typical distributed system and Figure 7.2 presents a client/ server system.

The client/server concept places computing power in the hands of the end users, while allowing them to choose their own front-end computer. This new architecture provides both new challenges and opportunities for managing the development of a software project. This chapter discusses client/server environments from the *software project manager's* perspective. For a basic understanding of client/server systems in general, the reader is directed to any of several available texts on the subject.[1]

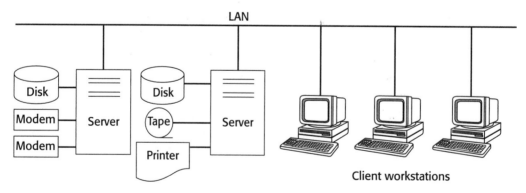

Figure 7.2   Client/server system.

[1]See Sinha's excellent summary for a comprehensive technical overview of client/server computing (Sinha 1992), or Inmon's text on the development of client/server systems (Inmon 1993).

7.1 An Introduction to Client/Server Environments

The client/server concept can be applied to two basic models: the development environment model and the application environment model. In the development environment, a client server system is a development tool facilitating the development of a software project. In the application environment, a client/server system provides a specific service. From a more general perspective both models can be perceived as overlapping, as clearly a development tool also provides a specific service. The following examples illustrate the difference between the two models.

The network presented in Figure 7.2 is a good example of a client/server development environment. In this example each software developer is provided with a client computer. The developers communicate with each other through the network of servers and client computers, and share the resources (e.g., disk space or printers) connected to the servers.

A network of automatic bank tellers (see Figure 7.3) is an example of an application client/server environment where each client is a teller computer and each server is a regional (or central) computer. Here the *client/server* concept is applied to an architecture that existed before the *client/server* term was coined. Though this example includes the basic components of a client/server application system, it does not include some of the added frills that come with modern client/server systems (such as direct communications between clients).

Another example of an application client/server environment is an inventory system where client computers are used for queries and transaction updates, and the server

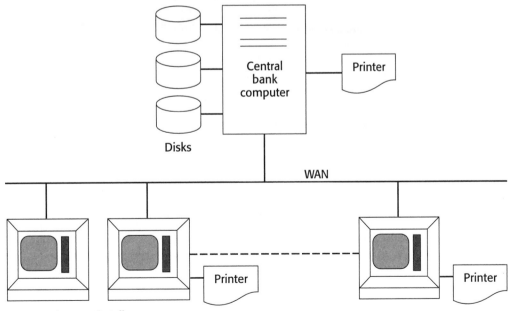

Figure 7.3 Automatic bank teller system.

computers (there may be several) are used to provide access to the data base and to the printers.

7.1.1 Definitions and Terminology

A client/server environment is a cooperative multiprocessing environment between processors (*clients*) and shared host processors (*servers*), in which each user is given a dedicated system perception.

The key terms in this definition are (a) *cooperative*, emphasizing the need for well-defined communication protocols, (b) *shared*, indicating the basic aspect of a client/server environment, and (c) *dedicated*, implying that each user (client) is not aware of the resources being consumed by other users.

Ideally, the users are provided with a single system image (SSI) so that they believe that they have the whole system to themselves. This dedicated system perception, in most cases, remains only an ideal. In reality, only the objectives of cooperative environments and shared resources are totally achieved.

There are many variations of the client/server environment. Sun workstations are frequently used as client/server development environments, and PC networks (such as Novell) are often used as application environments.[2] These environments may have multiple servers (see Figure 7.4) and occasionally servers may double as clients. In fact, in some client/server environments, any client may also be configured as a server, too.

Servers may communicate with each other either within a single client/server system or between separate client/server systems. In this wider context, client server systems may be hooked together via WANs (wide area networks) to logically form extremely large client/server systems (see Figure 7.5). For example, consider a multinational corporation that has development centers in several countries. While each country may have its own client/server system, the whole corporation may be linked via an international WAN. Thus a client in, say, France, may be able to share a resource located in the United States. With the vast improvement in global communications and with the expansion of large international corporations, this type of development environment is now becoming prevalent.

7.1.2 Client/Server Objectives

In a software development environment, let us consider how a client/server system compares to a centralized system (minicomputers or mainframes) and to individual computers (e.g., desktop PCs). In the latter case, several advantages are immediately apparent: the ability to share data files and to transfer information between users in real-time.

Centralized computer systems do not necessarily provide a development environment inferior to a client/server environment. The centralized environment has such advantages as the low cost of adding a user (the cost of a dumb terminal) and the rela-

---

[2]These examples should not be perceived as restricting how client/server systems can be used. Clearly Sun workstations can also be used in application environments and Novell is equally applicable to development and application environments.

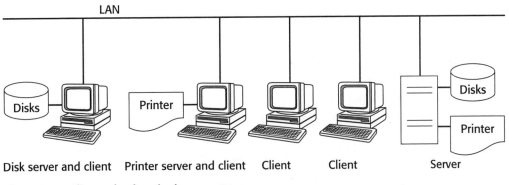

Figure 7.4 Clients also functioning as servers.

tively high power of the central processor. However, it is in the areas of versatility and low entry level cost that client/servers have the advantage. Ideally, the objective of a client/server development environment is to provide low-cost development workstations with a high degree of integration. At an entry level, a client/server environment is inexpensive. The initial investment is low and the addition of more workstations is relatively inexpensive (though admittedly more than the cost of a dumb terminal). The environment can grow virtually limitlessly.

The degree of integration between development workstations depends on the type of client/server system, the way it has been configured, the software packages being used, and the development standards being enforced. There are specific software packages (such as configuration management) that enforce a high degree of integration within a team of developers. However, ultimately it is the policy of the developing organization that determines just how tightly coupled the development activities will be.

In a non-development environment, application client/server systems have similar objectives. They provide a high degree of integration with a low-cost entry level for small systems. Consider the example of the automatic teller system discussed previously. Small banks and large can equally implement similar automatic teller systems, and best of all, can communicate among themselves to enable cross-bank transactions. Clearly the network of tellers is highly integrated, while the addition of a new teller machine is relatively simple and inexpensive.

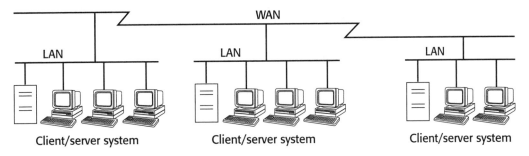

Figure 7.5 Client/server systems linked via a wide area network.

7.1.3 Functions of the Client

The client computer provides the interface between the system and the user. Modern client components will typically use a graphical user interface (GUI) such as that provided by MS-Windows, Windows NT, X-Windows, or Motif. This type of interface provides the user with an intuitive form of communication with the system that is both easy to use and easy to master.

The client is the mediator between the user and the server and it requests services from the server. On the most elementary level, the architecture looks like this:

$$\text{User} \leftrightarrow \text{Client computer} \leftrightarrow \text{Server computer}$$

One of the main differences between a simple terminal and a client is the client's ability to run its own software applications. The client usually hosts the presentation component of the overall system software and is therefore responsible for the reformatting and display of system outputs. The client also performs the initial manipulation and possibly also the initial processing of user inputs.

Different clients on the same client/server system may run different presentation software and they may use different GUIs. It is not uncommon to link an X-Station, a PC MS-Windows station, and a Macintosh to the same client/server network. In fact, any front-end computer can function as a client as long as it adheres to the client/server interface standards (commonly referred to as APIs or application programming interfaces).

7.1.4 Functions of the Server

One of the main functions of the server is to provide services to its clients. These services range from access to peripherals and networks to computing power on the server itself running remote applications. Ideally, the server will conceal the complexity of the client/server network from the client.

Another major function of the server is data access control. Servers commonly manage large data bases, which are accessed by clients or even other servers, in some cases, across large complex networks. The server in control of the data handles such functions as access control (e.g., password protection), data access contention (conflicting or competing requests primarily during data updates), and, of course, data base backup and recovery.

Within these large LANs and WANs (local area networks and wide area networks), the server functions as a gateway providing the client computers with access to the outside world. This important feature also provides access *from* the outside world to the client/server system from virtually anywhere. Access is provided either by permanently connecting to other linked networks or by dialing in (via modem) to other network nodes. Thus virtually any computer with a modem can function as a remote client.

Multiple servers do not necessarily mean multiple client/server systems. A single system may have more than one server. In a multi-server system, the servers function as a cooperative system dividing the tasks between them so that, for example, one server may handle the data base, another may handle communications, and a third may handle application processing. The complexity of this type of system is concealed by each server from the clients, making each client unaware of the existence of many servers.

Note that clients can also be servers. Any peripheral device connected to a client, or any other client resource, can be made available to other clients by setting up the client computer in the dual mode of client and server. Though not all client/server architectures support this dual mode feature, many do (such as IBM's PC network).

7.2 The Network

The network is the backbone of any client/server system and supports easy access and connectivity between nodes. This is provided through a layered network concept (see Table 7.1) referred to as an open systems interconnection (OSI) architecture. The OSI architecture is designed to allow for the interconnection of different types of systems. Though not exclusive to client/server systems, OSI provides one of its major strengths: the ability to easily link networks corporation-wide, nationwide, and even worldwide. The OSI architecture is common, though not essential, in client/server systems.

7.2.1 Network Protocols

Network links, be they for linking clients and servers or for linking between networks, require protocols: the rules by which networks and network elements talk to each other. One of the most common communications protocols is the Transmission Control Protocol/Internet Protocol, more commonly known as TCP/IP. TCP/IP is in fact a suite of protocols that supports LANs and WANs and that was originally developed for UNIX environments. For the client/server architecture, there is the Client/Server Internetwork Protocol (IP) that works together with TCP/IP.

There are many other network communications protocols on various levels, such as SNA (Systems network architecture), which is widely used by IBM, Novell NetWare, and Microsoft's LAN Manager. However, OSI, which was defined by the International Organization for Standardization (ISO) (see Chapter 9), is particularly of interest in client/server environments because of its ability to connect heterogeneous systems.

There are seven OSI layers that determine the different levels of network management, access, and application. These layers[3] are described in Table 7.1.

OSI does not mean only *interconnection*; it also means *open*. Open networks provide easy access to any network element that abides by a set of basic rules or standards. These standards govern the way data is stored and accessed and the way network elements behave. The basic assumption of being *open* is that any network element that conforms to the behavior and access rules can gain access to all other network elements (assuming that there are no security restrictions). Thus OSI is considered to be an ideal architecture for a client/server network.

---

[3]See Sinha (1992) for a detailed description of the OSI layers.

Table 7.1   The OSI Layered Model

LAYER NUMBER	LAYER NAME	TYPE OF INFORMATION	LAYER DESCRIPTION
7	Application	Messages	Provides application programming interface (API) to client/server application
6	Presentation	Messages	Translates data into user representation formats
5	Session	Messages	Provides services for communication between applications on different processors
4	Transport	Messages	Provides end to end control between nodes
3	Network	Packets	Switches and routes information across the network
2	Data link	Frames	Transfers units of information across the physical link
1	Physical	Bits	Transmits bit streams over a physical medium

7.2.2 Network Considerations

Easy interconnection is a significant benefit when managing a geographically distributed project, that is, when members of the development team are located at distant sites. Together with appropriate distributed development tools (e.g., configuration managers, error logs, access control, e-mail), it can provide the environment needed to create a single cohesive team from many separate groups.

For the project manager, open networks also ease the restriction of development platforms having to be the same. An open network may have remote developers using Sun workstations, PC workstations, or Macintoshes, and they may link Oracle or Informix data bases. This is by no means a recommendation for project managers to encourage the use of different platforms among their developers, but it is an indication that it can be done.

In application environments, the network also provides an excellent infrastructure for many distributed target systems, such as:

- Information networks
  - professional literature searching
  - crime prevention

- Financial systems
    - banking
    - credit approval
- Access control
    - identification systems
    - immigration control

These are basically data-driven systems in which there is no single central data base. It is the network that links the many data storage locations and integrates them into a single access system. Client/server architectures are well suited to handling this type of network application.

7.3 Project Management Advantages and Disadvantages of a Client/Server Environment

For the project manager, the client/server architecture, just like any other computer system architecture, has both advantages and disadvantages. These system qualities (or lack thereof) can impact the way a project is developed. They bear upon both the target environment and the development environment.

The advantages of a client/server architecture include:

Shared resources. Resources are more efficiently used due to the ability to share their use between users.

Reduced costs. The initial cost of a client/server system is less than most other types of multi-user systems. Also, the cost of expanding the capacity of the system may be less.

Start small and grow. It is not necessary for the project manager to initially determine the size of the system; it can start small and expand as the need arises.

Smaller systems (downsizing). It is relatively easy to reduce client/server systems in size, with minimal impact on end-user performance.

No single point failure. The risk of bringing down the whole system due to a single failure is significantly less than in other types of systems, as the failure of one client computer does not usually affect others.

Distributed data access. The client/server architecture is an excellent way of providing distributed data access for large numbers of users[4] by making server data bases accessible over large networks.

Adding clients is simple. Client/server systems can be expanded easily and virtually limitlessly by linking additional client computers to the network.

---

[4]See Microsoft (1992) for examples of client/server distributed data architectures.

Adding servers is relatively simple. There is no limit to the number of servers that can be linked to a client/server system, thus providing additional processing power, peripherals, data access power, and system management functions.

Unfortunately, the client/server architecture also has some disadvantages.

System administration. System administration rules can be difficult to enforce due to the large degree of freedom often available at the client station. For example, data may be stored locally on the client computer and not included in the system-wide backup.

Overloading a server. Though adding a server is relatively easy, this does not necessarily mean that servers are frequently added and removed. Thus, servers often become overloaded producing long resource queues when the capacity of the CPU is exceeded, or when the LAN or communications network is overloaded, or when disk space is exceeded. In general, response time during peak demand can become poor. Though these problems may occur in any system, they tend to be more serious in a client/server environment.

Limited number of users permitted to access packages. When clients share the use of an applications package (e.g., a graphics package or a CASE tool), they may be restricted by the number of computers licensed to use the package simultaneously. This means that an attempt to load an application package may occasionally be rejected.

Laborious maintenance. A large client/server system may include numerous computers, peripherals, and other hardware components: servers, clients, printers, disks, routers, etc. Hardware maintenance of such a plethora of components is often an extremely laborious task.

Difficult to manage. Management of a client/server development environment can be difficult, especially when the servers provide the developers with a large degree of system independence. This is especially true in a geographically distributed development environment.

Security. Security and access control can be difficult to control. There may be many data bases to secure at several different locations. Also, the large number of users with access to the system may be extremely difficult to track and control. It therefore takes more than one or two security measures to secure a client/server network completely (see Francis 1993).

The advantages and disadvantages of a business application client/server system from a business perspective are well summarized by Ullman (1993):

Client/Server Advantages

FEATURE	BENEFIT
Network webs of small powerful machines	If one machine goes down your business stays up.

Computer arrays with thousands of MIPS; clients aggregate MIPS beyond calculation	The system provides the power to get things done without monopolizing resources. End users are empowered to work locally.
Some workstations are as powerful as mainframes but cost one-tenth of the main-frame's price	By giving you more power for less money, the system offers you the flexibility to make other purchases or to increase your profits.
Open systems	You can pick and choose hardware, software, and services from various vendors.
System grows easily	It's easy to modernize your system as needs change.
Individual client	You can mix and match computer platforms to suit the needs of individual departments and users.

Client/Server Disadvantages

DISADVANTAGE	SIGNIFICANCE
Maintenance nightmare	Parts don't always work together. There are several possible culprits when something goes wrong.
Support tools lacking	With the client/server architecture, you locate or build support tools yourself.
Retraining required	The software development philosophy for a Macintosh or for a Windows environment is different from that for Cobol or C.

7.4 Selecting a Client/Server Environment

As we have seen, client/server environments are appropriate for organizations that need to start small and grow. Other considerations include:

- Budget: how much can be invested in the system?
- Functionality: what is the system expected to accomplish?
- Current status: what exists today?
- Users: what type of people will be operating the system?
- Future: what level of growth is expected?

Providing answers to these questions is often a project in itself.

Budget is one of the primary considerations in selecting a client/server development environment. The initial investment is small, and the cost for adding additional users is usually moderate. It is, however, important to remember that there will always be expansion steps at points along the way during which the investment will jump: the need for an additional server, an additional disk, additional communication ports, routers, etc.

The expansion of a client/server system, involves many considerations, as few systems are totally independent. The current computing status is often *the* deciding factor, meaning that the need to interface with other systems becomes a primary consideration. There are several levels of interfacing:

1. **Total compatibility.** On the highest system interface level, all major functions in the selected system must be identical to the existing system. The selected system must be capable of running the same software, it must have the same user interface, and it must use the same communications interfaces.

   On this level, the system user can move from one client workstation to another without noticing any difference.

2. **Integrated.** On an intermediate level, the selected system must be able to run similar functions (though not necessarily with the same software) and it must have similar communications interfaces.

   On this level, clients or workstations may work in the same way, but their user interfaces will not necessarily look the same.

3. **Connected.** On the lowest interfacing level, the selected system must have similar communications interfaces.

   The only condition assured at this level is that the system elements will be able to exchange information; they may not run the same applications, and when they do, the applications may not look the same to the user.

The first level clearly dictates the type of hardware to be used; the server processors may need to be identical (or compatible) to be able to run the same software. Examples are networks of PCs or Sun workstations. However, it may not be necessary to require all PCs to have the same 486 or Pentium processors, or all Sun workstations to be of the Sparc family.

From the project management perspective, the totally compatible networked development architecture is the ideal environment for the distributed development of a project. When the development team is split into several groups located in different places, totally compatible systems are helpful in enabling the groups to function as a single team.

On the integrated level, running similar functions may translate into similar data base software (e.g., either Oracle or Informix), but this software may run on different servers (e.g., HPs, Suns, or PCs). This type of architecture is suitable for large organizations with separate semi-autonomous divisions within which different development activities occur.

As we have seen, the third level just means that the selected system has the ability to communicate with the existing system for the exchange of information. This architecture is common between large independent networks that exchange information but do not cooperate in development.

7.5 Project Management

Project management has two very different perspectives in a client/server environment depending on whether we are developing *on* it or *for* it.

1. **The development perspective.** Is a client/server system a suitable development environment for the project to be developed?

2. **The target perspective.** Is a client/server system an appropriate architecture for the support of the application to be developed?

Strictly speaking, the target perspective is a project design consideration, while the development perspective is much more of a project management issue. However, whether developing a software system *on* or *for* a client/server environment, there are several potential problems that need to be addressed.

7.5.1 Project Control

As we have seen, client/server systems, due to their flexibility, can be both an advantage and a disadvantage to project management. Nowhere is this more evident than in the area of project control. Without adequate management tools, the project manager can easily lose control of the development activities.

So, if project control tools are required in all software projects, they are particularly required in client/server development environments. Some examples of these tools are:

Configuration management tools. As developers have their own workstations they have much more freedom in modifying project files (both text and code). A good distributed configuration management tool is needed to manage a central file library (usually located on one of the servers), and to monitor and control the check out and check in of project development files.

Time reporters. These types of tool report how much time has been devoted to various development activities. This is particularly important with a geographically distributed development team.

Online task monitors. This tool reports the activities and progress of the development team and is also important for distributed development teams.

Information disseminators. It is imperative for the project manager to be able to make announcements and notify quickly and clearly. It is equally important for the developer to be able to do so. Electronic mail is a simple but most valuable tool that provides this capability.

For the project manager, the solution to the client/server control problem is to be aware of it from the start. Many of the potential pitfalls can be avoided just by assuring adequate development processes and methods and ensuring that all developers abide by them.

7.5.2 Design Decisions

As a general rule, the project manager's design decisions should not be influenced by the type of development environment but rather by the type of target environment. However, like all rules, this one too has its exceptions.

One such exception is the need for the project manager to match the design to the development team. Strange as this consideration may appear, it does have some justification. In a geographically distributed development environment, it is important to decompose the project into well-defined loosely coupled components or subsystems. This is a design decision. In a distributed development environment, it is clearly much easier to manage a project that can be divided into independent components. If this cannot be done, then a distributed client/server environment may not be a feasible development environment.

A typical example would be a project with several computers performing different functions, such as a security access control system. If we assume that this project is being developed by a team of six developers, one group of two developers within the project team may develop the algorithms for the recognition and permission functions, another two developers may develop the software for the alarm and sensor controls, and a third group of two developers may be responsible for the permissions data base. Clearly, if these three function groups reside on separate computers or microprocessors, then they can be developed and tested without the need for extensive interaction between the three groups within the development team.[5]

As stated earlier, most design decisions are related to the target environment. Client/server environments are usually selected as target environments for very specific design reasons. Some examples follow:

1. **More Focus on the End-User.** A client/server target environment may be an ideal selection when the end-user is the most important consideration, such as in commercial customer systems (e.g., automatic bank tellers). These types of system are usually real-time interactive applications.

   At the other extreme, batch applications (such as salary systems) or non-independent interactive applications (such as security systems) would not necessarily be well designed around a client/server system. These applications would not necessarily take advantage of the client/server benefits, such as the independence of the end user client computer. For example, if a secure building entrance is out of order, we may want to declare the entire security system defective; however, if a single teller machine is out of order, it would be helpful if we could design the system so that all other teller machines would work.

2. **Partitioning of Application among Processors.** The ability to partition an application functionally is often a major design consideration. The automatic bank teller example demonstrates this concept well. Not only does the automatic teller system divide naturally into two separate major functions, it also partitions easily into separate platforms. Both these system qualities make a client/server design a natural choice.

---

[5]We can assume that project management, quality assurance, and configuration management will be performed from a single location.

3. **Segmentation of Data.** In distributed client/server systems, the distribution of data is an important consideration. Many modern commercial data bases provide the means to distribute data between remote locations over a network. However, it is important to assure that this is transparent to the developer or end user. Data store and retrieve functions, searches and updates, as well as data base applications, must function as if the data base was located in a single location. One area that must especially be evaluated is performance: how would a decision to distribute a large data base impact data access time?

4. **General Design Guidelines.** There are several general design principles that are often applicable to the management of a client/server-based project:

   - When merging several applications or functions into a single system, all client applications should be designed to have a similar look and feel, that is, a similar presentation, similar error handling, and similar command interface.

   - Client/server systems are often best designed so that the main processing is performed on the server, while the client provides the user interface functions.

   - The use of prototypes can be particularly helpful in the design of a client/ server system. A prototype can be used to model the user interface on the client and simple simulators can be used to replace the functions of the server.

   This type of prototype is an ideal aid in the design of the client/server system.

   - Object-oriented design approaches are often well suited for client/server systems. Being end-user oriented, these types of systems are often best designed by enabling the user to manipulate objects rather than the classic series of commands.

   - Another design consideration of client/server systems, derived directly from their being end-user oriented, is the use of windows. Client user interfaces commonly use a multi-window presentation, well suited to object oriented designs, with pull down menus and iconized objects (e.g., X-Windows, Motif, MS-Windows).

   - Another result of the end-user orientation in client/server systems is the increasing use of online context sensitive help. Good designs are directed toward ease of use, which means intuitive operation of client/server interfaces and easy guidance without having to trudge through forests of reference manuals. A good help feature responds quickly to user needs with minimal keystrokes.

7.5.3 Managing Test and Integration

Test and integration is often the most difficult phase in the development of any software project. This is especially true in client/server development environments, due to the independence of each developer (see Chapters 4 and 8 for a discussion on testing).

Configuration management and other project management support functions are vital for the successful test and integration of any software project, particularly for projects developed in a client/server environment. There are several project management guidelines that can make this phase easier:

■ In a distributed development environment, subsystem testing can be performed independently at each development location, provided the previous guidelines on project partitioning were followed.

■ Simulators are excellent tools for testing well-partitioned projects. For each subsystem, the simulators perform the basic interface functions of the other project subsystems. These tools should be defined at the beginning of the project and their development or deployment should be scheduled as a standard development task.

■ On the local client/server level, it is perfectly acceptable for developers to perform independent unit testing on their client workstations. However, higher levels of testing and integration, including subsystem and system testing, cannot be independent and are best controlled using a good client/server configuration management tool.

■ System level testing and integration requires the assignment of an integrator role. For large projects this is a dedicated assignment. In a client/server development environment, it is the responsibility of the integrator to assure that integration is performed as a centralized activity; in simple terms this means that developers cannot independently integrate system components on their workstation.

■ For target client/server systems, the testing and integration strategy will almost always be to integrate and test the client and server separately and then to integrate the two.

To summarize, we can say that all the guidelines for the testing and integration of a software system are especially applicable to client/server development environments; they must be more stringently followed when developers have more independent development facilities at their disposal.

7.6 Tips for Managing Client/Server Environments

The client/server environment is just one of many computer architectures. As we have seen, it can be an excellent choice for distributed processing or development; it can also be a hindrance if it is either unsuitably selected or incorrectly employed. This section provides a few tips for both client/server development environments and target environments that may make life a little easier for the project manager.

1. **Backups.** Backups are important on any computerized data system. Backups have added importance on client/server systems due to the fact that data is neither stored nor controlled from a single location.

   A backup procedure must be implemented not only for every server disk and file system, but also for every client local disk.

2. **Response Time.** There is a feeling that applications, users, and peripherals can always be added limitlessly. In theory this is true, but it is important to remember that, as the workload grows, at some point the system response time will degrade, unless the hardware grows too.

Response time is also impacted by the amount of data handled by the client/server system and by the bursts (temporary high loads) of data at specific times.

In a common client/server scenario, the system performs well at the beginning and deteriorates as it becomes increasingly overloaded. Therefore, system performance should be continuously monitored (many operating systems, such as UNIX, have real-time system performance monitors).

3. **Balancing between Server and Client.** For many applications there are functions that can be performed by either the server or the client. Overloading of the system, or poor performance due to data traffic congestion, can often be alleviated by restructuring the division of work between clients and server, or between server and server.

4. **Plan for Growth.** The expansion of a client/server environment can be compared to a step function. There are times when the addition of clients is relatively simple and inexpensive and there are other times when expansion is difficult and expensive. This is true also when adding peripherals to the server.

This step function is caused by the limited capacity of various system components, such as routers, backplane port sockets, disk space, memory, and the number of servers.

A common error is to assume that the addition of the next client station will be as easy as the addition of the last one. There should be a plan for growth that takes into account client/server system limitations and capacities, and application user restrictions (i.e., application vendors may have limited the number of permitted users). It is therefore important to ensure that clients and servers are expandable (e.g., they are not restricted by a low limit on installable memory or disk space), and that applications do not have too low a limit on user capacity.

7.7 Summary

A client/server environment is a cooperative multiprocessing environment between processors (clients) and shared host processors (servers), where each user is given a dedicated system perception. The client/server concept places computing power in the hands of the end users, while allowing them to choose their own front end computer.

Centralized computer systems do not necessarily provide a development environment inferior to a client/server environment. The centralized environment has such advantages as the low cost of adding a user (the cost of a dumb terminal) and the relatively high power of the central processor. However, it is in the areas of versatility and low entry level cost that client/servers have the advantage.

The client/server concept can be applied to two basic models: the development environment and the application environment. In the development environment a client/server system is a development tool facilitating the development of a software project. In the application environment a client/server system provides a specific service.

Ideally, the objective of a client/server development environment is to provide low-cost development stations with a high degree of integration. At the entry level, a client/server environment is inexpensive. The initial investment is low and the addition of more workstations is relatively inexpensive (though admittedly more than the cost of a dumb terminal). The environment can grow virtually limitlessly.

The network is the backbone of any client/server system. Ideally, the network should support easy access and connectivity between nodes. This is referred to as an open systems interconnection (OSI) network. The OSI network is based on a layered architecture designed to allow for the interconnection of different types of system.

For the project manager, there are both advantages and disadvantages in selecting the client/ server architecture. The advantages of a client/server architecture include:

- The ability to share resources
- Reduced initial system costs
- The ability to start small and grow
- Smaller systems (downsizing)
- No single point failure
- Distributed data access
- Adding clients is simple
- Adding servers is relatively simple

On the negative side, the disadvantages of a client/server architecture include:

- System administration is more complicated
- Servers are easily overloaded, degrading system performance
- A limited number of users is permitted to access packages
- Maintenance of many different hardware components is a laborious task
- A distributed system can be difficult to control
- Security is more difficult

The client/server architecture can be a suitable development environment for software projects, most especially for when the development team is distributed in several locations. However, this type of development environment can be difficult to control effectively. For the project manager, the solution to the client/server control problem is to be aware of it from the start. Many of the potential pitfalls can be avoided just by assuring adequate development processes and methods and assuring that all developers abide by them. In short, the general principles for the management of software development need to be applied to client/server projects, only more stringently.

Exercises

1. The New York Municipal Library is replacing its information system. Until now, the library has operated using a central computer with terminals in each reading room and in each book check-out center. This old system is now being replaced by a client/server system.

   Explain the advantages that will now be available to the library readers and librarians in moving from the old system to the new. Are there any disadvantages?

2. Suggest a design for the implementation of the New York Municipal Library's new client/server system. What potential problems need to be avoided? What design considerations need to be considered?

   Can you suggest more than one design? What are the differences between the various designs?

3. The New York Municipal Library has entered into agreements with the Municipal Library in Los Angeles, and with large libraries in London and in Paris. All the libraries have agreed to implement similar client/server systems, but they will not necessarily be identical. What new potential problems need to be avoided?

   Suggest a design for the overall network serving the four libraries.

4. All four libraries in New York, Los Angeles, London, and Paris have agreed to jointly allocate a budget for the development of the new library system. However, both London, and Paris have stipulated that parts of the system are to be developed in the UK and France as well as in the United States, with relative parts of the budget allocated to each country (e.g., half to the USA and a quarter each to the UK and France).

   Because the largest team will be located in the USA, the project manager will also be located there. You have just been hired as the project manager. Explain how you plan to set up your development team.

   How will you divide the project among the development groups? What potential problems are there and how do you intend to avoid them?

5. Class exercise: divide the class into three groups, representing the USA, UK and France. Elect a project manager from the US group. The project manager is to allocate part of the project to each group to design.

   Compare the three designs. Discuss the problems that arose due to the division of the team into three groups.

Project Support Functions

Project management is the application of knowledge, skills, tools, and techniques to project activities in order to meet or exceed stakeholder[1] needs and expectations from a project.[2] It includes planning, organizing, staffing, monitoring, controlling, and leading a project. Rarely can all these tasks be performed by the project manager; in fact, ideally they should not. Many control and monitoring activities can be assigned to project support groups. These support groups not only disburden the project manager and the development engineers from the support tasks; they also perform these tasks better by concentrating their efforts on specific support functions.

There are many types of project support functions. Legal counsel, document publication, administrative support, and procurement are examples of nontechnical support functions; testing, configuration control, systems engineering, integration management, and quality assurance are examples of technical support functions.

The larger and more complex a project, the more support functions will be required. For example, a large project will often have its own quality control organization, while a small project may have to share this function with other projects. Similarly, many organizations maintain an independent test group whose role is to test a software product before its release. In large projects, the independent test group is part of the project team and is involved in testing and test planning throughout the development cycle.

[1]A Stakeholder is an individual or organization who is involved in or may be affected by project activities.

[2]As defined by the Project Management Institute (PMI 1996).

This chapter describes the three major technical project support functions:

- Configuration control
- Software quality assurance
- Testing

These basic functions are required in every software development project. Configuration control manages the changes to the software product being developed, quality assurance monitors, and helps ensure the quality of the product, and testing verifies compliance with the product's requirements.

It is the project manager's responsibility to organize the project support groups and to document their planned activities in the project development plan (see Chapter 11). If these groups already exist within the organization, then their support needs to be coordinated and scheduled for the project. If the groups do not exist, then they must be established within the project development team.

The size of a support group is clearly dependent on the size of the project; for example, a large project may require a group of two or three configuration control engineers, a medium-size project may require one configuration control engineer, and a small project may assign this task part-time to a development engineer.

These decisions must be made by the project manager during the initial stages of the project. Project support functions that are well planned at the start of the project will contribute to effective project management throughout the project.

8.1 Software Configuration Control

Configuration control is a management support function that supports the many different activities related to changes to the software product. This includes program code changes, requirements and design changes, and version release changes. Configuration control is often regarded by developers as more of a hindrance than a benefit because it limits the freedom of the development team and places restrictions on what can and cannot be done. Configuration control does, however, provide an environment in which software can be developed in an orderly manner.

The term *configuration* is used here to describe the combination of software components to form an integrated system. When linked with the word *control*, the term is used to describe an efficient and orderly method by which this combination of components can be accomplished. Unfortunately, building software systems from low level components is no simple task. This is best illustrated by the following anecdote.

A large banking firm joined an international financial information exchange service. This service could provide the bank with online access to a central data base containing constantly updated information on world financial markets. In the modern world of fast electronic communications, this was an essential service for any modern banking institution. However, the bank's computer did not have the capability to interface with the financial service.

The bank assigned a project manager to develop the necessary software needed for the interface. After the integration phase began, one of the developers reported that a major milestone had been achieved: communications with the information service had been successfully established. The project manager reported this to his superiors and informed them that development was proceeding on schedule.

A week later, members of top management visited the project and asked for a demonstration of communications with the information service. However, the project manager was unable to provide the demonstration. The developer who had reported the milestone could not repeat his earlier success. This was because additional features had been added to the communications software and these were not yet working. Even the previous features were no longer working.

Clearly, the developer should have kept a copy of the communications software without the new features. In a well-organized project, the task of saving an earlier software version would have been performed by the configuration manager.

An interesting way of looking at configuration control is to regard it as a method of ensuring that the project moves forward (or at least does not move backward). In the above-related case, the project actually slipped backward.

Configuration control is essential for all developed items, including code, documentation, and integration of components. Figure 8.1 describes the flow of configuration control for the development of a software module. A similar flow would apply to documents generated by the project. Configuration control is also necessary during the maintenance phase to ensure that when a new system release is recalled due to severe defects, it can be replaced by the previous release.

8.1.1 Configuration Control Terminology

There are many terms used in relation to configuration control. Unfortunately, neither their usage nor their meanings have been standardized; several different terms are used to describe the same functions and ideas. One of the best attempts at standardization is contained in the IEEE's *Glossary of Software Engineering Terminology* (IEEE 1999). However, even this glossary reflects the lack of common interpretation and usage of these terms, as several configuration control terms appear with multiple definitions. The following is an explanation, rather than an accurate definition, of some of the basic terminology.

A *software configuration control item* (SCCI) is a software project item that is considered a unit for the purposes of configuration control. This may include such things as software modules, versions of software systems, or documents.

Change control is the process of controlling changes. This includes proposing the change, evaluating it, approving or rejecting it, scheduling and tracking it.

Version control, as applied to software development, is the process of controlling the release of software versions. This includes recording and saving each release, and documenting the differences between the releases.

Configuration control is the process of evaluating, approving or disapproving, and managing changes to configuration items. Configuration control also often includes version control functions.

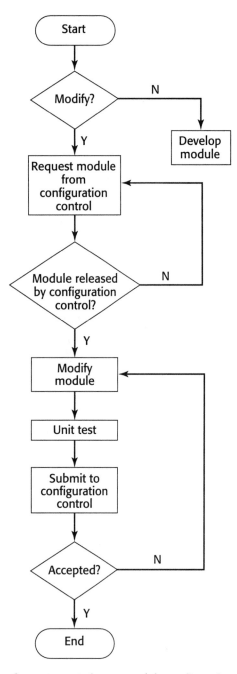

Figure 8.1   Software module configuration control flow.

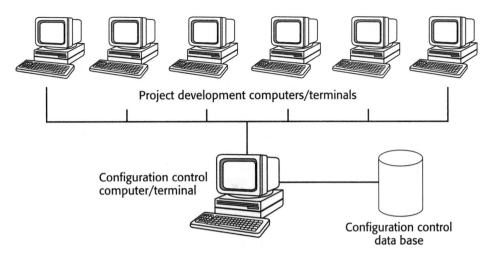

Project development computers/terminals

Configuration control
computer/terminal

Configuration control
data base

Figure 8.2   Networked configuration control.

Configuration management is the technical and administrative application of configuration control. This also includes the maintenance of a configuration control organization, change and version control standards, and configuration control facilities.

Other terms are the *configuration identification* designation used to identify configuration items, the *configuration control board* that approves or rejects engineering changes, and the *configuration audit*, which verifies compliance with configuration control standards.

The objective of configuration management is best defined not through the formal definitions of the IEEE glossary but rather through a more descriptive explanation, as provided in the foreword to IEEE standard 828 (1999) for software configuration management plans, which states:

> *Software configuration management (SCM) is a formal engineering discipline that, as part of overall system configuration management, provides the methods and tools to identify the software throughout its development and use. SCM activities include the identification and establishment of baselines; the review, approval, and control of changes; the tracking and reporting of such changes; the audits and reviews of the evolving software product; and the control of interface documentation and project supplier SCM.*
>
> *SCM is the means through which the integrity and traceability of the software system are recorded, communicated, and controlled during both development and maintenance.*

Some of the configuration management tasks overlap with the tasks of another support activity, software quality control (discussed later). In software projects in which quality control and configuration control are performed by separate groups, a clear definition of the division of responsibility is necessary.

8.1.2 Resources for Configuration Control

Configuration control is one of the first areas of software engineering that was recognized as a candidate for automation. Several configuration control activities, such as version control and change control, were automated in the early 1970s, with such tools as *make* and *SCCS* (see Rochkind 1975). Some of these tools migrated from the UNIX operating system, where they were first used, to other environments.

Many of the main configuration control activities are natural candidates for automated CASE (computer-aided software engineering) tools, as they are well defined, somewhat repetitive, and readily integrated into the development process. These tools can be easily interfaced with software code tools (e.g., editors and compilers) and word processors for the production of documents. Automated configuration control is best when used in a multi-user development environment such as a LAN. This way all controlled elements are stored in a central data base, and access by all developers is managed from a central configuration control system (see Figure 8.2).

Effective configuration control requires effective and well-defined organization. Any configuration control method must be based on the following four concepts:

1. A clearly defined configuration management authority must be established.

2. Configuration control standards, procedures, and guidelines must be produced and distributed to the developers.

3. Configuration control cannot be effective without the necessary tools and facilities.

4. A configuration management plan must be developed at the beginning of the project.

It is the project manager's responsibility to assign configuration management authority. This can range from a configuration control team in large projects to a part-time configuration control engineer in small projects. In either case, both the authority and the responsibility must be clearly defined. The configuration control engineer should be involved in all development activities, and must have the specific authority to approve or reject configuration items.

The development team members must be familiar with the configuration control standards, procedures, and guidelines, which should be comprehensive and clear. This will reduce the number of rejections by configuration control due to non-compliance with unfamiliar standards.

The configuration management environment consists of the resources necessary for the implementation of the configuration control plan. This includes:

- Configuration control tools, including:
    - automatic version control and change control tools
    - monitoring, auditing, and registration support utilities
- Storage facilities: a safe repository for all approved configuration items, including:
    - on-site storage for the day-to-day development process
    - on-site storage for catastrophe recovery

8.1.3 The Software Configuration Management Plan

The software configuration management plan (SCMP) is part of the project's software development plan. The SCMP may appear as a separate document or as a section within the project development plan. The SCMP documents the resources that are needed, how they are to be used, and which standards and procedures will be applied during the project. The SCMP then becomes the mandate for the configuration control group during project development. The issuance of this plan is the responsibility of the project manager, though in large projects it may be delegated to the configuration control manager.

Table 8.1 contains a list of the main subjects covered in the SCMP. When any of these subjects is covered elsewhere (e.g., in the software quality assurance plan), it can be

Table 8.1   Example of the Contents of a Software Configuration Management Plan

1. Software configuration management organization and resources
     Organization structure
     Personnel skill level and qualifications
     Resources
2. Standards, procedures, policies, and guidelines
3. Configuration identification
     Method for defining SCCIs
     Description of the SCCIs for this project
4. Identification methods (naming and marking of documents, software components, revisions, releases, etc.)
5. Submission of configuration items
     Approval/rejection procedure
6. Change control
     Change control procedures (method of submission, review, approval and rejection)
     Reporting documentation (change requests, problem reports)
     Change review procedures and review board
7. Version control
     Preparation of software and documentation versions
     Release approval procedure
8. Storage, handling, and delivery of project media
     Storage requirements
     Backups
9. Configuration control of subcontractors, vendors, and suppliers
10. Additional control
     Miscellaneous control procedures
     Project specific control (security, etc.)
11. Configuration status accounting
     Configuration audits and reviews
     Configuration status reporting procedures
12. Configuration management major milestones
13. Tools, techniques, and methodologies

omitted from the SCMP and replaced by a pointer to the document in which it is covered. Though most of the subjects in Table 8.1 are self-descriptive, the following are some guidelines:

- Configuration status accounting describes the way in which status information flows:
  - from the developers to the configuration management organization (audits and reviews)
  - from the configuration management organization to project management (status reporting procedures)
- Configuration identification describes the method for designating development items as SCCIs. This is part of the high level decomposition of the system into major development components (see Chapter 6).

The section on identification methods describes the way in which each component generated by the project is marked for unique identification.

- Security, restricted access, and classification refer to the secure development of sensitive products (such as documents, software, patents, military classified information, etc.). It is often convenient to assign many of these tasks to configuration control because of the need to be involved in the review and classification of documents and other related activities that are associated with security.

- Subcontractors, vendors, and suppliers may or may not implement their own configuration management plan. It is the project manager's responsibility to ensure either that subcontractors and external developers submit a CMP for review, or that the project's configuration manager assumes responsibility for their work.

The SCMP may also include diagrams and flow charts to describe procedures for submitting change requests, or for reporting problems (for a more detailed description of the SCMP, see IEEE Std 828 [IEEE 1999]). Figure 8.3 presents an example of a general configuration control flow chart.

8.1.4 Some General Guidelines

As a project management support function, the scope of configuration control covers many optional or elective activities. Configuration management organizes and controls all major project products and thus participates in reviews, audits, and customer presentations. These activities utilize the information available to the configuration manager: which product components are produced when, and by whom.

The keeping of records is important during all administrative project activities, but it is especially important in configuration control. The scourge of project management is the eternal dispute over misinterpreted or misunderstood verbal agreements. Poor change control is notorious for causing disputes between the customer and the developer. Similarly, poor version control can be catastrophic, especially when there are no records of the differences between versions.

Figure 8.4 contains an example of a change request form. These forms, which may be maintained in electronic format, record software changes from their initial submission,

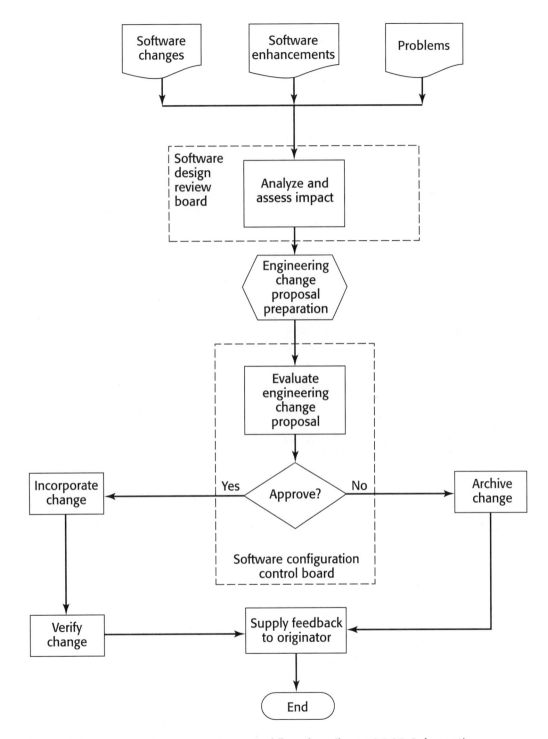

Figure 8.3 Example of a configuration control flow chart (from US DOD-Std-2167A).

SOFTWARE CHANGE REQUEST	SCR Number:	PAGE _____ OF _____

Name of originator:	Phone number:	Date:

Project:	System/Product:	Version/Release:

Reason for change:

Change description:

Reviewed by (name):	Signature:	Date:

Estimated person days:	Calendar time:	Schedule impact:

Estimates approved by (name):	Signature:	Date:

Change approval (YES/NO):	By (name):	Signature:	Date:

Figure 8.4   Example of a software change request form.

through approval or rejection, and finally to implementation and test (when approved). Note the need for signatures; even when the form is kept electronically, some kind of electronic signature is needed.

The following are some additional guidelines for effective configuration management. Some of these guidelines are equally applicable to other management support functions.

- Configuration management requires authority in order to be effective. This authority must be clearly delegated by the project manager to the responsible engineers. Any configuration management plan will become meaningless if the plan cannot be enforced.

  Blunt enforcement of any plan, policy, or standard is best avoided, whenever possible. One of the qualities of a good manager is the ability to apply policy with minimal enforcement. Whenever policies and standards are readily accepted by the developers, they are more willingly followed and there are fewer rejections of submitted material. This leads to a more efficient development process.

- Configuration management should be implemented from the start of a software project. Many of the formal documents issued during the initial concept phase are crucial for the requirements and design phases, and must be placed under configuration control.

  The early application of configuration management is especially important in rapid prototyping, spiral models, or other iterative development methodologies. These development approaches initially produce several versions of each product. Many different versions can become an engineering nightmare without orderly configuration control.

- Occasionally, some software configuration control activities may overlap with software quality assurance activities. In small projects, these two functions may be assigned to a single support engineer. Even in large projects, these two functions are sometimes performed by a single support group.

As a final general guideline, it should be noted that configuration management can be greatly exaggerated. The various configuration control activities are not an objective in themselves, they are a means. A typical example of the misapplication of configuration management (and misguided quality control), is a requirement to modify reused software to comply with current standards and procedures. Reused software is software developed previously in another project, and found suitable to be incorporated into the current project. In such cases it rarely makes sense to modify a complete and working product in order to make it comply with administrative standards intended to make it a complete and working product.

8.2 Software Quality Assurance (SQA)

Quality is difficult to define, especially when applied to a product development contract. Though not all software is developed under contract, quality still primarily remains a concern of the customer (and all projects ultimately have a customer).

The IEEE's standard glossary of software engineering terminology (IEEE 1999), contains two definitions for quality (see also Chapter 9):

1. The degree to which a system, component, or process meets specified requirements.

2. The degree to which a system, component, or process meets customer or user needs or expectations.

Quality should indeed be measured in terms of the customer's expectations. However, the customer's perspective is subjective. This section looks at quality control from the project manager's perspective, which must regard the achievement of quality control as an objective, systematic process.

8.2.1 Producing Quality Software

As we have seen, one of the main problems in producing quality software is the difficulty in determining the degree of quality within the software. As there is no single widely accepted definition for quality, and because different people perceive quality in different ways, both the developer and the customer must reach agreement on metrics for quality (this is discussed in more detail later). The method of measuring quality may differ for different projects.

This problem is discussed in a paper by Wesselius and Ververs (1990), in which they conclude that complete objectivity in quality assessment cannot be achieved. They identify three distinct components of quality:

- An objectively assessable component
- A subjectively assessable component
- A non-assessable component

The quality of a product is objectively assessable when the characteristics of the product, as stated in the requirements specification, can be identified.

The quality of a product is subjectively assessable when the characteristics of the product comply with the customer's expectations.

The quality of a product is non-assessable when it behaves according to our expectations in situations that have not been foreseen.

Wesselius and Ververs suggest that, for the quality of a software product to be assessable, as many characteristics as possible should be moved from the subjective and non-assessable components to the assessable component. Essentially, this means that the requirements specification must describe as many measurable characteristics of the product as possible.

Experience supports Wesselius and Ververs' conclusions. Badly defined requirements are always a source of dispute between developer and customer. Well-defined, detailed, and measurable requirements minimize disputes and disagreements when the development of the product is complete.

The IEEE has produced a standard for software quality metrics methodology (IEEE 1999) that attempts to provide guidelines for determining objective measurements for a software project. It is based on the specification of measurable quality requirements for each software project. Clearly, if this is achievable at the start of the project, with customer and developer in agreement, the measure of quality becomes much less controversial at the end of the project.

However, many development methods have a prolonged interval between the specification of requirements and the delivery of the product (refer to Chapter 4 for a discussion of the software development cycle) with numerous changes throughout the development cycle. This means that the quality requirements must change, too.

The establishment of effective quality control frequently encounters various misconceptions and myths, the most common of which is related to the cost effectiveness of quality control. Cobb and Mills (1990) list several of these myths, and suggest methods of combating them. Two of the more prevalent myths identified by Cobb and Mills are described below:

- **Myth: Quality costs money.** This is one of the most common myths (not only in software development). In fact, quality in software usually saves money. Poor quality breeds failure. There is a positive correlation between failures and cost, in that it is more expensive to remove execution failures designed into software than to design software to exclude execution failures.

- **Myth: Software failures are unavoidable.** This is one of the worst myths because the statement is partly true and is therefore often used as an excuse to justify poor-quality software. The claim that "there is always another bug" should never be a parameter in the design or implementation of software.

As these myths lose ground in modern approaches to software development, the demand for suitable quality control standards and procedures increases.

Two final myths can be added to the list:

- **Myth: Quality assurance is always an external function.** Modern approaches to quality assurance see this function as part of the development activity. In fact, new approaches to team structure include a quality assurance engineer as part of the development team. The advantage of integrated quality assurance is far greater than the risk of weakened quality control.

- **Myth: Quality assurance is an activity that occurs toward the end of a project**. The contrary is true. Quality assurance is an activity that accompanies software development from the very beginning of the development cycle to the final delivery of the product—and then goes on to the maintenance phase.

8.2.2 Resources for Quality Control

When the SQA mandate includes configuration control activities, the required resources will also include those required for configuration control. Merging SQA and configuration control is not uncommon, and can eliminate some duplication of assignments and activities. Two alternative organizational charts are shown in Figure 8.5. Note that for small projects, merging the two groups may mean simply assigning both responsibilities to the same person.

Though many tools are common to both quality control and configuration control, few tools are specifically designed for quality control. The following are some of the general support tools that can be useful in supporting SQA activities:

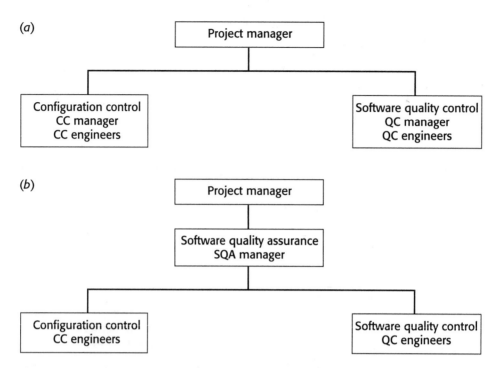

Figure 8.5 Configuration control and software quality control: (*a*) separate groups; (*b*) combined groups.

- Documentation utilities
- Software design tools
- Debugging aids
- Structured preprocessors
- File comparators
- Structure analyzers
- Standards auditors
- Simulators
- Execution analyzers
- Performance monitors
- Statistical analysis packages
- Integrated CASE tools
- Test drivers
- Test case generators

These tools support quality control in all phases of software development. Documentation aids can provide partially automatic document writers, spelling checkers and thesauruses, etc. Structured preprocessors (such as the UNIX utility *lint*) are useful both to standardize code listings, and to provide additional compile-time warnings that compilers often overlook. Early warnings regarding possible execution time problems can be provided by simulators, execution time analyzers, and performance monitors. Substantial software system testing can often be performed automatically by test suite generators and automatic test executors.

All SQA tools to be used during software development should be identified and described in the SQA plan. This plan includes a description of all required quality assurance resources and details of how they will be applied. Thus, at the start of the project SQA resources can be budgeted and procured as part of the required project development resources (see Chapter 11).

8.2.3 The Software Quality Assurance Plan

The software quality assurance plan (SQAP), like the software configuration plan, is also part of the overall software project development plan. The SQAP documents which resources are needed, how they should be used, and which standards and procedures will be applied during the project. The SQAP then becomes the mandate for the quality assurance group during project development. The issuance of this plan is the responsibility of the project manager, though in large projects it will usually be delegated to the quality assurance manager. The SQAP may appear as a separate document or as a section within the project development plan, and may include the configuration management plan (if this has not been documented separately).

Table 8.2 contains a list of the main subjects covered in the SQAP. When any of these subjects is covered elsewhere, such as in the software configuration management plan (SCMP), it can be omitted from the SQAP and replaced by a pointer to the document in which it is covered. However, the SCMP and the SQAP are concerned with different aspects of the controlled items. The SCMP is primarily concerned with the format of controlled items, while the SQAP is more involved with the contents of controlled items.

The SQAP must cover subcontractors, vendors, and suppliers, irrespective of whether or not these external entities have their own quality assurance organization. In any project, the quality of external components is ultimately the concern of the project manager and the SQA organization. When a system fails, it usually makes little difference whether the failure is due to an externally developed component or an in-house developed component. The plans for supervising these external groups must be adapted to the type of external components being provided (off-the-shelf or new development) and the type of organization (do they have their own quality assurance organization?).

The SQAP, as part of the project development plan, should be reviewed and updated periodically and whenever any requirements, project development procedures, methodologies, or other relevant activities are changed. The IEEE SQAP guide recommends periodic evaluation of two aspects of the plan: (1) the plan's content and (2) the plan's implementation.

The plan's content should be evaluated with regard to the specific SQAP standard used, to ensure the plan's continuing compliance with the standard even when the characteristics of the software project change.

Table 8.2 Example of the Contents of a Software Quality Assurance Plan

1. Software quality assurance organization and resources
     Organization structure
     Personnel skill level and qualifications
     Resources

2. SQA standards, procedures, policies, and guidelines

3. SQA documentation requirements
     List of all documentation subject to quality control
     Description of method of evaluation and approval

4. SQA software requirements
     Evaluation and approval of software
     Description of method of evaluation
     Evaluation of the software development process
     Evaluation of reused software
     Evaluation of non-deliverable software

5. Evaluation of storage, handling, and delivery
     Project documents
     Software
     Data files

6. Reviews and audits

7. Software configuration management (when not addressed in a separate document)

8. Problem reporting and corrective action

9. Evaluation of test procedures

10. Tools techniques and methodologies

11. Quality control of subcontractors, vendors, and suppliers

12. Additional control
     Miscellaneous control procedures
     Project specific control

13. SQA reporting, records, and documentation
     Status reporting procedures
     Maintenance
     Storage and security
     Retention period

The plan's implementation should be evaluated in terms of the changing scope of the project, including the tasks and responsibilities referenced in the plan, and other new or changed characteristics of the project.

When updating the SQAP, the following project activities and events should be considered:

- New or changed contractual requirements

- Additional standards and policies

- Additional project documents

- Changes in the project's organizational structure

- New tools and utilities

- Additional subcontractors and vendors

8.2.4 Software Quality Metrics

Much attention has been devoted to questions associated with the measurement of quality. How do we determine the extent to which a software product contains this vague attribute called "quality"? When is the quality of a software product high and when is it low?

One of the more recent developments in quality assurance (not only for software) is the realization that quality is not a binary attribute that either exists or does not exist. Kaposi and Myers (1990), in a paper on measurement-based quality assurance, have stated their belief that "the quality assurance of products and processes of software engineering *must be based on measurement*."[3] The earlier the measurement of quality begins, the earlier problems will be located. Cohen et al. (1986), in addressing the cost of removing errors during the early phases of software development, proclaim the existence of the famous *exponential law.*[4]

The quality of two products can be compared, and it is perfectly acceptable to claim that the quality of one product is greater than the quality of another. It is also acceptable to measure quality and deduce the extent of expected faults based on the measured result.

The set of measurable values associated with the quality of a product is referred to as the product's quality *metrics*. Software quality metrics can be used to determine the extent to which a software product meets its requirements. The use of quality metrics increases the objectivity of the evaluation of product quality. Human evaluation of quality is subjective, and is therefore a possible source of disagreement, particularly between customer and developer.

As discussed previously, the IEEE has produced a standard for software quality metrics methodology (IEEE 1999). It describes the purpose of metrics as *to make assessments throughout the software life cycle as to whether the software requirements are being met.* Quality is measured throughout the life cycle and not just at the end of the project.

Quality metrics, once defined, do indeed increase objectivity, but the definition itself is not necessarily objective and greatly depends upon the needs of the organization that produces the definition.

The basic approach for applying software quality metrics requires:

- The identification of all required software quality attributes. This is usually derived from the software requirements specification.

- Determination of measurable values to be associated with each quality attribute.

- A description of the method by which each measurable value will be measured.

- A procedure for documenting the results of measuring the quality of the software product.

---

[3]Italics added by this author.

[4]The cost of error removal increases exponentially as software development proceeds along the development cycle.

A set of many values can be used to determine the overall quality of a software product. However, a single measure can be created to represent the overall quality of the software product. This requires:

- A weighted method for combining the measured quality attributes into a single measure of quality for the product.

Some examples of software metrics are:

Reliability	The percentage of time that the system is successfully operational (e.g., 23 out of 24 hours produces: $100 \times (23/24)$ percent
Recoverability	The amount of time it takes for the system to recover after failure (e.g., one hour to reload from backups and 30 minutes to reinitialize the system)
User-friendliness	The amount of training time needed for a new user

The degree of quality should be measured at regular intervals during development. Thus, any major reduction in the overall measure of quality should warn the project manager that corrective action is required. High quality at the end of the project is achieved by ensuring high quality throughout the development of the project.

8.2.5 Some General Guidelines

Basic software quality assurance activities cover the review and approval of the development methodology, the software and documentation, and the support and approval of testing. Other SQA activities, such as the initiation of reviews, the selection and introduction of development tools, or the administration of configuration control, depend on the way SQA is adapted to a specific project. The size of the project is usually the determining factor. The following guidelines discuss some of the parameters to be considered for different types of project when planning SQA.

- In all types of projects the quality assurance engineer should be perceived as a member of the team or project. Quality assurance is performed by *insiders*, not *outsiders*. In large projects there may be several quality assurance engineers, with one in each team reporting to the team leader and dotted line (secondary reporting line) to the quality assurance manager.

- The main responsibility of the quality assurance engineer is not administration. It is enabling, facilitating, guiding, and leading the organization to higher levels of product quality.

- In small projects, many SQA activities can be performed by the project manager. This includes the organization and initiation of reviews and audits, the evaluation and selection of development tools, and the selection and application of standards.

8.3 Software Testing

The term *testing* has many meanings, but in its most common use the term is applied to the examination or evaluation of an object in order to determine the existence of certain properties. In software testing, these properties are associated with the software's predefined requirements. As we have seen, software testing is the process of determining the degree to which software satisfies specified requirements and achieves customer satisfaction. Therefore, software test plans are derived from the project's requirements specification.

In simpler words, *we cannot meaningfully test software if we do not know what the software is expected to do.*

Testing can be performed by the developer or by an independent test group. In most cases, software should never be tested by the programmer directly responsible for writing the code being tested. Programmers are rarely objective with respect to their own code, and their testing will not be effective. There are many ways to increase the objectivity of testing. The best way is to use an independent test group. Independent testers are engineers whose main assignment is to test the system according to formal test plans, objectively and rigorously, to ascertain compliance with the requirements specification.

8.3.1 Types of Software Testing

Full system testing is the last development activity of a software project. However, this does not mean that testing is conducted only at the end of a project. Software should be tested at each stage of its development.

The different types of software testing include:

- Unit testing
- Integration testing
- Subsystem testing
- System testing
- Regression testing
- Alpha testing
- Beta testing
- Acceptance testing

It is usually best to test software modules immediately after they are coded. This is one of the few cases where programmers test their own code. These initial module tests, called unit tests, are conducted by the programmer in order to determine whether they conform to a minimal set of requirements. They include such tests as:

- Entry and exit (no eternal loops) for a small basic set of input data.
- For given input, the output is reasonable.
- Subroutines are called in the correct sequence. This is tested by using stubs (empty subroutine shells).

After successful unit testing, the modules are submitted to configuration control. They are then released to integration, where they are assembled and tested as part of the integration test process. This includes the gradual assembly of the modules into a complete system by the integration team. As more modules are integrated into the system, all added functionality is tested. At this stage, previously tested functionality must be tested again to ensure that no new module has corrupted the system. This is referred to as *regression testing*.

In large software systems, the modules may be first assembled and integrated with hardware into subsystems. After the subsystems have been tested separately, they are combined into a complete system.

After system integration is complete, final tests are conducted. This includes alpha and beta testing and acceptance tests. Alpha testing is conducted with the complete system, but without live data. Beta testing uses live data, but requires constant supervision by members of the development team. Once the system is stable, acceptance tests are run, and if they are successful the system is released (these stages are further discussed in Chapter 4). The final stages of system testing are represented in the following example.

An automatic bank teller system is being developed for a large bank. When the teller subsystem is complete, it undergoes subsystem testing to ensure that the automatic teller features function correctly. Then the central computer subsystem is tested with test data to assure that it processes the data correctly. Finally, the communications subsystem is tested with a simulated teller on one end and a simulated central computer on the other.

The three subsystems are then integrated and full system testing is conducted to ensure that the automatic teller and the central computer communicate and function correctly.

After system testing, the fully integrated automatic teller system is tested in an alpha test environment. The system is tested with realistic test data, and the operation of all features is examined and compared to the requirements of the system. This task is assigned to the independent test group.

After the automatic teller system passes alpha tests, it is deemed sufficiently reliable to be able to process real data. This is the beta test. However, only a single automatic teller station is connected to the bank's computer, and the operation of the system is constantly monitored by members of the development team. Any problems are immediately located and corrected, and beta testing continues until the teller system runs error and fault free for a predefined period of time (e.g., one month). The supervision of the beta phase is also assigned to the independent test group.

After successful completion of beta tests, the teller system then enters final acceptance tests. Representatives of the bank's technical staff supervise a predetermined set of tests, and confirm or reject the success of the acceptance tests.

The automatic bank teller system has thus gone through all the major test phases. Not all of these phases are applicable to all projects. For example, alpha and beta testing may be applicable to commercial or user oriented systems, but not to the development of software for a communications satellite or for a mission-critical application. Another example is subsystem testing, which is obviously only applicable when the system is actually divided into subsystems.

In all cases, independent testing is highly recommended for the more advanced stages of testing (from system testing onward). Objective independent testing will often locate problems much earlier than subjective tests performed by the developers. This is of major benefit to the project, since the earlier problems are located, the less costly they are to correct.

8.3.2 Formal Testing Procedures and Plans

There are many different testing approaches and procedures for each stage of software testing. It is important to select the appropriate approach for each stage. Several formal software testing standards (see Chapter 4 and 9) include guidelines on how the standard is to be applied at each stage.

The IEEE standard for software test documentation (Std 829 ([IEEE 1999]) defines the following documents:

1. **Project Test Plan**: the overall plan that defines the approach, resources, and schedule of the testing activities.

2. **Test Design Specification**: refines the test approach and identifies the features to be tested.

3. **Test Case Specifications**: describes the test cases identified in the test design specification. Each test case includes a description of the item to be tested, input, expected output, environment, and dependencies.

4. **Test Procedure Specification**: specifies the steps for executing a set of test cases.

5. **Test Item Transmittal Report**: identifies the test item being transmitted for testing. Includes the person responsible for each item, its physical location, and its status.

6. **Test Log**: provides a chronological record of details about the execution of tests.

7. **Test Incident Report**: documents any event that occurs during the testing process that requires investigation.

8. **Test Summary Report**: summarizes the results of the designated testing activities and provides evaluations based on these results.

All or some of these documents may be implemented in a specific software project. For example the test design and test case specifications may be merged into one document and the test incident report and test summary may also be merged together.

Generally, all formal software testing procedures are based on four components: test planning, test description, test execution, and test reporting. Most test standards support these elements, even though they may differ in the amount of detail and documentation required.

The IEEE 829 standard contains a much more detailed description of the approach to software testing, including several examples and usage guidelines.

IEEE guidelines suggest the following approach to implementation of the testing standards:

1. Begin by introducing the planning and reporting documents. This will provide a foundation for the testing process and the recording of test results.

2. Introduce testing first on the system level.

3. Then introduce the remaining documents to the remaining levels. The sequence of introduction depends on the success in the previous phases.

Testing procedures are not just determined by the standards that are adopted. The actual test methods and techniques must be adapted to the type of project being developed and the testing environment and tools that are available. In addition to test planning and reporting, it is the responsibility of the test engineer (or test team) to select the appropriate techniques to be used during the testing of the software system (specific testing and integration techniques are discussed in Chapter 4).

8.3.3 Some General Guidelines

To be successful, testing must have a property called traceability: the ability to determine that each feature has a source in the requirements and each requirement has a corresponding implemented feature.[5] Though traceability is difficult to achieve, it does not in itself ensure good testing. Successful testing also requires full coverage, that is, the assurance that each requirement and implemented feature is completely tested—and this is where the difficulty lies: how to ensure that *all* aspects of the software's features are tested within a reasonable amount of time and with a reasonable amount of resources.

Testing occurs at the end of each phase of software development, with the most intense testing occurring, of course, toward the end. This is one of the basic principles of modern testing theory—that testing be done throughout and no longer just at the end of a project. This principle has led to the concept of *phase containment*: the detection and correction of errors within the development phase wherein they were introduced.

Phase containment's main objective is to prevent errors from propagating into other development phases, and thus to make the correction at the point where the cost is least (see Figure 8.6). This concept is applicable not only in the classic serial development life cycle but also in parallel and spiral life cycles where phases may overlap or may even be repeated.

Phase containment requires early testing of requirements, design, and code (before it runs on the target computer), as well as validation of both product and development documentation. This requires visual inspection of the output of each phase before it is permitted to pass on to the next phase. The concept of *inspections* was first formalized by Michael Fagan (and consequently is often called *Fagan Inspections*). Fagan published his theory of design and code inspections at IBM as far back as 1976, and since then the idea has gained support and has been adapted to all phases of software development (see Fagan 1976). The basic idea behind inspections (also called *peer-reviews*) is that the product of each phase is formally reviewed by the developer's colleagues to locate problems. The formal nature of the review is significant, as it promotes objectivity and completeness, and attempts to remove potential emotional conflict. However, successful reviews have been demonstrated to be a major factor in achieving effective phase containment.

The objective of phase containment is to reduce the number of problems found toward the end of the project and subsequently to reduce the amount of testing needed before the software product is released. In an attempt to reduce the amount of work required to run these final tests, many new tools and techniques have been developed to automate the final test phase.

---

[5]More precisely, traceability is a one-to-one mapping between requirements and implementation.

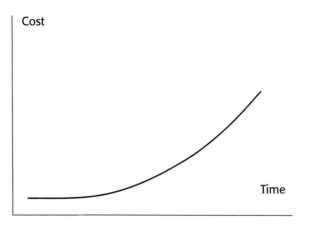

Cost

Time

Figure 8.6   Cost of correcting a software problem during development.

In any software project, there is a limit to what can and should be tested. Many test procedures are unreasonably complex and costly. It is important to adapt the intensity of the testing to the cost of an undiscovered system defect. An inventory system need not be tested to the same degree as the software for a medical life-support system.

Over-testing can also be misleading. Many test procedures require changes to the system being tested (e.g., online monitors, trace utilities, etc.), or the use of special test equipment. This may mean that the system being tested is not the system being delivered.

An interesting view of this problem was presented by Laplante (1990) in a paper linking Heisenberg's uncertainty principle (normally applied to physics) to software testing.[6] Laplante's theory states that the more closely a software system is examined, the more likely the examination process will affect the system being tested. This theory may have been suggested tongue in cheek, but it does bring home the basic message: at some advanced point in testing, the process of testing itself may change the behavior of the system.

What does a set of successful tests demonstrate? It shows one of two things: either a good system or bad tests. There are three basic requirements to ensure that it demonstrates the former (a good system):

- Well-written requirements
- Good test procedures
- Efficient testers

Good requirements are discussed in Chapters 4 and 9, but one of the basic conditions for a good requirement is that it must be testable. Therefore, formal requirements should always be written with testing in mind. A required feature that cannot be tested cannot be shown to exist, and should therefore have no place in the formal requirements specification for the project.

---

[6]Laplante suggests the following formula: $\Delta r \Delta s. \approx .H$ where Δr represents the uncertainty of the software code, Δs represents the uncertainty of the test specifications and H is some constant.

Test procedures are intended to demonstrate the fulfillment of the requirements. Therefore, they should be based on an approach called *negative testing*. This means that it is the test team's objective to find as many problems as possible. If the tests are conducted correctly, then when the testers fail, the project succeeds.[7] Testers should not be kind, because ultimately the users will not be kind either.

As we have seen, final system testing is best performed by an objective, independent test group. However, only large projects can support an independent test group. Small projects can share the services of independent test groups, and can even lend development engineers specifically for testing. Thus, a development engineer in one project can become a part-time objective tester in another project.

Another important necessity is that testing must be adequately documented. One of the worst types of test is a failed test that cannot be repeated. If a failure cannot be readily repeated, it often cannot be corrected. Therefore, the test documentation must be sufficient to enable the developers to repeat the sequence of events that led to the failure of the test.

Lastly, there are few greater follies than to release software without thorough testing. Any problem that is not found before the release will be found after the release and at a much greater cost. *In fact, there is no such thing as a software project without testing; it is only a question of when the testing is done.*

8.4 Summary

Project support groups not only provide critical assistance to the project manager and the development engineers for support tasks, they also perform these tasks better by concentrating their efforts on specific support functions. There are many types of project support function. Legal counsel, document publication, administrative support, and procurement are examples of non-technical support functions; testing, configuration control, systems engineering, integration management, and quality assurance are examples of technical support functions.

Three of the basic functions that are required in every software development project are:

- Configuration control: manages the changes to the software product being developed.

- Quality assurance: ensures the quality of the product being developed.

- Testing: verifies compliance with the product's formal requirements specification.

The software configuration management plan (SCMP) and the software quality assurance plan (SQAP) document the resources that are needed for each support group, how they are to be used, and which standards and procedures will be applied during the project. The SCMP and the SQAP then become the mandate for the two groups during project development.

---

[7]This demonstrates the point simplistically. Obviously, there are many other factors that also contribute to the success of a software project.

Software testing is the process of determining the degree to which software satisfies specified requirements and satisfies the customer. Test procedures are prepared in order to demonstrate the fulfillment (or lack of fulfillment) of the requirements. They should be based on an approach called *negative testing*. This means that it is the test team's objective to find as many problems as possible. If the tests are conducted correctly, then when the testers fail, the project succeeds.

Independent test groups are the preferred software system testers. Objective independent testing will often locate problems much earlier than subjective tests performed by the developers. This is of major benefit to the project, because the earlier problems are located the less costly they are to correct.

It is the project manager's responsibility to organize the project support groups, and to document their planned activities in the project development plan (which includes the SCMP and the SQAP). Project support functions that are well planned at the start of the project will contribute to effective project management throughout the project.

To be successful, testing must have a property called traceability: the ability to determine that each feature has a source in the requirement and each requirement has a corresponding implemented feature. Successful testing requires full coverage, that is, the assurance that each requirement and implemented feature is completely tested.

Testing occurs at the end of each phase of software development, with the most intense testing occurring, of course, toward the end. This is one of the basic principles of modern testing theory—that testing be done throughout and no longer just at the end of a project. This principle is called *phase containment*: the detection and correction of errors within the development phase wherein they were introduced. The objective of phase containment is to reduce the number of problems found toward the end of the project and subsequently to reduce the amount of testing needed before the software product is released.

Exercises

1. You have been designated project manager for the development of an inventory system for a large manufacturing company. The inventory system to be developed is to be based on the *sS ordering method* (when the inventory level for any item drops below *s*, then a quantity is ordered that will raise the level to *S*; each item has its own *sS* values).

   a. Suggest four intermediate versions of the system to be released internally for system testing, alpha testing, beta testing, and final release. What will be the functional difference between each version?

   b. Describe the version control procedures to be used, and suggest a version description form.

2. As project manager, define the configuration management and quality assurance organizations for the inventory system described in Exercise 1. How many people are required for these tasks, and what will the responsibilities of each person be? Explain your decisions.

3. As software quality assurance manager, write the reviews and audits chapter of the SQAP for the development of the inventory system described in Exercise 1. Which reviews and audits will be held, and when are they to be held? Describe the requirements for each review and audit and how each required item is to be approved. Describe the procedure for corrective action after each review and audit.

4. Plan the testing stages for the release of the inventory system described in Exercise 1. Which test stages do you suggest after the integration phase? Write the chapters in the test plan that describe each of these test stages. Which resources are required, and what test data is required? Assign the testers for each stage.

5. Define five major quality attributes of the inventory system described in Exercise 1, and define the quality metrics for these attributes. Explain the reasoning behind the metrics that you have defined.

6. Using the change request form described in Figure 8.4, fill out all entries in the form for the following changes: (1) an order monitoring feature is added for items that fall below level s, (2) the sS level for each item is to be added to the inventory report, (3) the requirement for a 6-second response to an inventory query has been relaxed to 20 seconds, and (4) the required capacity of the data base has been increased from 2,000 items to 5,000 items. Explain the problems and considerations related to each form.

Class exercise: divide the class into four groups. Assign Exercise 6 to each group. Discuss the differences between the way each group filled out the change request forms (e.g., discuss the difference in estimates). Discuss the different problems identified by each group and the considerations that were taken into account.

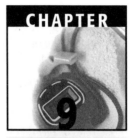

Software Development Standards: The Necessary Evil

There is a perception that standards are the straitjacket that restrains creativity. Unfortunately, this occasionally can be true, when they cease to be a means for achieving an objective and become an objective of their own. Standards must be reasonable, adaptable, and practical. A good rule is that a set of development standards must be the minimum needed to achieve their objective. A famous anecdote relates the case of the overzealous software manager who required his teams to hold weekly project meetings even for projects teams of one person.

Standards cannot be "one size fits all," and should be adapted to each individual project. The early US Department of Defense (DOD) software development standard 2167 (DOD 1988a) recognized this simple but important concept, and included a section for every standard called "tailoring," which referred to the removal of unnecessary sections of the standard. The IEEE software standards (IEEE 1999) also provided a wide range of flexibility and rarely defined any component as mandatory.

Standards are a necessary evil. They limit much of the software developer's freedom, as of course they are meant to do. They accompany the development cycle from beginning to end; there are design standards, documentation standards, coding standards, testing standards, and even standards for submitting and evaluating proposals (see Chapter 3).

Though standards can be regarded as a necessary evil, their application achieves a worthwhile result; it makes software development more manageable. This does not mean that only managers benefit from the use of standards. Standards promote a degree of tidiness and conformity that assists developers in understanding work produced by others and encourages them to produce work that is understandable by others.

To clarify the benefit that standards can provide to the software developer, let us consider the following real-life case.

Aereola, a major telecommunications corporation, has developed a sophisticated multimillion-dollar switching exchange, the XT2000, which has been delivered to a wide customer base worldwide. The XT2000's user interface is extremely cumbersome and it is difficult to operate, and customers regularly enter incorrect commands, causing poor performance of their phone system. They have urgently requested Aereola to produce a modern user-friendly graphic user interface for the XT2000.

The Aereola software development team estimates that it will take between one and a half and two years to develop a new user interface for the XT2000 due to the complexity related to producing a new release of the XT2000 software.

A bright young software engineer at Aereola has submitted a proposal whereby he and three colleagues would quickly develop a new user interface in two months on a PC computer that would connect to the existing XT2000 user interface, thus avoiding the need for a new XT2000 software release. This, they explain, would be a temporary solution until a new integrated user interface would be available on the XT2000 (presumably in one and half to two years) and therefore they would forgo the use of development standards and processes (to save time).

Due to the low cost of this proposal, the engineer and his three colleagues are given approval to proceed, and sure enough they produce the new PC-based user interface in just over two months, which they call the Slick Terminal (or ST). Two additional months are spent tuning and debugging the ST at one customer site before it is declared ready for delivery to all of Aereola's XT2000 customers.

Two years later there is still no new user interface on the XT2000 other than the ST, which has become a critical part of the XT2000 product and has been installed at 400 customer sites around the world. The ST has a list of over one hundred software faults awaiting correction and a second list of over forty changes that are needed. However, of the original team of four who developed the ST, only one remains at Aereola, and he is totally engrossed in another critical development project.

A new team is established to maintain the ST, but they have no idea how the ST was developed, nor do they know what its internal design looks like. Worse, even some of the ST's original source code is missing. In short there is no orderly development documentation for the ST. The new team has an almost impossible task.

This case, the likes of which is not uncommon, emphasizes the importance of enforcing standards for documenting and developing software. As we have seen, the overall penalty resulting from cutting all corners (commonly called *hacking*) far exceeds the additional cost required to document the software and follow an orderly development process.

In the real world, quick solutions are sometimes necessary. It is also true that there is often justification for relaxing standards and development procedures. However, when all development principles and values are thrown to the wind, the wind often blows them right back in an unruly manner. This was the case with the Slick Terminal.

While it is true that much software is still being developed today in the same way as in the Slick Terminal debacle, there is undoubtedly a growing awareness of the importance of development standards and orderly process (see Chapter 1). In fact, one of the main challenges facing the project manager is the selection of the right standard from a vast array of possibilities. Moore (1998), in his excellent overview of software standards, states that "Today's user of software engineering standards is presented with a bewildering array of choices, more than 300 standards developed and maintained by more than 50 different organizations, all approaching software engineering from different viewpoints and contexts."

This problem is resolved in cases where particular development standards are specified as requirements, as is often the case with government projects. In most other cases it is left to the development organization to select the most appropriate set of development standards. This chapter provides the software project manager with basic information to help make this selection. It discusses the vast array of software standards available today and centers on the merits of two of the most prevalent: the US-originated IEEE Software Engineering Standards and the European-originated ISO standards.

9.1 An Overview of Software Development Standards

The term *standard* has been broadly applied to various types of specification. Some standards may function as guidelines, suggesting or recommending development techniques or document formats. Other standards may function as a set of strict rules governing every aspect of the development activities. Figure 9.1 provides a basic example of the way in which software development standards relate to each other and how they are applied throughout the development cycle.

The European-based International Organization for Standardization (ISO) has made a significant contribution to standards in many areas of software engineering, manufacturing, and construction. ISO has produced many standards for software development, most notably the ISO 9000 quality standards (see Schmauch, 1995).

The Institute of Electrical and Electronics Engineers (IEEE) is an international technical professional society with branches in all major countries. The IEEE, based in the Unites States, has coordinated and led landmark research in many areas of software engineering and has produced numerous standards and guidelines (see IEEE 1999). ISO and the IEEE cooperate regularly in the development of standards to the extent that some of their software-related standards are, in effect, common.

The US Department of Defense (DOD) standard 2167 (see DOD 1988a) has been prominent for many years in the area of defense and mission critical software. Though the standard was developed to help ensure a common basis for the development of software for the US defense establishment, it became widely accepted by government-related agencies worldwide.

The above three sets of standards are discussed in detail below. There are, however, many other standards bodies worldwide producing software standards. Many of these

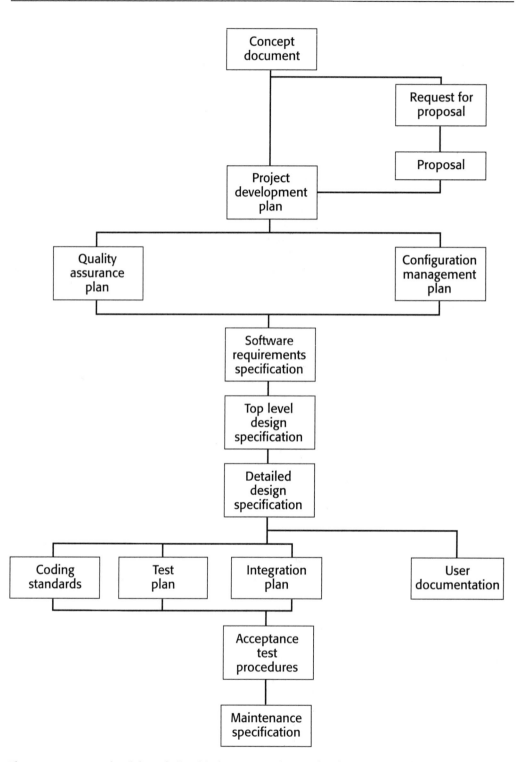

Figure 9.1   Example of the relationship between software development standards.

standards overlap and describe similar processes, though not always in the same manner. The use of terminology is also not always consistent.

This led to a general awareness in the software development community that all software engineers needed to speak some common language. This didn't mean that they needed to speak English or French. It meant that when engineers referred to *software fault tolerance* it would be desirable that the term had the same meaning for all.

Though it would be wishful to say that standardization of terminology for software engineering has been achieved, nonetheless significant progress has been made. One of the most noteworthy is the IEEE Standard Glossary of Software Engineering (see Section 9.2.4). The IEEE, understanding that their other standards would be difficult to produce without a common terminology, made the glossary one of their first projects.

ISO has also contributed significantly to the standardization of terminology, particularly in areas of Quality Management and Quality Assurance.[1] As the two organizations continue to increase cooperation between them, we can expect to see steps toward a single IEEE/ISO software engineering taxonomy.

Some things are more difficult to standardize than others, and this difficulty is represented by the multiple definitions provided for some of the more challenging concepts. For example, the difficulty in defining *software quality* was illustrated in an early version of the IEEE's glossary of terminology (IEEE 1987b), which contained no fewer than four separate definitions:

1. The totality of features and characteristics of a software product that bear on its ability to satisfy given needs; for example, conform to specifications.

2. The degree to which software possesses a desired combination of attributes.

3. The degree to which a customer or user perceives that software meets his or her composite expectations.

4. The composite characteristics of software that determine the degree to which the software in use will meet the expectations of the customer.

Software quality was defined by the US DOD (1988b) rather simply as:

1. The ability of a software product to satisfy its specified requirements.

While the IEEEs definitions 1 and 2 appear somewhat obscure, definitions 3 and 4 and the DOD's definition are subjective, and seem to suggest that quality, like beauty, is in the eyes of the beholder. It is interesting to note that in a later version of the IEEE glossary the controversial term *software quality* was removed (IEEE 1999) entirely, leaving only a definition for the general term *quality* (with *two* definitions).

Many US software organizations have adopted the terminology definitions of the IEEE. It is not uncommon for organizations to either adopt the IEEE or ISO standards outright, or where gaps exist, to base their own standards on them. In areas where the IEEE or ISO have left gaps, other institutes, such as the PMI or SEI (discussed later in the chapter), have stepped in with project management standards and with procedures for evaluating software organizations.

The following sections discuss the most prominent software engineering standards and the organizations that produce them.

---

[1]See ISO standard 8402:1994.

9.2 The IEEE Software Engineering Standards

In 1984, the Institute of Electrical and Electronics Engineers (IEEE) published their first set of software engineering standards (IEEE 1984). This set included four development standards that covered requirements, quality assurance, testing, and configuration management, and a fifth, long-awaited, standard glossary of software engineering terms.

The first set of standards, though far from complete, began a trend toward flexibility which was continued in later editions. The standards were more like a textbook and included many guidelines, examples, and recommendations.

Later editions covered other areas such as design, verification, and validation (V&V), and a standard specific to software development in Ada, the product of the DOD's abortive attempt to specify a standard programming language. As the number of standards began to grow, the IEEE also issued a standard about software standards, to be used as a method for planning the development and the evaluation of standards.

In 1999, the IEEE issued their landmark collection of software engineering standards contained in four volumes. This event was applauded by software developers worldwide. Admittedly, it was also regarded with some concern by some, who were fearful that software development would become regimented and process-heavy. However, this IEEE work was never intended as a set of edicts from which none should depart. Quite the opposite, the collection of standards were to be largely a source of reference, with significant flexibility provided to the developer within the context of each standard. This is stressed in the introductory text to the four volumes, which states: "Not only must the standards be technically excellent on an individual basis, but each must also take its place within a suite of standards that can be adopted in totality or in part by interested organizations."

9.2.1 Overview of the IEEE Standards

The stated intention of the IEEE Software Engineering Standards is to leave the development methodology up to the developer. The set of standards fits easily into many different software development paradigms, including the early phased Waterfall approach, the Spiral method, and the various forms of rapid prototyping (see Chapter 4).

There are four basic types of standard, each based on the objective of the standard, its level of specification, and the support information provided with it. Thus, an IEEE standard can be designated as either:

- A Recommended Practice
- A Guide
- A Standard
- Or, in some cases, a Supplement to a Standard

These classifications are themselves an indication of the supportive, almost textbook approach these standards take. They cover all phases of development from system level requirements (*Guide*: IEEE 1223), through software requirements and design (*Recom-*

mended Practice: IEEE 830, and 1016), to testing, user documentation, and mainte-nance (*Standards*: IEEE 829, 1063, and 1219).

A good example of the flexible quality of the standards is the IEEE 830 recommended practice for software requirements. In addition to detailed explanations and examples, the standard includes *eight* different possible outlines for the main body of the specification. The text of this standard provides excellent guidelines and will be discussed in more detail later.

The 1999 version of the IEEE software standards is contained in four volumes:

- Customer and Terminology Standards
- Process Standards
- Product Standards, and
- Resource and Technique Standards

The four volumes include forty software standards covering almost all aspects of software development.

9.2.2 A Synopsis of the IEEE Standards

The following tables (Tables 9.1 to 9.4) list the specific standards included in each of the four volumes. The organization of the collection of standards was determined by the IEEE's Computer Society Software Engineering Standards Committee (SESC), which

Table 9.1 IEEE 1999 Software Engineering Standards—Volume One: Customer and Terminology Standards

CUSTOMER AND TERMINOLOGY STANDARDS	
IEEE Std 610.12-1990	IEEE Standard Glossary of Software Engineering Terminology
IEEE Std 1062, 1998 Edition	IEEE Recommended Practice for Software Acquisition
IEEE Std 1220-1998	IEEE Standard for the Application and Management of the Systems Engineering Process
IEEE Std 1228-1994	IEEE Standard for Software Safety Plans
IEEE Std 1233, 1998 Edition	IEEE Guide for Developing System Requirements Specifications
IEEE Std 1362-1998	IEEE Guide for Information Technology—System Definition—Concept of Operations Document
IEEE/EIA Std 12207.0-1996	Software life cycle processes
IEEE/EIA Std 12207.1-1997	Software life cycle processes—Life cycle data
IEEE/EIA Std 12207.2-1997	Software life cycle processes—Implementation considerations

Table 9.2   IEEE 1999 Software Engineering Standards—Volume Two: Process Standards

PROCESS STANDARDS	
IEEE Std 730-1998	IEEE Standard for Software Quality Assurance Plans
IEEE Std 730.1-1995	IEEE Guide for Software Quality Assurance Planning
IEEE Std 828-1998	IEEE Standard for Software Configuration Management Plans
IEEE Std 1008-1987 (Reaffirmed 1993)	IEEE Standard for Software Unit Testing
IEEE Std 1012-1998	IEEE Standard for Software Verification and Validation
IEEE Std 1012a-1998	Supplement to IEEE Standard for Software Verification and Validation: Content Map to IEEE/EIA 12207.1-1997
IEEE Std 1028-1997	IEEE Standard for Software Reviews
IEEE Std 1042-1987 (Reaffirmed 1993)	IEEE Guide for Software Configuration Management
IEEE Std 1045-1992	IEEE Standard for Software Productivity Metrics
IEEE Std 1058-1998	IEEE Standard for Software Project Management Plans
IEEE Std 1059-1993	IEEE Guide for Software Verification and Validation Plans
IEEE Std 1074-1997	IEEE Standard for Developing Software Life Cycle Processes
IEEE Std 1219-1998	IEEE Standard for Software Maintenance
IEEE Std 1490-1998	IEEE Guide—Adoption of PMI Standard—A Guide to the Project Management Body of Knowledge

Table 9.3   IEEE 1999 Software Engineering Standards—Volume Three: Product Standards

PRODUCT STANDARDS	
IEEE Std 982.1-1988	IEEE Standard Dictionary of Measures to Produce Reliable Software
IEEE Std 982.2-1988	IEEE Guide for the Use of Standard Dictionary of Measures to Produce Reliable Software
IEEE Std 1061-1998	IEEE Standard for Software Quality Metrics Methodology
IEEE Std 1063-1987 (Reaffirmed 1993)	IEEE Standard for Software User Documentation
IEEE Std 1465-1998	IEEE Standard Adoption of International Standard ISO/IEC 12119:1994 (E)—Information Technology—Software Packages—Quality Requirements and Testing

Table 9.4   IEEE 1999 Software Engineering Standards—Volume Four: Resource and Technique Standards

RESOURCE AND TECHNIQUE STANDARDS	
IEEE Std 829-1998	IEEE Standard for Software Test Documentation
IEEE Std 830-1998	IEEE Recommended Practice for Software Requirements Specifications
IEEE Std 1016-1998	IEEE Recommended Practice for Software Design Descriptions
IEEE Std 1044-1993	IEEE Standard Classification for Software Anomalies
IEEE Std 1044.1-1995	IEEE Guide to Classification of Software Anomalies
IEEE Std 1320.1-1998	IEEE Standard for Functional Modeling Language—Syntax and Semantics for IDEF0
IEEE Std 1320.2-1998	IEEE Standard for Conceptial Modeling Language—Syntax and Semantics for IDEF1X$_{97}$ (IDEF$_{object}$)
IEEE Std 1348-1995	IEEE Recommended Practice for the Adoption of Computer-Aided Software Engineering (CASE) Tools
IEEE Std 1421.1-1995	IEEE Standard for Information Technology—Software Reuse—Data Model for Reuse Library Interoperability: Basic Interoperability Data Model (BIDM)
IEEE Std 1420.1a-1996	Supplement to IEEE Standard for Information Technology—Software Reuse—Data Model for Reuse Library Interoperability: Asset Certification Framework
IEEE Std 1430-1996	IEEE Guide for Information Technology—Software Reuse—Concept of Operations for Interoperating Reuse Libraries
IEEE Std 1462-1998	IEEE Standard Adoption of ISO/IEC 1410.2:1995—Information Technology—Guidelines for the Evaluation and Selection of CASE Tools

first determined the following six layers and then divided them between the four volumes as follows:

- The terminology layer provides terms for use in the entire set of standards and is part of volume one.

- The Overall Guide layer describes the collection and the relations between them and related disciplines. This layer is included in a separate companion book (Moore 1998).

- Three additional layers cover Principles, Element Standards, and Application Guides and they, in turn, are subdivided according to four basic objects of software engineering: Customer, Processes, Products, and Resources, which coincide with the four volumes.

■ The Techniques layer includes standards on detailed techniques, as companions to the other layers, and is included in volume four.

Examples of the six layers and how they relate to each other are described in Figure 9.2.

The six layers were intended to cover all aspects of a software system. The term *system* is a broad concept, which may include the software being developed in the project or a collection of software and hardware components that together form a system. The standards need to address this. They needed to be organized (layered) in such a fashion that they could be applied in all contexts that include software.

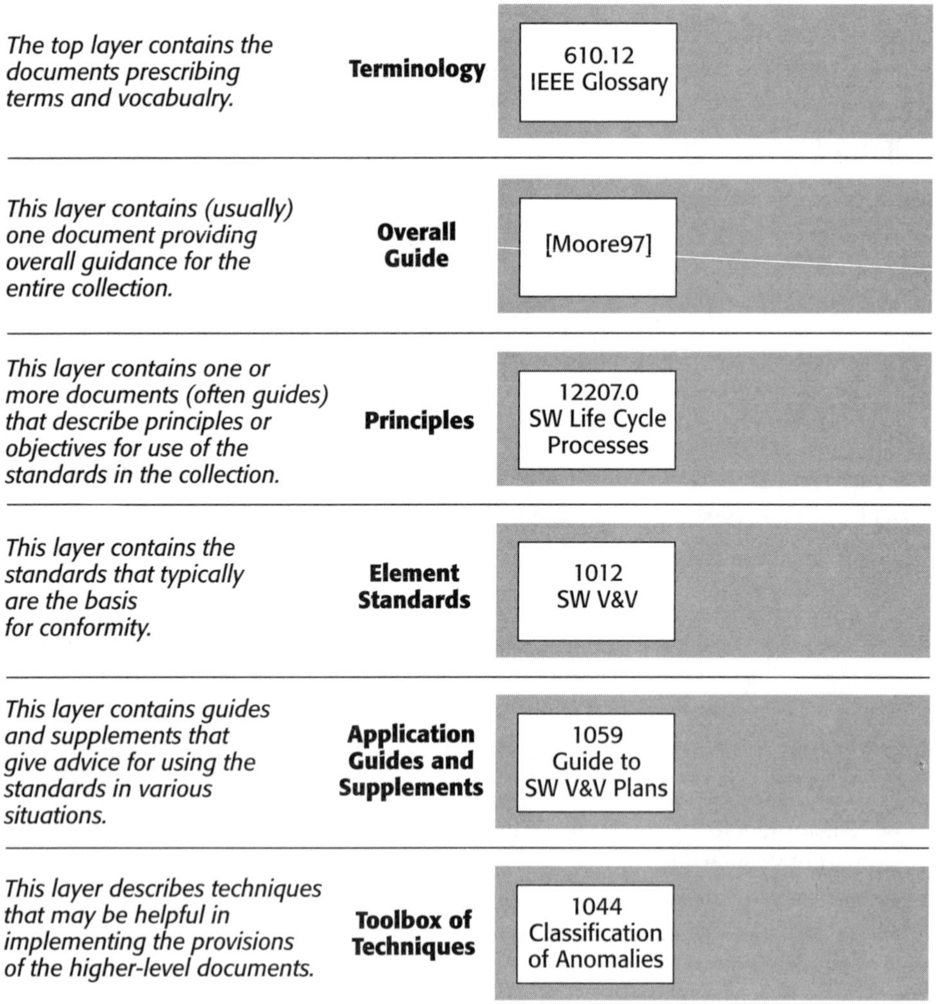

The top layer contains the documents prescribing terms and vocabualry.	**Terminology**	610.12 IEEE Glossary
This layer contains (usually) one document providing overall guidance for the entire collection.	**Overall Guide**	[Moore97]
This layer contains one or more documents (often guides) that describe principles or objectives for use of the standards in the collection.	**Principles**	12207.0 SW Life Cycle Processes
This layer contains the standards that typically are the basis for conformity.	**Element Standards**	1012 SW V&V
This layer contains guides and supplements that give advice for using the standards in various situations.	**Application Guides and Supplements**	1059 Guide to SW V&V Plans
This layer describes techniques that may be helpful in implementing the provisions of the higher-level documents.	**Toolbox of Techniques**	1044 Classification of Anomalies

Figure 9.2   Format of layer diagram using a part of the SESC collection as an example.

In 1998, the IEEE produced a standard that placed software in the context of a system. Standard 1233, a Guide for Developing System Requirements Specifications, provided the all-important link between the software components and the mechanical, electrical, chemical, and user-related components in a software intensive system. The system level specification also addressed broad concepts such as manufacturability and deployment.

By addressing requirements on a higher, system level, the specification intended to address the disparity between the customer and the technical community. The standard expressly states that it should ". . . act as the bridge between the two groups and must be understandable by both," referring to the customer and technical groups. The system level document is encouraged to be written using language and terminology that is understandable by a layman (a less technically oriented reader). There could be no bridge without a common understanding of the terminology and language.

While the system level documents provide a broad context for the software specific standards, they do not replace the need for separate hardware, electronic and user specifications, when needed. The system level document can be perceived as a high level specification that addresses all aspects of a system. Lower level specifications then address the software requirements, the hardware requirements, the user documentation, etc.

As discussed earlier, the IEEE standards include many guidelines and examples. The software design standard 1016 includes a set of recommended practices for design descriptions. The standard also includes a sample outline for a design specification document, as well as recommendations on the content of each paragraph in the document.

Both the requirements and the design phases of software development are somewhat bounded, in that they each have a reasonably well-defined beginning and end. This is less so for software testing, as modern approaches to software development perceive testing as an activity that continues in its many forms throughout the development cycle.

Testing has received considerable attention in the IEEE standards. Standard 829 covers the preparation of test documentation, standard 1008 covers software unit testing, and standard 1012 covers verification and validation throughout the development cycle. Standard 1012 includes a practical and detailed description that covers all project development testing activities (see Figures 9.3 and 9.4).

Of all the software standards, it would be challenging to choose one as representative of the complete set. However, one of the earlier standards, which covers software requirements (IEEE Std 830), could be perceived as a worthy candidate due to its seniority (it is one of the earliest IEEE software standards) and its wide recognition and use. It also aptly demonstrates the textbook nature of the set of standards. The following section describes the software requirements standard.

9.2.3 The IEEE Software Requirements Standard

The software requirements standard (IEEE Std 830) was included in the early 1983 set of software standards, and has since been significantly updated. It is an good illustration of a document that goes well beyond the basic function of a standard, providing many

Acquisition Process | **Supply Process** | **Development Process** | **Operation Process** | **Maintenance Process**

Acquisition Support V&V Activities

V&V Inputs
(1) Prel System Description
(2) Statement of Need
(3) RFP or Tender
(4) System Integrity Level Scheme
(5) Contract
(6) Supplier Development Plan and Schedules
(7) User Needs

V&V Tasks
(1) Scoping the V&V Effort
(2) Planning the Interface Between the V&V Effort and Supplier
(3) System Requirements Review

V&V Outputs
(1) SVP and Updates
(2) Task Report(s)
(3) Anomaly Report(s)

Planning V&V Activities

V&V Inputs
(1) SVVP
(2) Contract
(3) Supplier Development Plans and Schedules
(4) RFP or Tender
(5) User Needs

V&V Tasks
(1) Planning the Interface Between the V&V Effort and Supplier
(2) Contract Verification

V&V Outputs
(1) Updated SVVP
(2) Task Report(s)
(3) Anomaly Report(s)

Concept V&V Activities

V&V Inputs
(1) Concept Documentation
(2) Supplier Development Plans and Schedules
(3) User Needs
(4) Acquisition Needs
(5) Developer Integrity Levels Assignments
(6) Supplier Development Plan and Schedules
(7) V&V tasks results

V&V Tasks
(1) Concept Documentation Evaluation
(2) Criticality Analysis
(3) Hardware/Software/ User Reqmts Allocation Analysis
(4) Traceability Analysis
(5) Hazard Analysis
(6) Risk Analysis

V&V Outputs
(1) Task Report(s)
(2) Anomaly Report(s)

Requirements V&V Activities

V&V Inputs
(1) Concept Documentation
(2) SRS
(3) IRS
(4) Criticality Task Report (Rpt)
(5) User Documentation
(6) System Test Plan
(7) Acceptance Test Plan
(8) SW Config Mgmt Process Documentation
(9) Hazard Analysis Report
(10) Supplier Development Plans and Schedules
(11) V&V task results

V&V Tasks
(1) Traceability Analysis
(2) Software Reqmts Evaluation
(3) Interface Analysis
(4) Criticality Analysis
(5) System V&V Test Plan Generation/ Verification
(6) Acceptance V&V Test Plan Generation/ Verification
(7) Configuration Mgmt Assessment
(8) Hazard Analysis
(9) Risk Analysis

V&V Outputs
(1) Task Report(s)
(2) Anomaly Report(s)
(3) V&V Test Plans
    - System
    - Acceptance

Design V&V Activities

V&V Inputs
(1) SRS
(2) SDD
(3) IRS
(4) IDD
(5) Design Standards
(6) Concept Documentation
(7) Criticality Task Rpt
(8) Test Plans and Designs
(9) User Documentation
(10) Hazard Analysis Rpt
(11) Supplier Development Plans and Schedules
(12) V&V task results

V&V Tasks
(1) Traceability Analysis
(2) Software Design Evaluation
(3) Interface Analysis
(4) Criticality Analysis
(5) Component V&V Test Plan Generation/ Verification
(6) Integration V&V Test Plan Generation/ Verification
(7) V&V Test Design Generation/ Verification
(8) Hazard Analysis
(9) Risk Analysis

V&V Outputs
(1) Task Report(s)
(2) Anomaly Report(s)
(3) V&V Test Plans
    - Component
    - Integration
(4) V&V Test Design
    - Component
    - Integration
    - System
    - Acceptance

Implementation V&V Activities

V&V Inputs
(1) SDD
(2) IDD
(3) Source Code
(4) Coding Stds
(5) User Documentation
(6) Concept Documentation
(7) Criticality Task Rpt
(8) Test Designs/Cases
(9) Test Procedures
(10) Component Test Results
(11) Hazard Analysis Rpt
(12) Supplier Development Plans and Schedules
(13) V&V task results

V&V Tasks
(1) Traceability Analysis
(2) Source Code and Source Code Documentation Evaluation
(3) Interface Analysis
(4) Criticality Analysis
(5) V&V Test Case Generation/ Verification
(6) V&V Test Procedures Generation/ Verification
(7) Component Test Execution/ Verification
(8) Hazard Analysis
(9) Risk Analysis

V&V Outputs
(1) Task Report(s)
(2) Anomaly Report(s)
(3) V&V Test Cases
    - Component
    - Integration
    - System
    - Acceptance
(4) V&V Test Procedures
    - Component
    - Integration
    - System

Test V&V Activities

V&V Inputs
(1) Test Plans, Designs, Cases, and Procedures
(2) SDD
(3) IDD
(4) Source and Executable Code
(5) User Documentation
(6) Test Results
(7) Critical Task Rpt
(8) Hazard Analysis Rpt
(9) Supplier Development Plans and Schedules
(9) V&V task results

V&V Tasks
(1) Traceability Analysis
(2) Acceptance V&V Test Procedures Generation/ Verification
(3) Integration V&V Test Execution/ Verification
(4) System V&V Test Execution/ Verification
(5) Acceptance V&V Test Execution/ Verification
(6) Hazard Analysis
(7) Risk Analysis

V&V Outputs
(1) Task Report(s)
(2) Anomaly Report(s)
(3) V&V Test Procedures
    - Acceptance

Installation and Checkout V&V Activities

V&V Inputs
(1) Installation Package
(2) User Documentation
(3) Hazard Analysis Rpt
(4) Supplier Development Plans and Schedules
(5) V&V task reports
(6) V&V Activity Summary Reports

V&V Tasks
(1) Installation Configuration Audit
(2) Installation Checkout
(3) Hazard Analysis
(4) Risk Analysis
(5) V&V Final Report Generation

V&V Outputs
(1) Task Report(s)
(2) Anomaly Report(s)
(3) V&V Final Report

Operation V&V Activities

V&V Inputs
(1) SVVP
(2) New constraints
(3) Proposed Changes
(4) Installation Package
(5) Operating Procedures
(6) User Documentation
(7) Concept Documentation
(8) Hazard Analysis Rpt
(9) Supplier Development Plans and Schedules
(10) Operational Problem Report(s)
(11) V&V task results

V&V Tasks
(1) Evaluation of New Constraints
(2) Proposed Change Assessment
(3) Operating Procedure Evaluation
(4) Hazard Analysis
(5) Risk Analysis

V&V Outputs
(1) Task Report(s)
(2) Anomaly Report(s)

Maintenance V&V Activities

V&V Inputs
(1) SVVP
(2) Approved Changes
(3) Proposed Changes
(4) Hazard Analysis Rpt
(5) Supplier Development Plans and Schedules
(6) Proposed Changes
(7) Anomaly Report(s)
(8) Maintainer Integrity Levels
(9) Hazard Analysis Rpt
(10) Supplier Development Plans and Schedules
(10) Operation Problem Report(s)
(11) V&V task results

V&V Tasks
(1) SVVP Revision
(2) Proposed Change Assessment
(3) Anomaly Evaluation
(4) Criticality Analysis
(5) Migration Assessment
(6) Retirement Assessment
(7) Hazard Analysis
(8) Risk Analysis
(9) Task Iteration

V&V Outputs
(1) Updated SVVP
(2) Task Report(s)
(3) Anomaly Report(s)

Management of V&V Activities

V&V Inputs
(1) All V&V inputs
(2) All V&V outputs

V&V Tasks
(1) SVVP Generation
(2) Baseline Change Assessment
(3) Management Review of V&V
(4) Management and Technical Review Support
(5) Interface With Organizational and Supporting Processes

V&V Outputs
(1) SVVP and Updates
(2) Task Report(s)
(3) Anomaly Report(s)
(4) V&V Activity Summary Report(s)
(5) Recommendations to V&V Final Report

Note:
(1) The V&V tasks may be performed concurrently. The figure shows a sequential (waterfall) model as an example.
(2) V&V tasks listed in Figure 1 are the minimum for Software Integrity Level 4 (Highest Integrity Level).
(3) Table 2 contains a complete list of each V&V task description. Table 2 defines the minimum V&V tasks for each software integrity level.

Figure 9.3   An Example of software V&V overview.

196

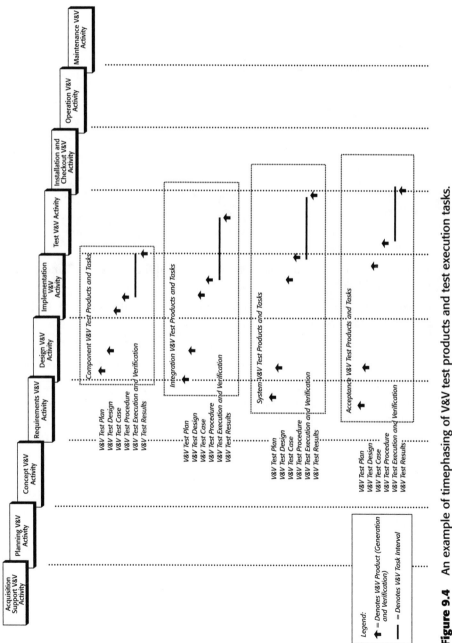

Figure 9.4 An example of timephasing of V&V test products and test execution tasks.

guidelines and examples. The standard states that it is intended to be a guide for the user toward the development of a "good software requirements specification" or SRS. It lists the basic characteristics of a good SRS as:

- Correct
- Unambiguous
- Complete
- Verifiable
- Consistent
- Ranked for importance and/or stability
- Modifiable
- Traceable
- Usable

This list can then be used as a checklist,[2] to evaluate the requirements specifications in the following manner:

1. Does each requirement accurately represent the expectation of the customer? (correct)

2. Is each requirement clear and does it have the same interpretation for all who read it? (unambiguous)

3. Are all requirements documented, have we ensured that no "verbal" understandings remain? (complete)

4. Can we prove in a reasonable manner, and at a reasonable expense, that each requirement has been met? (verifiable)

5. Does any requirement conflict with another requirement? (consistent)

6. In determining future trade-offs, has the relative importance of each requirement been assigned? (ranked)

7. Is the requirements specification documented in a way that will enable it to be easily corrected or changed later? (modifiable)

8. Are the origins of each requirement clear (backward traceability), and can the testing and design documents be later traced to requirements? (forward traceability)

9. Has the requirement specification been written so that it can be understood not only by the organization writing it, but also by the software maintenance organization? (usable)

---

[2]A rather obvious tenth characteristic is implementable, which implies that it must be possible to implement each requirement within the constraints of the project. Unimplementable requirements may refer to unattainable levels of reliability and performance or impossible interfacing between incompatible components.

The 830 requirements standard is best suited for software projects in which the requirements are fully known at the beginning of the project. In an evolutionary project (e.g., rapid prototyping or spiral paradigms), the standard may be less suitable (though the guidelines would remain valid). This would be an example where an organization may decide to modify and adapt the standard to its own needs, in this case to an evolutionary development cycle.

9.2.4 The IEEE Standard Glossary of Software Engineering Terminology

Occasionally, problems in software development can be attributed to issues of communication—not computer communication but rather human communication. What is a requirement? What does software quality mean? How do we define software performance, and what is the relationship between *up time* and *down time* on the one hand, and *mean time between failures* (or MTBF) and *mean time to repair* (or MTTR) on the other?

The importance of unambiguous language was further emphasized as standards began to evolve. Initially standards were relatively easy to define for such basic development activities as documentation and coding. More advanced development concepts such as design, testing, and reviews were more difficult to describe. It was easier to specify how instructions were to be written than to specify the elements of a good design. While everyone appeared to know what a program was, not everyone agreed on what a design was. Design was sometimes called *analysis*, or *software architecture*. Other concepts had multiple meanings, such as the term *process* or the term *testing*, which had many interpretations. Even the term *quality* meant different things to different people (it still does!). Clearly, these and other terms needed a single agreed definition. Thus, it became clear that a standard language was required.

The IEEE Standard Glossary of Software Engineering Terminology (IEEE Std 610.12) fulfilled that need. The glossary documents the existing terms and provides standard definitions for them. It covers some 1,300 terms in areas such as:

- Compilers and Programming
- Computer Performance Evaluation
- Configuration Management
- Data Types
- Errors, Faults, and Failures
- Evaluation Techniques
- Operating Systems
- Quality Attributes
- Software Documentation
- Testing

- Software Architecture and Design
- Software Development Process and Techniques, and
- Software Tools

Not all terms have a single definition. Understandably, the task of nailing down a single definition for each term would not have been easy. The Glossary resolves this problem by providing alternate definitions when no single accepted one exists. Thus, the term *quality* has two definitions, one related to requirements and the other related to customer expectations, and the term *patch* has four definitions, three of which address different concepts of software modification, and the fourth being the verb form of the term.

Some definitions provide tutorial-level descriptions, such as the term *system requirements review*, which is accompanied by a definition, which is, in effect, a description of the objectives of the review. Similarly, a software requirements review is described in detail, and the general concept of a review is explained.

Though widely accepted, the IEEE glossary is not the only set of definitions for software terminology. Additional valuable work on the standardization of software terminology was performed by other organizations, including ISO and the DOD.

9.2.5 The IEEE 12207 Software Life Cycle Standards

One of the more significant parts of the IEEE software engineering standards is a suite of three standards that describe the Software Life Cycle Processes (Std 12207). The stated purpose of these standards is

> . . . *to establish a common framework for software life cycle processes, with well defined terminology, that can be referenced by the software industry." The standard "contains processes, activities, and tasks that are to be applied during the acquisition of a system that contains software, a stand-alone software product, and software service and during the supply, development, operation, and maintenance of software products. (IEEE 1999).*

The 12207 standards are the result of significant cooperation between three organizations: the IEEE, the Electronic Industries Association (EIA), and the International Organization for Standardization (ISO). The EIA is a US-based association representing a broad range of companies involved in US electronics manufacturing, from companies that manufacture small electronics components to large multinational corporations. ISO, the leading international standards organization, is discussed in detail in Section 9.3. Much of the work in compiling the standards was accomplished by a joint technical committee of the EIA and ISO, referred to as JTC1 (see Section 9.3.2). The full designation of the standard is IEEE/EIA 12207, and its internal content is designated ISO/IEC 12207 so all contributing organizations are appropriately recognized.

The standard declares that it is intended to be used to:

a. Acquire, supply, develop, operate, and maintain software.

b. Support the above functions in the form of quality assurance, configuration management, joint reviews, audits, verification, validation, problem resolution, and documentation.

c. Manage and improve the organization's process and personnel.

d. Establish software management and engineering environments based upon the life cycle processes as adapted and tailored to serve business needs.

e. Foster improved understanding between customers and vendors and among the parties involved in the life cycle of a software product.

f. Facilitate world trade in software.

The 12207 suite of three standards includes the following parts:

1. 12207.0 *Standard for Information Technology—Software life cycle processes*: Contains ISO/IEC 12207 in its original form and five additional annexes: Basic concepts, Compliance, Life cycle process objectives, Life cycle data objectives, and Relationships.

2. 12207.1 *Guide for ISO/IEC 12207, Standard Information Technology—Software life cycle processes—Life cycle data*: Provides additional guidance on recording life cycle data.

3. 12207.2 *Guide for ISO/IEC 12207, Standards for Information Technology— Software life cycle processes—Implementation considerations*: Provides additions, alternatives, and clarifications to the ISO/IEC 12207's life cycle processes as derived from US practice.

Standard 12207 centers on five basic views of software life cycles:

■ The contract view, which includes acquisition and supply

■ The Engineering view, which covers the development process

■ The Operating view, which covers operating and maintenance processes

■ Supporting life cycle processes, which include documentation, configuration management, quality assurance, and other support processes, and

■ Organizational life cycle processes, which cover the management view, infrastructure, training, and the all-important improvement process

The relationships between the individual life cycle processes and views are illustrated in Figure 9.5.

The emergence of standard 12207 was an important milestone for organizations that are heavily involved in software procurement, such as government and pseudo-government agencies. This was particularly true for defense and military branches of government, and in fact the US Department of Defense adopted standard 12207 in 1998, as its sole standard for software acquisition (see Section 9.5.1).

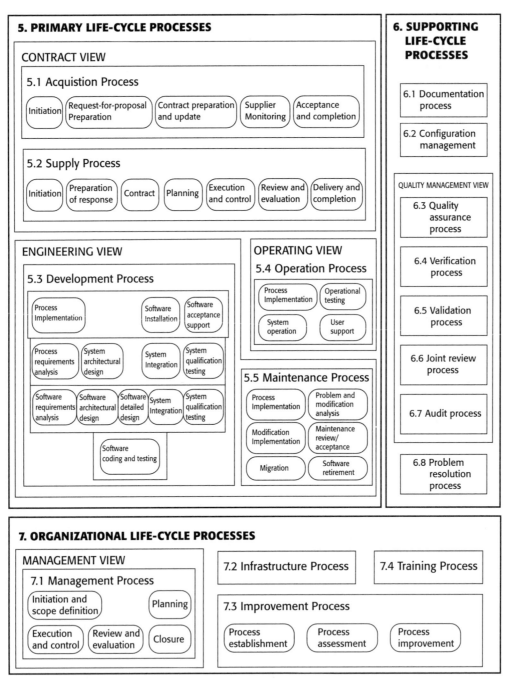

The position order of activities does not mean time order.
Names of activities in the Development Process are not names of development phases.

Figure 9.5   Software life-cycle processes, views, and activities.

9.3 The ISO Standards

The International Organization for Standardization (which uses the non-language-specific acronym "ISO") is probably best known for the widely used quality certification program, based on the ISO 9000[3] quality standards. ISO, initially regarded as a European organization, has since the early nineties been achieving increasing worldwide acceptance. This includes the United States, where ISO is also gaining a significant following, as is demonstrated by the growing cooperation between ISO and the IEEE.

ISO membership is typically offered to national bodies that represent countries. ISO standards are then applied and adapted to the needs of each member's country, with the right to bestow ISO certification commonly given to the national standards body in each country. The American National Standards Institute (ANSI) represents the United States in the ISO membership forum.

ISO does not carry out assessments to confirm that users are implementing its standards. This process, known as conformity assessment, is a matter for suppliers and their customers, and for regulatory bodies.

The international character of ISO has been advanced by the widely recognized ISO quality standards and, in fact, many national standards organizations started their relationship with ISO in this area. The software related ISO 9000 quality standards (also referred to as information technology quality standards) are arguably the most widely used quality standards in the world.

ISO's work goes well beyond the 9000 series quality standards. ISO standards cover most areas of software, including life cycle processes, software product evaluation, and maintenance, as well as many customer-related fields. These are discussed in more detail later in the chapter.

9.3.1 The ISO 9000 Standards

ISO states[4] that the *ISO 9000* set of standards is primarily concerned with *quality management*. The standardized definition of *quality* in ISO 9000 refers to all those features of a product (or service) which are required by the customer. *Quality management* is interpreted by ISO to mean that which the organization does to ensure that its products conform to the customer's requirements.

Three forms of the ISO 9000 standards exist (designated 9001, 9002, and 9003), and are related to the degree of development and production that exists in the organization seeking to adopt the standards:

- ISO 9001 sets out the requirements for an organization whose business processes range all the way from design and development, to production, installation and servicing;

- For an organization that does not carry out design and development, ISO 9002 is the appropriate standard, since it does not include the design control requirements of ISO 9001—otherwise, its requirements are identical;

[3]See Introduction to ISO, at: http://www.iso.ch/
[4]See http://www.iso.ch/9000e/9k14ke.htm

- ISO 9003 is the appropriate standard for an organization whose business processes do not include design control, process control, purchasing, or servicing, and which basically uses inspection and testing to ensure that final products and services meet specified requirements.

ISO 9000 is applied to software within the context of information technology. ISO 9001 identifies four basic categories of information technology products:

- Hardware
- Software
- Processed material, and
- Service

The overall guide for the standard is designated ISO 9000 and it includes four components that address specific questions on how the standard is to be applied. Then, in addition to the three variants of the standard (9001, 9002, and 9003), a fourth guide designated 9004 includes four components which describe the elements of quality management and quality systems. Four additional companion standards (designated 8402, 10005, 10007, and 10011) define quality terminology, and provide standards for quality plans, configuration management, and quality system audits. A summary of the ISO 9000 standards appears in Table 9.5.

The ISO 9000 standards are developed and maintained by the ISO Technical Committee 176 (ISO TC176). The American Society for Quality Control has adopted the ISO 9000 series standards and has designated them with similar ANSI standard identification numbers (e.g., ISO 9001 corresponds to ANSI/ASQC Q9001).

Not surprisingly, many of the areas covered by the ISO 9000 standard are similar to those covered by the corresponding IEEE standards, though the terminology is not always the same. The following review of some of the fundamental ISO 9000 terms explains how they are used within the ISO processes and how they relate to the principal software engineering activities, particularly when they differ from the IEEE and the US DOD concepts.

Management responsibility. This includes the definition and documentation of quality objectives and policy. It covers such areas as the organizational structure and management reviews.

Quality system. This activity covers the process by which quality is built into the software product during development, rather than it being discovered at the end of the process.

Internal quality system audits. Internal quality audits are carried out according to a predefined audit plan in order to verify whether quality activities comply with the quality plan and in order to determine their effectiveness.

Corrective action. This activity investigates the cause of non-conformance in a software product and defines the actions needed to correct the problem and to prevent recurrence.

Contract review. This process defines the requirements of a contract between supplier and purchaser. It covers such areas as contingencies and risks, discrepancies between tender and contract, subcontracting and terminology.

Purchaser's requirements specification. This process is similar to the corresponding IEEE and DOD standards.

Development planning. This process is similar to the corresponding IEEE and DOD standards.

Quality planning. This process defines the content of the quality plan, including measurable quality objectives, test activities, and quality responsibilities for configuration management.

Table 9.5 ISO 9000 Quality Standards

STANDARD DESCRIPTION	ISO STANDARD DESIGNATION	TITLE
This standard provides guidelines on application and use of the 9001, 9002, and 9003 standards, and is divided into the following four parts:	ISO 9000	
	ISO 9000-1	Quality management and quality assurance standards, Part 1: Guidelines for selection and use
	ISO 9000-2	Quality management and quality assurance standards, Part 2: Generic Guidelines for the application of ISO 9001, ISO 9002, and ISO 9003
	ISO 9000-3	Quality management and quality assurance standards, Part 3: Guidelines for the application of ISO 9001 to the development, supply, and maintenance of software
	ISO 9000-4	Quality management and quality assurance standards, Part 4: Guide to dependability program management
These are the three forms of the quality systems standards:	ISO 9001	Quality systems—Model for quality assurance design, development, production, installation, and servicing
	ISO 9002	Quality systems—Model for quality assurance in production, installation, and servicing
	ISO 9003	Quality systems—Model for quality assurance in final inspection and test

Table 9.5 (*continued*)

STANDARD DESCRIPTION	ISO STANDARD DESIGNATION	TITLE
This standard provides guidelines for quality management and is divided into the following four parts:	ISO 9004	
	ISO 9004-1	Quality management and quality systems elements—Part 1: Guidelines
	ISO 9004-2	Quality management and quality systems elements—Part 2: Guidelines for service
	ISO 9004-3	Quality management and quality systems elements—Part 3: Guidelines for processed materials
	ISO 9004-4	Quality management and quality systems elements—Part 4: Guidelines for quality improvement
Selection of terminology and toolbox quality related ISO standards	ISO 8402	Quality management and quality assurance—Vocabulary
	ISO 10005	Quality management—Guidelines for quality plans
	ISO 10007	Quality management—Guidelines for configuration management
	ISO 10011	Guidelines for auditing quality systems

Design and implementation. This process is similar to the corresponding IEEE and DOD standards.

Testing and validation. This process is similar to the corresponding IEEE and DOD standards.

Acceptance. This process refers to the acceptance tests (or criteria) for the delivery of a validated software product.

Replication, delivery and installation. Replication covers the copying of the software product: the number of copies, the storage media, documentation, etc.

Maintenance. This process is similar to the corresponding IEEE and DOD standards.

Configuration management. This process is similar to the corresponding IEEE and DOD standards.

Document control. This process covers the determination of documents to be controlled, approval and issuance procedures, and change and withdrawal procedures.

Quality records. The quality records process covers the procedures for the identification, collection, indexing, filing, storage, maintenance, and disposition of quality records. These records are used to demonstrate the achievement of the required quality level.

Measurement. This process covers the collection and reporting of quality measurements according to specific improvement goals. It also addresses the need for remedial action if metric levels grow worse or exceed established target levels.

Rules, practices, and convention. This set of processes covers a general area in which the supplier is required to set rules, practices and conventions in order to make the ISO 9000 quality standard effective.

Tools and techniques. This is also a very general process that covers the need to provide adequate tools, facilities, and techniques to make the ISO 9000 quality system effective.

Purchasing. This process covers the acquisition of software and hardware products for the development of, or for inclusion in, the final product. The process also covers the assessment of subcontractors.

Included software product. When existing products, either from the purchaser or from a third party, are required to be included in the supplier's system, this process addresses procedures covering how this is to be implemented. Areas addressed include validation and protection of the included product, as well as support for the included product after the final system is delivered.

Training. This process addresses the preparation of a training plan for the operation of the new system. It covers not only training in using the system being developed, but also training to acquire related skills that may be needed to use the system.

As cooperation expands between ISO and the IEEE, the use of different terminology will come to an end. This is already evident in the introduction of joint standards (e.g., standard 12207) as well as in other areas of software development standards.

9.3.2 The ISO/IEC JTC1 Software Development Standards

This section provides an overview of the work being conducted by various ISO groups on a broad range of software engineering standards. ISO has produced significant guides and standards in many areas that complement the ISO 9000 quality standards. This includes such fields as program language and data structure-related standards, consumer software documentation standards, and product evaluation standards.

ISO has also cooperated with other organizations, in addition to the IEEE, in developing software and computer system-related recommended practices and standards, most notably the International Electrotechnical Commission, or IEC, which is based in Switzerland. ISO and the IEC recognized in 1987 that significant overlap existed in their work, which led to the creation of a joint technical committee dedicated to standardization in the field of computer systems (or "information technology" as it was referred to by the two organizations). The joint technical committee was named JTC1. The United States is represented in the JTC1 by a technical advisory group (or TAG) affiliated with ANSI.

Since its founding, JTC1 has produced a wealth of guides, recommended practices, and standards in software and computer system-related fields, some of which are:

- Vocabulary
- Coded character sets
- Software engineering
- Data element principles
- Programming languages, their environments, and system software interfaces
- Computer graphics and image processing
- Interconnection of information technology equipment

The following two tables provide some insight into the work being conducted by the JTC1 in software engineering and the standards that are being produced. Table 9.6

Table 9.6   Software Engineering Fields for JTC1 Standards

1. Systems software development.	This covers documentation of software systems.
2. Tools and environments.	This covers tools and computer-aided software/ systems engineering (CASE) environments.
3. Evaluation and metrics.	Software products evaluation and metrics for software products and processes.
4. Life cycle management.	Management of the phases of software life cycles.
5. Support of life cycle processes.	As its title indicates, this covers standards intended to support the application of processes for software life cycles.
6. Software integrity.	Software integrity (ensuring the containment or confinement of risk) at the system and system interface level.
7. Software process assessment.	Methods, practices, and application of process assessment in software product procurement, development, delivery, operation, evolution, and related service support.
8. Software engineering data definition and representation.	Definition of the data used and produced by software engineering processes, its representation for communication by both humans and machines, and definition of data interchange formats.
9. Functional size measurement.	Establishment of a set of practical standards for functional size measurement, a general term for methods of sizing software from an external viewpoint.

describes the areas of software engineering in which the JTC1 has provided standards (see Moore 1998). These software engineering fields have been assigned by the JTC1 to individual work groups, who in turn are organized as a sub-committee of the JTC1, designated SC7. Temperance in using acronyms is apparently not one of the stronger points of the ISO and ISO affiliated organizations, for it is the ISO/IEC JTC1/SC7 that is the major source of international standards on software engineering, surpassing even the IEEE in the number of areas that have been covered. A selection of the SC7 standards appears in Table 9.7

Table 9.7 Selection of ISO/IEC JTC1/SC7 Software Engineering Standards

ISO/IEC STANDARD DESIGNATION	STANDARD TITLE
ISO/IEC 2382-1	Vocabulary—Part 1: Fundamental items
ISO/IEC 2382-7	Vocabulary—Part 7: Computer programming
ISO/IEC 2382-20	Vocabulary—Part 20: System development
ISO/IEC TR 12382	Permuted index of the vocabulary of information technology
ISO 5806	Information processing—Specification of single-hit decision tables
ISO 5807	Information processing—Documentation symbols and conventions for data, program and system flowcharts, program network charts, and system resource charts
ISO 6592	Information processing—Guidelines for the documentation of computer-based application systems
ISO 6593	Information processing—Program flow for processing sequential files in terms of record groups
ISO/IEC 8631	Program constructs and conventions for their representation
ISO 8790	Information processing systems—Computer system configuration diagram symbols and conventions
ISO/IEC 9126	Software product evaluation—Quality characteristics and guidelines for their use
ISO 9127	Information processing systems—User documentation and cover information for consumer software packages
ISO/IEC TR 9294	Guidelines for the management of software documentation
ISO/IEC 11411	Representation for human communication of state transition of software
ISO/IEC 12119	Software packages—Quality requirements and testing
ISO/IEC 12207	Software life cycle processes
ISO/IEC 14102	Guidelines for the evaluation and selection of CASE tools
ISO/IEC 14568	Diagram exchange language (DXL) for tree structured charts

The SC7 subcommittee produces standards according to a product plan produced by their Business Planning Group (see ISO/IEC 1996). The plan involves many years of work to complete an all-encompassing set of software engineering standards and guidelines[5] covering four main software engineering elements identified by the subcommittee: customer, process, product, and technology.

Clearly, there is considerable overlap between the work of the SC7 and ISO 9000 standards and the IEEE software engineering standards. As we have seen, there is significant cooperation between the two organizations. Nonetheless, each set of standards still retains specific flavors, and is perceived as having certain advantages and disadvantages (this perception is due, in no small part, to individual preferences and predispositions). The two sets of standards are compared in the following section.

9.4 Comparison of the IEEE and ISO Standards

As we have seen, both the IEEE and the ISO software standards are formidable pillars in the evolution of software development as an engineering discipline. However, there are differences between the styles and approaches taken by the two organizations. This section does not advocate either of the two to the exclusion of the other as either may be the preferred solution for different organizations, projects, or environments. Following is a brief summary of some of the advantages and disadvantages of the two sets of standards.

9.4.1 Advantages of the IEEE Standards

As a complete, integrated set of standards, the four IEEE volumes cover most, if not all, areas of software development.

As we have seen, the standards are a flexible set of principles, guidelines, and recommendations that can be applied to many different software development methodologies. One of their main advantages is that they are relatively easy to use. They also include many examples. Some of the standards (e.g., Software Requirements, Std 830) provide several variants and outlines representing different ways the standard can be implemented.

Though all IEEE software engineering standards are compatible, they have been developed so that in most cases the standards can be used individually. This means that many of the IEEE standards can be applied without the need to use them in conjunction with any other standard.

There are cases where the standards' advantages can also be perceived as disadvantages. They leave a great deal of freedom to the implementor, so that in many cases each organization must define the way they are to be implemented.

Worldwide, the IEEE set of standards is not truly perceived as a international standard. Nonetheless, they are widely used, particularly in the private sector.

There is no requirement or even expectation that all of the IEEE standards need to be used for all projects. As an example, not all projects need to implement a standard for

---

[5]For detailed information on the JTC1, see http://www.iso.ch/meme/JTC1.html. For information on the US JTC1 technical advisory group (TAG), see http://www.jtc1tag.org/.

Software Acquisition (Std 1062). Development tools need not be selected using the standard for the Adoption of CASE tools (Std 1348). Standards are intended to help with the development process without getting in the way. The IEEE standards should be applied as part of an overall company policy based on one basic principle: implement whatever is found to be helpful.

Finally, a software standard, just like any other convention, is a living entity. As software engineering matures and as development methods change, standards must change too. The IEEE software engineering standards are frequently updated and adapted to the real world: the world of the software development community both in business and in government. This continuous renewal of the standards is one of the reasons why they have been so widely accepted.

9.4.2 Advantages of the ISO Standards

The ISO standards cover virtually all major areas of software development. The ISO 9000 quality standards, coupled with the JTC1 standards, the ISO/IEC programming standards, and other software related ISO standards, constitute a formidable tour de force.

The standards cover many key programming and data processing areas, such as decision tables, conventions for data symbols, and areas of third-party product evaluation such as CASE tools, and evaluation of software products.

Though a number of ISO standards were adopted (and adapted) by the IEEE, there are distinct flavors to the approach each organization has taken. In many cases the ISO standards are more detailed, more defined, and less flexible. Implementation options and alternatives are less common, and textbook type clarifications are not as extensive as those provided by the IEEE.

An important consideration when selecting a standard is how widely and where it is used. In cases of international cooperation in the development of a project, this may be an important factor. ISO standards are widely perceived as a truly international set of standards. Though they originated in Europe, the ISO standards are used throughout the world, mainly due to ISO's policy of opening its committees to members of all countries. Thus, national standards institutes feel that they are part of the process that produces the ISO standards. Consequently, ISO, both by its name and by its national membership policy, has been able to achieve a more widely acknowledged aura of international standing than the IEEE.

An appealing aspect of the ISO quality standards is the ISO 9000 certification process. It is often important to know that the adoption of a standard can provide reputable recognition. The international facet of ISO is also illustrated by the fact that in many parts of the world ISO 9000 certification is fast becoming a requirement for companies that intend to provide computer systems (and other products).

9.5 The DOD and Other Software Standards

Though ISO and the IEEE almost entirely dominate the international software standards scene, they do not rule alone. Many other prominent national, research, and commercial organizations have produced noteworthy software standards, particularly in special purpose areas not considered adequately covered by the IEEE or ISO. Many government and pseudo-government agencies have produced their own software standards to regulate the way they procure software. Leading examples are the National Aeronautics and Space Administration (NASA), the European Space Agency (ESA), and the US Department of Defense (DOD).

For several decades, the US Department of Defense (DOD) has been a pioneer in standardizing software development. The DOD, a major customer for complex and large computer systems, found it impossible to control the quality and performance of its software products without a comprehensive set of development and acquisition standards. As most of the DOD computer systems were (and are) developed by outside suppliers, this led to the development of standards, which were primarily geared toward the control and supervision of contractors.

For much of the eighties and nineties, the US DOD standards were widely accepted as the authority for defense-related software development not only in the US, but also in numerous other countries worldwide. In many cases, these standards were also adopted by governments for other strategic and critical software systems such as aerospace programs, power and energy systems, and large national data base applications.

The following sections provide an overview of the DOD and other major standards organizations throughout the world.

9.5.1 The US DOD Software Standards

The history of the US Department of Defense software standards goes back to the early seventies when the US Navy and Air Force led the way. In 1985, the DOD issued Standard 2167 (DOD 1988a) for the development of all mission critical defense software systems, superseding the widely used Navy standard 1679A and MIL standard 1644B. The intention was for 2167 to become the only official standard for the development of defense system software for the US military. Standard 2167 and its adjuncts specified how software documentation was to be produced, how reviews were to be conducted, and described methods for adapting the standard for different types of projects.

DOD standard 2167 was considered by many more of a supervision tool than a development tool. It catered more to the customer organization than to the contractor or developer (see Section 9.5.2). The standard underwent a major revision in 1988 when it became 2167A,[6] which was much easier to use than its predecessor. The standard, in its various versions, dominated defense related software development for well over a decade.

By the mid-nineties, the DOD began recognizing that the work on standards being done in the private sector was overtaking the achievements of the DOD. It was clear that it was just a question of time before the DOD would adopt commercial standards. To this end, the DOD began strengthening its working relationship with the IEEE.

As an interim step toward the transition to commercial software standards, the DOD began using a standard called MIL-STD-498, in 1994, in parallel to standard 2167A (according to which many projects were still in development). The new standard 498

---

[6]For more information on DOD 2167A, see http://tecnet0.jcte.jcs.mil:9000/htdocs/teinfo/directives/soft/ds2167a.html

provided many advantages by incorporating years of experience learned from using the predecessor standards with major defense contracts.

The final step toward the introduction of commercial standards into the DOD occurred in 1998, when STD-498 was officially cancelled, standard 2167A was retired, and IEEE/EIA 12207 (see Section 9.2.5) was adopted as the DOD's software development standard.

Standard 2167 has left a major legacy for the software development community, not only in terminology (such as *CDR* for Critical Design Review, or *tailoring* for adapting standards to specific projects), but also in demonstrating how to manage very large projects. The standard was well suited for the hierarchical *divide and conquer* approach of breaking projects up into smaller manageable sub-projects.

Standard 2167 is worth studying because of its extensive use and the significant success it achieved. It unquestionably made software development more deterministic, though many felt it did so at a considerable cost in overhead.

9.5.2 Overview of Standard 2167A

The stated objective of DOD standard 2167A is to establish uniform requirements for software development that are applicable throughout the project life cycle. The standard is used together with several companion standards for configuration control, reviews and audits, and quality management.

Standard 2167A states that it is not intended to specify or discourage the use of any particular software development method (DOD 1988a). However, the standard is heavily inclined toward phased development methodologies, such as the Waterfall paradigm. The phased approach is inherent in the required development stages, specifying that system design is to be followed by software requirements, software design, implementation, and then testing. An illustration of this approac is reproduced in Figure 9.6.

In addition to the Waterfall methodology, the standard also mentions other models that can be used with the overall 2167A general concept, such as rapid prototyping. However, many basically different methodologies, such as the spiral model, are not easily adapted to the standard (see Chapter 4).

Standard 2167A includes a comprehensive set of project document standards called Data Item Descriptions (or DIDs). The DIDs cover all phases of software development, maintenance, and the production of user reference manuals. A section called *preparation instructions* provides a large degree of freedom by permitting tailoring of the document format and the use of alternate presentation styles. The full set of DIDs is described in Table 9.8.

Reviews and audits are one of the major control tools built into standard 2167A. This is because a successful review is usually a prerequisite for proceeding to the next development stage, particularly for defense-related contracts. Thus, a review formally affirms the customer's approval of the preceding development work, which is often related to a major payment milestone. This makes it a critical event both for the customer and for the contractor. Standard 2167A's main software project reviews and the relationships between them are shown in Figure 9.7.

Project reviews are also where major project development decisions are finalized. These critical decisions are documented in the development specification documents,

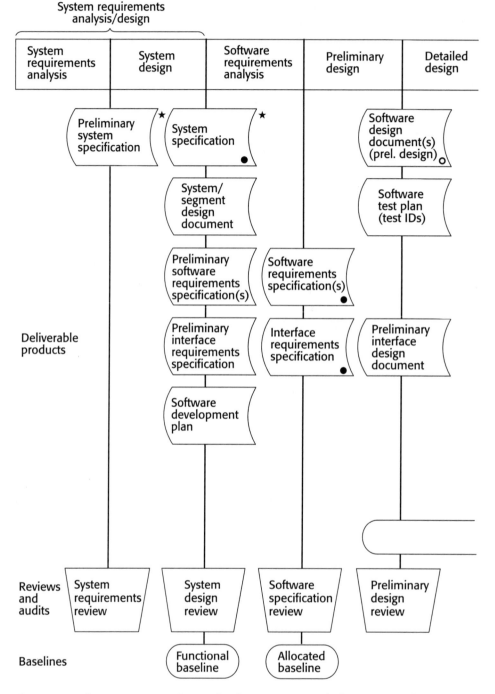

Figure 9.6   The DOD 2167A software development approach (from DOD-Std-2167A).

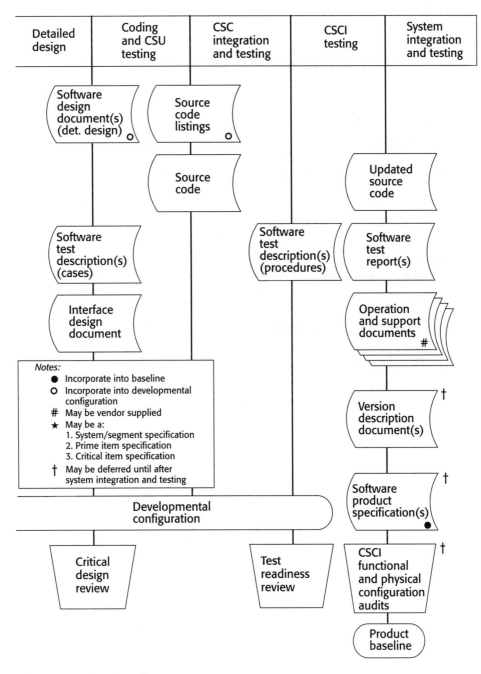

Figure 9.6   (continued)

Table 9.8   DOD Data Item Descriptions (DIDs)

DEVELOPMENT DOCUMENTATION

1. Software development plan
      System documentation
2. System/segment specification
3. System/segment design document
      Software design and requirements
4. Software requirements specification
5. Software design document
      Interface design and requirements
6. Interface requirements specification
7. Interface design document
      Version description
8. Version description document
      Test documentation
9. Software test plan
10. Software test description
11. Test report
      Release manuals
12. Computer system operator's manual
13. Software user's manual
14. Software programmer's manual
15. Firmware support manual
      Maintenance documentation and source code
16. Computer resources integrated support document
17. Software product specification

and are referred to as *baselines*.[7] The baselines then become the primary sources of reference for further development of the software product. There are three major baselines:

- The functional baseline; set at the system design review to finalize the system functional requirements (i.e., the user's view of the system).

- The allocated baseline; set at the software specification review to finalize the software requirements.

- The product baseline; this baseline is set at the conclusion of the development cycle and finalizes the development of the software product.

An additional intermediate baseline may be set at the critical design review (CDR) to finalize the design of the software product. Other intermediate baselines can be added to define the conclusion of important development activities.

---

[7]Baselines are further discussed in Chapter 11.

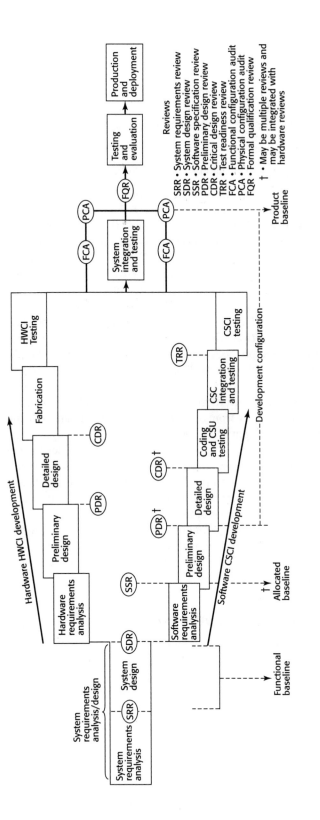

Figure 9.7 An example of DOD 2167 reviews and audits (from DOD-Std-2167A).

The three major baselines are common to all projects. The content of the baselines is not. The practice of tailoring determines how reviews, audits, and DID documents are produced for baseline reviews and how they are applied to specific software projects.

Tailoring of standard 2167A is not only encouraged, it is required. The DOD produced a guide for tailoring to be used as a reference source for adapting the standards to the type of project being developed.[8] Two basic principles apply to tailoring:

1. The tailoring process is the *deletion* of non-applicable requirements.

2. Tailoring of the standard should be carried out by the contracting agency.

The first principle means that these modifications can only include the deletion of requirements from the standard (and not changes to the requirements in the standard). The second principle means that the contractor (i.e., the developer) cannot tailor the standard without receiving permission from the contracting agency (i.e., the DOD).

One of the most frequent complaints about 2167 was that it created projects whose main product was paper and not software. In other words, a massive amount of time and effort was devoted to the generation of documentation. Subsequently, additional time needed to be devoted to keeping these documents constantly updated.

Other criticisms of the standard (see Polack 1990) included complaints that it prevented the application of iterative software development practices such as rapid prototyping and software reuse. As discussed previously, these methods can be applied to 2167A, though they may not fit naturally into the standard's general approach (see Overmyer 1990).

Standard 2167A is not easily applied to very small projects, as it requires substantial tailoring in order to reduce the overhead to a reasonable level. On the other hand, very large projects can benefit greatly from the standard, because it makes the projects more manageable and the development activities more visible.

Thus, one of the main benefits of Standard 2167 is that it provides the customer with significant visibility during all major stages of development. This can increase the likelihood of customer satisfaction with the final product. However, all this is at a price. Control, documentation, and reporting require the assignment of substantial resources, and these resources increase the cost of the development effort.

When other options are available, Standard 2167A would not be a developer's choice, as few developers would voluntarily choose its rigidity and overhead. As we have seen, it is more a customer's choice, because it supports the control of the development process from the customer's perspective.

9.5.3 Other Sources of Software Standards

As discussed previously, there are many organizations worldwide involved in the development of software and software-related standards. Chapter 10 discusses the work done at Carnegie Mellon University's Software Engineering Institute (SEI) in producing standards for measuring the maturity of a software development organization. The Project Management Institute (PMI) has produced important standards in areas of project management (see Section 10.3). The American Society for Quality Control (ASQC) has

---

[8]Tailoring guidelines can be found in DOD-HDBK-248 Guide for application and tailoring of requirements for defense material acquisition.

produced many guidelines, recommendations, and standards in the area of quality control (though the organization subscribes heavily to the ISO 9000 school). Internationally, the British Computer Society and the European Esprit consortium are just two examples[9] of several organizations that have made notable contributions in several areas of software development standards.

Many national standards institutes have also contributed significantly to the available material in software standards. In the English language, examples are the Canadian Standards Association (which uses the designation CAN), the British Standards Institution, and the Australian Standards Institute (see Thayer [1997] and Moore [1998] for extensive summaries of standards development organizations).

Though many national standards institutes have adopted ISO and IEEE standards, there are still a large number of standards being produced throughout the world. This led to a need for methods for evaluating standards.

Pfleeger has conducted research into methods for evaluating software engineering standards (Pfleeger et al. 1994). The aim was to provide a method for selecting a standard that would indeed be used. The intent of Pfleeger and his associate' research was to answer the following questions:

- What are the potential benefits of using a standard?

- Can we measure objectively the extent of any benefits that may result from its use?

- What are the related costs necessary to implement the standard?

- Do the costs exceed the benefits?

Pfleeger stipulated that "a standard is not good if there is no way of telling whether a particular organization, process, or piece of code complies with the standard." This is an important criterion for selecting standards, for it requires some method of ensuring compliance. The conclusion is that a standard has little value if there is no way of enforcing it.

Whatever the choice, many of the prevalent software standards are satisfactory if they are applied correctly. Probably the most important point to remember when selecting a suitable standard for a software project is that the development standard is a means, not an end. The standard must support the achievement of the objective: the successful development of quality software. If the standard interferes with the achievement of this objective, then it is most probably either the wrong standard or it is being applied incorrectly.

Standards are most successful when they flow with the current. Whenever possible, a standard should provide a formal framework for good practices already in existence. When existing practices are inefficient, the standard should support their replacement with practices that can easily be implemented. It will always be difficult to introduce a standard if it meets with the resistance of developers.

To summarize, software standards are like diet books: most of them work reasonably well if only you implement them. However, standards, like dieting, require discipline, which is not always easy to enforce.

---

[9]As an example, the British Computer Society has produced *TickIT*, or—as it is now called DT192 for the assessment of software development and maintenance, and the Esprit consortium has produced *Bootstrap*, a method for software process and improvement.

9.6 Summary

Though standards can be regarded as a necessary evil, their application achieves a worthwhile result: it makes software development more manageable. This does not mean that only managers benefit from the use of standards. Standards promote a degree of tidiness and conformity that assists developers in understanding work produced by others and encourages them to produce work that is understandable by others.

Two major organizations have made major contributions to software engineering standards: the US IEEE, and the International Organization for Standardization (ISO).

ISO, though based in Europe, has made a significant contribution to standards in many areas of software engineering, manufacturing, and construction. ISO has produced many standards for software development. The Institute of Electrical and Electronics Engineers (IEEE) is an international technical professional society with branches in all major countries. ISO and the IEEE cooperate regularly in the development of standards to the extent that some of their software related standards are, in effect, common.

In 1999, the IEEE issued their landmark collection of software engineering standards contained in four volumes. The collection of standards was to be a source of reference, with significant flexibility provided to the developer within the context of each standard.

An IEEE standard is either:

- A Recommended Practice
- A Guide
- A Standard
- Or, in some cases, a Supplement to a Standard

The Software Life Cycle Processes (Std 12207) is one of the more significant parts of the IEEE software engineering standards. The emergence of standard 12207 was an important milestone for organizations that are heavily involved in software procurement, such as government and pseudo-government agencies. This was particularly true for defense and military branches of government. In 1998 the US Department of Defense adopted standard 12207 as its sole standard for software acquisition.

ISO, the International Organization for Standardization, which was initially regarded as a European organization, has since the early nineties been achieving increasing worldwide acceptance. This includes the United States, where ISO is also gaining a significant following, as is demonstrated by the growing cooperation between ISO and the IEEE. ISO is probably best known for the widely used quality certification program, which is based on the ISO 9000 quality standards.

ISO membership is typically offered to national bodies that represent countries. ISO standards are then applied and adapted to the needs of each member's country, with the right to bestow ISO certification commonly given to the national standards body in each country. The American National Standards Institute (ANSI) represents the United States in the ISO membership forum.

Though a number of ISO standards were adopted (and adapted) by the IEEE, there are distinct flavors to the approach each organization has taken. In many cases the ISO standards are more detailed, more defined, and less flexible than the IEEE standards.

The US Department of Defense (DOD) has also produced many noteworthy software standards. As most of the DOD computer systems were (and are) developed by outside suppliers, the DOD has produced standard 2167, which is primarily geared toward the control and supervision of contractors. Though the standard was developed to help ensure a common basis for the development of software for the US defense establishment, it became widely accepted by government-related agencies worldwide. In 1998 the DOD converted to commercial standards and adopted IEEE/EIA 12207 as its sole standard for software development and procurement.

Many of the existing software standards are satisfactory if they are applied correctly. Probably the most important point to remember when selecting a suitable standard for a software project is that the development standard is a means, not an end. Whenever possible, a standard should provide a formal framework for good practices already in existence. When existing practices are inefficient, the standard should support their replacement with practices that can easily be implemented.

Exercises

1. Review the Aereola case study at the beginning of the chapter.

   (a) Suggest an interim solution that would avoid the problems created by the Slick Terminal development team but which would also resolve the XT2000 user interface problem within an acceptable time frame. Specify which standards would be required and what parts could be tailored out. Explain your decisions.

   (b) Given the situation produced by the development of the Slick Terminal, recommend a plan to support the 400 installations and how standards could be introduced. Consider two courses of action: (1) the improvement and long-term support of the ST, and (2) the replacement of the ST with a different solution. List the advantages and disadvantages of both courses of action and discuss the role of standards in each.

2. The DOD has assigned you as project manager to develop the software for a new inventory optimization utility that will replace one developed over a decade ago. The system receives information on specific military items, the number required of each, the locations, and the expected consumption rate of each item. The system then outputs recommended levels of inventory for each item, along with the location for each inventory stock. The new version will move from an old central computer to a client/server network and will use a modern graphic user interface.

   The system being replaced was developed according to standard 2167A and the new system will be developed according to the IEEE standards, including Standard 12207. Consider the following issue: will you rewrite all documents or will you use the 2167A documents as the basis for new documents? Explain your decision and provide a list of the ten most critical areas that will be affected by the application of the new standards. For example, will the new standards affect the retraining of maintenance engineers?

3. Compare the IEEE and ISO standards in relation to the project described in Exercise 2. Explain which standard you think is more suitable. Is there any area covered by the ISO 9000 standard that would make it preferable?

4. Prepare an outline of a requirements specification for the project described in Exercise 1. Based on the IEEE guideline for a good requirements specification, give examples for each of the nine characteristics described.

5. Tailoring is a basic feature of the DOD 2167A standard. Is tailoring as critical for the IEEE standards as it was for the 2167A standard? Explain. Prepare a proposal for a tailoring feature for the IEEE standards. How would your proposal be applied to the project in Exercise 2?

6. Review the professional literature and search the Internet for information on ISO 9000 software certification awarded to product organizations. Prepare a summary of the information you have found, including (1) the reasons organizations have pursued ISO 9000 software certification, (2) the annual increase in the number of organizations awarded certification, and (3) the preparation work required by a software organization to achieve certification.

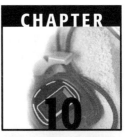
Organizational
Excellence

In previous chapters we have examined the importance of software project practices such as requirements analysis, design, configuration control, and testing. For these practices to be carried out, an appropriate organizational culture needs to exist. This includes implementing standards, training of development staff, establishing a quality assurance team, and more. Organizations need to be *built* to consistently produce good software, as the following example illustrates.

> *In the fall of 1999, a series of devastating storms hit the east coast of the United States. Among the hardest hit were the Carolinas. Houses and businesses were submerged, crops and livestock were lost, and many people lost their lives. A small software communications company had been established four years earlier and had grown to $65 million of annual revenue based on the development and maintenance of Internet web pages for large customers. All of the company's facilities were located in one office building right in the path of one of the storms. The storm completely destroyed the company's facilities and several key employees were incapacitated for several months.*
>
> *On December 31, 1999, the software company reported annual revenues of $72 million, and a profit $500,000 after taking a one-time charge of $4 million due to the storm. Everyone had expected the company to go out of business, or at best to report a loss. The most remarkable thing was that of the company's seventeen projects in process at the time of the storm, seven were completed on time,*

two were late by no more than five weeks, and the remaining eight were not due until the year 2000, and the company anticipated no delays.

How did the company survive the storm? Six months before the storm, the company had gone through an assessment to determine its maturity as a software development facility. It was classified at the highest level: level five. All of the company's projects were well documented, and backups of the documents and of the software were kept off-site. Teams were organized and trained to be able to provide assistance to one another when problems arose. Status reports documented the state of each project so that developers could take over tasks from their absent colleagues.

The company was able to survive because it was built to survive.

If you needed to select an organization to develop your project, you would seek a company like this one. But how can you tell? How do you measure the excellence of an organization?

This chapter deals with the organizational aspects of project management. It describes ways of measuring the ability of an organization to perform well and it examines the general concept of project management. The topics are covered through a discussion of the excellent work of two professional institutes: the Software Engineering Institute (SEI) and the Project Management Institute (PMI).

10.1 Why Measure?

If an organization wishes to improve its level of software development in any area, it must have a scale by which to measure itself. It must know where it is, and it must know where it wants to go. Simply stated: *If you cannot measure where you are, you cannot demonstrate that you are improving.*

Measurements, or as they are called, *metrics*, need to be collected throughout the project development process. These metrics help determine the level of a development organization by providing a means of measuring not only the organization itself, but also the software it produces. A mature organization uses its resources much more efficiently and finds it easier to overcome setbacks, such as the one experienced by the software company that survived the storm.

Though it is also true that successful software development may occasionally be accomplished without using an orderly process (like crossing Fifth Avenue in the Chapter 1 anecdote), it will be much more frequently accomplished with a good development engineering organization. And how do we know if we have a good organization? Well, *good* is measurable.

There have been several research projects to evaluate the benefits of improvement through measurement. Among the earlier, but thorough, works was one conducted by Herbsleb et al. in 1994. He reports that data from thirteen organizations was collected and analyzed to obtain information of software process improvement efforts. The organizations surveyed included Hewlett Packard, Motorola, Northrop, the US Air Force and Navy, as well as other major development organizations. The resulting measurements are summarized in Table 10.1.

Table 10.1   Summary of CMM-Based Process Improvement Survey Results

CATEGORY	RANGE	MEDIAN
Business Value (Return on Investment—ratio of measured benefits to measured costs)	4.0 to 8.8	5.0
Annual Investment per Engineer on Process Improvement	$490 to $2,004	$1,375
Annual Productivity Gain (based on LOC)	9% to 67%	35%
Annual Improvement in Early Detection of Faults	6% to 25%	22%
Annual Reduction in Development Time	15% to 23%	19%
Annual Quality Improvement (reduction in post-release defects)	10% to 94%	39%

Adapted from Herbsleb (1994)

Table 10.1 provides examples of aspects of an organization that can be measured and ways the results can be used. If we want to determine whether an organization is improving its testing process, we might examine the metric that represents improvement in the early detection of faults: is 19 percent good enough? What is our target for the next year? 25 percent? Is our cycle time reduction program performing as we expected? Is 19 percent reduction in development time good enough? What was our original target and did we meet it?

As we see, senior management of an organization can use measurement as a method for improving the quality of software produced by its development group. By setting high goals and applying objective evaluation at regular intervals, the organization's performance is gradually transformed. This is especially effective in a conservative organization.

Often, the management of the software group itself as a method of bringing about change initiates the evaluation.

In other cases, measurement of an organization is often required for contract organizations to qualify for proposal submission (see Chapter 3).

10.2 Measuring Your Software Organization

Since the early nineties, several measurement techniques have evolved for evaluating organizations, most notably ISO 9000 certification (see Chapter 9) and the SEI assessment. The assessment process is a formal procedure that requires preparation and some investment in time and resources.

Measuring a software organization's development capabilities is a means of assessing its likelihood of success in developing a project. Clearly, the organization's development capabilities are not the only factor in determining the likelihood of success, but it is undoubtedly a major factor.

This section describes the SEI Capability Maturity Model and the measurement scale by which software development organizations can be measured.

10.2.1 The SEI CMM Scale

In 1986 Carnegie Mellon University's Software Engineering Institute (SEI)[1] started working on a five-level scale for measuring what was initially referred to as *software process maturity*, and later as *software capability maturity*.

Paulk et al. (1993a and 1993b) explain the objective of SEI's Capability Maturity Model (CMM) as to "help organizations improve their software process" through "the progression from an immature unrepeatable software process to a mature, well-managed software process."

Paulk provides an excellent description of an immature versus a mature software organization:

> *Setting sensible goals for process improvement requires an understanding of the difference between immature and mature software organizations. In an immature software organization, software processes are generally improvised by practitioners and their management during the course of the project. Even if a software process has been specified, it is not rigorously followed or enforced. The immature software organization is reactionary, and managers are usually focused on solving immediate crises (better known as fire fighting). When hard deadlines are imposed, product functionality and quality are often compromised to meet the schedule.*
>
> *On the other hand, a mature software organization possess an organization-wide ability for managing software development and maintenance process. The software process is accurately communicated to both existing staff and [to] new employees, and work activities are carried out according to the planned process.*
>
> *In general, a disciplined process is consistently followed because all of the participants understand the value of doing so, and the necessary infrastructure exists to support the process.*

The five levels that measure the path from immaturity to maturity are presented in Figure 10.1, while Table 10.2 explains each of the CMM levels.

For an organization to be officially designated to have reached a CMM level, it requires a formal SEI assessment with trained assessors, using a formal set of procedures. However, trained assessors can do more than just conduct formal assessments. An organization may choose to train one of its engineers as a formal SEI assessor to guide it as it improves its process and moves up the SEI ladder.

In order for an organization to advance to a higher CMM level, it must focus on improvements in *key process* areas (see Figure 10.2). Each key process area identifies a group of related activities for reaching a set of goals that will enhance the organization's

---

[1]Information on SEI can be found at: www.sei.cmu.edu

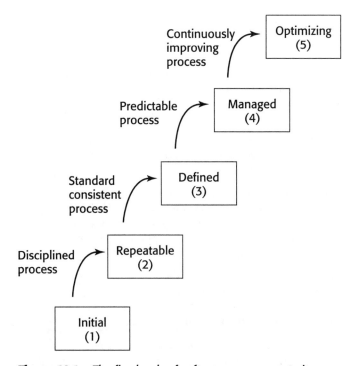

Figure 10.1 The five levels of software process maturity.
Reprinted with permission of The Software Engineering Institute.

process capability. When the goals for all key process areas for the next CMM level have been achieved, the organization is ready to attempt assessment at the next level.

A good practice is to conduct an informal assessment every six months or so, to evaluate the degree of improvement in each key process area. The main challenge is that the informal assessment must be objective. This is best achieved by taking a strict, uncompromising approach. Then, if the informal assessment confirms the attainment of the required level, the chances are that the formal assessment will do so, too.

Several surveys have been conducted both in the United States and throughout the world to try to assess informally how software organizations are distributed based on the five SEI CMM levels. Though various research papers have reported different results, most assessments agree that in the early 1990s, the large majority (80 to 90 percent) of software development organizations were at level 1. Between 6 and 12 percent were at level 2, and just a few percent were at level 3 and above. By the year 2000, organizations had improved, but the number of groups involved in software development also rose sharply. Consequently, the number of organizations at higher levels did increase but the ratio most likely did not.

There is broad agreement on the benefits to an organization in reaching levels 2 and 3. This covers both the business case and the engineering justification for moving up the SEI ladder. At level 2 (Repeatable) and above, software development can be planned and estimated with a reasonable degree of confidence, and success is not just achieved by chance. At level 3 (Defined), the process, with its standards and guidelines, is well

Table 10.2 SEI Software Process Maturity Levels Characterized

MATURITY LEVEL	LEVEL DESCRIPTION
1. Initial	The software process is characterized as ad hoc, and occasionally even chaotic. Few processes are defined, and success depends on individual effort.
2. Repeatable	Basic project management processes are established to track cost, schedule, and functionality. The necessary process discipline is in place to repeat earlier successes on projects with similar applications.
3. Defined	The defined process for both management and engineering activities is documented, standardized, and integrated into a standard software process for the organization. All projects use an approved, tailored version for the organization's standard software process for developing and maintaining software.
4. Managed	Detailed measures of the software process and product quality are collected. Both the software process and products are quantitatively understood and controlled.
5. Optimized	Continuous process improvement is enabled by quantitative feedback from the process and from piloting innovative ideas and technologies.

Reprinted with permission of The Software Engineering Institute

defined and is adhered to by all parts of the organization. This produces significant savings because similar methods and techniques are used for all projects throughout the organization.

Levels 4 (Managed) and 5 (Optimized) undoubtedly also come with a significant set of benefits to the organization. However, there has been much debate as to whether every organization actually needs these levels of excellence. As an example, the group that developed IBM's space shuttle program was at level 5, but all of IBM certainly was not.

In the early nineties, Motorola opened a new software development facility in Bangalore, India. To everyone's surprise, the Bangalore facility was formally assessed at SEI level 5. This was particularly remarkable because, at the time, other Motorola facilities were struggling to reach levels 2 and 3. Bangalore was the first Motorola facility to reach level 5. It had an advantage. It didn't know how to do things at levels 2, 3, or 4. It had started out with optimized processes already in place.

10.2.2 The Expansion of the CMM Concept

There are many variants of the SEI CMM scale, though, as an overall organization metric, the CMM scale is not the only measure available. The IEEE Standard 982 (IEEE 1999) provides a framework of Measures to Produce Reliable Software, the IEEE Stan-

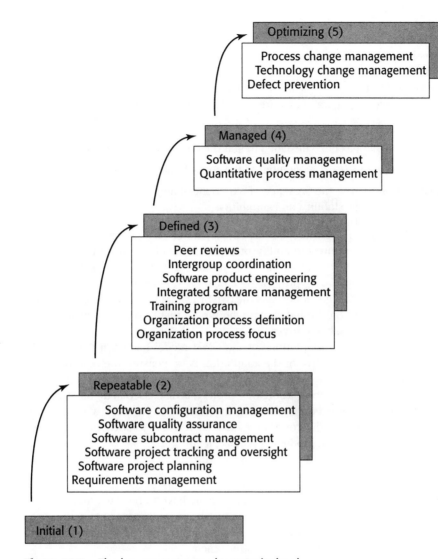

Figure 10.2   The key process areas by maturity level.
Reprinted with permission of The Software Engineering Institute.

dard 1061 (IEEE 1999) provides a basis for Software Quality Metrics Methodology, and the ISO 9126 standard (see Moore 1998) also outlines metrics for software quality. Nonetheless, the concept of measuring organizational maturity has gained significant popularity and has been expanded into other new areas.

This new work on improvement and maturity models is being performed through the SEI's two software engineering branches: the technical practices and the management practices.

Within the technical practices area, the institute develops processes and practices to help improve software development.

Within the management practices area, the institute has developed CMMs for both software development and software acquisition. It has also assisted other organizations to develop CMMs in such areas as systems engineering and integrated product development.

The CMM concept has been so successful that it has been adopted by others outside of the SEI. The concept appears to capture three basic attributes of a practical measuring tool:

- It is a *model*, that has been designed to suit the type of entity being measured.
- It measures *capability*, the potential of the entity to perform its task.
- It measures *maturity*, the presence of experienced and responsible mannerisms such as consistency, stability, and suitability.

The Project Management Institute, discussed later in this chapter, has adopted a similar maturity model to measure the ability of organizations to manage their projects (Schlichter 1999). Also, interestingly, a maturity model has been proposed to measure specification methods: how well project specification documents are created (see Fraser and Vaishnavi 1997). The model uses the five SEI CMM levels, from level 1 where documents are dependent on the individual who writes them, to level 5 where document formats are continuously improved.

One of the more practical adaptations of the CMM model has been developed by Sawyer et al. (1999). The objective of the adaptation is to measure the maturity of an organization's ability to produce software requirements. The status of requirements, as the single most important activity in a software project, is discussed in detail in the Epilogue to this book. It is in this context that the importance of Sawyer's work is recognized. If there is any one indicator that measures the capabilities of a software organization, it is the success in producing requirements.

Sawyer specifies three levels of requirements maturity:

1. **Initial.** The organization has an ad-hoc requirements process. It is difficult to estimate and control costs because requirements have to be reworked and consequently customers report poor satisfaction. The processes are not supported by planning and review procedures or documentation standards but are dependent on the skills of the individuals who produce them.

2. **Repeatable.** The organization has defined standards for requirements documents and has introduced policies and procedures for requirements management. Documents are more likely to be on time and high in quality due to the use of tools and methodologies.

3. **Defined.** The organization has a defined process model based on good practices and defined methods. There is an active process improvement plan and new methods and techniques are objectively assessed.

It seems reasonable that any organization would want to be at level 3. But Sawyer reports that most of the organizations he had surveyed were not there. How difficult, then, is it to reach the highest levels of CMM? For new organizations, the easiest way is to start off at the highest level (see the account of Motorola's India facility in the previous section). For existing organizations it is a question of commitment to change.

10.3 The General Concept of Project Management

As we have seen, there are numerous qualities that are distinctive in managing software (see Chapter 5). But for high technology projects, many aspects of planning are similar, and so are elements of quality management, documentation, and process improvement practices. One would wonder why these common elements of project management are not concentrated under a single roof.

They are. In 1969 the Project Management Institute (PMI)[2] was founded as a nonprofit professional association dedicated to furthering the interests of project management in such areas as standards, educational programs, and certification of organizations. PMI, though based in the United States, has a broad membership exceeding fifty thousand, worldwide. In an attempt to give the PMI a definite international character, the institute launched a Globalization Project in 1999. This was an important step, as it would bring the PMI closer to becoming an ISO-type international organization (see Chapter 9).

The PMI provides a broad range of services to project managers. It evaluates project management tools, it provides certification of project managers, it develops methods and practices and project management standards, the most notable of which is the Project Management Body of Knowledge.

10.3.1 The Project Management Body of Knowledge

Probably one of the most outstanding achievements of the PMI is the development of a standard designated The Project Management Body of Knowledge (PMBOK), which describes *the sum of knowledge within the framework of project management* (PMI 1996). This extensive work describes its purpose as:

> *To identify and describe that subset of the PMBOK which is generally accepted. With the term "generally accepted" meaning that the knowledge and practices described are applicable to most projects most of the time, and that there is widespread consensus about their value and usefulness.*

The work was adopted by both the American National Standards Institute (ANSI) and the IEEE as Std 1490.

The PMBOK text covers the general framework of project management, nine areas that contain relevant knowledge, and an excellent glossary of terms. At the outset, the guide describes such basic terms as *project* and *project management*:

> *A project is a temporary endeavor undertaken to create a unique product or service.*

The word *temporary* is intended to differentiate operations, which are ongoing and repetitive, from projects, which are temporary. The term *unique* means that the product or service is different in some distinguishing way from all similar projects or services.

> *Project management is the application of knowledge, skills, tools, and techniques to project activities in order to meet or exceed stakeholder needs and expectations from a project.*

[2]For more information on the PMI, see: www.pmi.org/

The text explains that meeting or exceeding stakeholder needs and expectations invariably involves balancing competing demands, such as:

- Scope, time, cost, and quality.
- Stakeholders with different needs and expectations.
- Identified requirements (needs) and unidentified requirements (expectations).

It is notable that prominence is given to the oft-forgotten consideration: expectations. However, in defining expectations as unidentified requirements, the problem becomes too technical. One tends to muse ". . . if only I had identified the requirement early!"

In reality, expectations are more multifaceted and would be better described as *unresolved requirements or preferences*. They are unresolved because there is often no agreement between the development team and the stakeholder (customer) on whether they should or should not be provided. That is the objective of a signed-off Requirements Specification: to reach such agreement. Unfortunately expectations are often related less to requirements and more to preferences. As we have seen, these issues are best resolved by customer involvement in the project development cycle (see Chapter 4).

The nine knowledge areas identified by the PMBOK are listed in Figure 10.3. The areas cover all major project management fields, many of which are directly applicable to software project management. The following overview from the PMI's PMBOK Guide describes the topics included in each of the nine areas. This overview is an excellent checklist for project managers to use to review their areas of activity.

Project Integration Management

A subset of project management that includes the processes required to ensure that the various elements of the project are properly coordinated. It consists of:

- **Project plan development:** taking the results of other planning processes and putting them into a consistent, coherent document.
- **Project plan execution:** carrying out the project plan by performing the activities included therein.
- **Overall change control:** coordinating changes across the entire project.

Project Scope Management[3]

A subset of project management that includes the processes required to ensure that the project includes all the work required, and only the work required, to complete the project successfully. It consists of:

- **Initiation:** committing the organization to begin the next phase of the project.
- **Scope planning:** developing a written scope statement as the basis for future project decisions.

---

[3]The term *scope* is often used elsewhere to describe estimation activities. In this context, the PMI uses the term scope to describe activities related to the decomposition of a project (see Chapter 4).

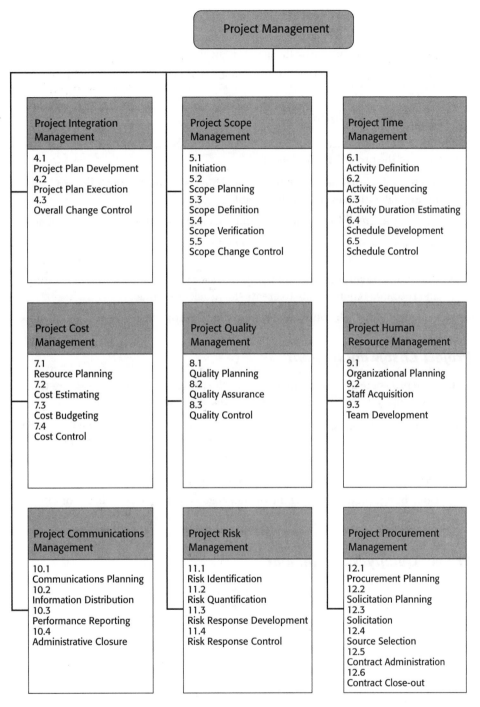

Figure 10.3   Overview of project management knowledge areas and project management processes.

Reprinted from the PMI *Guide to the Project Management Body of Knowledge* © Project Management Institute, with the permission of the PMI.

- **Scope definition:** subdividing the major project deliverables into smaller, more manageable components.
- **Scope verification:** formalizing acceptance of the project scope.
- **Scope change control:** controlling changes to project scope.

Project Time Management

A subset of project management that includes the processes required to ensure timely completion of the project. It consists of:

- **Activity definition:** identifying the specific activities that must be performed to produce the various project deliverables.
- **Activity sequencing:** identifying and documenting interactivity dependencies.
- **Activity duration estimating:** estimating the number of work periods that will be needed to complete the individual activities.
- **Schedule development:** analyzing the activity sequences, activity durations, and resource requirements to create the project schedule.
- **Schedule control:** controlling changes to the project schedule.

Project Cost Management

A subset of project management that includes the processes required to ensure that the project is completed within the approved budget. It consists of:

- **Resource planning:** determining what resources (people, equipment, materials) and what quantities of each should be used to perform project activities.
- **Cost estimating:** developing an approximation (estimate) of the costs of the resources needed to complete project activities.
- **Cost budgeting:** allocating the overall cost estimate to individual work items.
- **Cost control:** controlling changes to the project budget.

Project Quality Management

A subset of project management that includes the processes required to ensure that the project will satisfy the needs for which it was undertaken. It consists of:

- **Quality planning:** identifying which quality standards are relevant to the project and determining how to satisfy them.
- **Quality assurance:** evaluating overall project performance on a regular basis to provide confidence that the project will satisfy the relevant quality standards.
- **Quality control:** monitoring specific project results to determine if they comply with relevant quality standards and identifying ways to eliminate causes of unsatisfactory performance.

Project Human Resource Management

A subset of project management that includes the processes required to make the most effective use of the people involved with the project. It consists of:

- **Organizational planning:** identifying, documenting, and assigning project roles, responsibilities, and reporting relationships.

- **Staff acquisition:** getting the human resources that are needed assigned to and working on the project.

- **Team development:** developing individual and group skills to enhance project performance.

Project Communications Management

A subset of project management that includes the processes required to ensure timely and appropriate generation, collection, dissemination, storage, and ultimate disposition of project information. It consists of:

- **Communications planning:** determining the information and communications needs of the stakeholders: who needs what information, when will they need it, and how will it be given to them.

- **Information distribution:** making needed information available to project stakeholders in a timely manner.

- **Performance reporting:** collecting and disseminating performance information. This includes status reporting, progress measurement, and forecasting.

- **Administrative closure:** generating, gathering, and disseminating information to formalize phase or project completion.

Project Risk Management

A subset of project management that includes the processes concerned with identifying, analyzing, and responding to project risk. It consists of:

- **Risk identification:** determining which risks are likely to affect the project and documenting the characteristics of each.

- **Risk quantification:** evaluation risks and risk interactions to assess the range of possible project outcomes.

- **Risk response development:** defining enhancement steps for opportunities and responses to threats.

- **Risk response control:** responding to changes in risk over the course of the project.

Project Procurement Management

A subset of project management that includes the processes required to acquire goods and services from outside the performing organization. It consists of:

- **Procurement planning:** determining what to procure and when.

- **Solicitation planning:** documenting product requirements and identifying potential sources.

- **Solicitation:** obtaining quotations, bids, offers, or proposals as appropriate.

- **Source selection:** choosing from among potential sellers.

- **Contract administration:** managing the relationship with the seller.

- **Contract close-out:** completion and settlement of the contract, including resolution of any open items.

The terminology used in describing the topics covered by the PMBOK's nine knowledge areas is not always the same as that used by the IEEE, or ISO. The PMI, IEEE, and ISO glossaries are helpful when the interpretation of a term appears to be unclear.

The IEEE has also produced a standard for project management plans, specific to software—Std 1058 (IEEE 1999). This document does not rival the PMBOK but rather complements it. The IEEE document is more of a standard in the traditional sense; it defines the content of a formal software project management plan, and provides guidelines on how it should be prepared and maintained. The IEEE's definition of a software project is:

> *The set of work activities, both technical and managerial, required to satisfy the terms and conditions of a project agreement.*

The lengthy definition continues, describing the need for project start and end dates, and other critical ingredients such as budget and schedule, and concludes with a description of a project's scope and context.

Although the IEEE's definition is not totally in line with the PMI definition, it broadly captures both the essence and the spirit of software project management. The PMI definition may be somewhat more curt and philosophical. The common ground of both approaches is that project management is intended to meet the requirements or needs of the customer. Ultimately, that is what counts.

10.3.2 The PMI Maturity Model

The original SEI CMM model measured the ability of an organization to develop software. As we have seen, the general idea of measuring an organization's capabilities caught on, and other CMM models were proposed. PMI also envisions a capabilities model to measure an organization's ability to manage projects.

The evolution of the PM CMM is in process. A PMI focus group[4] has identified the following capabilities that contribute to effective organizational project management (see Schlichter 1999):

---

[4]The focus group was a part of PMI's Standards Program Work Session held in 1998.

- Project Management Methodologies and Processes
    - Defined existence of PM methodologies and processes
    - Recognition of best practices in the profession
    - Requirements for project status/forecast reporting
    - Internal project reviews
    - Approval/review process for major project changes
    - Quality control of methodologies and processes
    - Focal sponsorship for the organizational practices
- Human Resource Factors
    - Development of potential project managers
    - Project management training
    - Cross-training
    - Communications approaches for projects
    - Integrated product teams
    - Definition of team roles
    - Motivation, team building, leadership
    - Conflict management, issue resolution
    - Management of project time commitments by staff; stress management
- Organizational Support Structure for Projects
    - Technical, procurement, subcontractors, quality assurance, manufacturing, project accounting, contract administration
    - Multiproject staffing, assessment of multiproject needs, provision of the right people at the right time (until no longer needed)
    - Project support office
    - Project management and related system/tools, including selection, implementation, upgrades, and maintenance centers of excellence for practices and use of tools
- Alignment of Projects to Business Strategy
    - Project fit to strategic plans
    - PM involvement in business plans
    - Future value to technologies, competencies, and skills
    - Organizational fit, project risk, technical capability
    - Application of existing versus new technologies
    - Project sponsorship by internal management
    - Multiproject interactions and interfaces, assessments, and related decisions
    - Project priorities, decisions on organization resource/funding assignments
    - Management of project life cycles, including cancelling/closure
- Organizational Learning
    - Continuous improvement process implementation
    - Evaluation and feedback from project teams

- Post-project phase debriefs and feedback practices
- Changes to general organization systems/procedures to support improvements in PM capabilities
- Periodic review of PM effectiveness
- Reliability of status summaries and forecasts
- Metrics for project management effectiveness
- Standardization, productive and unproductive application
- Lessons learned and feedback into all capability areas

This is undoubtedly a broad mixed bag of PM capabilities, but it is also an excellent checklist for any organization. The list is a great place to start when looking for areas to improve.

10.3.3 The Context of Project Management

As we have seen, the PMI's Body of Knowledge concentrates on that which is common: practices which are applicable to most projects most of the time. Clearly the institute's work is not only applicable but also very beneficial to software project management. It is this that has led to its adoption by the IEEE software engineering standards group.

The IEEE's software engineering standards classifies the PMBOK Guide as an *umbrella* standard, and positions it among its general processes alongside its systems-level standards and its software project management plans standard. It is a high level guide written in a spirit similar to that found in the IEEE guides and using an almost textbook-like style.

The correct context of the PMBOK Guide and the IEEE standards for software PM plans is as follows: Project Management is a specialization of management in general. Software project management is a specialization of Project Management (see Figure 10.4).

Lastly, a note about the PMI's somewhat unique use of the term *stakeholder*. In most cases, the term has been interpreted here to correspond to the term customers, as described in Chapter 10. However, in the interest of accuracy, the PMI's definition follows:

Figure 10.4   Context of Software Project Management.

Project stakeholders are individuals and addition to the customer, organizations who are actively involved in the project, or whose interests may be positively, or negatively affected as a result of project completion.

One is almost tempted to add: or as a result of project non-completion.

10.4 Summary

The better a software organization, the greater the likelihood that it will produce good software. Hence, the improvement in our ability to produce successful software is represented by the improvement in the level of our software development organization.

Measuring a software organization's development capabilities produces a means of assessing its likelihood of success in developing a project. In 1986, Carnegie Mellon University's Software Engineering Institute (SEI) started working on a five-level scale for measuring what they referred to as the software capability maturity of a development organization. This scale provides the organization with the means of measuring improvement, and of determining its level of maturity in relation to other software development organizations. The five levels of the Capability Maturity Model (CMM) are:

1. Initial (lowest level)
2. Repeatable
3. Defined
4. Managed
5. Optimized (highest level)

For an organization to be officially designated to have reached a CMM level, it takes a formal SEI assessment with trained assessors, using a formal set of procedures. In order for an organization to advance to a higher CMM level, it must focus on improvements in *key process* areas. Each key process area identifies a group of related activities for reaching a set of goals that will enhance the organization's process capability. When the goals for all key process areas for the next CMM level have been achieved, the organization is ready to attempt assessment at the next level.

Probably one of the most outstanding achievements of the PMI is the development of a standard designated The Project Management Body of Knowledge (PMBOK), which describes *the sum of knowledge within the framework of project management.* The work was adopted by both the American National Standards Institute (ANSI) and the IEEE as Std 1490. The PMBOK text covers the general framework of project management, nine areas that contain relevant knowledge. They are:

- Project Integration Management
- Project Scope Management
- Project Time Management
- Project Cost Management
- Project Quality Management
- Project Human Resource Management

- Project Communications Management

- Project Risk Management

- Project Procurement Management

The correct context of the PMBOK Guide and the IEEE standards for software PM plans is as follows: Project Management is a specialization of management in general. Software project management is a specialization of Project Management.

If an organization wishes to improve its level of software development in any area, it must have a scale by which to measure itself. It must know where it is, and it must know where it wants to go. It is a well known fact that: *If you cannot measure where you are, you cannot demonstrate that you are improving.*

Exercises

1. Propose a CMM-type model for executive management. How would the five levels of CMM be applied to the measurement of the performance of a senior executive?

   Describe each level in detail, and provide key process areas for improvement at each level.

   What would the context of the Executive CMM model be in relation to the software related CMM? Explain.

2. Interpage Inc. is a company in South Carolina that develops and maintains Internet web pages for large customers. Review the story of Interpage in the introduction to this chapter. Describe the main elements of Interpage's project management plans that helped it survive the storm.

   Review the IEEE Standard 1058 for software project management plans. Which parts of the standard cover the areas that were most critical to Interpage's survival. Write an abridged software project management plan, based on IEEE Std. 1058, that contains only the sections that were most critical for Interpage's survival.

3. Review the PM Body of Knowledge Guide (it is available on the Internet). Refer to Appendix E, Application Area Extensions. Propose three areas into which the PMBOK could be extended, and justify why these extensions are needed. Select one proposed extension, and describe it in detail.

4. Class debate: How can new organizations succeed if maturity is necessary for success? Are new development organizations inevitably not mature (immature)?

   If a CMM model measures the *likelihood* for success, what happens if a level 5 organization fails? Does it negate the CMM theory? What does experience show?

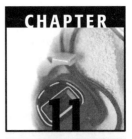

Project Scheduling

Any project can be completed, given an infinite amount of time and resources. Realistically, the amount of time available for project development is always finite. In fact, in most cases it is less than the project manager considers sufficient. Few projects are completed ahead of time; many projects overrun their schedule.

The following case history underscores some of the main elements of scheduling.

In the late 1970s, a large California-based defense contractor was developing a complex air defense system for the military. After the integration phase began, and for the following period of about six months, all efforts were directed toward the first major system test, to be conducted together with an East Coast subcontractor.

The subcontractor was to send up a plane that would communicate with the subcontractor's computer system on the East Coast, and that system in turn would communicate with the main contractor's test site in California. Many of the basic system functions were to be tried out during this costly system test. As the time approached for the test, every member of the team was under extreme pressure to assure that the test would be successful.

On the designated day for the test, all project personnel arrived at work early in the morning to ensure that the equipment was functioning correctly. The East Coast subcontractor sent up the plane, and the system was activated.

The test failed. Not only did it fail, in fact it never began. The reason was that no one had remembered to order dedicated communication lines from the phone company between the East Coast subcontractor's site and the California test site.

All attempts by management to have the phone company urgently install the lines on the day of the test failed because there just wasn't enough time. The total failure of the system test cost the contractor dearly, and probably cost some managers their jobs.

This anecdote underscores many of the problems of project planning and scheduling. Such errors may occur because of pressure of time due to unrealistic schedules, or because of poor assignment of personnel within the project organization.

Projects are almost always developed under pressure of time. There is pressure to "get going," and pressure to "show us something that works," and of course there is pressure to get the system installed and working. Probably the most common time-related pressure is "get that darned bug fixed quickly!" This kind of pressure can cause havoc with the project development plan, tempting the project manager to seek the quick fix or the short cut. And it is short cuts that lead to the kind of costly errors described above.

This chapter discusses methods for preparing a realistic schedule that project managers and the development team can reasonably commit to. However, preparing a realistic schedule is not enough; the schedule needs to be approved by senior management. Often, the project manager and senior management will not agree about the amount of time needed to develop the project. Gaining approval for a reasonable schedule, and other related problems, are also discussed later in the chapter.

11.1 The Project Development Plan

The project schedule is one of the most critical parts of the project development plan. The plan includes not only the scheduling of development activities, but also the scheduling of project resources, particularly people. This chapter discusses scheduling within the context of the project development plan.

The project plan is one of the first formal documents produced by the project team. This document describes:

- How the project will be developed

- What resources will be required

- How these resources will be used

The project development plan ensures that the development of the project is well charted before the main development activities begin. In addition to the basic development schedule, the plan addresses such issues as:

- The timely provision of equipment and tools so that they are available to developers when needed

- The availability of staff to perform the development tasks in accordance with the schedule

- Provision of contingency plans in the event that project risks materialize

- The designation of duties within the development team, and the assignment of these duties to the team members

The contents of the project development plan may be adapted to the size of the project; the plan may be a large document or just a few pages. Table 11.1 presents an outline of some of the subjects covered in the project development plan.

Not all of the subjects in Table 11.1 are applicable to all projects. For example, many projects do not administer their own budget. The interface with external sources is another area not applicable to all projects. The term external sources covers such activities as interfacing with subcontractors and vendors; and not all projects have external sources.

Many standards have been produced for the project development plan. The formal structure of the project development plan document differs, depending on the actual documentation standard used. For example, the IEEE standard 1058 (IEEE 1999) describes what is referred to as the software project management plan, which is essentially the same as the project development plan. The Project Management Institute

Table 11.1   Software Project Development Plan Items

1. System overview
2. Software development management
    Project organization and resources
    Development facilities
    Project organizational structure
    Personnel
3. Schedule and milestones
    Scheduled activities
    Milestones and baselines
    Activity network diagrams
    System component source
    Budget administration
      Milestone payments
      Major budgetary expenditures
      Expenditure authorization procedure
4. Risk analysis
5. Security
6. Interface with external sources
7. Procedure for formal reviews
8. Corrective action process
9. Problem change report
10. Software engineering
    Standards and procedures
    Development methodology
    Development resources
    Personnel—qualifications and function
11. Testing procedure
12. Software configuration management
13. Software quality assurance

describes in great detail the content of a general project management plan, not geared specifically to software (see Chapter 10).

This standard, too, provides the option of including configuration management and quality assurance plans, or of describing them in separate documents.

The project development plan should be prepared as a stand-alone document, in the sense that it should be read and understood without the need to refer to other documents. A general overview of the project is therefore usually included in the first section of the document.

References for additional detail, of course, should always be provided, including pointers to such documents as the project contract, the concept document, or the market research analysis.

The software development management section, which describes the organization and resources that will be used to develop the product, should always be included. The management section discusses how the facilities will be organized to support the development effort. This is one of the sections that provide much of the detail needed to prepare the heart of the development plan, namely the development schedule. The schedule provides answers to two basic planning questions: *what* and *when*, while much of the remaining sections discuss *how*.

The discussion in the *how* sections provides information on how the project will be organized, how risks will be handled, how reviews will be conducted, how standards will be applied, what development methodologies will be used, and how the product will be tested.

It is usually best to leave the completion of the schedule section (Section 3 in Table 11.1) for last. The schedule, being dependent on most of the other sections, is the most sensitive part of the development plan. After a first draft of the development plan is ready, an initial development schedule can then be prepared. As we shall see, the schedule will then be further refined as the development plan goes through progressive iterations.

11.2 Scheduled Activities and Milestones

A project development schedule is a list of activities and their expected time of implementation. There are many ways of representing a schedule: lists of activities, diagrams, graphs, etc. The most common methods of schedule representation are PERT network diagrams, Gantt charts, and lists of milestones (these methods are described later).

All methods of schedule representation should essentially provide the same basic information: activities and time of implementation. Therefore, the first step in preparing a schedule is the determination of the project activities.

As we have seen, the project development schedule is one of the most important elements of the project development plan, and this plan is required at the initial stages of the project. Unfortunately, a full list of activities is usually not available until well into the design phase.

Therefore, an initial version of the project schedule usually starts with a list of high level activities, and this initial schedule is repeatedly refined as more information becomes available. A full discussion of methods of refining the list of work activities appears in Chapter 6.

An initial schedule may contain only the basic phases of the software development cycle (requirements specification, design, implementation, etc.). This first version of the schedule is often produced together with the initial project estimates before the project is officially launched. As more detail becomes available, better estimates are produced and the schedule becomes more refined and more reliable. Project estimates are discussed in detail in Chapter 12.

11.2.1 The Scheduled Activity List

As we have seen, scheduling first requires a list of project activities. This list is often developed in conjunction with the work breakdown structure (WBS) table. The WBS breaks down all project activities to a much lower level, called *work tasks*. The WBS provides a method for monitoring actual work being performed by the development team and is especially useful for assigning low level work tasks to project personnel. The WBS is further discussed in Chapter 6.

Table 11.2 contains an example of part of a project schedule list of activities. The table refers to two major activities: integration and testing.

A schedule list of activities contains the following information:

1. *Activity ID*. This is a meaningful decimal identification, similar to the WBS task designation, and provides a method of identifying each activity according to the various work assignment classifications (see Figure 6.6).

2. *Activity name*. This is similar to numerical identification, and is used as a convenient activity reference.

3. *Description*. This is a short description of the activity.

4. *Start date*. This refers to the date the activity is scheduled to begin.

5. *Completion date*. This refers to the date the activity is scheduled to be completed.

6. *Dependencies*. This refers to other activities on which this activity is dependent. This activity cannot be completed until the dependency activities are completed.

7. *Assignment/responsibility*. This identifies the person who has been assigned responsibility for this activity.

All scheduled project activities are listed together with the above information. At this stage it is important to ensure that activities do not overlap; this means that no two high level activities include the same low level activity. Finally, the schedule list is sorted according to the start date of the activities. This procedure provides the most basic form of a project schedule.

11.2.2 Major Milestones and Baselines

Clearly, not all activities are of equal importance. Some activities signify major events in the project development cycle. The completion of the requirements specification is a major milestone, as is the completion of the design specification. Other major events may include the completion of a prototype or the installation of the first beta test system. Of course, the most important project event is the conclusion of the project, often

Table 11.2 Sample Activity List

ACTIVITY ID	ACTIVITY NAME	DESCRIPTION	START DATE	END DATE	DEPENDENCIES	ASSIGNMENT RESPONSIBILITY
5	Integration	System software and hardware integration				
5.1	Equipment	Procurement of integration equipment	Jan 10	Jan 31	5.3	J. Smith
5.2	Installation	Set up installation site	Jan 20	Feb 20	5.1	H. Baker
5.3	Integration plan	Prepare integration plan	Jan 1	Jan 28		R. Brown
5.4	Phase 1	Initial S/W integration phase	Feb 22	Mar 20	5.1	L. King
5.5	Demo 1	Initial integration milestone	Mar 21	Mar 22	5.4	L. King
5.6	Phase 2	S/W±H/W integration phase	Mar 15	Apr 30	5.4	L. King & J. Black
5.7	Demo 2	S/W±H/W integration milestone	May 1	May 2	5.6, 5.5	L. King & J. Black
5.8	Phase 3	Full system integration	Apr 20	May 31	5.6	L. King
5.9	Demo 3	Full system integration milestone	Jun 1	Jun 2	5.8, 5.7	L. King

ACTIVITY ID	ACTIVITY NAME	DESCRIPTION	START DATE	END DATE	DEPENDENCIES	ASSIGNMENT RESPONSIBILITY
6	Testing	System alpha, beta, and acceptance testing				
6.1	Test team	Establish test team	Apr 15	Apr 30		R. Brown
6.2	Test cases	Prepare testing proce-dures and test cases	May 1	May 31	6.1	R. Brown & B. Knight
6.3	Alpha equipment	Alpha site equipment procurement	Apr 1	Apr 30		J. Smith
6.4	Alpha installation	Install alpha site system	May 1	May 15	6.3	H. Baker
6.5	Alpha testing	Full functional system test at alpha site	May 15	Jun 30	6.2, 6.4	B. Knight & L. King
6.6	Beta installation	Install alpha equipment at beta site	Jul 1	Jul 5	6.5	H. Baker
6.7	Beta testing	Live system run in at beta site	Jul 6	Jul 31	6.6	B. Knight & L. King
6.8	TRR	Test readiness review for acceptance test	Jul 30	Jul 31	6.7	L. King
6.9	ATP	Acceptance test procedure to complete system development	Aug 1	Aug 4	6.8	L. King & R. Brown
6.10	Test report	Prepare ATP test reports	Aug 5	Aug 8	6.9	J. White

signified by the successful completion of the acceptance tests. These important events warrant special attention, and are recorded in a separate list of major project milestones.

Major project milestones often gain added importance due to their linkage to other events, such as development budget payments. Fixed price project payments are often linked by the customer to the successful completion of certain agreed milestones (see Chapter 3). This produces significant pressure on the project manager to complete the milestone on time (which undoubtedly was the customer's intention). However, schedules, just like any other part of the development plan, need to be updated periodically, and it is often in the project's best interest to modify the milestone completion dates, though the customer may not always see it this way. Changing completion dates usually means changing the project budget.

In-house projects often have a customer who is part of the same organization as the developer. In such cases, the customer may be the marketing department, or a group of users within the company (this is discussed in detail later). Budgetary modifications are then authorized by a common management authority that may be sensitive to the needs of both the in-house customer and the project development team.

Milestones are used not only as points of payment, but also for the measurement of progress on the project and for determining baselines.

If milestones have been described as major project events, then baselines can be described as major milestones. The IEEE definition for the term *baseline* includes the phrase "a formally agreed specification that then serves as the basis for further development." Baselines have important significance in the large contracts (especially contracts), where they refer to critical points during software development when major decisions are finalized. In such cases the approval procedures for software project baselines must be well formalized and the procedure for major decision making must also be clearly defined.

Often the first project baseline is the approved system requirements specification document, called the *functional baseline*. This document is the basis for all design and implementation, and in particular it is the basis for system testing and acceptance. Therefore, it is usually regarded as the most important project baseline. Examples of other project baselines are the system design and often the system prototype if it is approved as a basis for further project development (see Chapter 9).

11.3 Gantt Charts

Long before the advent of computers, Henry L. Gantt lent his name to a simple and very useful graphical representation of a project development schedule. The Gantt chart shows almost all of the information contained in the schedule activity list, but in a much more digestible way. The schedule information is more easily grasped and understood, and the activities can be easily compared. The Gantt chart enables us to see, at any given time, which activities should be occurring in the project.

Figure 11.1 is a typical example of a Gantt chart. The symbols used in the chart are widely accepted, though not standardized. The inverted triangle, for example, is commonly used to represent a significant event, such as a major milestone.

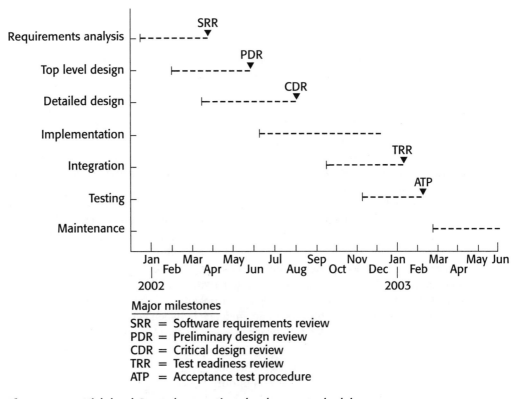

Figure 11.1 High level Gantt chart—project development schedule.

The Gantt chart in Figure 11.1 demonstrates the ease with which important schedule information can be quickly perceived. We can immediately see that, except for the maintenance phase, all phases overlap, and that from November to mid-December 2002 three high level activities overlap.

More detailed charts can also include the names of the engineers assigned to each activity, and the equipment that will be needed for each activity. This information can be added next to the activity time lines in the graph, or as an inserted reference table (similar to the list of major milestones in Figure 11.1). Some variations of the Gantt chart do include this type of information on the chart, but this can cause clutter, which is contrary to the main objective of the chart: to enable important schedule information to be grasped quickly.

It is also important to understand what Gantt charts do not provide. In a Gantt chart, it is difficult to provide information on the amount of resources required to complete each activity. A common mistake is to conclude that if five engineers are assigned to integration, and the integration activity starts in mid-September 2002 and ends in mid-January 2003 (four months), then integration requires 20 work months. In fact, integration may start with only one engineer, with one more joining during the second month, and the remaining three engineers joining during the third month. The integration team may then be reduced to three engineers during the fourth integration month.

Figure 11.1 includes only seven activities. As more detail becomes available, more lower level activities can be included on the chart. When the chart has more activities than it can reasonably carry (a subjective decision), additional charts may be added. For example, the design activity can be presented on a separate Gantt chart (see Figure 11.2).

Figure 11.2 presents both high and low level activities. For example, "Integrate phase I model" contains three low-level activities: "Integrate executive," "Integrate operating system," and "Integrate user interface." This provides the continuity link between the detailed Gantt chart (Figure 11.2) and the higher level chart (Figure 11.1).

Note that each period of one month in Figure 11.2 has been divided into four weeks. Though not completely accurate, this is a common approximation, used also in estimation (see Chapter 12), and apart from being convenient, it also provides some slack for minor scheduling adjustments.

Similar detailed Gantt charts can be prepared for each of the major project development phases. Nondevelopment activities will also appear on the Gantt chart, such as "Procurement of development tools," or "Market research." This is particularly useful when certain development activities are dependent on other nondevelopment activities, such as the procurement of development tools (e.g., a performance analyzer) that need to be completed before the implementation activities can begin. In cases where such dependent relationships may have been overlooked, they will often emerge from a review of the Gantt chart. This type of dependence between activities is best presented in another type of chart, called a *Network precedence chart* or a PERT *chart*.

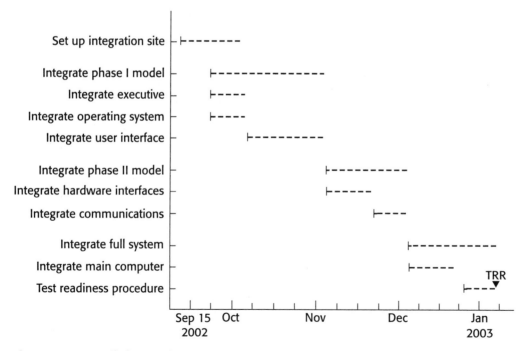

Figure 11.2   Detailed Gantt chart—integration schedule.

11.4 PERT Charts and the Critical Path

The air defense anecdote related at the beginning of this chapter provides an excellent example of the dependence between scheduled activities. Dependence exists when one activity cannot be completed unless another activity is completed. A graphical technique called *precedence network charts* can provide answers to two of the problems related in the anecdote: the need to identify dependencies, and the need to ensure that responsibility for each activity has been assigned.

The program evaluation and review technique (PERT)[1] uses a precedence network to plan project activities and to monitor their performance effectively. Like Gantt charts, there are many variations of PERT. The basic conventional PERT technique describes a network with nodes as events and activities as connections.

Each activity is associated with two related events, its start and its end. The end node of an activity can coincide with the beginning node of a second activity when the completion of the second is dependent on the completion of the first. This means that an activity can only be completed when all other activities ending in its start node have been completed.

Figure 11.3 presents an example of a PERT network chart representing the flow of project activities from start to end. Each event is represented by a numbered circle. The network begins with the start event, called the source node, and concludes with the end event, called the sink node. Each connecting line represents a project activity. Activity $A_{i,j}$ describes the activity that begins at event i and ends at event j. Attribute $D_{i,j}$ represents the amount of time that is scheduled to elapse between the beginning and end of activity $A_{i,j}$.

An important aspect of the PERT chart method is the concept of parallel activities. Each event node branches into a number of activities that can be performed in parallel. In Fig. 11.3, activities $A_{1,2}$, $A_{1,3}$, and $A_{1,4}$ can be performed in parallel. However, each of activities $A_{s,1}$ and $A_{10,E}$ cannot be performed in parallel with any other activity. We can also see from the chart that activity $A_{3,6}$ can be performed in parallel with either activity $A_{5,8}$ or activity $A_{8,10}$, but not both. Similarly, at any given time activity $A_{3,6}$ can be performed in parallel with only one of the following three activities: $A_{1,4}$, $A_{4,7}$, and $A_{7,9}$.

Figure 11.4 is an example of a PERT chart that includes numerical duration attributes. We can see from the chart that activity $A_{s,1}$ is scheduled to continue for five units of time (possibly weeks). When schedules need to be shortened, these duration values can be most helpful to the project manager. The duration values can assist in locating areas where additional effort is best directed.

11.4.1 The Critical Path

Close scrutiny of project development schedules is common, and should be expected by project managers. Large projects have many interested parties involved in scheduling, such as corporate management, the customer, subcontractors, vendors, users, the marketing department, and so forth. One of the most frequent criticisms refers to the need

---

[1]A detailed description of the PERT technique appears in Moder et al. (1995). See also: http://www.criticaltools.com/PERTMAIN.htm

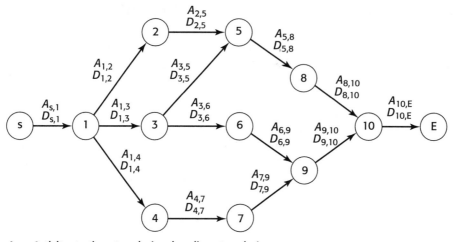

$A_{i,j}$ = Activity starting at node i and ending at node j
$D_{i,j}$ = Duration of activity $A_{i,j}$

Figure 11.3 A typical PERT chart.

to shorten the schedule. A common error on the part of the project manager is to assume that wherever additional effort is directed, it will shorten the schedule. However, in some cases, shortening activities will have absolutely no impact on the overall schedule duration.

In order to examine this phenomenon, we must first understand that in all non-trivial networks there are many ways of moving from the source node to the sink node. For example, in Figure 11.4 a possible path runs from node S to 1 to 3 to 6 to 9 to 10 to E.

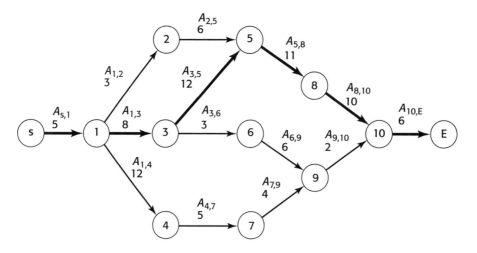

Figure 11.4 PERT chart showing the critical path.

Table 11.3 All Possible Paths from S to E (based on Figure 11.4)

PATH	LENGTH	CRITICAL PATH
1. S,1,2,5,8,10,E	41	
2. S,1,3,5,8,10,E	52	✓
3. S,1,3,6,9,10,E	30	
4. S,1,4,7,9,10,E	34	

Another possible path runs from node S to 1 to 2 to 5 to 8 to 10 to E. Each path can be characterized by a number that represents the total duration of the path, calculated by summing the durations for all activities along the path.

Table 11.3 contains a list of all possible paths from node S to node E in the PERT chart in Figure 11.4, together with the length of each path. Path 2 is the longest, 52 weeks. The longest path is referred to as the critical path, and it determines the duration of the project.

By shortening the duration of an activity along the critical path, we can usually shorten the duration of the whole project. There are a few extreme cases in which this will not occur, notably when there are two critical paths. However, one thing is certain: shortening an activity that is not on the critical path will not shorten the length of the whole project.

11.4.2 PERT Packages and Enhancements

Some enhanced versions of the PERT chart support additional planning activities, such as personnel assignment, resource allocation, and cost analysis. The chart can then draw attention to situations in which personnel are assigned more responsibilities than they can handle, or where allocation of resources conflicts.

An interesting adaptation of PERT, called flowgraph representation, which was developed by Riggs and Jones (1990), uses precedence networks to perform project life cycle cost analysis. The flowgraph technique analyzes project costs based on relationships between quantities, unit cost, time variables, staffing costs and learning, etc., all of which are represented on the PERT-like chart.

The flowgraph representation technique places a significant amount of information on the network graph. This information, just like the basic PERT information, must be kept constantly updated. A small change to a large PERT chart can require the complete redrawing of the chart and the recalculation of the critical path. The resulting tedium does not promote much enthusiasm for keeping the chart updated. For this reason, many computerized PERT utilities have been developed.

PERT software packages have been available for many years, but it is only during the past few years that good professional PERT computer packages have become available. These packages take much of the tedium out of the preparation of PERT charts, and also come with additional features such as various planning analyzers for activity assignment, "what if" scenarios and resource allocation. Computer utilities have been developed to perform flowgraph representation analysis that produces scheduled costs for major project activities.[2] These utilities have proven to be invaluable for project managers and release managers from laborious desk work, providing them with more time to actively manage the project.

11.5 Scheduling Human Resources

This section deals with the *scheduling* side of staffing and human resource management. The motivation and management of people is discussed in Chapter 5.

Essentially, the development team is a resource, just as development equipment is a resource. However, scheduling people is not the same as scheduling equipment. The project manager's most important and most valuable project resource is the development team, and therefore special attention must be given to the scheduling of the activities of team members. As the number of project activities varies, so the size of the development team varies throughout the project development life cycle. The team's organizational structure becomes more important as the size of the team grows.

11.5.1 The Development Team Size

The size of the development team is influenced not only by the number of activities, but also by the intensity of the activities. Some activities are intense at the beginning of the project and decline toward the end, and vice versa. For example, planning requires more human resources at the beginning of the project and fewer at the end, while configuration control requires fewer at the beginning and more at the end.

Figure 11.5 demonstrates this relationship between planning and management. As the intensity of planning decreases, fewer people will be required for this activity. Similarly, as the intensity of control increases, more people will be required for such activities as testing, quality assurance, and configuration management.

The team size often varies according to the familiar bell shaped normal distribution. This is demonstrated in Figure 11.6(*a*), which describes a small development team at the start of the project, a large development team during the mid-project phases, and then again a small team at the end of the project.

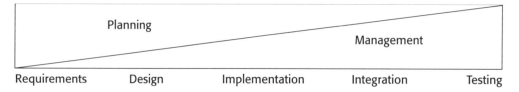

Figure 11.5   The relationship between planning and people management.

---

[2]Riggs and Jones (1990), in their paper on project cost analysis, describe the graphical economic cost analysis technique (GECAT) computer program. See also: http://www.criticaltools.com/PERTMAIN.htm

At either end of the development cycle, when the team size is small, many of the organizational functions are unnecessary. In many cases, team structures only become necessary toward the end of the requirements phase. As the project nears completion, teams may be disbanded, and one or two team members may assume responsibility for the development work of a whole team.

In some cases, Figure 11.6(a) may not represent the scheduling of the development team with sufficient accuracy. Figure 11.6(b) presents an asymmetric skewed curve similar to the normal distribution that describes a slower staffing rate at the start of the project and a more rapidly decreasing staff size toward the end. This is often typical of complex projects when the integration and test phases require a considerable effort. In fact, the skewed curve is generally more representative of staff scheduling than the normal curve, though the degree of inclination of the curve varies.

The way in which the maintenance phase is regarded also impacts the staffing curve. The staffing curve will look different if the maintenance phase is considered part of the

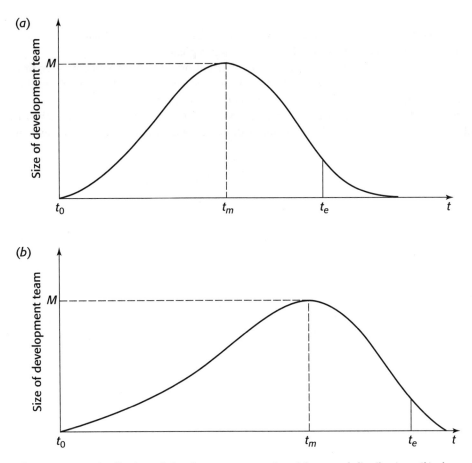

Figure 11.6 Distribution of development team size: (a) normal distribution; (b) skewed distribution. M = maximum size of development team, t_0 = start of project, t_m = maximum staffing point, t_e = end of project.

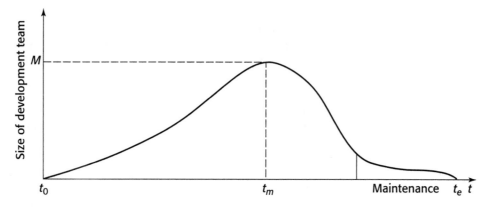

Figure 11.7   Distribution of team size, including maintenance. M = maximum size of development team, t_0 = start of project, t_m = maximum staffing point, t_e = end of project.

development cycle. The resulting curve, shown in Figure 11.7, has a lingering descending edge that continues throughout the maintenance phase.

Figure 11.8 describes a possible team size distribution function in a medium-size project with a maximum team size of 18. Initially, with a team size of three, configuration control and quality assurance will be handled by the project manager. As the team grows to eight, these responsibilities will be assigned to a team member, who may also fulfill other responsibilities. As the team grows to 12, a configuration control engineer

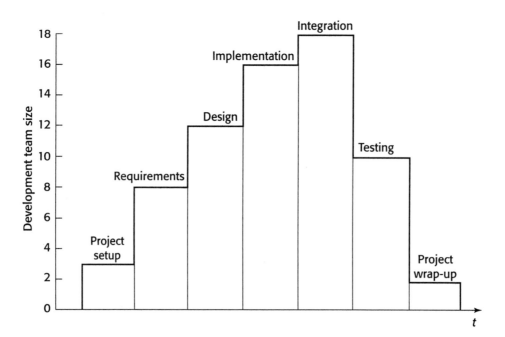

Figure 11.8   Example of development team size.

and a quality assurance engineer will be required, at least part-time. When the team reaches its peak size, these two engineers will probably be required full-time.

The team size is determined by the total number of people assigned to the project. However, in scheduling the team size, the allocation of two people, each for half of a full-time assignment, does not necessarily equal the assignment of one person full-time. It is difficult to deal with the allocation of half a person to an assignment. In such cases, as in quality assurance or configuration control, the expense to the project of assigning these activities can be reduced by sharing these functions with other projects. This is especially true for small projects.

Testing is another example of personnel resource sharing between projects. Many organizations have an independent test team that is not directly part of the project team. The independent test team becomes involved in the project mainly toward the end of the development cycle (although some test activities do start much earlier). Such teams can then move from one project to another provided, the test activities have been scheduled appropriately.

11.5.2 Skills and Experience

The scheduling of personnel is not just a case of allocating a number of people for each stage of the project. Specific skills are required for each activity and appropriately experienced professionals must be assigned the responsibility for these activities. Table 11.4 presents a list of some of the classes of personnel required for each project development stage. Not all projects require all classes of personnel, such as in the case of small projects, in which two or more of the project positions can be filled by one person.

Although Table 11.4 refers to different professional positions that require different qualifications, it is always an advantage when team members' qualifications are versatile. It is then possible to reassign team members within the project, thus saving much of the learning curve overhead that usually needs to be scheduled for new team members. A suitable training program can ensure that the project team members have a wide variety of skills. It is good practice to assign team members to different positions from time to time (from one project to the next). This is particularly true in the case of qual-

Table 11.4 Classification of Software Project Positions

CLASSIFICATION	PROJECT POSITIONS
Managers	Project manager, Team leaders, System engineers
Administrators	Administrative assistants
Configuration control	Configuration manager, Configuration controller
Quality assurance	Quality management, Quality assurance engineer
Software developers	Design engineers, Programmers
Technical writers	Documentation writers, Editors
Integration and Test	Independent test team, Test case developers

ity assurance: there is no better way to introduce team members to the importance of quality than to give them a *tour of duty* as quality engineers on a project.

Learning curve activities are often overlooked. Project familiarization for new team members is not the only case in which learning curve overhead exists. Training is an important factor that must be scheduled. However, not all training needs can be known during the initial stages of the project. Training requirements become evident as decisions are made regarding the development environment (such as programming language, development computers, etc.), and as the individual team members are selected and their skills and experience become known.

There are many problems related to the scheduling of people. Experience and skills of team members are not reliable measures of expected performance. The scheduling of engineers based on supposedly measurable qualities has long been a controversial subject. The substantial variation in software developer performance is discussed in Chapters 5 and 12.

11.5.3 The Infamous Man Month

Another common source of error, when scheduling people, is the difference in the way the term *man month* (or, as it is now called, *work month*) is used. If a project manager calculates that a specific scheduled activity requires six work months to complete, does that mean that if a suitable engineer is assigned for six months then the activity can be completed in six months?

Well, the answer is . . . maybe! In many cases the activity cannot be completed in six months, because a person seldom provides six months of work during a six-month calendar period. People take vacations, they celebrate holidays, and they are occasionally sick. Generally, people provide between eight and ten months of work during a twelve-month period. This must be taken into consideration when preparing a schedule.

When project managers inform their superiors that a project will require an investment of six years, they must be clear about the type of years they are talking about. Is it six calendar years, which means the project can only be completed six years from the starting date? Or is it six work years, which means that there are 72 months of work to be performed, which can be divided between a number of people? Or is it really 48 work months, with additional vacation, holidays, and sick leave?

Also, there is a maximum number of people that can be assigned to a project. Three hundred and sixty-five engineers cannot complete a one-year project in one day! And just as nine women cannot have a baby in one month, some projects take a specific amount of time, no matter how many people are assigned. Therefore, the significance of the duration of the project as well as the duration of each major activity must be clearly understood and presented as part of the schedule. The schedule should take into account absenteeism and overhead (discussions, meetings, and just plain talking), and it should explain which activities cannot be shortened and which can.

Reducing the duration of an activity has its price. Adding more people to a project generates more overhead. If five people can develop a project in two years, it does not follow that ten people can develop the project in one year. This is due to the additional communications between the team members; more meetings are necessary, more coordination is required, and more management and administration are required. And of course one cannot continue to reduce the duration of an activity by assigning more and more people to it. The law of diminishing returns is valid when assigning people to a project, and at some point people begin getting in each other's way. Zero or even negative contribution can be reached rather quickly when a project is well into development, and the learning curve becomes long and costly (see Brooks' classic *The Mythical Man Month* [Brooks 1982]).

11.6 Scheduling Resources

The previous section discussed the scheduling of the project's most important resource—the development team. But without the necessary tools, the development team cannot be expected to do a good job. If the project's target computer is not available when the integration phase is scheduled to begin, then the integration phase may very well not begin. A form of the critical path principle is also applicable to the availability of development resources. This means that if the availability of a critical scheduled resource is delayed, it will delay the completion of the project.

There are ways of dealing with availability problems for critical resources, such as risk analysis. The objective is to provide contingency plans in the event that critical resources are not available according to schedule. Risk analysis is described in Chapter 2.

11.6.1 Scheduling Workspace

At the outset of the project, workspace, particularly office space, is usually one of the first major resources required. The project area should be preassigned and well defined. As the project progresses, the required work area will increase.

The need for adequate workspace is often overlooked when scheduling development facilities. A well-defined and separate work area is an important factor in forming a development team. When project team members are dispersed throughout a large area and mixed in with other project teams, many problems arise. Communication between team members is more difficult, management becomes more complicated, and a team spirit does not develop.

Scheduling office and workspace is one of the first steps in scheduling resources. Space requirements are a function of the estimated personnel requirements, the equipment requirements, and the project staffing schedule.

Table 11.5 contains a checklist of some of the items to be considered when scheduling workspace. Of course, not all topics are applicable to all projects. Naturally, the actual space requirements depend on the size and type of each project. Many defense and security projects require special restricted-access areas, referred to in the checklist as a secure area. Another item, storage and inventory rooms, would be required only for projects that include large amounts of hardware and equipment.

11.6.2 Scheduling Equipment

With the right tools, the job can always be done better. But as we have seen, having the right tools is not enough: the tools must also be available at the right time. The objective

Table 11.5 Workspace Items—Checklist

1. Management office space
2. Secretarial administrative office space
3. Conference rooms
4. Development team rooms and desk space
5. Computer room
6. Laboratory
7. Test and integration areas
8. Lunch and recreation area
9. Storage and inventory room
10. Secure area

of the scheduling of equipment is to ensure that adequate development tools are available in sufficient quantity and when they are needed.

In the early years of software development, the basic tools included a programmer, a compiler, and a computer to run the code. Modern development tools include much more than a compiler and a computer. Software utilities ranging from integrated design tools to sophisticated test and debugging tools are now available. In fact, the computer has been harnessed as an aid to the developer to assist in specific development activities, producing the term *computer-aided software engineering* or CASE.

Clearly, not all computer projects are purely software projects. Many computer systems require the development of both software and hardware. This includes such projects as Internet software, communications systems, military systems, robotics, and various industrial systems. In such cases, special-purpose equipment is required for the test and integration phases. A central project office must then coordinate the planning and scheduling of software and hardware development to assure the timely availability of the development equipment.

Assuring the availability of adequate development equipment is an important part of good planning. Poor scheduling can lead to situations in which members of the development team are left idle or partly idle while they wait for the delivery of equipment. Even if team members can be reassigned temporarily, their efficiency and effectiveness as developers will be significantly reduced.

11.6.3 Vendors and Subcontractors

Not all scheduled activities are directly dependent on the project manager and the development team. Frequently, outside parties are also involved in project development. As we have seen, the timely delivery of equipment is crucial to the development schedule, and this often requires procurement from outside parties.

It is not uncommon, especially in large or complex projects, to subcontract certain parts of the project to companies that have specific expertise in relevant areas. This means that direct control of development may be delegated to the subcontractor.

It is difficult to schedule resources and activities over which the project manager does not have full control. In such situations the project manager has two alternatives:

1. Leave the scheduling to the subcontractor or vendor

2. Retain control over the subcontractor's or vendor's work

In the first case, when scheduling is left to the outside party, the project manager is at the mercy of a party over which he has no control. If the other party slips the delivery schedule, it may cause a schedule slippage for the whole project. This is best handled by:

1. Motivating the outside party to deliver on time (e.g., penalizing the party for late delivery or rewarding the party for on-time or early delivery)

2. Identifying late delivery as a project risk, and preparing contingency plans to handle the situation should it occur (see Chapter 2)

In the second case, when the project manager retains control over the outside party, many of the benefits of subcontracting are lost. For large projects, a position must be created for a supervisor of subcontractors and vendors. It is the responsibility of the supervisor to be constantly aware of the work being performed by outside parties, through:

- Visits to subcontractor and vendor sites

- Reviews and milestone evaluations

- Periodic reports from subcontractors and vendors

In addition, it is important for the supervisor to be able to motivate the outside party by linking payments to successfully completed milestones, and by imposing penalties for late delivery.

11.7 Monitoring and Updating the Schedule

The schedule is not a static document, and is therefore subject to constant change. An outdated schedule has little (if any) value. The schedule, as part of the project development plan, must be periodically updated. In order to enable the project manager to maintain an updated schedule, current information must flow regularly from the development team. This is achieved through periodic reports, reviews, and other monitoring activities.

11.7.1 Periodic Reports

Periodic reporting is one of the formal methods of ensuring a regular flow of information from the development team to the project manager. The recommended practice for preparing and submitting reports is described in Section 5.3.1.

Team members should submit their periodic reports to their team leader, who then summarizes the reports and submits the summary together with a copy of the individual reports to the project manager.

The project manager then summarizes the reports from the team leaders, together with reports from other project personnel, such as the head of the test group. The resulting document, which includes the project manager's report, forms the project progress report, and is an official project document that is submitted to top management. The distribution list for the project progress report may also include the individual development team members, the customer, and the project subcontractors.

The periodic reports are the basic channels of information used to evaluate and update the project development plan and, specifically, the project schedule. However, periodic reports should never be the only source of information for these activities. It is the responsibility of the project manager to verify the completeness and accuracy of the information reported.

The frequency of reporting is an issue to be decided by the project manager. Usually, a bi-weekly report is adequate for internal project needs, and a monthly report is adequate for external project needs. However, during critical phases of the project, more frequent reports may be necessary.

11.7.2 Other Schedule Monitoring Activities

One of the elements of good management is the establishment of personal contact between managers and staff. Personal contact supports many management goals, one of which is the verification of progress reports.

The main problems with periodic reports are those of objectivity, interpretation, and accuracy. The project schedule is not always interpreted or perceived in the same way by management as it is by the developers. The famous 90/50 syndrome discussed in Chapter 5 is illustrative of this situation. This, we may recall, states that "it takes 50 percent of the time to complete 90 percent of the work, and an additional 50 percent of the time to complete the remaining 10 percent of the work."

This means that when team members begin reporting that they have almost completed a task, it may well require a substantial amount of time to really finish the task. This is because it is often relatively easy to get something going, but the tedious drudgery required to wrap up a task requires a significant amount of work. And this, of course, is in addition to the natural optimism of the developer in expecting that nothing will go wrong.

There are many methods for monitoring progress that involve personal contact between the project manager and the development team. Weekly project and team meetings are good opportunities to discuss progress, and informal reviews of specific activities enable the project manager to see and evaluate the actual work that has been produced.

When a schedule is not being achieved, it is sometimes a sign that the team member entrusted with a specific activity does not support the schedule. Such situations underscore the importance of having the development team involved in the preparation of the schedule. It is usually easier to have a developer commit to a schedule when he or she was involved in its preparation.

11.7.3 Updating the Schedule

As we have seen, the project development plan must be reviewed periodically. The schedule should be updated whenever the periodic review justifies it or whenever a significant event occurs. For example, if the review shows that many activities are behind

Table 11.6   Schedule Update Checklist

1. Activity list
2. Personnel assignments
3. Risk list and risk analysis
4. Resource allocation
5. Third party status (subcontractors, vendors, suppliers)
6. Schedule chart (Gantt)
7. Precedence network (PERT)
8. Approved requirements and design changes

(or ahead of) schedule, or that several new activities need to be added to the activity list, then a new schedule should be produced. Also, if the development of part of the project is replaced by purchasing a similar off-the-shelf component, then the schedule should be modified to reflect a smaller development effort (a rare occurrence indeed!).

Table 11.6 contains a checklist of scheduled items that should be reviewed (and possibly updated) periodically, or whenever a significant project event occurs.

The first item in Table 11.6 refers to updating the activity list. This task, in effect, is derived from other items in the checklist, such as reviewing the approved requirements and design changes or updating the list of project risks. After all items have been reviewed and, if necessary, updated, then the schedule representation medium should be updated (Gantt chart, PERT chart, etc.). As in the preparation of the initial schedule, it is always good practice to have members of the development team review the new schedule before its release. Scheduling errors, omissions, and conflicts can thus be identified and corrected before the schedule is distributed.

11.8 Some General Guidelines for Scheduling and Planning

Planning begins with the start of the project, and in some cases even before. As we have seen in Section 11.1, all project activity should be planned. The lack of planning is frequently the principal reason for failure. A good first step in planning a project is to prepare a project development plan outline, as described in Table 11.1, and gradually begin to fill in the sections.

11.8.1 Refining the Initial Activity List

As we have seen, the initial list of activities, together with the projected dates to accomplish the activities, produces an initial schedule. The refinement of the activity list is an iterative process that will eventually produce the detailed project development schedule.

As the schedule progresses and becomes more detailed, the activity list will contain low level activities that will be assigned to specific team members. It is therefore most important for the project manager to include the relevant team members in this phase. It is always preferable to have engineers propose a schedule for their area of responsibility rather than to dictate the schedule to them. Team members always feel much more committed to a schedule that they prepared than to one dictated for them.

A common technique is to hand detailed activity lists to the members of the development team and have them submit a proposal for the completion dates. The project manager should then call a meeting with the various development groups in order to resolve any disagreements and problems. This process should then be iterated until an acceptable and agreed schedule is produced. Only if agreement cannot be reached should the project manager exercise his or her authority and set the parts of the schedule that remain in discord.

Table 11.7 summarizes some of the basic guidelines for the production and maintenance of a detailed development schedule.

11.8.2 Gaining Approval for the Schedule

Preparing a realistic schedule is not the project manager's only objective; getting the schedule approved is just as important. Too often, a realistic schedule is painstakingly prepared by the project manager and submitted to corporate management, only to have it rejected for business reasons. This underscores the importance of project managers being aware of the broader corporate or business picture, and not just restricting themselves to the narrow technical perspective.

When preparing the overall project development plan, the project manager should naturally expect pressure in two basic areas: (1) the completion date and (2) development costs. Other pressures may also be brought to bear, but these two basic areas are universal.

For the project manager, the best way to respond to such pressure is to attempt to view the project from other non-technical perspectives.

If pressure is brought to bear by the customer, the project manager should try to understand the customer's concerns and attempt to address these concerns within a

Table 11.7 Schedule Guidelines

1. Promote team involvement
2. Iterate from high level to detailed schedule
3. Be aware of needs of customer, management, users, and marketing
4. Schedule not only activities, but resources and personnel, too
5. Resist pressure to commit to an unreasonable schedule
6. Use computerized scheduling tools
7. Schedule contingency plans for risks
8. Update the schedule periodically or after major project events

realistic schedule. Will the customer accept an early delivery of a partial system? Is there an off-the-shelf solution that will suffice for a while until the full system is completed?

If pressure originates from higher management, the project manager should try to discover the reason for the pressure. Has the project become far too large for the available budget? If so, can the project be implemented in phases, with many of the sophistications delayed until more financing is available?

Wishful thinking and self-delusion is usually the worst policy. It is always best to stick to a reasonably achievable schedule. The best approach for the project manager is to be honest. *Never promise anything you do not expect to be able to deliver!*

A proven and effective approach is always to present a problem together with a solution. This means that when the schedule cannot support the expectations of the customer or of higher management, the problem should be presented and explained, and an alternative schedule should be suggested together with a modified set of objectives. The following example will demonstrate this approach.

> *ACO, a well-established company, has been involved in retail support services for many years. They recently decided to develop a new networked computerized system that would interface with the existing cash register systems in order to provide a wide variety of services to the stores and their customers. Two things were clear from the outset: first, there was a definite demand for these services, and second, this company was not the only one aware of this demand.*
>
> *BCO, the company that was offered the development contract, realized that the system was far from trivial. Realizing that ACO wanted to beat the market, BCO submitted the shortest realistic schedule that they felt they could commit to. However, the schedule was rejected by ACO.*
>
> *After further investigation by BCO, it became evident that ACO had already committed to delivery dates for the system to some of their customers. ACO also felt that there was a window of opportunity in the market, and that it would close and they would lose their customers if they could not deliver on time.*
>
> *BCO proposed an intermediate system that would not be networked between stores and that would have reduced functionality. This intermediate system would run on the same hardware, and all its functions would be compatible with the final fully functional system. This intermediate system would be delivered to ACO's customers earlier, and would be replaced later by the full system. This was acceptable to ACO.*
>
> *BCO resisted the temptation of promising an impossible delivery date in order to assure that they would be awarded the contract. They explained the problem to ACO and suggested a solution that addressed ACOs problems with their customers. By choosing this course, BCO also gained the confidence of ACO, which proved to be helpful throughout the project.*

No one, be they customer or management, can justifiably expect the impossible. Therefore, in order to gain approval for the project development schedule, the recommended course of action is:

1. Do not present the schedule in a vacuum. The schedule must be part of an overall project development plan.

2. Learn the perspective of your audience, including the customer, top management, and sales and marketing. Study their viewpoints and understand their concerns.

3. Ensure that the schedule is reasonable, and well prepared. Be ready to justify all milestones.

4. Seek support from other experts and professional reference sources in order to substantiate any problems that you present.

5. Always present a problem together with a proposed solution.

6. Be confident within yourself that you are right. If you doubt your own assertions, then you are not ready to present the schedule or the plan.

A realistic schedule approved by management (or by the customer) is a major step toward the successful development of a project. When a schedule is unrealistic, it is often camouflaged with such terms as "tight," "aggressive," or "challenging." However, tight, aggressive, and challenging schedules are rarely conducive to successful projects.

11.8.3 The Relationship between Schedule, Resources, Quality, and Functionality

As we have seen, the project development plan charts a course from the current situation to the project objective. The plan describes the resources necessary to achieve the objective within a specified schedule. The required resources and the schedule can both be calculated (or estimated) based on the declared objective of the project.

The project objectives, being the functionality described in the requirements specification, are not necessarily the only requirements of the project. A specific schedule may also be required (e.g., to develop the project within one year). If the required schedule is too short, then this additional requirement may be an unfeasible requirement. However, if the required schedule is not too short, then, together with the functionality, it will determine the required resources.

The resources may also be a requirement (a maximum development team size, or a specific development computer). If the resources are unsuitable, then this additional requirement may be an unfeasible requirement. When the required resources are suitable, then, together with the functionality, they will determine the schedule.

The question that remains is what happens if both the resources and the schedule are required? Usually this means that the extent of the functionality is then determined by the schedule and the resources. This means that within a given schedule, and with given resources, the amount of functionality is limited.

Another way of looking at this triangle of dependent project attributes (functionality, schedule, and resources) is to introduce a fourth attribute: quality. This means that if all of the previous three attributes are predetermined, then the quality of the software product is also determined. However, the project manager enters dangerous ground when all four attributes are predetermined (see Figure 11.9).

The determination of at least one (preferably two) attributes must be left to the project manager. It is perfectly valid for the customer or for higher management to ask what functionality can be provided with a given budget and given resources and at a given quality level.

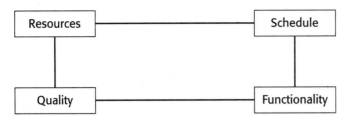

Figure 11.9   The four attributes of a development project (any three determine the fourth).

Similarly, the project manager can be asked what resources are needed in order to develop a given functionality within 18 months at a given quality level.

11.8.4 The Customer Perspective

As we have seen, the customer is a central figure in project scheduling. In fact, the customer is the central figure in all respects.

There are three basic customer-related principles in software project planning. Leading the list is: (1) *Without exception, every software project has a customer*. Simply stated, the customer is the entity for whom the software is being developed.

Because the customer is the reason for the project, it follows that (2) *the customer is the most important project entity*. It is amazing how often developers and project managers forget this basic principle.

Having identified the customer, the third basic principle can be established: (3) *The success of a software project is measured by the degree of its customer's satisfaction*. As we have seen, this is also a measure of software quality (see Chapter 9, which discusses the IEEE's definition of software quality as a measure of customer satisfaction).

The link between a software project and its customer is not always clear. The litmus test to identify the customer is to ask this question: if the entity did not exist would the project still be needed? If the answer is yes, then that entity is most probably the customer.

What should be done to promote customer satisfaction? It is all a question of having the right perspective. The following approach helps maintain a customer perspective:

1. Manage customer expectations through honest commitments. Do not commit to a schedule that has little chance of being achieved (see Chapter 4).

2. Maintain continuous communications with the customer. Have the customer participate in the preparation of the project plan.

3. Give priority to delivering a reliable software product. Do not provide a short schedule at the expense of a quality product. Ensure that all phases of testing have been included in the project plan.

4. Give priority to delivering an easy-to-use product. Examples are context sensitive help and realtime data validation. Do not make a system cumbersome to use in order to shorten the schedule.

5. Understand the different needs of different customers. There is no one set of rules governing business needs, strategic constraints, budgets, and schedules. They depend on each individual customer. You can plan your project for as close a match as possible to your customer's needs, if first you take the time to understand them.

11.9 Summary

The project schedule is one of the most important parts of the project development plan. This plan is often the first formal document generated within the project, and includes not only the scheduling of development activities but also the scheduling of project resources, particularly people.

The project development plan describes in detail how the project manager plans to develop the project, what resources will be required, and how these resources will be applied.

A schedule is a list of activities and their anticipated time of implementation. There are many ways of representing a schedule: lists of activities, diagrams, graphs, etc. The most common methods of schedule representation are precedence network diagrams (such as PERT), Gantt charts, and lists of milestones.

It is a common error to assume that wherever additional effort is directed, it will shorten the schedule. Shortening activities will have absolutely no impact on the overall schedule duration if these activities are not on the project's critical path. The critical path is the longest path through the network precedence chart, from the start node to the end node.

Scheduling resources is just as important as scheduling activities. Development resources include facilities, workspace, equipment, and human resources.

The project manager's most important project resource is the development team. As the number of project activities varies, so the size of the development team varies throughout the project development life cycle. The team's organizational structure becomes more important as the size of the team grows.

An outdated schedule has little value. The schedule, as part of the overall project development plan, must be periodically updated. In order to enable the project manager to maintain an updated schedule, current information must flow regularly from the development team. This is achieved through periodic reports, reviews, and other monitoring activities.

A realistic schedule approved by management (or by the customer) is a major step toward the successful development of a project. When a schedule is unrealistic, it is often camouflaged with such terms as "tight," "aggressive," or "challenging." However, tight, aggressive, and challenging schedules are rarely conducive to successful projects.

There are three basic customer-related principles in software project planning. (1) *Without exception, every software project has a customer*, (2) *the customer is the most important project entity*, and (3) *the success of a software project is measured by the degree of its customer's satisfaction*.

The following approach helps maintain a customer perspective:

1. Manage customer expectations through honest commitments.

2. Maintain continuous communications with the customer.

3. Give priority to delivering a reliable software product.

4. Give priority to delivering an easy-to-use product.

5. Understand the different needs of different customers.

Exercises

1. You have been designated project manager for a large truck delivery company's dispatching and routing system. Each truck will be equipped with a digital communications device that will communicate with a central computer.

   Your project will develop the software to communicate with the trucks and dispatch them according to optimum routing algorithms. The system will also maintain a detailed data base that will include information regarding the company's trucks, their current location, their drivers, and the delivery routes. The system will also provide online query and update capabilities, as well as report generators. Prepare an activity list for this project. Identify the major milestones and define the project's baselines.

2. Prepare a high level Gantt chart for the project described in Exercise 1. Prepare a detailed Gantt chart for two of the high level activities. Explain any overlap between activities.

3. Prepare a high level PERT chart for the project described in Exercise 1. Include all development and nondevelopment activities. Locate all paths through the network and identify the critical path.

   Demonstrate how the critical path can change when a single duration attribute changes. Explain the dependencies as they are represented in the chart.

4. Prepare a staffing schedule for the project described in Exercise 1. Describe how many team members will be needed at each stage, what their skills should be, and what their assignments will be within the project.

5. Prepare a resource schedule for the project described in Exercise 1. Describe each development resource and explain why and when it will be required.

   Discuss the implications for the project development effort of not being able to obtain each resource.

6. Consider which elements of the project in Exercise 1 may be dependent on outside parties. Discuss which development activities can be considered for subcontracting and which components can possibly be purchased off-the-shelf.

7. Consider the problems that may be expected during the integration phase of the project described in Exercise 1. Prepare a sample project progress report that is being submitted two weeks after integration begins.

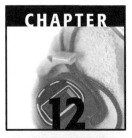
The Preparation of Estimates: Methods and Techniques

Estimation is concerned with the prediction of uncertainties. It is more dignified than fortune-telling, though not always more accurate. This can best be illustrated by the following anecdote.

In the early 1980s, a major American defense contractor was awarded a US Department of Defense software development contract. The company had been divided into small "profit centers," and each such center was required to justify its existence by being profitable. On being informed of the contract award, engineers from the profit center, after initial celebration, set about planning the launch of the project. Only then did they discover that the expected development cost used in their proposal was based on their original estimate of 80 work years, while their new calculations produced an estimate of 120 work years. This would potentially cause a budget overrun of 50 percent!

The additional 40 work years would cost the company about $4 million, and while this amount would not break a major corporation, it was a significant amount for the profit center and could cost a number of senior managers their jobs.

The profit center management sent a letter to the Department of Defense stating that they had miscalculated the cost of developing the project, and requested that they be permitted to resubmit a corrected proposal. If their request was rejected, they stated, they would be willing to withdraw and permit the contract to be awarded to the company that had submitted the next best proposal. The answer they received stated that not only would they not be permitted to resub-

mit their proposal, but should they try to withdraw, the Department of Defense would take legal action against the company that would cost them well in excess of their anticipated loss.

At this stage, the managers of the profit center were probably ready to clean out their desks when a suggestion was put forward by one of the engineers. He suggested that a super-team of developers be established that would be composed of the best engineers in the profit center. These engineers would be pulled out of other projects that were well under way and where their contribution was no longer essential. Then the super-team would be assigned to the new project in an attempt to complete the project with as small an overrun of the original estimate as possible.

The plan was approved, and the best possible development team was assembled. The super-team members were requested to make every effort to complete the project in less than the 120 work year estimate, with the objective of reducing the 80 work year estimate overrun to the extent possible.

So the project was developed over a three-year period by the best team the profit center could put together, and the outcome was that the project was developed in 60 work years!

This short anecdote highlights the basic questions related to the preparation of estimates.

How are professional estimates prepared? What was the correct estimate in this case: 80, 120, or 60 work years?

What good is an estimate in work years if it is so heavily dependent on the identity of the person doing the work?

Is the motivation of the developers a factor in estimating the resources necessary for the development of a project?

And lastly, how can a manager budget a project if professional estimates can be off by as much as 100 percent?

This chapter addresses these and other related questions, and provides tools that enable such concerns to be taken into account in the preparation of project development estimates.

12.1 Project Estimates

Any unknown quantity can be estimated, whereas known quantities do not need to be estimated. For the software project manager, there are many unknown quantities that must be estimated. These are associated with such areas as:

- Project development costs
- Project development schedule
- The size of the project development team
- The amount of software to be developed
- The required hardware resources

How to estimate these quantities is not the only problem that needs to be addressed; the units used to measure these quantities must also be considered.

Project development costs are best measured in monetary units, such as dollars, pounds, or shekels. However, it is acceptable for an initial estimate to be prepared in an intermediate measure that is later converted into monetary units. A common intermediate unit for project development costs is *work months* (or *man months* or *engineer months*, etc.). In some cases, this can later be converted into monetary terms by estimating the cost of a single work month (more about this in Section 12.5).

A project development schedule is obviously estimated in units of time such as days, weeks, months, or years. The schedule, like most plans, must have a beginning and an end. Often, when a project is being planned, the formal beginning is not known, and hence the end is also unknown. In such cases the acronym ARO (After Receipt of Order) is commonly used, and the schedule is constructed using such designations as: *End of design phase*—4 months ARO. A more detailed discussion of software project development schedules appears in Chapter 11.

Estimates of the development staff required for the project are clearly in units of people. However, the development personnel should be grouped according to some common classification, such as software engineers, documentation writers and support staff, and each group should be estimated separately. The time on the project of each person should also be estimated by identifying their entry into the project and their exit from the project. This can commonly be represented by a bell shaped curve with a small development staff at the start and end of the project and a maximum staff size close to the middle[1] [see Figure 11.6(*a*)].

The amount of software to be developed is a measure of project size. It is also a factor in estimating project schedules, as will be discussed later. The software to be developed is commonly estimated in either of two measures: by lines of code or by kilobytes or megabytes of memory. Both methods have their advantages and disadvantages. The number of lines of code is a more representative measure of the degree of development effort, but it is also heavily language dependent in that a hundred lines of high level language code does not require the same degree of effort as a hundred lines of assembler code. "Kbytes of memory" is representative of the amount of software and may be relatively independent of the source programming language, but a single high level READ instruction can generate much more machine code than a complex mathematical algorithm.

The amount of hardware resources is measured in various units depending on the particular resource being considered (this is discussed in more detail in Section 12.8).

12.2 Estimation Techniques

If you wanted to estimate a software project, how would you begin? If you had not done this before, you would probably ask someone who had. This is not a bad technique.

Early estimation techniques were simply based on experience. This worked reasonably well as long as the next project was similar to the previous one and the experienced resources continued to be available. Because this was often not the case, new methods

---

[1]The distribution of the development team size is further discussed in Section 10.5.1.

needed to be developed to identify areas of a project that were unique and original and for which little or no experience existed within the development organization. This led to methods that combed the project looking for areas that were difficult to estimate (see Section 12.3). These areas were then given special attention, while the rest of the project was estimated based on experience.

Though experience continues to play a central role in most modern estimation techniques, the methods have become more formal and less subjective. Leaders in the development of software engineering theory have attempted to produce an algorithm that, if followed systematically, will always produce reasonably good estimates.

In 1981, Barry Boehm first published his celebrated *Software Engineering Economics*, which documented the Constructive Cost Model, or COCOMO (see Section 12.5). Boehm, a professor of software engineering at the University of Southern California, has led a growing following of COCOMO enthusiasts in research supported by such leading corporations as AT&T, Raytheon, and Motorola, and by branches of the US military. Clearly, many organizations were recognizing that estimation techniques needed to be improved.

Boehm produced COCOMO II in 1995 (which led to the retro-naming of the first model as COCOMO 81). The new COCOMO II[2] signified the coming of age of the COCOMO technique which continued to be fine-tuned until its formal release by USC in 1997. Further development of the COCOMO concept is ensured through the COCOMO Affiliates Program (see USC [1995]) which includes several aerospace and other commercial companies, as well as a number of government and nonprofit organizations.

In his first paper on COCOMO II, Boehm (1995) declared his objectives as:

- To develop a software cost and schedule estimation model tuned to the life cycle practices of the 1990s and 2000s.

- To develop software cost database and tool support capabilities for continuous model improvement.

- To provide a quantitative analytic framework, and set of tools and techniques for evaluating the effects of software technology improvements on software life cycle costs and schedules.

There has also been much progress in methods based on counting product features, as well as historical data collection, statistical application, and promotion of use. Function Point Analysis (FPA) was one of the first product feature-counting methods (see Section 12.6). In recent years this has expanded to include algorithmic approaches to convert subsystems, modules, and objects such as screens, dialogs, data tables, reports, messages, and such into estimates of product size. FPA, the initiatory feature-counting method, has maintained its popularity and the method now has an international users group dedicated to its refinement and improvement.[3]

In parallel, new perspectives have focused on understanding the reasons for lateness in software project delivery and have resulted in a new understanding of a broader set

[2]See the University of Southern California COCOMO II website at http://sunset.usc.edu/COCOMOII/cocomo.html

[3]See http://www.ifpug.org and http://ourworld.compuserve.com/homepages/softcomp/fpfaq.htm

of parameters. In an analysis of software project management, Tsoi (1999) concludes that technical solutions alone cannot solve the estimation problem. Many broader factors such as human relationships and senior management commitment strongly influence the performance of a development team. This concept is excellently demonstrated in Ben Rich's recounting of Lockheed's Stealth fighter plane project (Rich and Janos 1994), in which he relates the story of how small, dedicated development teams were able to achieve almost incredulous results in both schedule, efficiency, and product.[4] This clearly demonstrates how the estimate is closely linked to the quality of management and to the motivation of the team.

One example of the relationship between management style and the estimated schedule is the results of *management by decree*. This style of management basically states: *thou shalt deliver on a given date no matter what!* This means that the software product will ship on a certain date irrespective of its status. This poor product release policy has probably been one of the most prevalent reasons for product failure. It is an example of one of David Carney's tongue-in-cheek Chinese quotes, which can be found in *Quotations from Chairman David* (Carney 1998):

> *The anxious farmer brings his crops to the market early. How can he do this? By picking them too soon, when they are not yet ripe.*

Getting the produce to the market too early does not save time. In fact, it usually takes more time. Estimates cannot be set by decree. If an estimated schedule is too long, it is best shortened by reducing functionality (see Figure 11.9). There are several estimation tools available that can help evaluate such scenarios by enabling the project manager to ask: *how would the estimate change if I removed these features?*

The remainder of this chapter provides a more detailed presentation of software estimation techniques and tools, including methods based on experience, prototyping, statistical methods, the variants of COCOMO, and feature point analysis.

12.3 Stepwise Estimation

Many estimation methods are based on the ability of the development organization to collect and maintain historical data about previous development projects (see Figure 12.1). When such data is available, experience can play a major role in producing good estimates. This requires the separation of a project into elements for which experience can be applied and elements that require other approaches to estimation.

These project elements may be identified using the "divide and conquer" approach, which is often applied in many different areas of software engineering (see Chapter 6). This method, which divides a large problem into numerous smaller problems, is also used in most estimating techniques. The basic approach is to decompose the project into well-defined components, and then to iterate step-by-step until only small units remain, which can then be more easily estimated.

---

[4]The wide span of human output has been recognized for many years (see Sackman et al. [1968]), but it has not always been understood that a person's position within the span is strongly influenced by management behavior and attitude.

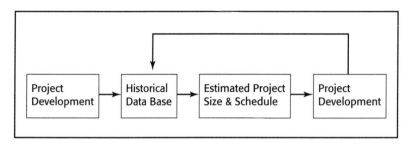

Figure 12.1   Maintaining historical development data.

The first step in project decomposition is the division of the project into the following four categories (see Figure 12.2):

1. *Off-the-shelf* components
2. *Full-experience* components
3. *Partial-experience* components
4. *New development*

Each category represents a class of development activities that can be estimated separately, using different methods of estimation. As we shall see, each category is also associated with the degree of *risk* involved in the development of the software.

For the purpose of this discussion, we will consider only components of actual software development, and not their related activities, such as management, configuration control, or quality assurance, which are discussed later.

12.3.1 Off-the-Shelf Components

An off-the-shelf component is any piece of existing software that can be incorporated into the current project with little or no modification. Off-the-shelf components are often elements of the project that have been previously developed as part of other projects or that have been acquired externally, a process often called reuse or component-based development (see Chapter 6). Examples of off-the-shelf components are mathematical subroutine libraries, software test cases (test suites), hardware peripheral drivers, various algorithms, and even major project components such as the user interface.

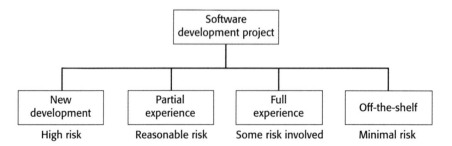

Figure 12.2   Software project development categories by degree of risk.

The risk involved in using off-the-shelf components is minimal. The components are often well evaluated and tested. Incorporating this category of components into the project in most cases lowers the development cost of the project by reducing the amount of development work.

Minimal risk is still different from no risk, and a price is paid for using off-the-shelf components. The price is in often having to make do with less functionality or suitability than would be provided by redeveloping the components specifically for the project. This is similar to buying an inexpensive off-the-rack ready-made suit instead of a much more expensive tailor-made suit. Sometimes the ready-made suit may be a perfect fit, but often some compromises must be made.

Off-the-shelf components often require, to some extent, adapting the project to the component rather than adapting the component to the project.

12.3.2 Full-Experience Components

Full-experience components are the essence of what companies are really all about. Companies usually specialize, meaning that Boeing makes planes and not televisions and IBM makes computers and not planes. But both develop software. Similarly, two organizations may have the same expertise in one area of software (say data bases), while one may specialize in some area (say communications systems) and the other may specialize in another area (say accountancy systems). In business, companies exist by becoming expert in certain fields that represent their *core competency.*

This is certainly true of software development. Most software projects contain components that are similar to components in previously developed projects. Examples of these components, called *full-experience* components, are Internet applications, professional packages (billing systems or inventory systems), and even major subsystems such as communication networks and data base systems.

A full-experience component is any part of the software project about which we can say "We have done something similar in the past." However, it is most important to emphasize that the term *full experience* is valid *only if the experience has been retained.* That means that some of the developers who were involved in the previous similar projects are still available (they have not left the company) and the information regarding the previous projects exists and is documented. The fact that a company has previously developed a telephone billing package is not in itself sufficient grounds to classify the development of a cellular billing package as a full-experience activity, particularly if the members of the earlier development project have resigned from the company and have left neither development nor historical documentation behind. Often, when historical development information is lost, so is core expertise and, hence, the ability to estimate effectively (see Heemstra 1992).

Full experience requires the capability to repeat previously successful activities.

There is relatively little risk in the development of full-experience components. There is a basic assumption that if we have done it before we can do it again. This is not always so. The main risk is in errors of classification. This refers to cases where components only *look* similar, but are in fact quite different. An example would be the classification of the development of a cellular phone billing application based on experience developing a telephone billing application. Both involve billing calculations for phone calls and the maintenance of a subscriber data base, but cellular phone billing involves airtime, roaming, and other considerations that are very different from those related to regular phone billing. The correct approach would be the classification of the activity in this case as *partial experience*, which is discussed in the next section.

12.3.3 Partial-Experience Components

The advancement of technology would be much slower if development groups did not widen their areas of expertise from time to time. This is often done in an evolutionary manner, whereby new projects take steps in innovative directions while building upon prior experience. Hence, the experience level in the new project is partial.

Partial experience refers to components that are in part similar to components developed in previous projects. An example of partial-experience would be the development of a payroll system by a team who had previously developed a time and attendance system. The team would have accumulated experience in handling employee records, but not in complex salary and tax calculations. Another example (described at the end of the previous section) is the development of a cellular billing application based on the previous development of a telephone billing application.

A partial-experience component is a part of the software project that we can say we are familiar with, though we have not actually developed something similar in the past.

There is a reasonable degree of risk involved in the development of partial-experience components, and it is the willingness to assume this risk that leads companies to expand their expertise gradually in evolutionary stages. However, in this instance too there is a danger of erroneous classification. Being partially familiar with a task is a subjective condition. There are few tasks within which we cannot find *something* we are familiar with. So the classification of a component as partial experience depends on the classifier. A possible solution is to require agreement by more than one estimator on the classification of components in this category, and in fact, as we shall see later, this approach is recommended for many of the techniques used in estimation.

The main requirement in classifying a component as partial experience is the ability to identify both familiar and new elements within the component.

12.3.4 New Development

New development is involved with the development of components when no significant experience exists within the development team. This definition can be somewhat tempered, based on the fact that computer companies seldom build automobiles, and automobile companies seldom build computers. So new development may have some previous experience to draw upon, and we will assume that the *basic skills* needed to perform the required tasks are available.

Not all research and development is evolutionary in nature. A perfect example is the US space program, which was inspired by President Kennedy's prophetic declaration that by the end of the decade (the 1960s) the United States would land a man on the Moon. Nothing similar had ever been undertaken before—so this was most certainly new development.

New development is obviously the most difficult class of components to estimate, and contains the highest degree of risk. Owing to rapid advances in computer science over the past few decades, computer projects are more apt to contain new development components than are other branches of technology. This is especially true of software projects and is one of the main reasons why computer projects have demonstrated such a poor track record in project estimation.

Thus, new development usually lacks a reliable basis for estimation and requires the application of specific methods to enable adequate estimates to be made. This will be discussed in detail in the next section.

12.3.5 Project Decomposition by Level of Risk

As we have seen, the initial decomposition of a software project identifies four major categories, with different degrees of development risk associated with each. After the first step of project decomposition, we end up with project components that (1) we have available (off-the-shelf), (2) we know how to develop (full experience), (3) we are at least partially familiar with (partial experience), or (4) are completely new to us (new development).

The objective of the next step in project decomposition is to further identify familiar and unfamiliar tasks. This leads us to re-examine the partial experience category (see Figure 12.3).

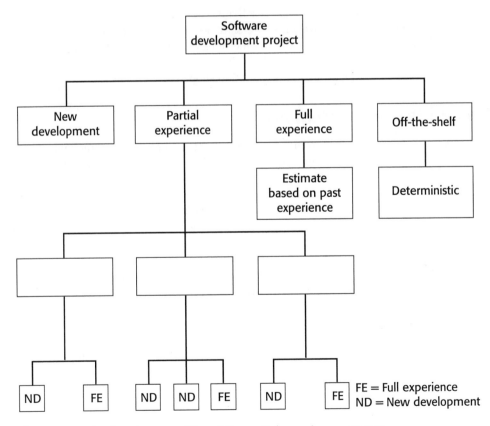

Figure 12.3 Further decomposition of the partial-experience category.

The partial-experience category has been described as containing project components that are in part similar to components developed in previous projects. We therefore expect to be able to decompose these components further into smaller new development and full-experience components. In some cases, off-the-shelf components may also be identified during further decomposition of the partial-experience category.

By applying stepwise refinement, we can thus iterate and identify all new components of the project. In so doing, we have also identified all project components for which we can apply relatively reliable methods of estimation, based on our previous experience. This will increase the reliability of our overall project estimates.

12.4 Estimating New Development

When we do not have the benefit of experience to draw upon in preparing estimates, we must seek additional information in order to progress from the "out of the hat" or "ballpark" estimate to something more reliable. Two common approaches are:

1. Prototype methods
2. Statistical methods

Both methods involve some common activities, such as the need to build something to base our estimates on. However, as we shall see, the prototype methods are more engineering oriented while the statistical methods are more scientific. For those who favor engineering over science, it should suffice to say that many projects that started with prototypes never made it to the production shop.

12.4.1 Prototype Methods

Software prototypes differ from prototypes in other branches of technology. An advanced prototype airplane may be very similar to the final production airplane, and may be used as a model for the construction of the production line. Software, however, is built only once (though it may be modified later). Once the software is developed, subsequent products can be immediately created just by copying the software that was produced. This is a unique feature of software (though written text is somewhat similar because of its reproducibility).

The concept of prototypes assumes a slightly different meaning when applied to software. Software prototypes are reduced functional versions of the full product.

In addition to the reduced functionality of a software prototype, the development standards may be relaxed so that less formal development methods and standards are required. Also, the functionality that is retained in the prototype may be more crude than in the full product: for example, the user interface may be less user-friendly. All this provides for a fast development cycle that quickly produces an initial version of the full software product. This procedure is commonly referred to as *rapid prototyping*.

The following example demonstrates the use of prototyping in the preparation of software development estimates.

Computer Developers Inc. (CDI) had been successfully marketing an expert system for lawyers that provided them with instant access to information on legal cases and precedents, laws and legal procedures, and lists of legal experts in various areas of law. The system acted as a very fast and reliable legal aide, and in some cases was even capable of suggesting solutions to legal problems.

Based on their success in the legal field, CDI management was contemplating broadening their share of the expert system market, and decided to evaluate the risk in developing an expert system for medical doctors. To enable them to evaluate the risk efficiently, the management of CDI needed estimates on the size and cost of the development of a medical expert system.

Clearly the medical expert system contained all of the project risk categories described in the previous section:

- *Off-the-shelf components from the legal system (such as data retrieval and identification of experts)*
- *Full-experience components (such as data maintenance and case history features)*
- *Partial-experience components (such as recommendation logic and user interface)*
- *New development (such as medical diagnosis and drug interaction monitoring)*

The complexity of the medical diagnosis component would render it difficult to estimate. Therefore, building a computerized prototype medical diagnosis assistant would be effective in providing information on the amount of work necessary to develop a full version of the system.

The medical diagnosis prototype would exclude much of the user-friendly interface necessary to appeal successfully to doctors as potential users of the system. It would also exclude much of the required medical data and algorithms, and would be a stand-alone program that need not be integrated with the other features of the expert system.

The actual functionality of the prototype is dependent on the time and budget available for its development. Obviously the larger the budget and the longer the development time permitted, the more useful the prototype becomes as a tool for estimating the full system. In the extreme, the prototype would contain all of the functionality of the full system, and would thus provide an accurate estimate of the development resources required. This, essentially, is the same as developing the project first and estimating it after it is complete. This estimate is accurate but useless.

In many instances, the prototype is not a throw-away, and is later refined and incorporated into the full system. In such cases there is a risk of using substandard or poor-quality software in the final product, as documentation may be lacking and coding and design practices may be inferior. This can be avoided if a decision is made before the development of the prototype to maintain development standards to the extent that would enable the prototype to be used later as part of the production software.

To summarize, a prototype of new development components is an excellent tool that can provide the additional information necessary to prepare reliable estimates. However, a prototype can be costly, and in fact the more supportive it is of a reliable estimate, the more costly it is to develop.

12.4.2 Statistical Methods

Statistical methods employ sampling techniques in the estimation of project components. At the lowest level of project decomposition, representative units or modules are selected. These units are then actually developed and thus they provide information on the expected effort required for the development of the components they represent. This method includes the following basic stages:

1. Identify all new development software components.

2. Prepare an initial design of each component by identifying the software modules that will implement the component.

3. Divide the modules into similar categories, according to:
   - complexity (degree of difficulty)
   - function (such as communications, data base, human interface, etc.)
   - type (screen, operating system, library utility, service task, etc.)

4. From each category, select one module that is representative of the others.

5. Implement the selected modules.

6. Based on the information derived from the implementation of the selected modules, estimate the resources required for each category.

7. Combine the estimates for each category, thus obtaining an estimate for all new development software.

For large projects, the selection of more than one module from each category will provide a more accurate estimate. The dilemma here is similar to prototyping. The more modules selected from each category, the more accurate the estimate. However, in the extreme we would be estimating a component based on the full development of that component. Once again, this would provide an accurate but useless estimate.

The selection of the module categories and the assignment of modules to these categories requires extensive experience in software development. The selection of representative modules also requires relevant experience. These activities are best carried out by three or four professionals who compare notes and attempt to reach agreement on the classification and selection decisions.

The initial design of the components, in stage 2, is a critical activity. Design is a major phase in software development, though the decomposition of the components into modules should suffice at this stage. Even this is no easy task, and for large projects may require a substantial effort. The initial design coupled with the implementation of the selected modules may sometimes be reusable in the full development of the system.

Many tools are available for generating various classes of prototypes. For rapid prototypes that will later become products, there are tool sets such as Rational's integrated suite (see Bawtree 1999), or Research Systems' Integrated Data Language (see Fox 1999). Screen generators, 4GL languages, and other VHL (Very High Level) languages are also excellent tools for prototyping.

12.5 The Constructive Cost Models

The anecdote related at the beginning of this chapter illustrates the many factors that affect the extent of resources required to develop a software project. Clearly, a good development team will complete a project earlier and at a lower development cost than an average development team. Many other factors can be considered when estimating the cost of software development.

The more common factors are:

- Level of personnel
- Level of complexity
- Project size
- Development environment
- Reliability level

Similar factors were originally presented by Boehm (1981) and were included in his constructive cost model, later referred to as the COCOMO 81 method, for the preparation of software cost estimates. Similar models, such as the one presented here, have since been further developed and modified, primarily in the selection of the effort formulae used by the model (see Jeffery and Low [1990], Anderson [1990] and Balda and Gustafson [1990]). The COCOMO 81 model is an algorithm that takes into account the above five factors (and possibly others) and produces estimates associated with the quantification of risk. Several computer programs are available that perform much of the tedious work required by the model (further described in Section 12.6).

The COCOMO 81 model starts from an existing estimate of the number of software lines of code to be developed. It then provides tools for the estimation of cost, schedule, and the size of the development staff. The number of lines of code may be estimated using the project decomposition and statistical methods described at the beginning of this chapter.

The COCOMO 81 model requires a set of formulae, one for each of the factors being used to produce the estimate. Examples of such formulae follow.

As discussed in Section 12.2, more advanced versions of COCOMO have been developed by teams led by Barry Boehm. COCOMO II has taken a more object oriented approach in estimating project size and uses Object Points (screens, reports, etc.) and Function Points to determine software size (see Section 12.6).

The following description of the COCOMO models is to some extent generic and its objective is to explain the foundation for the basic model. Several of the COCOMO II enhancements are also discussed. Many COCOMO tools exist (this will be discussed later), but in the unlikely event that readers would want to create their own COCOMO II estimation tool, a full, detailed description of the method can be found in Boehm et al. (1995) and Chulani et al. (1998).

12.5.1 Level of Personnel

In discussing the type of software developers, Boehm (1995) provides a stunning view of the software practices marketplace[5] in the first decade of the twenty-first century.

---

[5]Extrapolated from US Government statistics and other surveys, see Boehm (1995).

- End-user programming will be 55 million practitioners in the US alone,
- while application generators and composition aids will have six hundred thousand practitioners,
- systems and applications—seven hundred thousand,
- system integration of large scale systems—seven hundred thousand,
- and infrastructure—seven hundred and fifty thousand practitioners.

Boehm covers a wide range of software developers, from high-end users to low-end practitioners. As the number of practitioners grow, the wide range in performance may be expected to grow, too. Therefore, estimates for each level of software development must take into consideration the skills, knowledge, and expected performance of the developers.

It is not uncommon to observe a variation of software performance of hundreds of percent. Assuming an orderly development methodology is being used, a variation of up to 400 percent may occur. This means that, on an average, we may observe an experienced, intelligent, and motivated software engineer producing up to four times as much as a beginner (or mediocre) software engineer, or even in some cases, another engineer with the same level of experience.

The larger a project, the less impact individual performance will have, as this factor tends to average out based on personnel interaction and general statistical averaging theories.

Table 12.1 presents an example of the tabular function

$$PL = f \ (\Sigma EP, \ N, \ KSLOC)$$

which represents the personnel level (*PL*), using *KSLOC* as a measure of the size of a project[6] (thousand source lines of code) and *EP* as the expected performance assigned between 1 and 4 for each engineer, summed over *N*, the total number of engineers on the project.

This function produces a value between 0 and 4 that serves as a factor to be applied to the cost of the development effort. A *PL* value below 1 indicates a good development team while a *PL* value above 1 indicates a weak development team. A *PL* value of 1 indicates an average development team, and will not cause the cost estimate to change.

Note that as the project size increases, the impact of the level of personnel on project cost variation lessens. However, an average personnel level of 1 produces a worst case factor for all project sizes, which in Table 12.1 is represented as a factor of 4.

Other similar functions may give more consideration to the contribution of the level of personnel by producing a wider span of values. In the extreme, we may assume that in some cases a development team with all level 1 engineers may never complete a large

---

[6]Boehm (1981) uses KDSI (thousand delivered source instructions) in the various formulae he uses. However, project development costs are not based on the number of lines delivered but rather the number of lines actually developed. The two are often not the same, as delivered lines of code may originate from off-the-shelf (reuse) components (see Section 12.2), and developed code may not be delivered for various reasons (e.g., test code). See also Ratcliff and Rollo's (1990) discussion on the ambiguity associated with KDSI.

Table 12.1   Cost Multipliers for the Level of Personnel

| (ΣEP)/N | PL = F(ΣEP, N, KSLOC) | | |
	KSLOC < 5	25< KSLOC < 300	300 < KSLOC
4	0.33	0.50	0.75
3.5	0.45	0.65	0.81
3	0.66	0.85	0.90
2.5	1.00	1.00	1.00
2	2.20	1.80	1.50
1.5	3.50	2.50	2.20
1	4.00	4.00	4.00

project. The actual numbers in Table 12.1 represent an improvement on a straight unfactored cost estimate. However, these numbers should be regarded as an example, and a refinement of the table should be based upon the actual experience accumulated in the organization within which the project is to be developed.

An additional improvement of Table 12.1 may also be achieved by refining the project size steps. Table 12.1 uses three project size steps, $KSLOC < 25$, $25 > KSLOC < 300$, 300, and $300 < KSLOC$. A more detailed set of step sizes may use 25, 100, 300, and 500.

We shall consider three examples based on three project sizes with three groups of engineers.

Consider the following projects:

- Project A with 10,000 estimated *SLOC*s
- Project B with 100,000 estimated *SLOC*s
- Project C with 500,000 estimated *SLOC*s

We shall assign the values to:

- Beginner engineers
- Average engineers
- High-level engineers
- Exceptional engineers

It is reasonable to expect most project engineers to be on a level of 2 or 3. Many projects permit one or two beginners and many projects will have one or two gurus. Note that in the case related in the introduction to this chapter, we can assume the team that was assembled comprised 3 and 4 level engineers.

For Project A we will assume 3 software engineers (this includes system designers, programmers, etc.): none at level 1, 1 at level 2, 1 at level 3 and 1 at level 4.

For Project B we will assume 35 software engineers: 9 at level 1, 18 at level 2, 6 at level 3, and 2 at level 4.

Table 12.2 *PL* Cost Factors Calculated for Three Projects

	A	B	C
KSLOC	10	100	500
N	3	35	190
ΣEP	9	71	435
(ΣEP)/N	3.0	2.0	2.3
PL	0.66	1.80	1.00

For Project C we will assume 190 software engineers: 20 at level 1, 100 at level 2, 65 at level 3, and 5 at level 4.

Table 12.2 summarizes the calculation of the PL project cost factor, based on the values in Table 12.1.

The *PL* value for Project C is rounded to the closest value in Table 12.1. A linear interpolation between values of (ΣEP)/N could also be used to determine the value of *PL* for Project C.

The results presented in Table 12.2 show that Project A is supported by a superior development team that brings the estimated project development costs down by one third. On the other hand, Project B has a weak development team that almost doubles the cost of project development. Project C has an average development team.

Exercise 4 at the end of this chapter deals with improved functions for factoring the level of personnel into the calculation of cost estimates.

The COCOMO II model goes a step beyond the level of individual team members by addressing *team cohesion,* a measure of the ability of a group of developers to work well together. This measure also produces an effort multiplier that ranges from *very low*—5 (very difficult interactions)—to *extra high*—0 (seamless interactions).

The COCOMO II model also considers such additional factors as Personnel Continuity (PCON), defined as the annual personnel turnover. This produces a factor influencing the final estimate which ranges from 3 percent to 48 percent.

The impact of team factors on project estimates provides a powerful argument for the decomposition of projects into smaller independent sub-projects, and also for maintaining small dedicated development teams (see Rich and Janos 1994).

12.5.2 Level of Complexity

The level of software complexity is a significant factor in the preparation of project estimates. It is obvious that some classes of software are much more difficult to develop than others. Generally, communication applications are more complex than typical data processing systems, so that the number of lines of code would not serve as an effective means of comparison for the development of two such systems. It is therefore reasonable to divide software components into classes according to their level of complexity, and to assign different measures of complexity to each class.

Boehm (1981) originally chose three levels of program complexity: organic, semi-detached, and embedded. We will consider the following four classes of complexity:

1. **System software:** this class of software includes any software that is close to the hardware, such as operating systems and communications software.

2. **Algorithmic software:** this class includes any software that is heavily dependent on complex logic and algorithms, such as scientific programs, sort utilities, and fault tolerant software.

3. **Service software:** this includes basic utilities such as editors, word processors, and graphics programs.

4. **Data processing software:** this class includes general data base applications, such as inventory programs, report generators, and spreadsheets.

These four classes of software represent the main levels of software complexity. In some cases, it will not be immediately evident to which class some programs belong. In such cases we must assign the program to the class that is *closest* in complexity. An example might be the development of a compiler. The complexity of compilers is mainly due to the complex algorithms that are involved in such areas as syntax analysis, parsing, optimization, etc. Therefore compilers would be classified as algorithmic software.

The following formulae are somewhat similar to those proposed by Boehm, except that *KSLOC* is used instead of *KDSI*, and four classes of complexity are used instead of three. Each formula produces the estimated number of software engineer months (*SEM*) based on the estimated number of lines of code and the class of software complexity.

System software: $$SEM = 3.6 \times (KSLOC)^{1.20}$$

Algorithmic software: $$SEM = 3.2 \times (KSLOC)^{1.15}$$

Service software: $$SEM = 2.8 \times (KSLOC)^{1.10}$$

Data processing software: $$SEM = 2.4 \times (KSLOC)^{1.05}$$

The graphs of these functions demonstrate the divergence of the estimated effort (software engineer months) as the size of the project in lines of code grows. This means that in the preparation of estimates, the classification of software becomes more important as the size of the project grows. Above 100,000 lines of code it becomes significant, and above 300,000 lines of code the difference between the two extremes (system and data processing) can be over 200 percent.

Many projects contain software components that belong to different classes of complexity. The most efficient way to apply the above formulae is to decompose the software into components, assign each component to its class of complexity, and then estimate each class of components separately. The resulting set of estimates is then combined to provide a single estimate for the overall project.

In the COCOMO II model (Table 12.3), object types are also classified into levels of complexity to provide complexity weights for computing software size.

These weights can be adapted to each development organization and calibrated based on historical data. They can also be expanded to include additional objects such as data base objects, dialogs, messages, and so forth.

Table 12.3 COCOMO II Complexity-Weights (from Boehm 1999)

OBJECT TYPE	COMPLEXITY-WEIGHT		
	SIMPLE	MEDIUM	DIFFICULT
Screen	1	2	3
Report	2	5	8
3GL Component			10

In the discussions above, the term *software engineer months* (*SEM*) refers to all types of software professionals involved in software development. It is important to note that an engineer month is not the same as a calendar month. It may take six weeks to achieve one engineer month of effort, due to the fact that engineers, similar to other employees, occasionally tend to be sick, take vacations, and usually do not work on national holidays. These topics are discussed further in Chapter 11.

12.5.3 The Reliability Factor

The required level of reliability in a software project can have a major impact on development costs. Reliability, similar to the complexity factor discussed previously, can also produce an increase in development costs of more than 200 percent.

Reliability is an expensive quality in computer systems, and can be achieved through hardware, through software, or through a combination of both. Reliability is also difficult to implement and should be heavily factored into development cost estimates. Fault tolerant systems require costly integration and test phases. This is due to the fact that fault tolerance and other levels of reliability are difficult to test.

Before considering reliability multipliers for the development of software, a decision must be made about the number of reliability levels that will be used. Boehm (1981) uses five reliability levels, based on the effect of system failure:

- Slight inconvenience
- Losses easily recovered
- Moderately difficult to recover losses
- High financial loss
- Risk to human life

It is comforting to find human life classified higher than high financial loss.

The basic approach is to divide the reliability of the system into levels that range from minimal (no specific effort devoted to reliability), to the highest level of reliability (maximum fault tolerance).

In order to introduce a reliability factor into the cost estimates for the development of a software project, an initial decomposition stage is required, similar to the method described in Section 12.3. However, the objective now is to decompose the system into classes of components by level of reliability.

After the initial decomposition, a table of reliability effort multipliers is then applied to each component and calculated for each level, yielding the reliability effort multiplier (*REM*). The values in the reliability table are based upon experience accumulated by the company or organization responsible for the development of the software project. A reliability effort function, similar to the one below, can be used to generate the reliability factor table.

$$REM = 0.75 + (L - 1) \times 1.25/(2 \times N - L - 1)$$

In this function, N is the number of reliability levels and L is the level of the multiplier being calculated. The reliability multipliers produced by this function for five levels are presented in Table 12.4.

In the above example, the reliability effort multipliers grow by 0.18 from level 1 to level 2 and by 0.5 from level 4 to level 5. This indicates that as reliability becomes more critical to the project, the associated effort increases non-linearly. Actually, fully fault tolerant systems (level 5) require a major part of the development effort to be invested in the provision of reliability. It is also worth noting that the above function introduces a range of close to 200 percent in the cost of implementing different levels of reliability (0.75 to 2.00). This means that a high reliability system could cost up to three times as much to develop as a system requiring no effort invested in reliability. In some cases the factor could even be higher.

After determining the reliability effort multipliers, these values are applied to the *SEM* estimates (refer to the previous discussion on project complexity) for each component within each class, thus factoring reliability into the estimates. The estimates for all components are then combined to produce an overall cost estimate for the project.

12.5.4 The Development Environment

Anyone who has ever attempted to make some minor home or car repairs has observed that tasks are easier to perform when the right tools are available.

How long does it take to mow the lawn? Well, it depends on the size of the lawn. However, it also depends on whether you are using a push lawnmower or a motor-driven lawnmower (we have already seen that it also depends on the person behind the mower). Not surprisingly, this observation is also true of software development.

Table 12.4   Reliability Multipliers for Five Reliability Levels

LEVEL OF RELIABILITY	RELIABILITY MULTIPLIERS
1. No effort required	0.75
2. Low	0.93
3. Data integrity preserved	1.17
4. High reliability required	1.50
5. Full fault tolerance	2.00

One of the most common contributors to the development environment factor is the use of high level languages. As programming languages become more efficient, it becomes less desirable to develop software in assembler languages, except for rare cases. Both productivity and reliability of code are many times higher when using high level languages as compared to assembler. This single consideration bears so much on the cost of software development that it is often factored into the development cost separately.

The programming language is but a single example of the effect the development environment can have on productivity. The hardware environment is also significant, as are the software tools that are available on the development hardware. If special-purpose hardware is being developed for the project, then good debuggers and other software analysis tools become essential for effective testing and integration. Goldberg (1983) discusses the significant contribution of a good computer-aided software engineering (CASE) environment to development productivity.

In contrast to the previous factors discussed, the impact of the development environment on productivity is not necessarily affected by project size. Good development environments are necessary in large and small projects alike. Based on this assumption, a single table of multipliers for different levels of the development environment is used to apply this factor to project development cost.

We shall consider three development environment levels:

1. A poor development environment, with few development tools and inadequate development hardware facilities.

2. An adequate development environment, with good development tools and a good hardware development platform.

3. An excellent development environment, with CASE tools and separate hardware development facilities for each engineer.

We will assume that a good development environment can increase development efficiency by 50 percent, and a bad development environment can decrease efficiency by 50 percent. The resulting set of multipliers is presented in Table 12.5.

This table can be refined by including five levels of multiplier, one between levels 1 and 2 (for environments with some basic, but yet inadequate, tools), and one between levels 2 and 3 (for environments with a good, but not excellent, set of tools). An additional refinement of the table would be the inclusion of project size in the factor. This would require increasing the impact of the development level as the project increases in

Table 12.5   Development Environment Multipliers

PROJECT COST MULTIPLIER	DEVELOPMENT ENVIRONMENT LEVEL
1. (poor)	1.5
2. (adequate)	1.0
3. (excellent)	0.5

size. In projects where new hardware is being developed, this may well be the case, as inadequate facilities could make the integration phase in large projects almost impossible to complete.

12.5.5 Subsystems

The first decomposition step for large software systems often yields independent high-level system components, referred to as subsystems (this is discussed further in Chapter 6). Subsystems are components of a system that can be viewed as systems themselves. We can take advantage of the relative independence of subsystems in improving the cost estimate for the whole system.

Subsystems can be characterized by complexity, reliability requirements, and other attributes, in a manner similar to the way low level system components have been classified. An automatic bank teller system may comprise the central communications subsystem, the teller subsystem, and the bank data base interface subsystem. Two of these subsystems are heavily communications dependent, and one is heavily data base and data processing dependent.

The attributes of subsystems can be factored into the system cost estimate using methods similar to those described for the complete system. The subsystem is not decomposed further, but rather is considered as a single unit, focusing on subsystem level activities such as integration and test.

In the above automatic bank teller example, we apply a table of reliability multipliers similar to Table 12.4, but these multipliers are applied to the subsystem only, as a single unit (see Table 12.6).

The data base subsystem in the previous example may be assigned reliability level 3 to ensure data integrity, as we would be slightly inconvenienced if our bank was unable to provide us immediately with our account balance, but we would be most dissatisfied if our bank occasionally sent us erroneous bank statements. The central communications subsystem may be classified as level 5, because a failure in that system would cause a failure in all automatic teller machines. The teller subsystem may be classified as level 4, even though no permanent data base resides within the teller machine, because the bank would most probably like to avoid errors in dispensing cash to their customers.

Table 12.6   Subsystem Reliability Multipliers for Five Reliability Levels

LEVEL OF RELIABILITY	SUBSYSTEM RELIABILITY MULTIPLIER
1. No effort required	0.80
2. Low	0.95
3. Data integrity preserved	1.10
4. High reliability required	1.25
5. Full fault tolerance	1.40

The appropriate multipliers would then be applied to each subsystem, in order to factor the reliability level into the cost estimate.

Note that the deviation of values for the subsystem multipliers is significantly less than for the low level components (compare with Table 12.4). This has been done to compensate for the reliability factor that has already been introduced on the lower level.

The complexity of subsystem (are they simple or complicated to develop?) can be factored into development costs in a similar manner. Complexity multipliers may be assigned to each subsystem. On the subsystem level, program size is not taken into consideration (this has already been factored in on the system level).

Attributes that are not subsystem dependent should not be applied on the subsystem level. In most cases, the level of personnel should *not* be factored into development cost estimates, as this factor would normally not vary on a subsystem level. When completely different personnel are assigned to each subsystem, we would normally regard each subsystem as a separate system for purposes of estimating development cost.

12.5.6 The Basic COCOMO Cost Estimation Algorithm

The following algorithm is derived from Boehm's original COCOMO 81 model (Boehm 1981), and consists of 10 basic steps for the generation of project development cost estimates. These steps cover the decomposition of the project into components, the application of the effort formula to each component, and the combination of all the data produced into a single project cost estimate.

The basic algorithm comprises the following steps:

1. Decompose the software system using stepwise refinement, into subsystems and then decompose each subsystem into low level software modules (the term *software module* is synonymous in this context with the lowest level software decomposition unit).

2. Use a size estimation method (such as Stepwise Estimation described in Section 12.3) to estimate the size of each module. Then combine the estimates for each module, thus producing estimates for the size of each subsystem, and for the full system.

3. Determine effort multipliers for each module, using methods similar to those described at the beginning of this section. The effort multipliers used should at least include formulae for:

   - Level of personnel
   - Size of project
   - Reliability
   - Development environment
   - Module complexity

4. Apply the effort multipliers to each module using methods such as those described at the beginning of this section, thus producing estimates for each module.

5. Determine subsystem effort multipliers for each subsystem (remember: these are in addition to the other multipliers that were established in Step 3 for the whole software system or program).

6. Combine the estimates for the modules in each subsystem with the subsystem effort multipliers, thus producing estimates for each subsystem.

7. Combine the estimates for all subsystems, thus producing an estimate for the whole system.

8. Review all factors that were considered on a module and subsystem level. Seek interaction between factors, between modules, and between subsystems, and allow for the interaction.

9. Seek additional costs that were omitted from the system estimate, such as market analysis, overhead, etc., and combine them with the system estimate that was produced.

10. Have a second (and if possible a third) independent estimate prepared. Compare the estimates produced by each group, and examine any substantial differences. Resolve any differences and produce a single agreed project cost estimate.

This algorithm produces project development cost estimates taking all major factors into consideration. Step 10 also addresses individual errors of estimation by requiring major differences to be explained and resolved.

Step 8 attempts to identify factors that have been partially or fully duplicated in the estimate. An example of full duplication would be the assignment of a complexity factor to a software component because of high reliability requirements, since the provision of reliability often requires complex logic. This would result in the estimate for the component being increased twice, each time for the same reason.

Additional factors may be included in Steps 3 and 5, based on the characteristics of the actual project being estimated. This could include such factors as the complexity of the programming language (if, for example, C++ was being used for the first time), or familiarity with target hardware (if special hardware is being developed and the integration phase would therefore be more difficult). A complete implementation of this algorithm should have all the above effort formulae included.

It is important to remember that the classification of the software components is *different* for each factor. This means that when applying the reliability multipliers to classes of components, these classes will most probably be different from those produced when the complexity multipliers are applied. Therefore each set of multipliers is applied individually to each decomposition component. This is where a computer could be most helpful and, as stated earlier, a number of COCOMO computer packages are available to perform these tedious tasks.

The basic COCOMO algorithm (also called the COCOMO 81 algorithm) is heavily dependent on subjective decisions made by the estimator. This has led to the development of many variants of COCOMO, and the effort formula (see Jeffery and Low [1990], Anderson [1990] and Balda and Gustafson [1990]) which in turn led to COCOMO II.

12.5.7 Some COCOMO II Distinctions

As we have seen, COCOMO II is an enhanced version of the first COCOMO model. It includes many new cost drivers and effort multipliers as well as an early estimation algorithm. While these enhancements certainly have the potential to improve the performance of the model they also require additional work by the estimator in collecting and inputting data.

COCOMO II's early estimation algorithm estimates the number of person months (PM) in a project based on counting object points. This algorithm is used as an initial estimating mechanism before the application of cost modeling (i.e., before applying effort multipliers). The following is an overview of this algorithm, called the Baseline Object Point Estimation Procedure (there are tools available to perform the calculations automatically):[7]

1. Estimate the number of objects in the application: screens, reports, 3GL components, etc.

2. Classify each object's level of complexity (simple, medium, difficult) using a classification scheme (Boehm provides a scheme for screens—the number of views in relation to source data tables, and for reports—the number of sections in relation to source data tables).

3. Determine complexity weights for each object (Boehm provides examples of complexity weight tables).

4. Calculate the *Object-Point Count* by adding all weighted objects to produce a single number.

5. Estimate percentage of reuse in the project and compute the *New Object Points* (*NOP*) to be developed:

$$NOP = (\text{Object Points}) \times (100 - \% \text{ reuse}) / 100$$

6. Determine a productivity rate, defined as the number of new object points per person month. A proposed scheme is provided with the algorithm based on the developers' experience and capability and on the development environment's (ICASE) maturity and capability:

	VERY LOW	LOW	NOMINAL	HIGH	VERY HIGH
PROD	4	7	13	25	50

7. Compute the estimated number of person months for the project: $PM = NOP/PROD$

As mentioned earlier, this algorithm produces a preliminary estimate that does not yet show the results of the application of the cost drivers. As more information becomes available on the characteristics of the project, the cost-based COCOMO II model can be used. The COCOMO II model produces an estimate of PM by calculating:

$$PMestimated = (\Pi EM_i) \times A \times (Size)^B$$

where *PM* is the estimated number of person months, EM_i are the effort multipliers, *A* is a constant used to capture the linear effects on effort with projects of increasing size, and B is a scale exponent produced from the scale factors.

---

[7]Tools for the implementation of COCOMO and COCOMO II are available at the official COCOMO website: http://sunset.usc.edu/COCOMOII/cocomo.html and by Softstar systems at: http://www.SoftwareSystems.com and by SPC at: http://www.spc.ca/products/estimate/technical.htm

These calculations do not need to be manually computed. Tools for the implementation of COCOMO 81 and COCOMO II are available from many sources, though most notably from the University of Southern California, where this model was pioneered. The name of USC's software tool package is based on its year of release and its version (e.g., *USC COCOMO II.1997.1*).

The COCOMO tools calculate the project estimate based on input of the project attributes and preset effort multipliers. The multipliers can be calibrated based on experience, trial and error, or recommended settings.

For a precise and detailed description of the COCOMO II estimate model and its many cost drivers and scaling factors, see Boehm (1995) or Devani-Chulani (1998).

12.6 Function Point Analysis

There is considerable controversy regarding the value of "source lines of code" as the sole measure of project size (see Ratcliff and Rollo [1990] and Jeffery and Low [1990]). There is no common definition for the measure *SLOC*; it may or may not include test code or reused code, or in some cases even library code. Also, does *SLOC* really mean the same for assembler and C++ code? Or Java and C code? Can a single factor really be applied (see the COCOMO factors) to make all program languages comparable?

These questions can be sidestepped by directing the estimating process to other types of project characteristics that can be converted into a measure of project size. As discussed earlier, Feature Point Analysis represents a set of techniques that can provide a more representative measure of project size. This includes counting function points, object points, and other characteristics of the software to be developed.

One of the first feature point methods, Function Point Analysis (FPA), gained a significant following as a successful technique to produce project estimates based on the problem size. This method was incorporated into COCOMO as early as the first COCOMO 81 versions.[8]

FPA has gained quite an impressive following and an international users group has been established, the IFPUG (International Function Point Users Group),[9] to "promote and support function point analysis and other software measurement techniques" (see Section 12.2).

Problem size is a measure derived from the initial project phases, in particular the requirements phase. The amount of functionality in the project determines the problem size, which is represented by a numerical value (the FPA value).

The FPA value of a project can be used to:

- Compare the complexity of projects
- Compare the relative effort required to complete a project
- Generate other project measures (such as *SLOC*s)[10]

---

[8]See Heemstra (1992).

[9]The IFPUG can be accessed on the web at http://www.ifpug.org/ifpug.

[10]Jeffery and Low (1990) describe a program called CLAIR used to convert function points (FP) to *SLOC*.

There are many variations of the FPA technique. Many of these variations attempt to adapt the technique to specific types of projects, or to increase accuracy by adding more project attributes to the FPA process.

12.6.1 The Basic FPA Steps

The basic FPA process includes eight steps. Two of the steps can be prepared independently of the project being estimated, because they are involved with determining lists of function types and complexity attributes to be used to classify the characteristics of the project.

The eight basic FPA steps are:

1. Determine a list of input/output dependent function categories. This may include:[11]
   - External input/inquiry functions
     – User inputs of data or controls
     – User inquiries requiring a response
   - External output functions
     – Distinct data or signal output functions
   - Logical internal file functions
     – Data or control information
   - External interface file functions
     – Shared files, data and control information

2. The number of basic software functions of each type is identified. A function should be counted if it is expected to require special processing.

3. Each function counted in Step 2 is classified as:
   - **Simple:** Minimal file accesses, few different data types, and minimal user involvement.
   - **Average:** This classification is designated for functions between simple and complex. "Average" can be subdivided into more than one intermediate classification.
   - **Complex:** Many file accesses, many different data types, and extensive user involvement.

4. A numerical weighted value is attributed to each classification set in Step 3 (e.g., simple = 6, average = 8, complex = 10, or average can be extended over 7, 8, and 9). Each function category can have a different set of weights.

   The values of all weighted functions are added, providing the unadjusted FPA value (the UFP).

5. The attributes of the processing complexity are identified. These may include:
   - Data communications functions
     – Data and control transmitted, local and remote

---

[11] These function categories are similar to those suggested by Albrecht and Gaffney (1983).

- Distributed functions
  - Distributed data functions
  - Distributed processing functions
- Performance
  - Performance objectives, such as the influence of throughput or responsiveness on development activities
- Utilization of the configuration
  - The degree of usage of the hardware; communications lines
- Transaction rate
  - The degree to which the transaction rate influences development
- Online data entry
  - The degree to which online data functions are handled by the system
- End user efficiency
  - The required efficiency of the handling of online data functions performed by the end user
- Online update
  - The degree of updating required for logical internal files
- Complex processing
  - The degree of influence of complex processing on development. This includes interrupt handlers, re-entrant code, complex algorithms, I/O, etc.
- Reusability
  - The degree to which the code must be developed as reusable for other systems
- Installation ease
  - The degree to which installation ease impacts development
- Operational ease
  - The required degree of ease in such functions as backup and restore, recovery, human interface, etc.
- Multiple sites
  - The degree to which the system will be developed for different sites and different types of user
- Facilitate change
  - The degree to which the software must be developed to support functional changes easily

Table 12.7   FPA Values for Different Types of Project

PROJECT	UFP	CAF	AFP
Time and attendance system	1200	0.42	504
Access control system	680	0.87	592

6. Each processing degree of influence for each complexity factor is designated based on one of the following values:

0: non-existent

1: insignificant

2: moderate

3: average

4: significant

5: strong

and the total of all the complexity factor values is calculated, providing the total degree of influence (TGI).

7. The total degree of influence value is converted to a complexity adjustment factor (CAF). A simple conversion function may be

$$CAF = \frac{TGI}{5 \times (\text{number of complex factors})}$$

8. The adjusted function point measure (AFP) for the project is then calculated as:

$$AFP = CAF \times UFP$$

An example of the values produced by function point analysis appears in Table 12.7. The values in the table demonstrate the importance of the function point value adjustment. A large commercial data processing system provides a much higher UFP than a real-time system, but the complexity adjustment produces a higher adjusted value for the real-time system. The conclusion is that even though the time and attendance system has almost twice the number of functions as the access control system, the complexity of the access control system indicates that it will require more effort to develop.

12.6.2 The Application of FPA

When and where can function point analysis be successfully used? The advocates of FPA claim that the method can be useful in most types of software development project (see SCT 1997). As we have seen, the FPA measure is useful for comparing the effort of projects. It does not directly provide a method for estimating the cost of a project.

Based on the assumption that there is a high correlation between cost and effort, a function can be applied to the FPA value to produce a cost estimate. A simple function can be based on past experience; for example, a previous project with an AFP value of 1,000 cost \$1,500,000 to develop, and another previous project with an AFP value of 850 cost \$900,000. If we assume a linear correlation, then if the current project being estimated produces an AFP value of 920, we will estimate its cost at \$1,180,000.

For more sophisticated methods of calculating function points and deriving effort (work hours) and software size, see Garmus and Herron (1995), whose text is consistent with the IFPUG's release 4.0 of their Function Point Counting Practices Manual.

The COCOMO method can be applied together with function point analysis to achieve two important goals:

1. To ensure that the estimates are reasonable (no major divergence of results)

2. To produce a more comprehensive set of estimates (comparison values and cost values)

There are many tools available to perform Function Point Analysis. SCT's FAQ paper (SCT 1997) provides an impressive list of Function Point software packages though only two in the list are IFPUG approved: *Productivity Manager for Windows* from the Productivity Management Group, and *S.M.A.R.T. Counter* by DDB Software. Also, many implementations of the COCOMO models also include Function Point Analysis software.

12.7 The Estimate as a Range

If asked how long it would take to develop a single software module, an experienced programmer would probably respond, "It depends." As we have seen, it depends on the programming language, on the complexity of the logic, on the individual programmer, and possibly on other factors. If pressed for a specific answer, the same programmer might respond that it could take anywhere between two days and two weeks. This is a valid answer.

Estimates are often presented as a *range*. A range is a helpful estimate in planning for the development of a project. Management will often be willing to accept an initial estimate that states that a project will cost no less than $400,000 and no more than $750,000. These types of estimates are frequently used in the planning stages of a project. As more information becomes available, the range becomes narrower, until eventually it becomes a single number.

The statistical theory behind this approach deals with the concept of *confidence intervals*. If a variable x has probability p of being between two values a and b, then we say that the interval (a, b) is a p-confidence interval for x.

As an example, if (2, 14) is a 95 percent confidence interval for the number of days it takes to develop a module, then we are 95 percent sure that the development of the module will take more than 2 and less than 14 days to develop.[12]

A word on being 95 percent sure. If we are 95 percent sure of something, then, out of 100 instances, we expect to be right 95 times and wrong 5 times.

The range considered here will be the range of estimates for a given project attribute, such as *SLOC*s, development cost, size of development team, development time, and so on.

We will assume a normal distribution of estimates. This means that if 20 software professionals are requested to estimate the number of days required to develop a specific software module, we expect a result similar in distribution to the following:

1 person will estimate 2 days

2 will estimate 5 days

4 will estimate 7 days

[12]Strictly speaking, the mathematical definition of probability refers to a function that produces a value between 0 and 1. However, in the real world, especially in the business world, probabilities are often expressed as percentages. In fact, in this author's own experience, percentages are to be preferred when presenting estimates to management as they are more easily grasped.

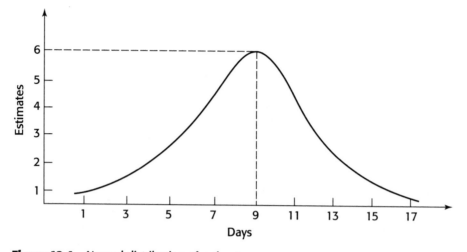

Figure 12.4 Normal distribution of estimates.

6 will estimate 9 days

4 will estimate 11 days

2 will estimate 13 days

1 will estimate 16 days

Figure 12.4 presents a graph of the above numbers. The resulting curve is referred to in statistics as the graph of a *normal distribution* function.[13] The normal distribution is characterized by a bell-shaped graph with an even distribution of occurrences around the average. In the above example, the average estimate is 9 days, with as many estimating below the average as above. And, most importantly, both the frequency and distance of estimates below the average are similar to those above the average. Many frequently occurring events in nature occur as a normal distribution, for example, the height of male (or female) students in a school class, or the number of rainy days in April (excluding England, where it is always 30).

Let us now consider a second possible set of responses by a group of software professionals to the same question:

1 person will estimate 7 days

4 will estimate 9 days

10 will estimate 11 days

4 will estimate 13 days

1 will estimate 15 days

Figure 12.5 presents a graph of these new results. The curve, representing these results, undoubtedly also represents a normal distribution. However, the bell-shaped

---

[13] For the mathematically minded, strictly speaking, the normal distribution is a continuous distribution. For simplicity, we will also include the discrete approximation of the normal distribution.

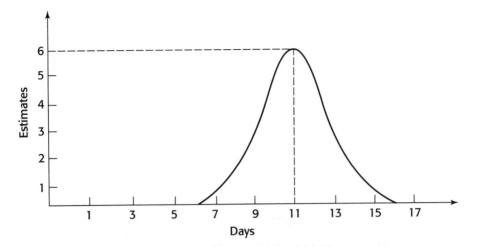

Figure 12.5 Normal distribution of estimates with small deviation.

curve is thinner and taller than in the first example. In this case the divergence of responses was less than in the first example. Also, the average has moved: it is now 11 days.

All normal distributions are characterized by these two parameters, the average and the degree of divergence. The average is referred to as the expected value, μ, and the degree of divergence is referred to as the standard deviation, σ.

We shall use approximations to calculate the normal distribution parameters of various software project estimates.

The first step is the calculation of a *worst case estimate* and a *best case estimate*. These can be calculated by a single person or by a group of people. If we estimate that the development of a synchronous communications driver would take at best four weeks, and at worst 12 weeks, then the best case estimate would be four weeks and the worst case estimate would be 12 weeks (this is not yet a confidence interval, because we do not yet know the probability of our estimate being correct). The two values, best case and worst case, approximate the two extremes of the normal distribution curve.

We now need to calculate values between the two extreme cases. The more estimates we can produce between the two extremes, the more accurate the normal curve will be. However, we will approximate with a single intermediate value, the *most likely case*. In the above example, if four weeks was the best case estimate and 12 weeks was the worst case estimate, we might conclude that seven weeks is a reasonable time for the development of the synchronous communications driver, so that seven weeks is the most likely case (note that the most likely case is an independent estimate and is not an average derived from the best case and worst case estimates). In using the three estimates, best case, most likely case, and worst case, we will assign probabilities to each case as follows:[14]

---

[14]Both Nienburg (1989) and Sodhi (1990) use the following similar approximation: μ=(worst case +4, 6 most likely + best case)/6.

$$P(\text{best case}) = 0.2$$
$$P(\text{most likely}) = 0.6$$
$$P(\text{worst case}) = 0.2$$

The discrete definition of the expected value μ is

$$\mu = E(x) = \Sigma x P(x)$$

Therefore, the approximation of the expected value in the previous example would be

$$\mu = E(x) = 0.2 \times 4 + 0.6 \times 7 + 0.2 \times 12 = 7.4$$

A simple approximation for the standard deviation would be the difference of the extremes multiplied by their probability:

$$\sigma = (\text{worst case}) \times P(\text{worst case}) - (\text{best case}) \times P(\text{best case}),$$

which, in the previous example, would produce:

$$\sigma = 0.2 \times 12 - 0.2\,6\,4 = 1.6$$

We can use common normal distribution tables to discover that:

$(\mu - \sigma, \mu + \sigma)$ produces a 68 percent confidence interval
$(\mu - 2\sigma, \mu + 2\sigma)$ produces a 95 percent confidence interval
$(\mu - 3\sigma, \mu + 3\sigma)$ produces a 99 percent confidence interval

This means, that, in the above example, we can estimate the time to develop the synchronous communications driver as between 4.2 days and 10.6 days, and we are 95 percent confident of our estimate. We can also estimate the development time as being between 5.8 days and 9 days, but then we would only be 68 percent confident of our estimate.

One of the qualities of statistics is that the results can only be as good as the data on which they are based (a form of "garbage in, garbage out"). It is therefore important to devote the necessary time and effort to the development of three effective estimates. A solid, though laborious, approach is to request a number of software engineers (say six) to prepare individual estimates for the worst, best, and most likely cases. The worst case estimate and the best case estimate would be the two extremes produced, while the most likely would be either the average, the median, or the most frequent (the mode).

12.8 Estimating Hardware Resources

In many applications the amount of hardware is limited. This may occur not only in small electronic devices (such as palm-held computers) but also in aerospace systems and other real-time applications. When hardware is significantly limited, software must be designed to fit comfortably into its host environment. The host environment is comprised of the target hardware and its various attributes. Poor software design may result in an overload of the CPU capacity or it may exceed the available memory or mass storage capacity. This can sometimes, but not always, be remedied by expanding the target hardware.

Hardware resources are measured in units of the particular resource being considered: for communications, bits (or bytes) per second; for storage devices, kilobytes or megabytes (or even gigabytes), for a specific CPU, a percentage of the CPU load. A major resource that is heavily dependent on hardware, though it is not in fact hardware itself, is response time. Response time estimates describe our expectations regarding the performance of the system to be developed, and are often required in the early planning phase of the project.

We will consider methods for estimating the following three main resources:

1. CPU load

2. Data storage

3. Response time

Response time, though more an attribute than a resource, will be considered as a resource for the purpose of this discussion.

12.8.1 The CPU Load

Estimation of the CPU load can be quite complex, especially in a multi-process environment, where at any given time more than one process may be competing for the CPU. This is similar to a service queue, in which a number of service requesters await service to be provided by one or more service providers. In our context, the service requesters are the processes and the service providers are the CPUs. The service queue problem is a common problem in operations research, and is handled with the aid of statistics. For a full discussion of queue theory refer to Gross and Harris (1997).

We will consider the CPU load in a slightly more deterministic environment. We will assume that, at any given time, we can determine which demands can be made for CPU processing resources. Without this assumption, the CPU load estimate cannot be calculated, and can only be derived by simulating the actual environment and observing the result.

The CPU load is estimated as a percentage. We say that a system has a 75 percent CPU load, meaning that 25 percent of the processing power is available for additional tasks.

The CPU load is always measured in a worst case situation. A 75 percent CPU load means that, at any given time, no more than 75 percent of the CPU is being utilized. This, however, is paradoxical, as in effect we know that at all times one hundred percent of the CPU is being utilized. We must therefore define what we mean by CPU utilization for purposes of estimation.

First, the CPU load is always measured within a specific time window. This means that within a specific interval of time (which, for example, may be 10 milliseconds long) we measure the amount of time utilized by the CPU. One of the main tasks, then, is the selection of an appropriate time window.

In determining the utilization of the CPU within the time window, we consider only those tasks that cannot be processed at any other time. In a system where diagnostics are performed in the background whenever the CPU has no other task to process, we would not consider the diagnostic tasks in the calculation of the CPU load.

A system that has a 60 percent CPU load in a 10 millisecond window can accept an additional 4 millisecond task if that task can tolerate a maximum 10 millisecond delay.

As an example, we will consider data input from a communications port. If the port has a data transfer rate of 1,200 bits per second, then a byte can be available at the input port approximately every 7 milliseconds, and we must be ready to retrieve a byte from the port before the next byte becomes available. The communication port driver can therefore tolerate a maximum 6 millisecond delay (assuming 1 millisecond processing time).

CPU load estimates are most often required in real-time systems. They are rarely required in commercial data processing systems. Real-time systems are frequently characterized by a basic system loop, often referred to as the main loop, or the executive. This is a low level task that loops endlessly, executing a set of synchronous tasks that drive the system. In many cases, the low level loop is actually part of the operating system that can be configured based on the required cycle time for the loop. This low-level loop may be selected as the time window for the calculation of the CPU load. If the main loop comprises even lower level *fast loops*, then the smallest fast loop may be selected as the time window (see Figure 12.6).

The following set of steps describes the method for calculating the CPU load. This method requires an initial decomposition of the system into its major software tasks and the estimated execution time for each task.

1. Determine the lowest level system loop, and derive from that the time window to be used for estimating the CPU load.

2. Perform a timing analysis of the system and identify all tasks that may require processing within the time window.

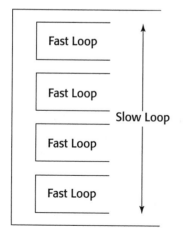

Figure 12.6   Real-time executive with slow and fast loops.

3. Combine the estimated execution times for all tasks identified in Step 2.

4. Divide the result of Step 3 by the size of the time window.

Note that Step 2 requires the identification of any task that *may* require (not just request) CPU time within the time window. This includes operating system tasks.

Consider the following example. A computerized intensive care monitoring system includes the following main components:

- Data input from monitoring equipment

- An alarm

- A user interface component

- An executive loop for reading the monitor equipment

The executive loop consists of:

- A main loop that reads two complex inputs that also require some logic processing every 400 ms. These tasks are estimated to take 60 ms each.

- A fast loop that reads two inputs every 40 ms. These tasks are estimated to take 10 ms each.

There are 10 fast loops within the main loop. We will select a time window of 40 ms. In calculating the worst case, within the time window, we will first consider the fast loop tasks. They immediately use up 20 ms of the 40 ms available. That means that of the 400 ms main loop, only 200 ms are left for other tasks. Of this, 120 ms are required for the two main loop tasks, which can be accommodated easily. If we divide the main loop tasks evenly between the fast loops, then an additional 12 ms will be required from the time window, for a total of 32 ms.

We can assume that when the alarm task is executed, all other tasks are aborted, so that we need not consider the execution time for this task. The user interface component is not a real-time activity (compared to the monitoring equipment input tasks), and we can assume that the user interface will be handled by the main loop spare of 80 ms, in the background. The executive loops are relatively simple, and are estimated to require less than 1 ms, and will therefore also be excluded from the calculation.

The CPU load for the intensive care monitoring system is

$$32/40 = 0.80$$

which means that the CPU load is 80 percent within a 40 ms time window. This example is illustrated in Figure 12.7.

An interesting situation arises when the CPU load calculation provides a result greater than 1.00. This means that the CPU load is more than 100 percent! The obvious conclusion then is that the processor is incapable of performing the tasks required. In such cases there are two possible remedies: either the system requirements should be reduced or a faster processor should be used.

If a 100 percent CPU load poses a problem, a 90 percent CPU load is usually no less of a problem. This is due to the fact that the CPU load is rarely accurately estimated. Also, the changing requirements during project development often increase the CPU load. Another consideration is the need to reserve CPU resources for future expansion

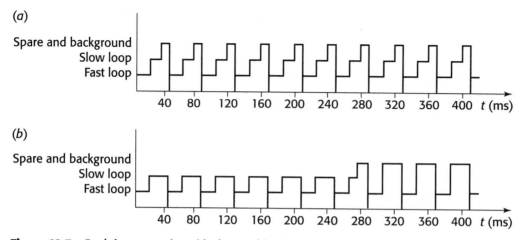

Figure 12.7   Real-time executive with slow and fast loops: *(a)* timing analysis perception; *(b)* actual execution timing.

of the system. It is always good practice to design a software system in such a way that initially it does not require more than a 60 percent CPU load.

12.8.2 Data Storage

We will use the term *data storage* to cover both software storage and data storage. Data storage utilization is essentially a design issue, and frequently has but limited bearing on the requirements for the system. Requirements may consider data storage from the aspect of cost, because inefficient data storage design may require excessive storage facilities, such as memory and disk drives. Such unnecessary facilities result in added cost.

Requirements may also address data storage from the spare perspective. A requirement that the system must provide 30 percent spare memory or disk space may have considerable impact on data storage design, especially in a system where operational memory consumption is close to the limit.

By and large, data storage utilization is not visible to the user, and is therefore mainly determined during the design phase. However, initial rough estimates are required at early phases of the project to ensure that the target hardware configuration is capable of supporting the software system being developed.

Measures of the amount of software to be developed, as discussed earlier in Section 12.1, may be lines of code (*KSLOCs*), or Kbytes of memory. Memory storage is estimated only in units of Kbytes. The first step involves system decomposition, similar to the stepwise estimation method described in Section 12.3. This time the objective is to estimate the amount of memory required by each module at execution time.

The low level software components are combined into concurrent memory resident groups of modules. Then other factors are also considered, such as dynamic memory allocation, operating system requirements, and various memory-resident buffers and tables.

The following method produces memory estimates based on the worst case memory utilization during system execution.

1. Decompose the system into low level modules and estimate the memory requirements for each module at execution time.

2. Identify the indirect memory requirements of each module with respect to:
    - dynamic and static memory work areas
    - memory resident tables
    - buffers

3. Identify the set of memory modules with the largest combined memory requirements that will be memory-resident at any given time.

4. Review the correlation between the memory modules and remove duplicate memory requirements.

5. Repeat Steps 3 and 4 until the largest expected memory utilization is identified.

6. Identify system level memory requirements, such as:
    - memory resident tables
    - file buffers
    - stack size

7. Calculate the total operating system memory utilization.

8. Combine the results of Steps 5, 6, and 7 to produce the total memory storage estimate.

Step 7 should exclude memory requirements that have already been considered in Steps 5 and 6 (e.g., the same file buffers should not be considered both in Step 2 and in Step 6).

The use of overlays can reduce memory requirements, but this is achieved at the expense of additional resources, such as disk I/O, CPU load, and execution speed. The trade-off between memory and response time (or speed) is a common factor in most software systems.

Estimates of mass storage requirements are less critical than estimates of memory requirements. Computer memory is much more limited than disk storage. Disk storage is often restricted only by the cost of the disk storage device.

Estimates of disk storage utilization must take into account the following disk storage consumers:

- Fixed operating system and service utilities
- Variable operating system requirements (overlay and swap areas, system files, etc.)
- Project software
- Data files

For the purpose of this discussion, we will include service packages, such as data bases and communication programs, as part of the operating system. Information regarding the operating system disk utilization is commonly provided by the operating system vendor. If, however, the operating system is being developed as part of the project, then it must be estimated either as a separate system, or as part of the project software (as a subsystem).

Variable operating system requirements are dependent on the specific operating system configuration and on the project software. As an example, disk space for overlays is both a function of the operating system and of the actual software design. Advanced operating systems often provide utilities for estimating disk overhead (both in terms of storage and access) when using overlays. Swap areas for multi-user applications can usually also be sized based on standard operating system utilities. These utilities are commonly part of the operating system tuning or configuration tools.

Estimates for the disk requirements of the project software are straightforward and are produced by the system decomposition. The total of all estimates for each module produces the disk requirements for all project software being developed.

The preparation of estimates for all data file sizes is a tedious task, and is based on the size of individual records and the maximum number of records for each file. This becomes more complicated when records are of variable length. In such cases, maximum or average record sizes should be used. All data files have an overhead, which includes indexes and directories. These must also be factored into the estimate, and are heavily dependent on the data base or file system being used.

In many cases, mass storage data estimates need not be based on a worst case scenario. This is primarily because of the relative ease with which additional mass memory can be added to the configuration. Therefore, in many cases the average mass storage requirements may suffice. Obviously, there are some cases in which a worst case scenario must be used, such as when mass storage utilization grows very fast.

Design estimates for data storage requirements must also make allowances for spare. This is especially true of memory estimates, where the design should provide for about 33 percent spare. This spare memory must be available to cover errors in estimation, changes in the requirements, and future development.

12.8.3 Response Time

The speed of a system is measured in terms of response time. This is often based on a very stringent set of requirements that define system response to specific events.

An example might be the requirement that the user interface must respond to user input in no more than three seconds. It is extremely frustrating having to wait in front of an automatic bank teller machine for a response to a request. Many such teller machines have alleviated the frustration of having to wait by providing background noise that sounds as if money is mechanically being counted, or at least as if something is happening. A simpler solution is to display a flashing message that says "Transaction being processed."

Hatley and Pirbhai (1988), in their pioneering book on real-time systems, differentiated between *external timing* and *internal timing*. Internal timing is a design issue, while external timing is a requirements issue. External timing, then, would refer to response time. Hatley and Pirbhai proposed a diagram (which they call a *timing requirements picture*) to assist in the analysis of the system timing constraints.

In their analysis of internal timing, Hatley and Pirbhai include activities that are not directly related to response time. We will consider here only the timing issues that are directly related to response time, as viewed externally by system users.

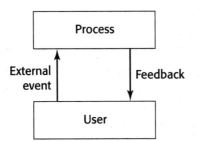

Figure 12.8 Response time perceived as feedback.

Response time can be perceived as system feedback generated by an external event; this is illustrated in Figure 12.8. It is therefore reasonable to divide response time into three basic components:

1. The time from the end of the occurrence of the event until the event is identified by the system
2. Event processing time
3. The time from the conclusion of event processing to the beginning of the external response

Note that response time does not include the time it takes to perform the events on both ends; it includes only the interval of time between the two events (see Figure 12.9).

When estimating response time, the perspective then becomes one of input, processing, and output. The input component refers to the time it takes for the system to receive information regarding the end of an event and to identify it.

The output component refers to the time it takes the system to take the result of processing and to communicate it to the external response generator.

The event processing component includes all activities within the system that are required to generate the response. This also includes delays caused by higher priority activities, and by external devices, such as disk drives, that must be accessed for relevant information.

Response time is usually provided both as a worse case response and an average response.

In the previous example, the automatic teller responds to key input by the user. The last keypress of a transaction (usually *enter*) starts the response time interval. The screen display or the cash dispenser ends the interval as soon as it begins to operate. As

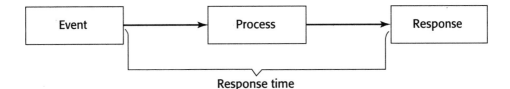

Figure 12.9 The response time interval.

Table 12.7 Example of a Response Time Distribution Table

RESPONSE TIME (SECONDS)	PERCENTAGE
0–3	20%
3–6	60%
6–9	39%
9–15	1%

we have seen, the system designer may "cheat" by responding with a "please wait" message before the real response is ready. This is a perfectly valid practice, and does make the system appear more user-friendly. However, a flashing message that announces "Please wait, now processing request" can also become irritating if it is displayed for too long.

An average automatic teller response to a balance inquiry may require a response time of 5 seconds. On some occasions, when the teller system is at peak utilization, the same inquiry may take 15 seconds. The average response time would then be 5 seconds, and the worst case response time would be 15 seconds. Although a 15-second response delay may be irritating to the user, it may be acceptable to the bank if it does not occur too often. It is therefore necessary, when presenting response time estimates, to include an estimate of the percentage of time in which the worst case can be expected to occur. We may state, for example:

Estimated average response time: 5 seconds

Estimated worst case response time: 15 seconds in 1 percent of transactions

A more detailed description of the estimated response time is frequently required. In the above example, 10 percent of the response delays may take 14.5 seconds, which would not be acceptable, but which may fit into the above figures. In such cases a distribution table would be preferred (see Table 12.7).

12.9 Nondevelopment Overhead

Good estimates are based on the most current and comprehensive data available. It is therefore important to update all project estimates periodically. This should at least be done at major project milestones such as the major software project reviews. Updated estimates should be part of the required deliverables at these reviews.

After the end of the design phase, estimates should be revised before integration begins, and then again before testing begins. Also, any unexpected event that occurs during the development cycle may require the recalculation of estimates. An example of such an event may be the substitution of an off-the-shelf component for a new development component, or a major unscheduled project delay.

Also, any changes to the project requirements specification must always be accompanied by an analysis of the impact of that change on the project schedule. All changes, with very few exceptions, require cost changes. Even the removal of a requirement will produce a change in the estimated project cost.

A certain amount of change to the requirements specification is often taken into account during the preparation of project estimates. This is included in the estimate in the form of a *safety factor*. The safety factor can also be used to compensate for other circumstances, such as errors of estimation and unexpected delays.

Commonly used safety factors range from 20–40 percent, depending on the degree of confidence in the estimates, the expectancy of requirements changes, and the possible delays that could occur.

Similar factors are also sometimes used to include nondevelopment activities into the estimates, such as project management, configuration control, and quality assurance. However, the extent of these tasks is also dependent on other project characteristics. A very small project may not require any direct management, while a large project would be doomed without it.

Table 12.8 presents overhead factors for nondevelopment software project activities. The numbers in Table 12.8 indicate that a software project with a team of 100 engineers would require approximately 10 full-time managers. This includes such tasks as project manager, deputy project manager, team leaders (who may devote part of their time to development work), and so forth. In a small three-person project, one of the team members would be expected to devote about one third of his or her time to the management of the project.

Similarly, in a software project developed by a team of 100 engineers, we would expect to assign two configuration control engineers and three software quality assurance engineers. A more general statement would be that in a 100 work year project, two work years would be devoted to configuration control and three work years would be devoted to general quality assurance.

The numbers in Table 12.8 may be slightly influenced by project size and by the factors discussed in Section 12.5. A complex project will require more overhead than a relatively simple project.

The total project overhead for these activities totals about 15 percent. It is important to remember that this refers only to *direct* project overhead, and does not take into account time invested by senior management, administrative assistants, etc.

Table 12.8 Overhead of Nondevelopment Activities

	OVERHEAD
Management	0.1
Configuration control	0.02
Software quality assurance	0.03

12.10 Good Estimates

The techniques discussed in the previous sections do not, themselves, ensure that good estimates will be produced. After all, what is a good estimate? It is a project development forecast that materializes in reality. It takes everything into consideration: work, team, resources, management, atmosphere, motivation, risks, and others.

Good estimation techniques must be applied *together* with good development processes if there is to be some similarity between the estimates and the project that is subsequently developed. To what extent is this being done? This section discusses how senior management and customers perceive the ability of software project managers to estimate their project.

As we have seen, software projects have a poor reputation for meeting estimates and many customers and senior managers believe that one of the most common shortcomings in software development is the inability to deliver on time. Estimation of software schedules is considered a mystery in the executive boardroom. A business executive recently lamented to his newly recruited software manager:

I ask my software managers to estimate the schedule for their project. I then apply a generous factor to their estimates and only then do I commit to a delivery date. And after all that, they are still appallingly late. Even when I further increase the factor based on my experiences with the developers, they still miss their delivery dates. Why does this happen? Is there no way to successfully estimate the completion of a software project?

Laments like these cause skepticism regarding the ability to meaningfully estimation of software development. Gaining acceptance for estimates means demonstrating that the estimates can be met. For senior management and for customers this, first and foremost, means meeting delivery dates.

Meeting delivery dates is very closely related to meeting commitments. In many instances in which software is delivered late, the cause could have been factored into the estimated schedule (see Chapter 11) thus producing a later, but achievable, delivery date. Techniques such as risk analysis can also help the project manager identify problems ahead of time and factor the likelihood that they will occur into the schedule (see Chapter 2).

A simple rule of thumb states: *The secret of meeting customer commitments is never to make a commitment that you cannot meet.* The rule primarily applies to situations in which you *know* that there is little chance of meeting a dictated schedule and therefore you should avoid committing to it. Unfortunately, life is not that simple and there are innumerable pressures and demands that are difficult for project managers to ignore.

In an interesting true case, a project manager recounted how, many years ago, he lobbied for an important project for his team. The decision lay with a vice president at Motorola who was responsible for new business at one of the company's larger divisions. Initial estimates indicated that if the project was launched in March of that year it could be completed no earlier than April of the following year (a thirteen-month project).

This project manager accompanied the busy vice president first down and then back up the elevator, all the while explaining why his team should be assigned the project. At one point the vice president turned to the project manager and said: "Okay, you can have the project. But only if you commit to deliver it in December of this year."

The response was polite but resolute. "Sir, if you are looking for a project manager who will tell you that the project will be ready in December, you'll probably find one. But my team and I have done our homework and we can show you that there is no way that the project can be delivered in December, no matter what anyone tells you. If you give the project to my team, I can tell that it will be completed in April, and I firmly commit to you that it will." He got the project!

Admittedly, it is not easy for a project manager to withstand the onslaught on the estimates and schedule at the beginning of a project. Chapter 1 discusses ways to do this and to survive. A conclusion from experience states that:

It is better to withstand the assault on a schedule at the beginning of a project and be applauded when it is completed on time, than to be applauded at the beginning of a project for accepting an impossible schedule and being rebuked at the end for failing to deliver it on time.

12.11 Summary

This chapter illustrates how estimation is applied in the prediction of uncertainties. Any unknown quantity can be estimated, while known quantities do not need to be estimated. For the software project manager, there are many unknown quantities that must be estimated.

These are associated with such areas as:

- Project development costs
- Project development schedule
- The size of the project development team
- The amount of software to be developed
- The required hardware resources

Stepwise estimation, often referred to as the "divide and conquer" approach, divides a large problem into numerous smaller problems, and is used in most estimating techniques. The basic approach is to decompose the project into well-defined components, and then to iterate step-by-step until only small units remain that can then be more easily estimated.

The initial decomposition of a software project identifies four major categories, with different degrees of development risk associated with them. The first step of project decomposition produces project components that (1) we have available (off-the-shelf), (2) we know how to develop (full experience), (3) we are at least partially familiar with (partial experience), or (4) are completely new to us (new development). Specific estimation techniques can then be applied for each different type of project component.

Another method, called the constructive cost algorithm (COCOMO), has several tools available for its application. The original COCOMO model consists of 10 basic steps covering the decomposition of the project into components, the application of effort multipliers to each component, and the combination of all the data produced into a single project cost estimate. The more recent COCOMO II model uses a much more sophisticated algorithm and many new effort multipliers.

Function point analysis (FPA) produces project estimates based on the problem size. The amount of functionality in the project determines the problem size, which is represented by a numerical value (the FPA value). The FPA value of a project can be used to:

- Compare the complexity of projects

- Compare the relative effort required to complete a project

- Generate other project measures (such as *SLOCs*)

Estimates are also often presented as a *range*. A range is a helpful estimate in planning for the development of a project. The statistical theory behind this approach deals with the concept of *confidence intervals*, which provides a probability that development costs will fall into a given range.

In many applications the amount of hardware is limited. This may occur not only in small electronic devices (such as palm-held computers) but also in aerospace systems and other real-time applications. When hardware is significantly limited, software must be designed to fit comfortably into its host environment. Methods for estimating CPU load, data storage, and response time are based on decomposition of the software into estimable modules. These estimates are then combined with a safety factor. Commonly used safety factors range from 20–40 percent, depending on the degree of confidence in the estimates and the expectancy of requirements changes.

Good estimates are based on the most current and comprehensive data available. It is therefore important to update all project estimates periodically. However, no matter which method of estimation is used, it is always important to remember that an estimate can only be as good as the data on which it is based.

Exercises

1. Analyze a warehouse inventory system being developed by a company that has previously developed a department store inventory system. Using stepwise estimation, decompose the system into the four categories of components. Then decompose the partial experience components into full-experience components and new development components. Specify any assumptions made.

2. Further develop the problem in Exercise 1, and prepare a plan for the estimation of new development components using statistical sampling. Define a group of categories, and assign each new development component to its relevant category. Select representative modules from each category for implementation. Explain the rationale behind the assignment of categories and the selections made.

3. Based on your experience, assign reasonable numbers of *KSLOCs* to each component in Exercise 2. Assume one development person for each 5 *KSLOCs*.

Assume that 10 percent of the personnel are level 1, 30 percent level 2, 45 percent level 3 and 15 percent level 4. Compute the *PL* factor for the development project. Discuss the impact of the *PL* value on project development costs.

4. Review Table 12.1, which is concerned with the calculation of the *PL* factor. Suggest a different table of values, based on additional *KSLOC* levels and a wider range of multipliers. Discuss the reasons you chose the numbers in your table. Recalculate the values in Table 12.2, based on the table you have proposed.

5. Decompose the warehouse inventory system described in Exercise 1 into components by level of complexity. Based on the *KSLOC* numbers assigned in Exercise 3, calculate the *SEM* for each class of components and combine the results to produce an estimated number of *SEM*s for the whole project.

6. Decompose the warehouse inventory system described in Exercise 1 into components by level of reliability. Use five reliability levels to factor reliability into the *SEM* estimate calculated in Exercise 5.

7. (a) Suggest a five level table of multipliers for the level of the development environment, based on three levels of project size:

   $KSLOC < 25,\ 25 < KSLOC < 300,\ 300 < KSLOC$

   (b) Suggest a table of multipliers to factor subsystem complexity. Discuss whether project size should also be considered.

8. Calculate the cost estimate for the warehouse inventory system described in Exercise 1 using the results of Exercises 3, 5, 6, and 7.

9. (a) Consider the application of the function point analysis algorithm to the warehouse inventory system described in Exercise 1. What are the advantages and what are the disadvantages in using the FPA method? Compare FPA to COCOMO for this specific project and discuss how both can be used together.

   (b) Review the literature (library, Internet, etc.) to identify the various types of feature point analysis. Prepare a table of the advantages and disadvantages of each.

10. Class assignment: based on the different individual results produced for Exercise 8, calculate 68 percent and 95 percent confidence intervals for the range of the development cost for the warehouse inventory system.

11. (a) Review the CPU load example in Section 12.8.1. Assume that the equipment input is driven by interrupts. Each interrupt has an overhead of 0.5 ms. What is the CPU load?

    (b) What would the CPU load be if the fast loop had three inputs instead of two? Discuss the implications of the result.

Pulling It All Together

Now that we know all the elements of software project management we can successfully manage any project. Can we? Rumor has it that it is not that easy. There are major challenges in deciding just how much process should be used and how it should be introduced.

Naturally, processes, methods, and techniques are worthless if they are not used. But a common error is to over-use these processes. The following case illustrates how this can happen.

The following is a true account of a large multinational aerospace corporation with a poor software development record. Every problem mentioned in this book and more had been plaguing the company's software division for many years. Business had been good and the software division had grown at an astronomical rate. While business was good the software problems appeared to be bearable, but gradually the company's business began to suffer and market share began to shrink. This was due in no small way to the higher quality of software being provided by the company's competitors.

This sounded an alarm at corporate headquarters. The company launched a search for a seasoned software development professional and eventually recruited a senior executive with an impressive software development background.

The executive went right to work establishing a new organization structure for the division, introducing orderly development processes, initiating frequent development reviews, applying standards, and organizing mandatory training classes for the software engineers. Within less than a year the results were evident: the quality of software improved, customer satisfaction was on the rise, and market share stabilized at an acceptable level. The new executive was applauded throughout the company. Then three years later he was fired.

To describe what happened next, consider a single coordinate axis with negative infinity represented by total chaos and plus infinity represented by total bureaucracy, and with zero at the center (see Figure Epi.1).

The executive was recruited at the *start* point, and was applauded as he led the software division to point zero (the point of equilibrium where just the right amount of process and organization exists). However, he did not stop at that point, and instead continued leading the division into the domain on the other side of point zero, toward higher and higher levels of control, supervision, and bureaucracy. This was the domain where reviews ran rampant, paperwork was excessive, and meetings took up whatever little time remained for constructive work. The improvement in quality that the division had seen began taking its toll on productivity.

The executive was not exactly fired; he was transferred to a very different position and a new manager was brought in to find a more equitable balance between the two extremes (closer to point zero on the axis).

The lesson is clear. Too much medicine can kill the patient. Applying good process requires an understanding of what is possible; it requires the ability to focus on the essentials and above all it requires common sense.

The above story is an illustration of a new concept referred to as *analysis paralysis*: the syndrome of over-process. Hanscome (1999) reports on a recent survey that found that over 65 percent of software development professionals have experienced this condition in which excessive detail obsures the view of a project's original goal. Hanscome also points to the opposite syndrome, *paralysis paranoia*, in which developers are so afraid of over-process that they practically avoid it altogether .

There is a variant of the over-process syndrome caused by the wealth of guides, standards, techniques, and methods that have accompanied the maturity of software engineering. A common mistake made by software project managers is the belief that all of this material must be used in their development organization, and on their software project, no matter what the status of their project may be. Another real-life example illustrates this phenomenon.

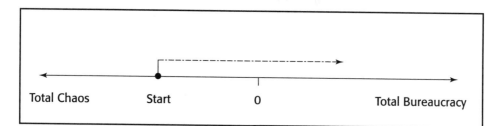

Figure Epi.1   Rushing past the goal line.

In the mid-nineties, an electric power company developed a large software application to monitor the maintenance of its power plants. The software was developed by its in-house development team. The project changed project managers three times in two years and at the end of a two-year period the team was struggling to release its first version of the software.

The team had proudly implemented several basic processes activities, including detailed design of the software. However, the detailed design was poor; it was difficult to understand, it had been built patch upon patch, and it was almost impossible to maintain. Nonetheless, the project manager dutifully had his team continue to update the design document at a considerable cost in time and effort. But the design document was worthless.

The team kept trying to update the design because it was inconceivable to them that their project would have no formal design. Without a design document, they had learned, they would not be able to produce a high quality product.

It was not until the project reached total chaos that a full reevaluation was conducted and a plan was produced to salvage the project. As part of the project recovery plan, the detailed design document was abandoned.

Process is a delicate balance between orderly development and common sense. As the preceding story illustrates, it is essential to focus on the most important goals remembering that the means are not the goals. This is achieved through:

1. *Continuous re-evaluation of the validity of the organization's process related practices and procedures.* A good example is the common dilemma about whether paper copies of documents are required when everyone has access to electronic versions and a good backup process is in place.

2. *Measuring results of techniques and methods and determining their value based on actual performance data.* This refers to the elimination of the *gut feeling* syndrome in which a person's subjective opinion is used as the basis for decisions. Chapters 8 and 10 explain the advantage of measuring results based on data.

3. *Discarding burdensome and bureaucratic practices.* This is not just an issue of submitting forms in triplicate when copying machines are readily available. It also refers to micro-management practices where each minor decision needs to be decided by a committee. A good example is the need to decide when a change must go through a change review board, and when a minor change can be approved through a simple fast-track procedure.

4. *Establishing a culture within which process is kept to the absolute minimum needed to successfully achieve the organization's objectives.*

5. *Avoiding slipping back into the reverse syndrome, paralysis paranoia, by establishing a basic set of rules which cannot be easily discarded (e.g., "software corrections are never released without an acceptable level of testing," or "no changes to requirements will be implemented without formal approval").*

6. *A repeat of the above. Continuous validation of all procedures to ensure that they are geared toward the organization's goal.*

This strategy is best represented by the last (sixth) principle: the importance of always keeping focused on the organization's goal. And, in virtually all cases, the goal is customer satisfaction. For as we have seen it is the customer in the end who determines the success of the project.

If You Don't Do Anything Else, Do This

Brooks claims that all software developers are optimists who believe in happy endings and fairy godmothers. They often hope that if they work hard enough, their problems will go away. But working hard is not enough. In their inspiring book, *Hope Is Not a Method*, Sullivan and Harper (1996) state:

> *Doing the same things you have always done—no matter how much you improve it—will get you only what you had before. The old ways lead to the same old failures.*

But introducing change is not easy. Participants at a round table debate on software project management recently discussed where one should start. The question being debated was:

> *In an organization with ad hoc software development practices and no orderly process, what is the first step that should be introduced?*

The consensus opinion is best illustrated by considering a similar question about how one would embark on a journey. What would be the single most important aspect of the trip that would be required for the journey to succeed? The answer is simple: knowing where you need to go!

The analogy in software development is: specifying software requirements.

The following list proposes a sequence of basic steps for the evolutionary introduction of orderly process into a development organization:

1. **Requirements Specifications.** Though not a guarantee of success, it is unlikely that a project will succeed without clear requirements. *In an organization with no orderly process in place, this should always be the first step. For organizations unreceptive or suspicious of documentation, a good practice is to let a small team from the organization define their own specifications template.* Though the first version of the template may be crude, it will make it easier to introduce an industry standard later on (see Chapter 9).

2. **Project Development Plan.** The essence of a development plan is estimates, schedules, milestones, and resources (see Chapters 10 and 11). This should be included in the first version of the template for a plan. Later on, additional content can be added such as external dependencies and risk analysis (see Chapter 2). Eventually, an industry standard plan can be introduced (see Chapter 9).

3. **Change Control.** It is arguable whether change control is more or less critical than a project plan. Though the need for a project schedule is indeed essential, it

is also true that uncontrolled changes is one of the most common reasons for project failure (see Chapter 1). It would be most desirable *to introduce formal change control in parallel with the introduction of the first formal document* (see Chapter 8). Therefore, change control should be introduced as close on the heels of the Development Plan as possible, and preferably in parallel with it.

4. **Test Plans.** Testing validates the system. Partial testing validates only part of the system. It is not uncommon for testing to cover only part of the system. Then, if the part being tested is acceptable, the system gets released. This can be avoided with comprehensive test plans that cover all of the requirements.

   Partial testing is like looking at part of a picture. This brings to mind the ancient Indian story of five blind men feeling an elephant. One touches the trunk and believes that an elephant is like a serpent, one touches a leg and believes that an elephant is like a tree, one touches the tail and believes that an elephant is like a rope, and on it goes. The lesson is that unless a full orderly set of tests is planned, the full software system will not be validated.

   Though modern practices require testing throughout the development cycle of a software project, undoubtedly the most important testing occurs at the end. Thus, for an existing organization with no orderly test plans, *the specification of the release test criteria is a good place to start.* An excellent way of doing this is with an independent (external) test team. Full testing throughout all phases of development can then be implemented in stages (see Chapter 8) and the concept of phase containment can be introduced.

New methods of software management are continually being developed and existing theories are constantly being reevaluated. This leads to the fifth item on the software project manager's list:

5. **Improve—constantly.** The pursuit of improvement must include the willingness to discard old methods and adopt better ones. A successful development organization is dynamic; it is always learning from its past successes and failures, always willing to seek new methods and techniques for building better software products. This is the essence of an SEI level 5 organization (see Chapter 10).

If a project manager does nothing else other than introduce the above five activities, then the project will have a reasonable chance for success. All other activities described in this book simply improve the odds.

References

Albrecht, A.J., and J.E. Gaffney, Jr. (1983). Software function, source lines of code, and development effort prediction: a software science validation. *IEEE Transactions*, SE-9, No. 6. November.

Allen, P., S. Frost, and E. Yourdon (1998). *Component-Based Development for Enterprise Systems: Applying the Select Perspective*. (Managing Object Technology Series, No 12). Cambridge University Press.

Ambriola, V., L. Bendix, and P. Ciancarini (1990). The evolution of configuration management and version control. *Software Engineering Journal*, Vol. 5, No. 6.

Anderson, O. (1990). The use of software engineering data in support of project management. *Software Engineering Journal*, Vol. 5, No. 6.

Balda, D.M., and D.A. Gustafson (1990). Cost estimation models for the reuse of prototype software development life-cycles. *ACM Sigsoft, Software Engineering Notes*, Vol. 15, No. 3, July.

Balzer, R. (1985). A 15-year perspective on automatic programming. *IEEE Transactions on Software Engineering*, SE-11, No. 11, November.

Barber, W., and A. Badre (1998). Culturability: the merging of culture and usability. *Proceedings, 4th Conference on Human Factors and the Web*. June 5.

Bawtree, H. (1999). Rational Suite 1.0. *Software Development*, Vol. 7, No. 6, June.

Bennatan, E.M. (1987). Artificial intelligence in software engineering: a survey of projects and initiatives. *Desarrollo De Sistemas Informaticos (DSISA) S.A.*, Madrid.

Boehm, B. (1995). Cost models for future software life cycle processes. COCOMO 2.0. *Annals of Software Engineering Special Volume on Software Process and Product*

Measurement. J.D. Arthur and S.M. Henry (Eds.). J.C. Blazer AG, Science Publishers, Vol. 1.

Boehm, B. (1999). Making RAD work for your project. *IEEE Computer*, March.

Boehm, B., et al. (1995). *The COCOMO 2.0 Software Cost Estimation Model*, Research Paper, USC Center for Software Engineering, Litton Data Systems, UC Irvine, Amadeus Software Research.

Boehm, B.W. (1981). *Software Engineering Economics*. Prentice-Hall.

Boehm, B.W. (1988). A spiral model of software development and enhancement. *IEEE Computer*, May.

Boehm, B.W., and T. DeMarco (1997). Software risk management, *IEEE Software*, Vol. 14, No. 3, May–June.

Brooks, F.P., Jr. (1982). *The Mythical Man Month*, Addision-Wesley Publishing Company.

BSI (1991). *British Standard 5750*, British Standards Institution, 1991, London.

Carlow, G.D. (1984). Architecture of the space shuttle primary avionics software system. *Communications of the ACM*, Vol. 27, No. 9, September.

Carney, D. (1998). *Quotations from Chairman David*, Software Engineering Institute, Carnegie Mellon University, July 1.

Chulani, S., B. Boehm, and B. Steece (1998). *Calibrating Software Cost Models Using Bayesian Analysis*, University of Southern California, CSE 1998.

Chulani, S., B. Boehm, and B. Steece (1998). *Calibrating the COCOMO II Post Architecture Model*. Center for Software Engineering, Computer Science Department, University of Southern California, April.

Cobb, R.H., and H.D. Mills (1990). Engineering software under statistical quality control. *IEEE Software*, November.

Cohen, B., T.W. Hartwood, and M.I. Jackson (1986). *The Specification of Complex Systems*. Addison-Wesley.

Comer, E.R. (1997). *Alternative Software Life Cycle Models*, Software Engineering, IEEE Computer Society Press.

Cox, B.J. (1990). Planning the software industrial revolution. *IEEE Software*, November.

DeMarco, T. (1979). *Structured Analysis and System Specification*. Prentice-Hall.

Devani-Chulani, S. (1998). *Modeling Software Defect Introduction*. USC Center for Software Engineering. 1998.

Dijkstra, E. (1972). *Notes on Structured Programming*. Academic Press.

DOD-STD-2167 and DOD-STD-2167A (1988a). *Military Standard, Defense System Software Development*. US Department of Defense (1984, 1985, and 1988).

DOD-STD-2168 (1988b). *Military Standard, Defense System Software Quality Program*. US Department of Defense.

Dorfman, M., and R.H. Thayer, eds. (1997). *Software Engineering*. IEEE Computer Society Press.

Fagan, M.E. (1976). Design and code inspections to reduce errors in program development. *IBM Systems Journal*, Vol. 15, No. 3.

Fairly, R. (1985). *Software Engineering Concepts*. McGraw-Hill.

Fishman, S. (1998). *Software Development: A Legal Guide*. 2nd ed. Nolo.com

Fox, P. (1999). Software reviews: IDL data visualization broadly upgraded. *IEEE Spectrum*, June.

Francis, B. (1993). The search for client/server security, *Datamation*, 1 May.

Fraser, D. (1976). *Probability and Statistics, Theory and Application*. Duxbury Press.

Fraser, M.D., and V.K. Vaishnavi (1997). A formal specifications maturity model. *Communications of the ACM*, Vol. 40, No. 12, December.

Frenkel, K.A. (1985). Toward automating the software development cycle. *Communications of the ACM*, Vol. 28, No. 6, June.

Garmus, D., and D. Herron (1995). *Measuring the Software Process: A Practical Guide to Functional Measurement*. Prentice-Hall.

Gemmer, A. (1997). Risk management: moving beyond process, *IEEE Computer*, May.

Gibbs, W.W. (1994). Software's chronic crisis. *Scientific American*, September.

Giegold, W.C. (1982). *Practical Management Skills for Engineers and Scientists*. Lifetime Learning Publications.

Gillett, B. (1976). *Introduction to Operations Research: A Computer-Oriented Algorithmic Approach*. McGraw-Hill.

Goldberg, A. (1983). *Proceedings of the 1983 ACM Computer Science Conference*, ACM.

Graham, L. (1999). Act quickly to avoid losing patents. *IEEE Software*, March/April.

Gross, D., and C.M. Harris (1997). *Fundamentals of Queueing Theory*. John Wiley & Sons.

Hanscome, B. (1999). Paralysis paranoia. *Software Development*. Vol. 7, No. 6, June.

Hatley, D.J., and I.A. Pirbhai (1988). *Strategies for Real-Time System Specification*. Dorset House.

Heemstra, F.J. (1992). Software cost estimation. *Information and Software Technology*, Vol. 34, No. 10, October.

Herbsleb, J., A. Carleton, J. Rozum, J. Siegel, and D. Zubrow (1994). *Benefits of CMM-Based Software Process Improvement: Initial Results*. Software Engineering Institute, August 1994.

Herbsleb, J., et al. (1996). *Benefits of CMM-Based Software Process Improvement: Initial Results*. Software Engineering Institute, Carnegie Mellon University.

Higuera, R.P., and Y.Y. Haimes (1996). *Software Risk Management*. Software Engineering Institute, Technical Report CMU/SEI-96-TR-012, ESC-TR-96-012, June.

Humphrey, W. (1999a). *Checkpoint Restart—Part 1*, Software Engineering Institute, Carnegie Mellon University, Online Articles, March 11.

Humphrey, W. (1999b). *The Changing World of Software*, Software Engineering Institute, Carnegie Mellon University, Online Articles, March 11.

Humphrey, W. (1999c). Bugs or defects? *Software Engineering Institute Interactive*, Vol. 2, No. 1, March 11.

IEEE (1984). *Software Engineering Standards*. The Institute of Electrical and Electronics Engineers, Inc., New York.

IEEE (1987a). *Standard for Software Project Management Plans*. The Institute of Electrical and Electronics Engineers, Inc., New York (IEEE Std-1058.1-1987).

IEEE (1987b). *Software Engineering Standards*. The Institute of Electrical and Electronics Engineers, Inc., New York.

IEEE (1990a). Draft of *Standards for a Software Quality Metrics Methodology*. The Institute of Electrical and Electronics Engineers, Inc., New York.

IEEE (1990b). *Standard for Software Productivity Metrics*. The Institute of Electrical and Electronics Engineers, Inc., New York (IEEE Std-1045-1990).

IEEE (1990c). *Standard for a Software Quality Metrics Methodology*. The Institute of Electrical and Electronics Engineers, Inc., New York (IEEE Std-1061-1990).

IEEE (1993). *Software Engineering, IEEE Standards Collection*, The Institute of Electrical and Electronics Engineers, Inc., New York.

IEEE (1993). Std 1058, Standard for Software Project Management Plans, The Institute of Electrical and Electronics Engineers, Inc, New York.

IEEE (1999). *Software Engineering Standards, Volumes 1–4*, The Institute of Electrical and Electronics Engineers, Inc., New York.

Inmon, W.H. (1993). *Developing Client/Server Applications*. John Wiley & Sons.

ISO (1990). *Quality Management of Quality Assurance Standards*. The International Organization for Standardization (Standard 9000–3).

ISO/IEC (1996). JTC1/SC7 Business Planning Group, *Product Plan for ISO/IEC Software Engineering Standards*, 1st edition, (Approval Draft).

Jackson, M.A. (1975). *Principles of Programming Design*. Academic Press.

Jeffery, D.R., and G. Low (1990). Calibrating estimation tools for software development. *Software Engineering Journal*, Vol. 5, No. 4, July.

Jell, T. (1998). *Component-Based Software Engineering* (Managing Object Technology Series, No 10). SIGS Books, Cambridge Press.

Johnson, J. (1995). Chaos: the dollar drain of IT project failures. *Application Development Trends*, Vol. 2, No. 1.

Jones, C. (1994). *Assessment and Control of Software Risks*. Prentice-Hall.

Kaposi, A.A., and M. Myers (1990). Quality assuring specification and design. *Software Engineering Journal*, Vol. 5, No. 1, January.

Keil, M., et al. (1998). A framework for identifying software project risks, *Communications of the ACM*, Vol. 41, No. 11, November.

Krieger, D., and R.M. Adler (1998). The emergence of distributed component platforms, *IEEE Computer*, March.

Laplante, P.A. (1990). The Heisenberg uncertainty principle and its application to software engineering. *ACM Sigsoft, Software Engineering Notes*, Vol. 15, No. 5, October.

Macro, A., and J. Buxton (1987). *The Craft of Software Engineering*. Addison-Wesley.

Madden, W.A., and K.Y. Rone (1984). Design, development, integration: space shuttle primary flight software system. *Communications of the ACM*, Vol. 27, No. 9, September.

Madsen, K.H. (1999). The diversity of usability practices. *Communications of the ACM*, Vol. 42, No. 5, May.

Microsoft (1992). Designing client–server applications for enterprise database connectivity. *Microsoft Technical Notes*, Vol. 3, No. 14.

Moder, J.J., C.R. Phillips, and E.W. Davis (1995). *Project Management with CPM, PERT & Precedence Diagramming*. Blitz Publishing Co.

Moore, J.W. (1998). *Software Engineering Standards: A User's Road Map*. IEEE Computer Society.

Nichols, K. (1999). The age of software patents. *IEEE Computer*, April.

Nienburg, R.E. (1989). *Effective Skills for Technical Managers*. Learning Tree International.

Nolan, A.J. (1999). Learning from success. *IEEE Software*, January/February.

Overmyer, S.P. (1990). The impact of DOD-STD-2167A on iterative design methodologies: help or hinder. *ACM Sigsoft, Software Engineering Notes*, Vol. 55, No. 5, October.

Parnas, D.L. (1972). On criteria to be used in decomposing systems into modules. *CACM*, Vol. 14, No. 1, April.

Paulk, P.C., B. Curtis, M.B. Chrissie, and C.V. Weber (1993a). *Capability Maturity Model for Software*, Version 1.1, Software Engineering Institute, Carnegie Mellon University, CMU/SEI-93-TR-24.

Paulk, P.C., B. Curtis, M.B. Chrissie, and C.V. Weber (1993b). *Key Practices of the Capability Maturity Model*, Version 1.1, Software Engineering Institute, Carnegie Mellon University, CMU/SEI-93-TR-25.

Peter, L.J., and R. Hull (1970). *The Peter Principle*. Pan Books.

Pfleeger, S.L., N. Fenton, and S. Page (1994). Evaluating software engineering standards. *IEEE Software*, Vol. 11, No. 5, September.

Philips, R.A. (1998). *Guide to Software Export: A Handbook for International Software Sales*. International Business Press.

Pinto, J.K., and S.J. Mantel (1990). The causes of project failure. *IEEE Transactions on Engineering Management*, Vol. 37, No. 4, November.

Polack, A.J. (1990). Practical applications of CASE tools on DOD projects. *ACM Sigsoft, Software Engineering Notes*, Vol. 15, No. 1, January.

Pressman, R.S. (1992). *Software Engineering: A Practitioner's Approach*, 3rd ed. McGraw-Hill.

Project Management Institute (1996). *A Guide to the Project Management Body of Knowledge*. PMI Publishing Division.

Ratcliff, B., and A.L. Rollo (1990). Adapting function point analysis to Jackson system development. *Software Engineering Journal*, Vol. 5, No. 1, January.

Rich, B., and L. Janos (1994). *Skunk Works: A Personal Memoir of My Years at Lockheed*. Little, Brown and Company.

Riggs, J.L., and D. Jones (1990). Flowgraph representation of life cycle cost methodology—a new perspective for project managers. *IEEE Transactions on Engineering Management*, Vol. 37, No. 2, May.

Rochkind, M.J. (1975). The source control system. *IEEE Transactions*, Se-1, No. 4.

Royce, W.W. (1970). Managing the development of large software systems: concepts and techniques. *WESCON Technical Papers*, Vol. 14.

Russo, P., and S. Boor (1993). How fluent is your interface?: designing for international users. *Proceedings of the Conference on Human Factors in Computing Systems*. Association for Computing Machinery.

Sackman, H., et al. (1968). Exploratory experimental studies comparing offline and online programming performance. *Communications of the ACM*, Vol. 11, No. 1, January.

Sawyer, P., I. Sommerville, and S. Viller (1999). Capturing the benefits of requirements engineering. *IEEE Software*, March/April.

Sawyer, S., and P.J. Guinan (1998). Software development processes and performance. *IBM Systems Journal*, Vol. 37, No. 4.

Schlichter, J. (1999). *Surveying Project Management Capabilities*. PM Network, April.

Schmauch, C.H. (1995). *ISO 9000 for Software Developers*. American Society for Quality.

SCT (1997). Function point FAQ: frequently asked questions (and answers) regarding function point analysis. *Software Composition Technologies Inc.*, June 25, 1997; also available on the web at http://ourworld.compuserve.com/homepages/softcomp/fpfaq.htm

Shaw, M. (1990). Prospects for an engineering discipline of software. *IEEE Software,* November.

Silver, H. (1986). *Technical Marketing and Proposal Preparation.* HSA Publication.

Sinha, A. (1992). Client–server computing. *Communications of the ACM,* Vol. 35, No. 7, July.

Sodhi, J. (1990). *Computer Systems Techniques.* TAB Professional and Reference Books.

Sullivan, G.R., and M.V. Harper (1996). *Hope Is Not a Method.* Times Business.

Symons, C.R. (1988). Function points analysis: difficulties and improvements. *IEEE Transactions,* SE-14, No. 1.

Tahvanainen, V., and K. Smolander (1990). An annotated CASE bibliography. *ACM Sigsoft, Software Engineering Notes,* Vol. 15, No. 1, January.

Thayer, R.H. (1997). *Software Enginneering Standards.* Software Engineering, IEEE Computer Society.

Tsoi, H.L. (1999). A framework for management of software project development. *Proceedings of the 1999 ACM Symposium on Applied Computing.*

Ullman, E. (1993). Client/server frees data. *Byte,* June.

USC Center for Software Engineering and UC Irvine Research Unit in Software (1995). *Prospectus COCOMO 2.0 Program.* September 1995, Version 1.5.

Ward, P.T., and S.J. Mellor (1986). *Structured Development for Real-Time Systems.* Yourdon Press.

Warnier, J.D., and K.T. Orr (1977). *Structured Systems Development.* Yourdon Press.

Weinberg, G.M. (1998). *The Psychology of Computer Programming: Silver Anniversary Edition.* Dorset House Publishing.

Weinberg, J. (1992). *Quality Software Management, Volume 1: Systems Thinking.* Dorset House Publishing.

Wesselius, J., and F. Ververs (1990). Some elementary questions on software quality control. *Software Engineering Journal,* Vol. 5, No. 6, January.

Wilson, D.N., and M.J. Sifer (1990). Structured planning: deriving project views. *Software Engineering Journal,* Vol. 5, No. 2, March.

Yourdon, E., and L.L. Constantine (1978). *Structured Design.* Yourdon Press.

Zimmer, B. (1991). Implementing productivity managers. *IEEE Software,* January.

Index